Appomattox Commander

General E.O.C. Ord. U.S. Signal Corps photo No. B-4550. *(Brady Collection)*
National Archives.

Appomattox Commander

The Story of General E.O.C. Ord

★★★★★

Bernarr Cresap

SAN DIEGO • NEW YORK
A. S. BARNES & COMPANY, INC.
IN LONDON:
THE TANTIVY PRESS

First Edition
Manufactured in the United States of America

For information write to:
A.S. Barnes & Company, Inc.
P.O. Box 3051
La Jolla, California 92038

The Tantivy Press
Magdalen House
136-148 Tooley Street
London, SE1 2TT, England

Library of Congress Cataloging in Publication Data

Cresap, Bernarr, 1919-
  Appomattox commander.

  Bibliography: p.
  Includes index.
  1. Ord, Edward Otho Cresap, 1818-1883. 2. Appomattox
Campaign, 1865. 3 United States — History — Civil War,
1861-1865 — Campaigns and battles. 4. Generals — United
States — Biography. 5. United States. Army — Biography.
E467.1.07C69   973.7'3'0924 [B]   79-15102
ISBN 0-498-02432-6

1 2 3 4 5 6 7 8 9 84 83 82 81

To Dorothy, Michael and Elizabeth

Contents

List of Illustrations

Acknowledgments

Grateful acknowledgment is made to the following members of the Ord family for placing at the author's disposal their valuable collections of family papers: the late Miss Ellen F. Ord, Berkeley, California; Mrs. Vida Ord Alexander, Washington, D.C.; Mr. A. Murray Preston, Washington, D.C.; Mrs. Rebecca Ord Radford, La Jolla, California; and the late Mr. James Ord, San Francisco.

The author expresses thanks to the courteous personnel of the several libraries and government depositories who served him so efficiently. The staff members of the following institutions placed before him the archival material, manuscripts, newspapers and books used in the preparation of this volume: the old War Records Office and, more recently, the Civil War Branch of the National Archives; Manuscript and Serials Divisions of the Library of Congress; Bancroft Library of the University of California, Berkeley; Rutherford B. Hayes Library, Fremont, Ohio; Library of the United States Military Academy, West Point, New York; Joint University Libraries, Nashville, Tennesee; University of North Carolina Library, Chapel Hill; Duke University Library, Durham, North Carolina; Mississippi Department of Archives and History, Jackson; Collier Library, University of North Alabama, Florence; Georgetown University Library, Washington, D.C.; Tennessee State Library, Nashville; Library of the Sons of the American Revolution, San Francisco; Missouri Historical Society, St. Louis; Stanford University Libraries, Stanford, California; University of Rochester Library, Rochester, New York; New York Historical Society,

New York; Newberry Library, Chicago; Smithsonian Institution Archives, Washington, D.C.; Historical Society of Pennsylvania, Philadelphia; Chicago Historical Society, Chicago; Minnesota Historical Society, St. Paul.

Grateful acknowledgment is made to the publishers of two periodicals for permission to quote portions of my previously published articles on General Ord. These are: "Early California as Described by Edward O.C. Ord," *Pacific Historical Review, XXI* (1952): 329–40; and "Captain Edward O.C. Ord in the Rogue River Indian War," *Oregon Historical Quarterly*, LIV (1954): 83–90.

Thanks are due the late Professors Frank L. Owsley, William C. Binkley and Daniel M. Robison, and to Professors Henry L. Swint and Paul Hardacre, all of the History Department of Vanderbilt University at the time this study was undertaken. The author is under obligation to Miss Clara Mae Brown, formerly reference librarian of the Joint University Libraries, Nashville, for assistance with the research; to Mrs. Hershel Marks of Florence, Alabama, for aiding in the preparation of the manuscript; and to Mr. Edgar Lowe of Gallatin, Tennessee, for preparing the maps.

Finally, the author is grateful to his wife for assistance in countless important ways, but especially for the encouragement which kept him to the task.

Appomattox Commander

1

★★★★★

A Jesuit's Son

CUMBERLAND, Maryland, lay sheltered and inconspicuous, a mountain retreat far from the din of battle. The year was 1814, the war a thousand miles away in the swamps below New Orleans. The not-too-distant Allegheny mountains, their verdure subdued by winter, encircled the town as though to defy intrusion. Yet, the place was bustling, and there was access, for Cumberland was a center of trade for western Maryland. From the east, roads from Baltimore and Washington converged at Frederick to bring a steady flow of men, women, children, animals and goods; while the National Road, the grand federal highway thrusting through The Narrows westward, daily reached further into the wilderness.

Cumberland was not completely without a reminder that the nation was at war, for the townspeople had become accustomed to the presence of a recruiting officer, First Lieutenant James Ord of the Thirty-sixth United States Infantry Regiment. They were impressed by his serious but kindly manner. His uniform lent a dash of color as he strode down Washington Street. Not a few young bucks of the vicinity, adventure-prone, had signed up to win glory on some distant battlefield.

Lieutenant Ord was a man of mystery, and mystery would shroud his origins to the day of his death. He was small of stature, about twenty-eight years of age, of grave and scholarly demeanor, and of mild, even pious, deportment. Though he was commissioned in the regular army, he seemed strangely ill-suited to the part he was playing. The quiet of a cloister rather than the hurly-burly of secular life seemed his proper sphere. Indeed, a scant three years before, Ord had been a member of the Jesuit Order and, under its first vows, pledged to the priesthood of the Roman Catholic Church.[1]

Who was James Ord? The man himself would ask that question throughout his adult life, and the uncertainty of the answer would torment him to the day of his death. He was born in London, England, in 1786; of that there seems no doubt. His alleged parents were Mary (née Ord) and Ralph Ord of a London family described as rigid adherents to the Catholic faith. But by other accounts, he was the son of George, Prince of Wales, and his morganatic wife, the Catholic Mrs. Maria Fitzherbert. The prince, later to be King George IV, and Mrs. Fitzherbert, born Maria Smythe, were married by an Anglican priest in 1785, a ceremony eventually recognized in secret by the pope as canonically valid. There were rumors that Mrs. Fitzherbert was with child. Was James Ord the offspring of this union?[2]

There is evidence to suggest that a member of the royal family disposed of an infant in 1786. Quietly, an approach was made to Catholic circles in London to place a male child with a Catholic family. M.E. Coen, Catholic priest of St. Mary and St. Michael's Church, Commercial Road East, London, became the intermediary in this transaction. The circumstances of the Ords fitted the need precisely, and Coen was well-acquainted with their situation.

Ralph Ord, the reputed father, married Mary Ord on 4 July 1785 at St. George's in the East, Cannon Street Road, London. James Ord, son of Ralph and Mary, was baptized 9 April 1786 by M.E. Coen in St. Mary and St. Michael's Church. Ralph Ord did not live long after his marriage, and the infant, James, whom he probably never saw, lived only a short time. Mary Ord, bereft of husband and child, then lived with her mother, Helen Ord, and Mary's unmarried brother, also named James Ord. The arrangements for the transfer of a child to the Ords were made by a member of the royal family and a Mr. Farmer. They entered into negotiations with James Ord the elder as head of the household. Ord was told very little about the infant. He understood that the child was from one of the sons of King George III. The elder James assumed guardianship of the infant who became his namesake. His sister Mary was doubtless eager to have a surrogate for her lost son.

Forces moved strangely and swiftly to take the Ords out of England. James Ord the elder, an experienced ship's captain and naval architect, contracted on 28 September 1786 to serve the King of Spain for four years as inspector of the dockyard and vessels at Bilbao, Spain. By one account, arrangements for this position were made by the Duke of York. Thus, Captain James Ord betook himself to Catholic Spain with his sister Mary, their mother Helen, and the infant James.

★★★★★

Across the Atlantic, far from Bilbao, the struggling Catholic community in Maryland had reached a milestone with the appointment of John Carroll as first Catholic bishop for the United States. The urbane and polished Carroll had been educated in Europe, had joined the Jesuit Order, and had served as tutor and chaplain to noble Catholic families in England. Returning to England for his consecration, he was elevated to the bishopric on 15 August 1790 in the chapel of Lulworth Castle. Lulworth was the place of the Weld family, the seat of Edward Weld, Mrs. Fitzherbert's deceased first husband.

By remarkable coincidence, Captain James Ord's contract to serve the King of Spain expired at about the same moment. One can imagine the Ords, torn by homesickness, in a quandary as to their future. Should they remain in exile in this strange foreign land? A return to England was out of the question. At this juncture, there was certainly some communication between Bishop Carroll and the Ords out of which came a proposal that they emigrate to the United States. Bishop Carroll reached Baltimore on 7 December 1790. The Ords either accompanied him or followed soon after, for, late in 1790 or early in 1791, they took up residence in Norfolk, Virginia, where Captain James Ord was employed in shipbuilding by John Brent, a nephew of Bishop Carroll.

Successive tragedies quickly altered the family's situation. In October 1791, Helen Ord died in Norfolk County, and Mary Ord died there a year or two later. James the younger, then seven years of age, was taken into the Brent family. He attended school in Norfolk until 1795 or 1796 when John Brent returned with his family to his old home near Port Tobacco, Charles County, Maryland. The Ords, uncle and nephew, accompanied them.

As a young boy, James Ord had heard his playmates discussing their birthdays. It had occurred to him that he did not know his own. With natural curiosity he asked his uncle about the matter. "I do not know, James," was the reply. "If you had your rights in England you would be something very great. God forgive those who have wronged you." These words and the solemn manner in which they were spoken made a lasting impression on a boy too young to understand their meaning. Later, at a more responsible age, the younger James asked his uncle to explain his unusual statement. The uncle acknowledged that the youth was not his nephew and that, shortly after birth, he had been adopted by the elder James's sister who had lost her own child and her husband. He would give no further particulars at that time and told the young man that it would not be for his happiness to know more. The young James was led to believe that the elder was under a vow of secrecy. This reticence, taken with such statements as his foster uncle had made, caused James to conclude that he was an illegitimate child. The thought was so painful and humiliating to him that he never again discussed the matter with his uncle.

The Ords lived with the Brents near Port Tobacco until 1799, when the young James was sent to live for a brief period with Notley Young on his estate called "Non Such" near Washington. The move was probably made in pursuit of further education for the young man, for, on 12 April 1800, at the age of fourteen, James was enrolled in Georgetown College, a Jesuit institution founded by Bishop Carroll in 1791 in nearby Georgetown, D.C. Bishop Carroll paid young Ord's expenses at the college. Notley Young, Carroll's brother-in-law, was one of the professors there.[3] The elder Ord meanwhile had secured a position as naval constructor at the Navy Yard, Washington, D.C.

James Ord, along with other students, took up residence in the new college building at Georgetown which afforded facilities for lodging as well as a refectory. This structure was situated on an eminence in a beautiful setting. The rolling waters of the Potomac, hastening toward the Chesapeake, swirled below. To the rear of the building, wooded walks led to the next higher elevation and to dense forests beyond. To the front lay the nation's capital, its nascent grandeur rising from the wilderness.

At Georgetown College, James pursued his studies seriously and determined to enter the priesthood. This course was warmly endorsed by his uncle, who had often expressed the hope that the youth would join the Jesuit Order. In 1806, at the age of twenty, the younger James joined the Jesuits, taking the first vows in 1808 and becoming a teacher in the college. For young Ord, life at Georgetown was virtually a monastic existence. The routine began before the break of day—prayers, followed by the saying of religious offices, classroom instruction and study. These were carried out in a peaceful sylvan retreat.

Suddenly the young man's steady routine of life at the college was shattered. A courier dispatched from the Navy Yard breathlessly arrived at Georgetown with the intelligence that the elder Ord had been suddenly stricken with an illness. The young cleric must come at once. Hastening to the yard, James reached his uncle's side. The elder Ord recognized his nephew and began to speak: "James, I have something of the greatest importance to communicate to you." But his life was slipping away, and he could not muster sufficient strength to continue. In a few minutes, he lapsed into unconsciousness and never spoke again.

What inner turmoil the young Jesuit must have suffered with the passing of his uncle and the nagging mystery surrounding his origin! Torn by uncertainty, he passed through a spiritual crisis. Less than a year after the death of his uncle, James Ord quit the Jesuit Order and departed from Georgetown College.[4] The emergence of the young man from the protective cloisters of Georgetown into the rough and tumble of secular life must have been a shocking experience. Ord was entirely without family connections in the United States; his sole acquaintances, according to his own statement, were the Brents, for, with the exception of an occasional day spent at the Navy Yard with his uncle, he had been at the college continuously for eleven years. He was equipped with a thorough classical education.[5]

Fortune favored the inexperienced Ord. He left the college in May 1811, and, by 9 June, had secured an appointment as midshipman in the United States Navy. The outbreak of war with England a year later found him still in the service, but a cruise on the frigate *Congress* convinced him that the sea was not to his liking. He resigned his commission on 13 April 1813 and, a few days later (30 April), was commissioned a first lieutenant of the Thirty–sixth United States Infantry Regiment. Fortune indeed! Ord never knew to whom he was indebted for these rapid-fire appointments, but he supposed it was to the Brent family.

Lieutenant Ord performed most of his military service on recruiting duty, and it was in the interest of securing raw material for the army that he was sent into the mountain metropolis of western Maryland. His term of service in Cumberland evidently lasted for some months, long enough, at least, for him to take a wife. He was married 29 September 1814 to Rebecca Ruth Cresap of Allegany County.

The twenty-year-old Rebecca, member of the first family to settle in the area, was her husband's opposite in many respects. In contrast to the mild James, she was spirited and forceful, with "flashing brown eyes" and a "Cresap temper." And, very important, she was a Protestant. For this latter reason, the Brents, who had always treated James as a member of their own family, were much opposed to the marriage, but the lieutenant would not be deterred.

Rebecca Cresap was a great-granddaughter of Colonel Thomas Cresap, who had settled about 1742 with his family at Oldtown, a few miles from Cumberland. Cresap, a native of Skipton, Yorkshire, England, had come to the colonies as a youth. He had a good education, was possessed of boundless energy and ambition, and had more luck than any ten men might reasonably have expected in the course of a life that stretched over nearly a century. As agent for Lord Baltimore in the Maryland-Pennsylvania boundary dispute of the 1730s, he had been burned out of his house by angry Pennsylvanians and taken in chains to repose for some months in a Philadelphia jail. Finally settling at Oldtown, he built a home, with a stockade for protection, which was for many years the westernmost outpost of settlement in Maryland. Colonel Cresap was Indian trader, land speculator, surveyor, member of the Ohio Company and member of the Maryland Assembly.[6]

Cresap's three sons were active in various colonial and Revolutionary affairs. Thomas, Jr., was killed in an action with the Indians in the French and Indian War. Michael, trader and Indian fighter, led the first company of soldiers to arrive in

Cambridge from a Southern colony to join Washington's army in 1775. Daniel Cresap, grandfather of Rebecca Ruth, was a man of domestic habits, "the patriarch of the day and country in which he lived." By his extensive land holdings near Cumberland he acquired great wealth.

Daniel Cresap, Jr., father of Rebecca Ruth, was among the numerous children of the patriarchal Daniel and his second wife Ruth Swearingen. At twenty-two, he had marched to Cambridge as a lieutenant in his uncle Michael's company. Surviving the war, he had returned home to agricultural pursuits and was colonel of the militia of Allegany County. He commanded a regiment in the famous "Whiskey Rebellion" in western Pennsylvania in 1794. Suffering from hardships and exposure, Daniel died in December 1794, shortly after his return home from this campaign. Surviving him were his wife and several children, the youngest, Rebecca Ruth, being but six weeks old.[7]

Rebecca's heritage was of Indian fighters and Revolutionary soldiers, but the military life was not for her scholarly husband. James Ord resigned his commission on 14 February 1815, and, with his bride, took up residence at the Cresap home, presumably to engage in farming. They lived in Allegany County until 1819, and here were born the first three of their twelve children, eight of whom lived to maturity. The names chosen for the children reflected the contrasting influences of Rebecca and James. The former, being of a more practical turn of mind chose Cresap family names—Daniel, Edward Otho, Mary Elizabeth. James, on the other hand, though naming three of the sons for members of the Brent family, attached names of classical or religious significance to several of the other children. Thus, the family roster reveals such names as Pacificus, Raphael, Placidus, James Lycurgus, the seventh child named Septimus, William Marcellus and John Stephen.[8]

The third child of James and Rebecca, a son, was born in Cumberland on 18 October 1818 and given the name Edward Otho Cresap in honor of Rebecca's elder brother, who had died the year before in Kentucky. For reasons not clear, the Ords were at this moment at an inn known as Faw's Tavern on Greene Street in Cumberland. The infant born at Faw's was to be the venturesome one, restless and energetic, and with qualities of mind and spirit that were to set him apart from the ordinary.

Allegany County was not to be the scene of Edward's childhood. Before another year had elapsed, James Ord had moved his rapidly growing family from the mountains of western Maryland to the restless political center of Washington, D.C. For the young Edward, "home" was to be the nation's capital.

At the time the Ords took up residence in Washington, the city had largely recovered from the destruction wrought by the British torch. The President's House had been rebuilt, and the burned portions of the Capitol reconstructed to accommodate the meetings of Congress. The aristocratic James Monroe was president, and the social life was elegant and formal. The city was animated when Congress was in session, desolate when it was not. In Washington, James Ord held minor government positions and was a magistrate from 1821 to 1837. He was able to provide for his large family, though his economic circumstances were never more than moderate.

What distinguishing qualities did Edward Ord inherit? What part did chance play in his upbringing that we can say, "His destiny was shaped by this or that turn of fortune?" These mysteries elude us in some measure even as we attempt to grasp them. For young Edward Ord, as for anyone, we paint in broad strokes those shaping forces and delineaments of character which make a personality.

Edward grew up in a pleasant family circle. Rebecca was a center of strength, James a reservoir of quiet steadiness. The family members were openly affectionate. Edward and the other children were expected to be mutually helpful, and they developed a sense of responsibility for the well-being of one another. Edward himself was usually cheerful and often jocular when among close associates. With those not so close, he was inclined to be somewhat constrained.

There was a distinctiveness about this youngster, a pronounced quality of individualism. Eccentric in his habits, his later associates would say. He marched to the beat of his own drum; conformity had no charms for him. The most obvious manifestation of his singularity was a carelessness of appearance and dress. He was energetic and restless, eager for adventure and action. When action was called for, he was aggressive, and, in the face of danger, courageous to the point of foolhardiness. Even as a youth, his endurance and perseverance were proverbial, and there was a quality of hardness, a toughness,

about him. His mind was quick, not ordinary; his imagination
fertile. He was inventive and his talent in mathematics was
outstanding—even to genius—by the testimony of qualified
observers.

Edward was of average height and build, strong and agile,
as he reached full physical development. His appearance was
striking. A shock of unruly black hair contrasted with bluish-
gray eyes and a ruddy complexion. His features were well-
defined—nose straight, chin cleanly formed—giving an impression of determination.

The youngster's imagination was stirred by the Cresap
heritage, with its stories of adventure on the frontier and of
heroic actions in the forest and on the battlefield. Here was
inspiration to action and to achievement. More immediate and
more continuous as a shaping force from day to day was the
guiding hand of James Ord. Edward and the other children
were reared as Catholics. The pious James was untiring in his
efforts to train them in their religious duty and was firm in his
instruction. However, there were sometimes ways to circumvent his good intentions for them. Sent to attend a particular
mass on Sunday, the Ord brothers, Edward and Pacificus,
would wrestle or engage in some other test of strength with
their friends, the loser being required to attend the service. The
unlucky contender was obliged to listen carefully to the Gospel
for the Day and report to his companions, for James Ord was
certain to quiz his sons on this point upon their return home.
On the whole, the father's efforts at moral instruction were
successful. The Ord children, though not always good
churchmen, were honest and upright.

Edward was ten years of age when Democracy triumphed
under the leadership of Andrew Jackson. This event occurred
only after a vicious campaign in which the incumbent, John
Quincy Adams, was charged with corruption and gambling,
while his opponent was portrayed as a lecherous murderer.
Discounting campaign sins, James Ord was a strong adherent
of Jackson. "Old Hickory's" victory in 1828 was, no doubt, a
significant event in the Ord household, and the fortunes of the
Democratic party figured strongly among the impressions of
Edward's childhood and youth. It is not surprising that he
"grew up" a Democrat.

That Edward Ord was born south of the Mason-Dixon line
was significant. He was to refer to himself on more than one

occasion as a Southerner. But Maryland was the border South, and the District of Columbia, "neutral ground." Perhaps his residence here removed him somewhat from the influence of extreme sectionalism. In the developing sectional controversy, James Ord early adopted a stance of nationalism in keeping with the tenets of Old Hickory himself. Following this example, the younger Ord was unwavering in his attachment to the Union.

In his schooling in Washington, Edward demonstrated extraordinary mental capability, and it seemed proper for him to go on to higher education. Open to him were the halls of Georgetown College, but he had little appetite for its classical curriculum. His natural talent being particularly in mathematics, he was drawn to the possibility of securing an appointment to the United States Military Academy.

Through acquaintances of the Ord family, and very likely through the Brent connection, Edward was able to secure the support of influential persons in his endeavor. By appointment on the night of 6 March 1835, he called at the home of Colonel Sylvanus Thayer, famous superintendent of the Military Academy from 1817 to 1833. Ushered into the parlor, the stripling of sixteen faced the stern colonel and was subjected to a long and searching inquiry into his studies. "He is a very intelligent youth," Thayer reported, "&, if I am not deceived, possesses genius of a high order especially for Mathematics."[9] The colonel, with sixteen years of experience handling West Point cadets, was not likely to be deceived.

A second letter of recommendation was secured from one very close to the throne of "King Andrew." President Jackson's staunch friend, Richard M. Johnson, was a member of the House of Representatives from Kentucky. Johnson had known a brilliant career as leader of mounted riflemen in the War of 1812. As a member of Congress, he had been prominent on the House Committee on Military Affairs and a strong advocate of both military and civil education. He was soon to be Jackson's choice for the vice-presidency under Martin Van Buren. Johnson's recommendation also stated that Edward was "peculiarly gifted" with mathematical talents.[10] These letters were impressive, and the appointment appears to have come from the secretary of war, Lewis Cass, himself. Ord lost no time in accepting it, for scarcely a month remained in which to make preparations for his journey to the heights overlooking the Hudson.[11]

2

★★★★★

Restless Soldier

EDWARD Ord disembarked at the West Point boat landing on a September day in 1835 to begin his four years of training in the profession of arms. He surveyed a scene of rugged beauty. The Hudson channel narrowed here, the Point occupying a commanding position in the densely wooded highlands overlooking the river. Up the hill on West Point plain were the Academy buildings. Learning that his baggage would be delivered to him upon payment of a charge of fifty cents, Edward frugally shouldered his small trunk and trudged up the steep road.

This pinched financial condition was to plague young Ord for the next four years. He had been settled in the routine of cadet life for some little time when he wrote one of his brothers reciting some of his troubles. "In the first place," he said, "I have got no drawers, but that is nothing for if I had them I would not wear them half the time." He described himself, after studying hard all day, sneaking in at night "between one sheet" and sleeping under a piece of comforter which, when tucked in on one side, came up on the other. He confessed to being sixty-seven dollars in debt. His letter concluded with a laconic and unenlightening, "P.S. Same as before in all my studies."[1]

The studies encountered by Ord were mathematics, ethics, engineering, natural and experimental philosophy, tactics, artillery, French, drawing, chemistry and mineralogy and sword exercise.[2] Later he was to be critical of the academic encounter, charging that West Point afforded very few facilities for gaining practical knowledge. The "nice" instruments at the Academy were used only by the professors. "In a word," he said, "the course of studies at West Point is . . . eminently theoretical." He chanced to visit Kemble's foundry, which gave him more knowledge of cannon casting than all of the books in the course. He commanded a company on infantry drill once or twice, but in other arms not at all. He studied French, but was not called upon to speak it. He later learned more Spanish from a Mexican señorita in two months, he said, than French at the Point in two years.[3] He excelled in astronomy, his interest and mathematical aptitude serving him well, and he became a favorite of the professor, Benjamin Alvord.[4]

For Ord, there was pleasant association with the members of his own class, the Class of 1839, as well as those preceding and following. A roster of cadets in attendance between 1835 and 1839 would reveal the names of a great many famous men. Ord knew some of them very well, others only slightly. He formed a very warm friendship with a red-haired youth from Ohio, William Tecumseh Sherman, a friendship which was to last to the day of his death. Sherman belonged to the Class of 1840. Upon his arrival at the Academy in June of 1836, Sherman shared the same tent with Ord in the summer training activities. In this same class were George H. Thomas, Richard S. Ewell and Bushrod R. Johnson. In the Class of 1841 was another particular friend, Julius Peter Garesché of Delaware. This group also included Horatio G. Wright, Josiah Gorgas, John F. Reynolds and Don Carlos Buell. Of the Class of 1838, Pierre G. T. Beauregard was a friend. In his own class, Ord was well acquainted with the top-ranking cadets, Isaac I. Stevens and Henry W. Halleck. Others attending the Academy during Ord's time were Irvin McDowell, Braxton Bragg, Jubal A. Early, Joseph Hooker, E.R.S. Canby, D.H. Hill and James Longstreet.

Ord's record at West Point reveals something of his character. Despite his talents, his academic standing was only middling. He was never chosen a cadet officer or noncommissioned officer. Whatever merit he acquired academically seems to have been offset by demerits in conduct. In his first three years, he held steadily to his ranking of twenty-first in his class, though its membership diminished from fifty-eight to thirty-three. In his senior year, he moved up to seventeenth in a class of thirty-one graduates. His conduct grew steadily worse over the four years. In his final year, he managed somehow to amass 192 demerits and stood fifth from the bottom of the list—227th out of a cadet corps of 231. This was a poor record, but there is no evidence that he was involved in any serious escapades. He appears to have been careless and indifferent in matters of punctuality and neatness.[5] The Academy had deeply etched in him the fundamental habits of obedience and command, but he possessed a certain resistance to the trivia of regimentation, an individualism he would not abandon.

Upon graduating, Ord was commissioned second lieutenant in June 1839 and spent a three months' leave with his family in Sault Sainte Marie, Michigan. James Ord had moved in 1837 from Washington to this northern outpost, where he held the position of Indian agent. Here, Edward informed the adjutant general of his preference for the artillery and was assigned to Company H of the Third Regiment. This choice assured the venturesome Ord of an immediate field of action, for the Seminole Indian War was in progress, and the Third Artillery was then serving in Florida.[6]

In November, Ord reached his company at Fort Brooke located in a beautiful setting on the west coast near Tampa Bay. Though barely more than twenty-one, he found himself immediately in command of his company. Subsequently stationed at various forts along the east coast, he commanded not only his company but also a depot post, and he served at various times as assistant quartermaster and assistant commissary. After some lessons from the experienced sergeants, he was able to make out his rolls, returns and reports—after a fashion.[7]

Ord found himself in a dangerous situation. The Seminole Indians had sought refuge in the wilderness of the Everglades and were stubbornly resisting the efforts of the United States to subdue them. For many years the government had been removing the various Indian tribes from eastern areas and consolidating them on western reservations. The Seminoles, alternately agreeing and refusing to be moved, had come into conflict with their white neighbors and with the United States army.[8]

In December 1840, with a detachment of his regiment, Ord joined an expedition into the Everglades organized by Lieutenant Colonel William S. Harney of the Second Regiment of Dragoons. The command of about 100 men equipped with canoes set out from Fort Dallas on what the regimental report described as "a perilous and most arduous expedition into the everglades where no white man has ever been known to go before. . . ."⁹ The young lieutenant quickly learned of the brutality of Indian warfare, for Harney, humiliated by the Indians in previous encounters, was in no frame of mind to show mercy. The expedition came upon two canoes of Indians, eight of whom were captured and two "hung to a tree." Harney ordered Lieutenants Ord and James L. Rankin to push on with their detachments in canoes to the island of the Indian Chakaika. They reached their destination undetected until they dashed into the Indian camp. One warrior was shot, and two others were captured. Chakaika, a principal leader of the hostiles, was overtaken and killed. Ord, with a small detachment, pursued two warriors who had escaped to an island two miles away. As he approached on foot to the attack, several more Indians appeared holding out white flags. Ord continued the approach until within about forty yards of the Indians when they fired upon his party, killing one soldier and wounding the guide and another soldier.

The arms and ammunition of Ord's force had been damaged as the men waded through the water to the island, and, unable to return the fire effectively, they retired under cover. Rankin's detachment soon joined Ord's, its arms also useless. An attempt was made to charge the Indians, which resulted in the wounding of three more soldiers and the retirement of Rankin's force to cover. The arrival of Harney with twenty men relieved the situation, but the Indians meanwhile had made good their escape from the opposite side of the island. The next day three Indians were killed, and eleven women and children captured. The expedition reached the head of Shark River and descended it to the Gulf of Mexico, having spent twelve days and nights crossing through the Everglades.¹⁰

Ord was sent on scouting and other difficult forays into the Everglades during 1841. "I was sent ahead, on dangerous expeditions, so often," he wrote, "that one of the staff officers told me he thought the Col. had some designs against my safety. . . ."¹¹ Ord thought he and his fellow officers should be brevetted for their sufferings, "& have a years leave of absence . . . to polish up and see the ladies."¹² Indeed, Ord's reputation in the army for enduring dangers and hardships was established quite early and came to the attention eventually of higher authorities, even to General Winfield Scott himself.

According to Sherman, Ord would plunge into a stream or scale a height rather than waste time with devious ways of negotiating such obstacles.[13]

The hoped for brevet was not forthcoming, although Ord had been recommended for one. He did receive a routine promotion to first lieutenant and the coveted leave of absence early in 1842. The Third Artillery had served in Florida for a number of years and, the war being nearly over, was now in line for relief from combat duty. Ord's company was directed to report to Fort Macon, Beaufort, North Carolina, which he called one of the "d--d--st mean posts on the Atlantic."[14]

Fort Macon was a big fort, surrounded by a deep moat, solitary in its location overlooking Beaufort Inlet. Lieutenant Ord set out to explore the vicinity and to become acquainted with the people. His findings were hardly an omen of future contentment in his new station. The people of nearby New Bern were so poor and spiritless, he wrote, that "it takes half a dozen of them to hollow hurrah for Jackson." A farmer having an apple tree must "wait for the chill to come on before he can shake the apples off."[15] The citizens of Beaufort were no more satisfactory to him than those at New Bern, though he admitted that the fashionable people were all away to escape the fever and ague season.

Garrison life was "dull business" to Ord, especially after two years of roving, and he found it difficult to settle down to books and drilling. He hoped to learn in the near future of his transfer to St. Augustine or Charleston. At the same time, he had an idea of transferring to one of the prairie regiments. In short, Ord was restless and dissatisfied. He despaired of receiving a brevet and supposed that he would be a lieutenant for the next fifteen years. He saw little chance of a staff appointment and was emphatic in saying that he did not intend to spend his next fifteen years at Fort Macon.[16]

A jaunt to Charleston to see about transferring there was fruitless, and, upon his return, Ord settled down, as he phrased it, in the back room of one of the fort's dungeon-like recesses, "a complete cynic, hypocondriac [sic], miser, and misanthrope," with the intention of letting his pay accumulate "as long as Uncle Sam will furnish it." He pictured himself at the end of ten years "a lean leftenant fit only to make out a muster roll or gallant simple spinsters to meeting and back again."[17] As he had nowhere to go, Ord took to reading. He also began to study French and cursed himself for not filling his mind with all sorts of knowledge at West Point when he had the chance. [18]

Indeed, Ord had sunk into a severe state of depression. His discontent seemed to affect him like a fever with ever-mounting intensity. His stay at Fort Macon can be described as no less than torture. He had been endowed with a superabundance of energy; he must be constantly active, constantly moving among new scenes and into new adventures. He was not without understanding of his own character. "The fact is I want excitement, travel, or novelty of some kind," he said, ". . . or a little of Gods correction to the dissatisfied and mutinous spirits, ie [sic], misfortune would no doubt cure me. . . ."[19]

Coupled with his restlessness and melancholia, Ord had a somewhat fiery temperament. "I believe we have all got a little of mothers temper in us, (God bless her for it)," he wrote his brother Pacificus, "for I notice that those whom I can hurt take d--n good care not to make me so [angry] again." This characteristic Ord did not consider extreme, for he concluded: "I don't think any of us get mad at trifles. . . ."[20] In any event, neither brooding nor temper were able to obscure a fine sense of humor and a jocularity which must have given his associates much pleasure. Even in the depths of melancholy, his expression often took a humorous turn.

At the age of twenty-five, Lieutenant Ord was in the full vigor of maturity and eager for action. His weaknesses stood revealed and recognized—a tendency toward depression, occasional ill-temper, and dissatisfaction with inactivity. His strong points well outweighed his weaknesses; he was intelligent, energetic, courageous and possessed of a fine sense of humor. His rigorous Catholic training had also had its effect. "God Almighty & Pa have made us too honorable," he wrote Pacificus. "Well there is some consolation in knowing it is not our fault."[21]

Ord was ambitious. When not plagued by his temperamental weaknesses, his self-confidence and determination were boundless. "If it were not for my fits of ill nature, disgust, and almost want of hope I believe I could succeed at anything I should turn my hand to," he said emphatically.[22] "It is d----d provoking that our troubles like bad luck generally should all come in a lump. Never mind! We must show our perseverance, & the indomitable courage of the good old stock by rising the higher after every fall. I think I shall succeed in my efforts for I'll be damned if I shall stop at trifles."[23] Ord was well equipped mentally, physically and morally to make his mark; he needed a field of action.

It was with great satisfaction that Ord learned in November 1844 of his long-hoped-for transfer from Fort Macon. His new post was Baltimore's famed Fort McHenry on Whetstone Point jutting into the Patapsco River. Here Company F was assigned for instruction in light artillery. In his new round of activities, Ord rode into Baltimore two or three times a week, as he put it, to take off "the Ft. Macon rust and disgust."[24]

In February 1845, while on leave in Washington, Ord called upon Lieutenant and Brevet Captain John C. Frémont in an unsuccessful attempt to join Frémont's third exploring expedition to the West. Later the same year, always on the lookout for a change, he managed to be relieved of command of his company and was ordered to temporary duty at the Coast Survey Office in Washington.[25]

Ord's chronic ailments, restlessness and ambition, continued to plague him. Perhaps a small war would develop, he thought, in which he might get "chopt up for Glory." The "small war" which Ord envisioned was a possibility, for the two pressing political questions of the day, Oregon and Texas, threatened to involve the United States in clashes with England and Mexico.

These were the great days of "Manifest Destiny." Ord was not unaffected by the expansionist fever abroad in the land, but his views on territorial acquisition were unsettled—now moderate, now extreme. In addition, his views of expansionist wars had more than a touch of cynicism about them. The politicians who would get the nation into a war of conquest would be generals and colonels, get money and patronage out of it, and leave all the hard knocks to the regulars, he wrote.[26]

Nevertheless, Ord urged his brother, Placidus, then a member of the Michigan Assembly, to come out strongly in legislative resolutions for all of Oregon and the extension of our free institutions. He did not think war with England likely, however, and seemed more interested in impressing President James K. Polk and General Lewis Cass with Ord support for expansionism than with the actual expansion itself.[27] The Oregon matter was soon settled with England by division of the territory at the forty-ninth parallel.

The Texas question was not so easily resolved. At the time of Ord's visit with Frémont in Washington, Ord noted that the bill for the annexation of the Republic of Texas was all the talk. "I shall be glad if it passes," he wrote, "as it may give us something to do, tho I think its playing a grab game."[28] The grab was accomplished on 1 March 1845, when President John Tyler signed the joint resolution of Congress providing for annexation. The passage of the bill resulted in the severance of diplomatic relations between the United States and Mexico. The republic below the Rio Grande had never given up its claim to Texas. The territorial problem was further complicated by the desire of President Polk to possess California. Later Ord came around to an even more extreme view that the United States should have not only California, but ought to seize all of Mexico—again not so much for the territory as for the fact that anarchy prevailed there under a succession of tyrants who stripped honest citizens of their substance. Our democratic system would be a blessing to the whole country, he believed.[29]

In preparation for the anticipated extension of U.S. boundaries, Ord set about to equip himself to take part in the matter by studying Spanish. "The Companies (Army) will be increased," he wrote, "one new Regt raised, and probably a row with Mexico, in which case I shall be 'thar.' "[30] On 10 May news arrived in Washington that Mexicans had crossed the Rio Grande and attacked an American force under General Zachary Taylor. President Polk sent his war message to Congress on 11 May, and, on 13 May, war was declared upon Mexico.

Ord, as usual, was eager to be off to battle, but his enthusiasm seems to have been prompted strictly by personal and professional ambition. As a good Democrat, he told his brother Pacificus, he was strong for war, besides which war was his trade and he liked the excitement of it. Through the losses of war he might gain. At the same time, he expressed contempt for the politicians responsible for bringing on the conflict. President Polk had called for 20,000 volunteers, and Edward warned Pacificus not to volunteer. Volunteers, he said, were merely puppets to satisfy the ambition of political demagogues. He thought the president would not get 10,000 volunteers, as he did not think there were so many "d----d fools" in the country. Moreover, he went on, the citizen soldier had no idea what a mean, disgusting business soldiering is or the "'many dangers that do environ the man who meddles with cold iron.'"[31]

Edward applied all around—to the secretary of war and the adjutant general—for a transfer that would get him into action quickly. Ever resourceful, he requested the adjutant general at the same time for permission to go recruiting to fill Company F. He was off to Fort McHenry to pick up the recruiting detail and, on 26 May, arrived at his destination—his native town, Cumberland, Maryland! "Here I am at last," he wrote to Pacificus, "on same errand as Pa 34 years ago."[32] Prospects for recruiting seemed fairly good. He found a town of 7,000 inhabitants very lively. Cumberland now possessed a courthouse, jail, bank, church, barber shop, warehouses, shops and many substantial brick homes. The people, he noted, were "plenty but not ardently" fond of Texas.[33]

There were numerous Cresap relatives in Cumberland and vicinity, and the lieutenant made an effort to see as many of them as possible. "They were very hospitable," he wrote to his brother, "and Mothers black eye and animated, vigorous face shone out in two or three of them." In the area he was so well received generally that he boasted that he would make himself popular enough to run for Congress some day.[34]

In the meantime, Company F was placed under orders for California. Completing his recruiting duty in June, Ord repaired with the company to Fort Columbus on Governor's Island, New York, to make preparations for the long voyage by sea around Cape Horn to the faraway Pacific Coast.

An interesting party began to join Ord at Fort Columbus for the passage. His brother, Dr. James L. Ord, just graduated from the Medical College of the University of Pennsylvania, appeared as acting assistant surgeon (though remaining a civilian). Ord had written his good friend Lieutenant William T. Sherman to apply for the California voyage, but Sherman, without committing himself, had merely applied for any active service. Sherman was assigned to Company F. Yet another friend, "Old Brains" of Ord's class at West Point, First Lieutenant Henry Wager Halleck of the Corps of Engineers, was attached to Company F for the voyage. Thus on 14 July 1846, with a notable party on board, the store ship *Lexington* weighed anchor in New York harbor and put out to sea.[35]

3

★★★★★

California:
Conquest and Gold

EDWARD Ord was enthusiastic as he began his travels. With full sails billowing overhead and the outline of New York City diminishing in the distance, he had no doubt that this was the good life for him. Not only was there adventure, new experiences, and new and strange scenes on sea and land ahead, but also, at the end of the voyage, there was an exotic country, a veritable *terra incognita*, in which fame and promotion might be won. For Lieutenant Ord there could scarcely have been a more enticing prospect.

Aboard the *Lexington*, the company of officers in the wardroom proved to be a congenial group. Ord shared a stateroom with Sherman and found the accommodations comfortable. The *Lexington* was a slow but strong ship with a usual speed of six knots. She had formerly been a twenty-four-gun sloop of war, but because of her dull sailing, had been converted into a store ship.[1]

The first leg of the passage, 7,000 miles from New York to Rio de Janeiro, Brazil, required fifty-nine days. Ord admitted that the journey was pleasant under the circumstances, but grumbled that "the sea don't improve on acquaintance." As the *Lexington* sailed into the beautiful harbor of Rio de Janeiro, Ord and the party aboard had before them more than two weeks of pleasant recreation amid the strange sights and sounds of Rio and its vicinity. The lieutenant rode all about the town, making his way through narrow streets, past thick-walled stuccoed houses with barred windows. Gangs of Negroes trotted along carrying coffee, bananas and oranges. Indeed, the city seemed to be made up of Negroes and mulattoes with a sprinkling of French, English and Yankee merchants. Churches were profusely scattered on the surrounding hills. Ord and Sherman visited the botanical garden of Emperor Dom Pedro II, pulling specimens of rare plants and eating fruit from the trees. The young officers rode boldly up to the imperial palace itself, their uniforms passing them by the sentinel unchallenged. Ord made yet another horseback excursion, this one to the top of the Corcovado, one of the highest peaks near Rio. On his return, a farewell visit to the home of United States Minister Henry A. Wise, a Virginian, evoked in Ord a longing for his own home and family.

Aboard ship, all hands were at work hoisting sails and weighing anchor. Ord watched the hills of Rio fade from sight as the *Lexington* headed south to round Cape Horn. The passage to the Horn was monotonous, though the weather was becoming colder. Rounding the Horn proved to be extremely hazardous and difficult. For nearly a month, the *Lexington* fought against a mighty storm. The members of the crew were nearly exhausted from the constant struggle on decks covered with ice and snow. All the fresh food was gone, and the water allowance was down to two quarts per man each day. Ord and his associates spent their time in a little stateroom six feet square, where, by lighting three or four candles, they made it warm enough to play cards. At last the *Lexington* shook off the gales of the Horn and headed northwesterly up the coast of Chile.

For several weeks the men aboard the *Lexington* had been isolated in their own small world. Ord wondered about the progress of the Mexican War and was impatient for news. With fair winds along the Chilean Coast the *Lexington* put into Valparaiso harbor on 24 November. The news here was rather uncertain and not up-to-date. Ord was pleased to learn that a more vigorous prosecution of the war was promised by the sending of Commodore Robert F. Stockton to command the naval and land forces. In the meantime, he had to reconcile himself to nearly two more months of slow sailing from Valparaiso to California. Finally, after a voyage of more than six months, the *Lexington* sailed into Monterey Bay on 27 January 1847, and Company F occupied Monterey Redoubt.[2]

Monterey was a picturesque old town which had served as the capital of California under Spanish and Mexican rule. The settlement lay in a beautiful setting at the southern end of the bay. The fort was situated on a hill about 100 feet above the sea and commanded the anchorage. Ord was quartered there with the troops, while Sherman and Dr. James L. Ord had more comfortable accommodations in the customhouse. The town held about 800 people, mostly Mexicans and Indians with a sprinkling of English, Scottish and American inhabitants.[3]

Ord must have been considerably chagrined to learn upon landing that the last shot in the conquest of California, actually the reconquest of southern California, had been fired a scant three weeks before, and that he had been denied a part in the conflict. He had momentary hope that more action might develop, but the people of the region turned out to be remarkably polite and friendly. With all the fighting over, Ord and Company F settled down to a routine existence at Monterey not at all pleasing to the lieutenant or his soldiers. They were set to work building a fort, a disagreeable task which made the men grumble and desert.[4]

Ord and Sherman were impatient to have a look inland, and, after securing permission, started out on horseback for the Mission of San Juan Bautista, some twenty-five miles to the northeast. Through the strange and picturesque land they traveled, taking advantage of Californian hospitality—usually a meal of beef and a bed on the dirt floor of a one-room adobe house. "We were officers and *caballeros*," said Sherman, "and could not be ignored."[5] The young lieutenants arrived at the mission on a Sunday morning and saw several horses hitched about and heard church music. Ord, "somewhat of a Catholic," as Sherman described him, created a sensation as he strode into the church in uniform with spurs clanking and knelt down to join in the worship.[6]

Ord's impressions of California were varied. A pretty country, he called it: "All mountains with now and then a valley." And then, later: "This country has been much overrated. Tis only fit for cattle grazing." The native Californians stood well in his estimation. "I don't circulate . . . much but like the people & the place. Tis something like St. Augustine

Fla—the men drive and kill cattle & ride horses & gamble; the women dance & have children at an early age."[7] There was a shortage of food and supplies of all sorts, and prices were exorbitant. Ord, Sherman, Halleck and Dr. Murray Warner sought to economize by boarding in the home of Don Manuel Jimeno and his wife Doña Augustina, members of a prominent Monterey family.[8]

Not long after his arrival in California, there occurred a change in Ord's status calculated to put him in a better frame of mind. The commanding officer of Company F, Captain Christopher Q. Tompkins, a Virginian, decided to go home. This gave Ord command of the company, and a new army bill brought him close to a captaincy. On 30 April 1847, he assumed command with Sherman as his second.[9]

A state of hostilities with Mexico continued to exist until 2 February 1848, when the Treaty of Guadalupe Hidalgo was signed. Life in California was not to return to any semblance of prewar stability, however, for, shortly before the signing of the treaty, gold was discovered in northern California.

Ord wrote to his family back East of the mania for getting gold dust, for a mania it truly was, with ever-increasing intensity. The forces of law and order in California, already weak, were now subjected to unbearable strain as thousands of immigrants began pouring in from every part of the globe. No civil government could be established while the peace treaty was pending. Even after its signing, the Congress was slow to define California's status. Meanwhile, a tiny military establishment was expected to police this vast area. Colonel Richard B. Mason, commanding the Tenth Military Department and serving as military governor of California in Monterey, had under his command three bodies of United States troops— Colonel John D. Stevenson's regiment of New York Volunteers, soon to be discharged; and two companies of regulars, Company C of the First Dragoons and Ord's Company F of the Third Artillery. The latter company numbered sixty-two, present and absent, but scarcely a day passed that one or more did not desert.[10]

Colonel Mason, with several attendants, set out on a tour of observation of the gold region. The few steady workmen sorely needed in building up the villages and in improving land had either preceded or followed him. Even the Indians, upon whom the army depended for supplies of bread, corn and beans, were being enticed away by high wages. Dr. James L. Ord, in company with some of the most prominent Californians, had left Santa Barbara for the mines. Lieutenant Sherman, now adjutant to Colonel Mason, the governor, was off to make his fortune. Sherman took up a lot of shirts and other clothing to sell, and carried his pick and shovel with the intention of going to work. "I wouldn't be much surprised if Col. Mason, the Governor himself was now hard at work hunting for the big lumps," Ord wrote.[11] Some six months after the discovery, Ord described conditions in Monterey and vicinity: "The farmers have left their crops, husbands their wives & families, tradesmen and merchants their shops until there is no one here scarcely except soldiers and women. I am afraid even the soldiers and women will all clear out."[12]

In the midst of this mad rush to the gold fields, as men forgot the restraints of a more stable social order, lawlessness became rampant throughout California. "At the present time," Ord said, "there is, as the best disposed citizens will tell you, no law in California except the law of the rifle. Every man goes armed. Robbery, theft, and even murders take place between here and the mines every week, and there is not even the slightest attempt made to overtake or punish the offenders."[13]

Very soon after Ord wrote of this miserable state of affairs, a shocking crime occurred at the Mission of San Miguel ninety miles south of Monterey. This abandoned mission had been leased to a man named Reed who occupied the premises with his wife, several children, and servants—ten in all. The mail rider from the south, making his way to Monterey, stopped at the mission as usual and discovered that all ten occupants of the place, men, women and children, had been brutally murdered. Riding posthaste to Monterey, the courier reported to Colonel Mason, who dispatched Ord with a detachment of soldiers to pursue the murderers to the death. Ord was off with a couple of men before midnight and reached San Miguel the next day. He ascertained the facts in the case, found the trail of the murderers, and overtook them just south of Santa Barbara. Ord and his men had a running fight with the criminals, five in number, killed their leader, and captured the others. The murderers were all deserters from the war sloop *Warren* at Monterey. They were brought to Santa Barbara to stand trial. Colonel Mason told Ord to inform the alcalde that if the evidence in the case was clear and the sentence of the jury was death, he might carry out the sentence without referring the matter to the military governor. The trial was held, the sentence was death, and they were shot. Ord and his detachment were present but did not assist in the execution. Colonel Mason urged upon his superiors in Washington the need for an early creation of a territorial government for the newly acquired province. [14]

The military establishment itself steadily diminished in the face of the need for law and order. The regiment of New York Volunteers, some 300 strong, had been turned loose upon Monterey to await discharge. They were disorderly and insubordinate toward their officers and proceeded to rob and plunder every unprotected house. Desertion among the regulars increased through 1848, as recruits brought from the states to fill the regular companies promptly headed for the gold fields. By October, Ord's company had dwindled to thirty, while only five dragoons remained. [15]

Sometime during 1848, probably in late July and early August, Ord paid a brief visit to the gold mines. Perhaps he was after deserters. If so, his efforts were fruitless. "Tis useless to ask questions as to who passed," he wrote with evident despair, "when some 10 or 15 hundred of all classes went on up the road the week before! And parties of discharged and runaway soldiers, sailors, & marines line the road, clear to the mines and mountains & there scatter amongst the thousands nearly all of whom have also run away from some service or other." Ord was especially indignant at the desertion of native Americans. "I have been some fifteen years in service and have had to manage all sorts of characters," he wrote, "and had I to lead a forlorn hope or defend a desperate pass I would rather have a picked body of Irishmen than any other men I have met." [16]

The military situation steadily deteriorated until, early in 1849, Colonel Mason initiated a policy of liberal furloughs to all soldiers desiring them. This amounted to a virtual abandonment of any attempt to maintain the military establishment in California. Five men of Company F volunteered to stay on duty. "No desertions under the new system," Ord drily observed to Sherman. [17]

The ugly condition in California brought Ord to a complete disapproval of the recent war. His language was not gentle as he expressed his views to Pacificus: "The plain truth of the matter is, that we have, having been set on by an interested knave [President Polk], choked Mexico until she has disgorged two very rotten members [California and New Mexico], which the filthy appetite of our President took a fancy to, and if the Government of the United States are wise they will avoid such offensive matter at all events till the maggots have left."[18]

Tied down to a token Company F, Ord was in unhappy circumstances. He complained that he was getting poorer, while everyone else was going to the mines and getting rich. Though the prospect was unpleasant, he determined to hold on until the spring of 1849 when he expected to receive a six months' leave of absence and then make "a bold push for a small fortune and home."[19]

Ord began his leave in April and immediately headed north to the gold region. He took a brief turn at gold mining, apparently without much luck.[20] Calling upon his Coast Survey experience, he then teamed up with Sherman to engage in surveying in the vicinity of Stockton. From here, they went to the village of Sacramento and surveyed for Captain John A. Sutter. After a couple of months, they had accumulated $7,000.00, not a fortune, but at least a hedge against the soaring cost of living.[21]

Ord discovered that his talent as a surveyor was in further demand. The Ayuntamiento, or council, of the town of Los Angeles had requested that the military government send a surveyor to make a map of the town. The request was in pursuance of an order by Brevet Brigadier General Bennett Riley, successor to Colonel Mason as military governor, requiring the town to have a survey made in order that vacant lots might be allocated. Ord was selected for the task and proceeded to Los Angeles to confer with the officials.[22]

Los Angeles was built close to the hills on the north side of Los Angeles River Valley. The "pueblo" consisted of "an old adobe church, and about a hundred adobe houses scattered around a dusty plaza, and along three or four broad streets leading thereto." Until the discovery of gold, the population had been about 3,000, including some retired trappers and a number of vagabond Indians once attached to the missions. Upon conferring with the officials, Ord contracted to make the first survey of the town and provide a map for the sum of three thousand dollars in coin. He completed his task within six weeks of the date of the contract.[23]

Ord returned to Monterey to make preparations for a special mission under orders from General Riley. The general instructed Ord to proceed to Los Angeles and from there to

Cajon Pass, some fifty miles to the east, to select a point for the establishment of a military force to restrain Indians prone to come through the pass to steal horses in the area around Los Angeles. In addition, Riley verbally requested Ord to report on the possibility of constructing a rail or other road between the southeast corner of California and the valley of the upper Rio Grande.[24]

Ord took the steamer from Monterey to San Diego and there began his reconnaissance. The port at San Diego he described as a good frigate harbor and recommended that it be surveyed. The town itself contained about twenty badly built adobe houses and two good ones. He visited the nearby Mission of San Diego whose walls were tumbling down and where everything within was going to ruin. The library, he suggested, should be placed in charge of someone interested in its preservation.[25]

Picking up a guide in San Diego, Ord struck out northward on horseback in the direction of Los Angeles. The old Spanish missions were of interest to him, and, indeed, his journey seemed to be a progress from one abandoned mission to another. He passed the deserted Mission of San Luis Rey, its people all dead or gone away. He thought someone should be sent there to protect the woodwork and gardens. Proceeding north, he made his way to the missions of Las Flores and San Juan Capistrano, both falling into ruins. Skirting Los Angeles, he headed inland to Cajon Pass, one of the several important passes through the Sierra Madre.

In accordance with his instructions, Ord contracted for troops' quarters and corn at some of the ranchos near the pass. On his return, he stopped at the remains of the Mission of San Gabriel near Los Angeles, once one of the richest of the stations of California. A few more miles brought him to the "pueblo" of Los Angeles which he had surveyed a few weeks before. In the town, he spoke to the judge, the alcaldes, Benjamin D. Wilson, John Temple, Pio Pico, Manuel Riquena and other principal inhabitants, urging them to form a volunteer company for local protection against marauding Indians. All were in favor of this measure. The lieutenant then returned to San Diego and boarded the steamer for Monterey.

Back at his post in Monterey, Ord set himself to the task of preparing a report for General Riley on the possibility of constructing a railroad from southern California to the upper Rio

Grande which might become part of a future transcontinental railroad. The sectional question as to whether the proposed transcontinental road should follow a southern or a northern route complicated the matter. Ord proposed an intermediate route roughly along the thirty-fifth parallel.[26]

As the end of 1849 approached, Ord looked forward to an extended leave of absence which would permit him to return to the East, where he hoped to secure authorization to make the topographical examination of the route between New Mexico and California. In this hope he was disappointed. General Winfield Scott gave a favorable endorsement, but higher authority failed to act.

The steamer on which Ord sailed on 1 January 1850, bound for Panama, had a distinguished complement of passengers aboard. Among the army officers returning home were Ord's friends, Sherman, Andrew J. Smith and Daniel H. Rucker. Another passenger was John C. Frémont, about whom Ord had said many harsh words for his conduct in defying regular army authority in the conquest and occupation of California. Also among the travelers was William M. Gwin, a Tennessean with whom Ord developed a cordial friendship. Frémont and Gwin had been elected as California's first United States senators and were now on their way to Washington, bearing a copy of the newly framed state constitution. They hoped to promote the admission of California into the Union as a free state and their own admission into the Senate.[27]

As Ord reached the nation's capital, a critical debate was in progress in the Congress; the slavery controversy was threatening to undermine the very foundations of the Union. On 29 January 1850, Henry Clay had introduced his famous compromise bill into the Senate in an effort to settle the several outstanding issues. The first of Clay's measures provided for the admission of California into the Union, leaving the slavery question to be decided by the people there; but the Californians soon had before Congress a constitution expressly forbidding slavery. Speculation as to the status of California was ended by the passage of the Compromise of 1850. The bill to admit California as a free state was signed by the president on 9 September 1850.

Ord himself was a professed proslavery advocate at this time.[28] While in Washington he "conversed with many of the wise men there," he said. Almost certainly, Senator Jefferson

Davis of Mississippi was among those sages. On 3 July 1850, the Mississippi lawmaker secured the printing of Ord's reports of the southern California reconnaissance and of the suggested railroad route in the *Senate Executive Documents*.[29] Davis and Ord are known to have carried on a correspondence at this time. Nearly three years later, a bill for a transcontinental railroad was before the Senate, and Senator Gwin was pushing hard for the immediate construction of a road along the very route described by Ord. Gwin read Ord's report in the Senate and termed it *"conclusive* on the subject."[30] Under Gwin's leadership the Senate shortly was persuaded with House concurrence to authorize the secretary of war to make preliminary surveys to determine the best route from the Mississippi River to the Pacific Ocean. The surveys were made in 1853 under the direction of Jefferson Davis, who was, by this time, secretary of war. Lieutenant Amiel W. Whipple and his party explored the route along the thirty-fifth parallel described by Ord in his report. Whipple followed a course almost identical with that outlined by Ord and reached the Pacific coastal plain through Cajon Pass.[31]

On 13 July 1850, Ord embarked from New York aboard a dirty and uncomfortable steamer to return to California. Three days out, a terrific gale struck the ship, sweeping away staterooms, berths, and part of the wheelhouse, and flooding the engine room. "I wondered on to what beach our bodies would float & how they'd look," Ord wrote. "I went to work at pumps; in intervals tried to calm passengers. . . . Knew God Almighty would do as he pleased."[32] The storm finally abated its fury, and the ensuing days were pleasant.

Ord was fond of going aloft to scan the waters and the horizon, and, on one occasion, recorded that he "had a pleasant time thinking of the world of waters and of the land beyond and people on it. . . . [I] thought a great deal," he wrote. "Getting quite serious now. Didn't used to think so much." Upon passing an island which he believed was the first land seen by Columbus, Ord began thinking about the hard time Columbus had, wondering what the discoverer thought upon seeing land, and wishing that he could have been in Columbus's place. "Great man, Columbus," he mused, "greatest ever lived—I think—barring our Savior."[33]

Arrived at last at Chagres, Ord boarded a river steamer for the first leg of the Isthmus crossing. From the steamer, he transferred to a small boat poled by natives. "Had to pole myself some," he wrote. "Astonished the natives with the facility with which I handled the pole and jabbered Spanish."[34] In this fashion, he reached Cruces, continuing by muleback for the remainder of the crossing to the city of Panama on the Pacific Ocean, where he boarded the steamer for Monterey.

Soon after his arrival, Ord received the welcome news of his promotion to captain of Company B, Third Artillery. As his new company was in garrison at Fort Independence, Boston, Massachusetts, the promotion meant a return to the East. The new captain assumed command of his company early in 1851. The fort was located on a rocky little island in the bay some three miles from Boston. Ord managed to visit the city once or twice a week, but his warm nature was not at home among the New Englanders. The Yankee temperament repelled him—or perhaps the fault lay with his own impetuosity. He soon began to build up a surplus of restlessness and discontent. Fort Independence was becoming another Fort Macon. He complained of the cold and of the bleak island. "Don't like it," he wrote Placidus, "nothing to do; want to be roving."[35] On top of his dissatisfaction, Ord was at odds with his immediate superior, Major Francis O. Wyse. Charges and countercharges flew back and forth, and Ord was placed under arrest. The matter was finally resolved without court-martial, but this did not render his situation more tolerable.[36] Finally, a cooperative surgeon furnished Ord with a certificate recommending removal to a drier climate or a sick leave. The certificate procured for the captain a leave of five months.

In this interim, Ord managed to arrange a return to the Coast Survey, and orders shortly came for him in March 1853 to repair to Savannah, Georgia, to continue the triangulation of the Savannah River. In the course of the next three months, he surveyed thirty square miles.[37] Returning in June to Washington he prepared for another assignment: California! He was directed to take charge of the triangulation of the islands along the West Coast. In the latter part of 1853, Ord began his work near San Pedro and reported in July 1854 that his survey had covered about 421 square miles. There was yet much more to be done.[38]

★★★★★

Captain Ord found time, in spite of his pressing Coast Survey duties, to attend to affairs of the heart. This was not a new venture for him, for he had courted many young ladies.

He confessed to having run through his winter's pay pursuing the ladies while stationed at Fort McHenry. He had broken his New England exile at Fort Independence by journeying once a month to visit a young lady in New York City. His frequent changes of station no doubt militated against a permanent attachment. He was now thirty-six, a ripe age for a bachelor. His captaincy meant that matrimony was now feasible—at least economically.

Ord gave his attention to twenty-three-year-old Mary Mercer Thompson, daughter of the Honorable Robert Augustine Thompson, a leading lawyer of San Francisco. The Thompsons were Virginians, and the family had been prominent land and slaveholders for several generations in Culpeper County in the Old Dominion. In Virginia, Robert Augustine Thompson had married Mary Ann Slaughter, by whom he had six children, Mary Mercer being the second child. He was married a second time in 1847 to Mrs. Elizabeth Jane Early Woods, sister of Major Jubal A. Early. From the second marriage, three children were added to the family. Thompson had begun a political career in Virginia, serving as a member of Congress from that state. He forsook Virginia politics to make a new start in California, setting up in San Francisco for the practice of law and serving for several years as judge in the courts of the state.[39]

Captain Ord's courtship of "Molly" Thompson, the judge's daughter, was successful, and on 15 October 1854, they were married in San Francisco. The marriage vows were read by the Right Reverend William I. Kip, first Protestant Episcopal Bishop of California, only recently arrived in the state.

Molly Ord was a beautiful woman, open-hearted, vivacious and self-controlled. She and Edward were a good match, as they were mutually helpful to one another in many ways. This was especially apparent in those all-too-frequent intervals when his military duties kept them apart. In these times of separation, he advised her on practical matters, exhorted her to walk for exercise and to keep busy to keep the blues away. On her part, she expressed sincere affection and Christian sentiments which inspired him to be more patient and self-disciplined. Her religious convictions ran deep; she sent him a Bible on one occasion. In letters to her, he mentioned reading the Scriptures and acknowledged that she had had great influence in making him a better Christian. Her influence was too much for the captain's father, however, who, after the lapse of a year, was deploring the fact that Edward had not attended mass since his marriage, but rather had frequented Protestant services. "Pray for his return to the true Church," James Ord enjoined Placidus, "and for the conversion of your sister-in-law."[40]

The Ords' family life was affectionate, openly sentimental, and had much good humor. A glimpse of this life was described by Captain Erasmus D. Keyes, detailed as a member of a court-martial convened at Fort Miller, California, in 1858: "Captain E.O.C. Ord was the commanding officer, and his family were with him at his post. They entertained the members of the court-martial bountifully, and the loving harmony of that household was delightful to observe. Ord was cheerful and domestic in his habits, and his accomplished wife told me that her life had been joyous."[41]

Family responsibilities were good for Ord, and he engaged in such domestic pursuits as gardening and was fond of going fishing occasionally. It must be said, however, that, for all its beneficial effects, domesticity failed to cure his wanderlust. He was always looking for a change of station, always eager to get into action!

Edward and Molly Ord were blessed with many children. There were thirteen in all, though only seven lived to maturity. The three sons were Catholics, the four daughters Episcopalians—an arrangement which seemed to suit all around. Besides showing much affection for his children, Ord's influence upon them was positive in other ways. He encouraged them, sometimes exhorted them, and indulged them—perhaps too much. But they turned out well, and that, it would seem, is the mark of the successful parent.

★★★★★

Molly Ord was now embraced within the larger family circle of James and Rebecca Ord and their children. The Ords were a warmly affectionate family, comfortable and relaxed with one another. They maintained an admirable sense of unity. Letter writing was frequent, and the recipient of a letter quite often added one of his own to the paper and passed it on to a third, and so on in chain-letter fashion. Or generous extracts would be made from a letter and passed along. James

Ord was an inveterate copier of letters which thus made the rounds of the family. There was a spirit of loyalty, cooperation, and helpfulness among the Ords, and Edward, as one of the older children, early assumed responsibility in family matters. During West Point days, he thought of subscribing to the *Philadelphia Gazette*, principally to send it to his father. He contributed a share of financial assistance to his parents, assistance in the education of the younger children, and advice about schooling and work.

By 1854, six of James Ord's seven sons were in California. Pacificus was United States district attorney in San Francisco, James Lycurgus was practicing medicine at Monterey, Robert and John were farming near Sacramento, and William Marcellus was assisting Edward on the Coast Survey. In 1855, James and Rebecca, with their youngest child and only daughter, Georgiana, left their home in Washington and made the passage to California. By this time, the railroad across the Isthmus of Panama was in use, making the journey much easier. Not long afterward, Placidus brought his family to California, thus completing the remarkable migration of all of the Ord family from the East to the West Coast.[42] "It seems my fate to settle here," Edward had said after one of his many transfers to California,[43] and so it proved to be the fate of the entire Ord clan.

4

★★★★★

Indian Wars

CAPTAIN Ord was relieved of Coast Survey duties in May 1855 and assumed command of Company B, Third Artillery, at Benicia Barracks some twenty miles northeast of San Francisco. A few months after he took his post, the tedium of garrison life was interrupted by an outbreak of Indian hostilities in the recently organized Washington Territory. There had been a great influx of American immigrants into the Oregon country in the 1840s and 1850s. As the white settlers and miners moved in to dispute the Indians' claim to the land, the red man resisted the encroachment. This brought about the usual pattern of outrage and retaliation. Ord was called into action in the territory for the Yakima War (1855-59).[1]

Ord, with his company, reached Camp Yakima near the Columbia River, where an expedition under the command of Major Gabriel J. Rains was being assembled. Ord was given special responsibility for three mountain howitzers. The force moved out on 30 October 1855 for a drive into the Yakima Indian country. Rains's command was composed of 351 artillerymen, infantrymen and dragoons with 19 officers, including Captain Christopher C. Augur and Lieutenant Philip H. Sheridan. The column was augmented by 488 Independent Oregon Volunteers under the command of Colonel James W. Nesmith.[2]

The expedition moved northeasterly toward the Yakima River with its destination the Yakima Mission on the Atahnam

River. Upon reaching the mission the soldiers by chance discovered a cache of gunpowder. They jumped to the conclusion
that the mission priest, Father J. Charles Pandoza, had furnished powder to the Indians, and in their fury they destroyed
the mission. This destruction and the Indians' driving off fifty-
four army mules were the only noteworthy events of the
expedition.[3]

Ord chafed under Rains's mismanagement of the affair but
was powerless to do anything about it. Major Rains, Ord
wrote, was "a good Christian and man of personal valour," but
he would not act, nor would he allow anyone else to act for
him, and the time for action, according to Ord, was all the
time.[4] Rains was ordered to conclude the campaign and return
to Fort Dalles on the Columbia River. The troops reached the
latter place late in November, having marched 175 miles.
Everyone generally conceded that the expedition was a miserable failure, though Major Rains attempted to lay the blame on
everyone else and to smooth over the fiasco.[5]

Upon his return to Benicia, Ord, highly exasperated at
Rains's conduct, preferred charges of incompetency against
him. Rains promptly made counter-charges, accusing Ord of
stealing a pair of shoes from Father Pandoza at the time the
mission was destroyed. As related by Sheridan, a rumor of
such a theft had circulated through the camp as a jest, occasioned by the fact that Ord, "who was somewhat eccentric in
his habits, and had started on the expedition rather indiffer-
ently shod in carpet-slippers, here came out in a brand-new
pair of shoes."[6] The charges against Ord, of course, were
ignored. General John E. Wool could not spare a sufficient
number of officers of rank to constitute a court-martial in the
case of Rains, and the latter escaped with a transfer to another
field.

Meanwhile, the Rogue River Indians in southern Oregon
were on the warpath again. They had been involved in inter-
mittent trouble with whites since 1850. The latest flare-up was
provoked by outrages against them by miners and territorial
volunteers. Letters and reports of General Wool and his officers
were full of accounts of such acts of violence, to the dismay of
the territorial authorities and inhabitants. The San Francisco
press took the side of the United States military officers, while
the territorial press furiously denounced the army for its slowness and inefficiency and pressed for a more vigorous prosecution of the war. Ord was right in the middle of the fray, writing

his views in a letter to the *New York Herald* and in an article in *Harper's New Monthly Magazine* in which he laid the responsibility for the war upon the whites. The captain, with wry humor, suggested that all the gold-hunters might be put on a reservation and paid to stay there, leaving the God-forsaken country to the Indians.[7]

The war was at hand for whatever cause, and Ord and his company, along with other companies, were ordered north. The troops were packed "as thickly as books on a library shelf" on a little steamer which proceeded to land detachments at various places between San Francisco and Puget Sound. Ord's company was dropped off at Crescent City, California, a half-moon of shore ringed with shanties serving the needs of miners, now made idle by the Indian troubles. In a few days, Ord and his men set out up the coast toward the mouth of Rogue River in Oregon. A portion of the march was through a forest of huge redwood trees, which greatly impressed Ord. Some of these giants, he wrote, "appeared to have been growing since before the birth of our Savior."[8] Beneath these trees, the ground was covered with great, green ferns upon which the sun had never shone. Ord's column encountered other natural features, some in the nature of obstacles. They came to a river which had to be forded. The captain ordered the men to take off their lower garments, leaving their coats on, and to put clothing, rations, and ammunition on their shoulders. Ord and another officer stationed themselves in the deepest place to assist any who might be swept off their feet. The soldiers plunged into the swiftly flowing stream whose waters were waist-deep and ice-cold. One or two had to be fished out by the officers, and only four got their ammunition wet.[9]

At the mouth of the Chetco River, Ord was met by Colonel Robert C. Buchanan whose command he was to join, and the force marched to the mouth of Rogue River. There were Indians in the immediate vicinity. Colonel Buchanan chose a camp site; Ord protested that the location was exposed, and the colonel moved. Again Ord objected, and again the colonel moved. During the night, a corporal was shot by a recruit on guard. Several shots followed, and the camp was in panic. Ord brought in the wounded man and went around reassuring the soldiers. "Very bad practice sending recruits to fight Indians," he wrote in his diary. "Generally do more harm than good."[10]

Under orders from Colonel Buchanan, Ord set out from the camp at the mouth of Rogue River on 26 March 1856 to lead an expedition upstream a few miles to destroy the Macanoote-nay village of the Rogue River Indians. The force was made up of Ord's company under Lieutenant John Drysdale and a company of infantry of Captain Delancey Floyd Jones, totalling 112 men. The soldiers were mostly raw fellows, many of whom had never handled a musket before leaving Crescent City. The battalion reached the village about 2 P.M. "after a hard march (especially on the recruits)."[11]

The just-deserted village was located in a small and almost inaccessible river bottom with protection on all sides. To the south was Rogue River, wide, rapid, and deep; to the north, thickly wooded, steep slopes; to the west, a thick growth of swamp willows; and, to the east, where Ord's party entered, were steep wooded spurs. Into this box-like trap, Ord boldly moved his troops and put the torch to the thirteen houses along the river.

At this moment, the Indians appeared in some force on the opposite side of the river upstream and began crossing in canoes, obviously intending to attack from the wooded spurs and slopes to the north and east. Ord had disposed of his troops at four points: Captain Jones and his company in the willows to the west, Lieutenant Drysdale along the wooded slope to the north, a small guard for the baggage and mules on a spur to the east, while Ord himself with a small advance guard was, under cover of the burning houses, watching the river crossing. Realizing that the Indians would attack from the east and north, Ord quickly ordered Captain Jones to charge the wooded spurs to the east. Though the Indians had already reached there, Jones attacked and drove them before him. Ord then directed Drysdale to strike the Indians by a flanking movement to the north of the baggage from which the Indians had driven the guard. This movement was quickly executed. A few Indians had penetrated into the box-like bottom, and Ord and the advance guard, picking up the baggage guard, charged them, helped along by some "hard swearing" on Ord's part. These Indians were driven into Drysdale's cross fire, and several were killed. A few more rushed into the wooded knolls to the east and the Indians were driven back to their boats. Ord now commanded their crossing, and, as the Indians were paddling to the other side of the river, three more were killed.

The entire action had lasted an hour and a half, and Ord estimated that 60 to 100 Indians had been engaged against his force. Ten Indians had been killed and several wounded, while

Ord had amazingly suffered the loss of only one man wounded. The men were "fagged out, and I was very tired," said Ord, but there could be no rest in such an enclosure.[12]

Ord put his column in motion for a march to a suitable camp site about two and one-half miles from the village. He had considerable difficulty urging on his nearly exhausted troops and gave up his saddle mule to a soldier who had fallen behind. As First Sergeant Nash of Ord's company was putting the man on the mule, the Indians fired upon them, wounding the sergeant severely. The trail was so rough, a litter proved ineffectual, and it became necessary for Ord to carry the wounded sergeant before him on his mule.[13] A trying march of six hours was required to cover the two and one-half miles to the camp site. On the following day, the expedition returned to the mouth of Rogue River.

"Officers all congratulated me and think I will get a Brevet," Ord wrote.[14] Indeed, he had shown considerable skill and daring, and the effect of the action was to raise his prestige considerably in the army and among the people of the Pacific Coast. But the importance of the fight was more than personal. The *San Francisco Daily Herald* called the action "the first regular defeat of the Indians" in the war and noted that it was the first time the whites had charged the Indians after being attacked by them. "This, with a little more powder and ball is expected to bring them to terms. . . . "[15]

In April, Ord was sent down the coast to take command of an escort for a large supply train. He surprised a large body of Indians at the mouth of the Chetco River. Though outnumbered, Ord showed his characteristic aggressiveness by going at the Indians promptly and rapidly and following them so closely that they scarcely had time to fire. Five or six Indians were killed or wounded, and several captured, along with a quantity of provisions, while one soldier was killed and another wounded.[16]

Late in May, Ord stated that he was gratified at having seen some service, but he believed the war almost over, since nearly all of the Indians were sending in delegates to talk peace. On 23 May, Ord had marched his men up to the south side of Rogue River to a point where they could cross when he unexpectedly encountered the Indian Chief George and his band on the other side. George sent word for Ord to come and have a "good talk." Ord said he would talk as soon as his men were over. Ord crossed, but kept his men ready. He then sent

word to George that, if he wanted to talk, he must come to
Ord. George advanced with a considerable escort. Ord advanced, self-consciously aware that his rough attire, in tatters
from hard service, would not make a very strong impression.
He tried to make up for the deficiency by adopting his most
military posture and his sternest countenance. The Indians
approached, and George extended his hand. Ord was not
entirely at ease as they talked and kept one hand on the hilt of
his knife and the other near his pistol. George said that he and
his people wanted to come in. After their conference, the two
shook hands and parted.[17]

Arrangements were made shortly for the surrender of
George and his people, and, on 30 May, Ord received them at
the bend of Rogue River. There were 100 women, 35 men and
several children. They had to be conducted to Port Orford,
some twenty-five miles north of the mouth of Rogue River, and
for Ord this proved to be an unhappy task. He described the
Indians as "poor devils" and sympathized with them in their
suffering, particularly the women and children. "It almost
makes me shed tears to listen to their wailing." No wonder
their men fight so desperately, he thought.[18] His sympathy for
the Indians led him to suggest that they ought to be taken out
of the hands of politicians who cheated them and who played
up to Indian haters. The army could handle the Indians better,
he wrote; at least the military would "care a little" for them.[19]

On the march, the Indians presented a pitiable spectacle
which touched the captain deeply. He described a portion of
the march in the cryptic language of the diarist:

> We marched down river 2 ms. and turned up a steep hill; rather
> rough on the old squaws. One old fellow and his blind wife
> already behind. Poor old woman begins to fall down before we
> begin to climb the mountain, and she broke down completely
> short distance up. . . . Went and got a horse. Old squaw fell off. I
> then took her in front of me. Pretty hard to stand it. . . . Gave up
> my mule to lame girl and broken down old squaw. Girl quite
> childishly happy; first time maybe in her life she has had so much
> kindness shown her.[20]

Ord was next ordered to the mouth of Rogue River to
receive other Indians who desired to surrender and to conduct
them to Port Orford. Receiving the Indians became a delicate
task, as a recent battle in which Captains Smith and Augur had

been engaged had greatly angered the soldiers. "Tis difficult to show any quarter; the men are disposed to kill all," Ord wrote.[21] Upon his arrival at the mouth of the river, he found many Indians already there, and, during the following week, many others followed. On 23 June, Ord reached Port Orford with 242 Indians.[22]

Among the last of the Indians to surrender was the notorious Old John with his people. Old John was noted for his treachery and for his reluctance to give up the struggle. Ord was directed to proceed to a camp near Reinhart's to await the arrival of this group and to conduct them to Port Orford. The captain looked askance at the thought that being sent to meet the worst Indians was a compliment. Old John and his party, about two hundred strong, came in on 28 June. "I advanced a short distance up hill from camp and shook hands with him," Ord wrote. The warriors, one by one, gave up their rifles, "some rather with a look of defiance." The captain then took the chief into his tent and gave him a drink. The Indians were escorted to Port Orford where Ord remained a few days and improved his acquaintance with Old John by having him to Sunday lunch and dinner.[23] This was Ord's final act in the Rogue River hostilities. The war being over, he returned with his company to Benicia Barracks.

Ord's return coincided with the reign of the great Vigilance Committee of 1856 in San Francisco. Angered by the prevalence of crime, several thousand citizens formed the committee and had taken law enforcement into their own hands. Ord was directed by General Wool to take post with his company at the Presidio of San Francisco, apparently to safeguard United States property. There were no difficulties, though Ord remained at the Presidio during August, September and October.[24]

The captain returned to Benicia Barracks where he spent all of 1857. Early in 1858, he was transferred from Company B to Company K of the Third Artillery, which meant a move from Benicia to Fort Miller in the San Joaquin Valley.

★★★★★

A recurrence of the Yakima War in Washington Territory brought Ord back into the field in 1858. The Indians were giving trouble in the Colville gold region in eastern

Washington. A sizeable expedition sent into the area under the command of Colonel Edward J. Steptoe had been driven back in defeat. Ord was ordered to join a much stronger expedition of six hundred regulars equipped with new long-range rifles under the command of Colonel George Wright. The column was assembled at a camp near Fort Walla Walla, and Ord with Company K joined the battalion of the Third Artillery under the command of Captain E.D. Keyes. In August, the force moved into the heart of the Indian lands generally following a course northeasterly in the direction of the Coeur d'Alene Mission. The country presented a forbidding aspect with extensive burnt districts. Hostile Indians in increasing numbers appeared on the flanks of the column.[25]

On 31 August, a long hard march of twenty miles was made through a rugged country under the hot sun and without water. About two o'clock in the afternoon, the men were staggering with fatigue and heat, and the Indians were threatening a general attack. Ord, who had started out with a canteen of coffee, now divided the precious beverage among the most fatigued men. The Indians withheld their blow, but, for the next three hours, Ord was "an awfully thirsty soldier." After a good deal of searching, he found a hole with about two quarts of water among the bushes and weeds. He stuck his head down and drank nearly all of it, "wigglers varmints and all."[26]

On the following morning at "Four Lakes," the Indians were gathered on the summit of a high hill some two miles distant from Wright's camp, and the colonel ordered the troops under arms to drive them from their position. Wright moved with two squadrons of the First Dragoons, Captain Keyes's battalion of the Third Artillery, including Ord's company, a battalion of the Ninth Infantry, one mountain howitzer, and thirty friendly Nez Percé Indians.[27]

Ord's company, with other artillerymen, infantrymen and friendly Indians, was marched to the right of the hill to gain a position for an easy ascent, while the dragoons were sent to the north and east around the base of the hill to intercept the retreat of the Indians after the foot troops had driven them from the summit. Significantly, Ord's company was sent up the hill first and, with the help of a squadron of dragoons, drove the Indians off the hill to its base where they rallied under cover. As Ord reached the crest of the rise, there lay before him an extensive plain with a large body of mounted warriors apparently eager for battle. To the right, at the foot of the hill in the pine forest, other Indians were seen in large numbers. There were the braves of the Spokane, Coeur d'Alene and Palouse tribes.

Deploying his troops along the crest of the hill behind the dragoons and in front of the pine forest on the right, and with a howitzer emplaced on the hillside, Wright ordered an advance. The colonel himself remained on the hill and retained Ord's company as his personal escort. Ord was thus able to observe the action very closely. Captain Keyes on the left drove the Indians steadily before him on to the plain. The dragoons were suddenly mounted and charged through the foot troops upon the Indians. The mounted warriors were dispersed and several killed, and, within a few minutes, not an Indian was seen on the plain. On the right the Indians were driven out of the forest and out of sight. The battle of Four Lakes was over. Not a single soldier was killed or wounded in the action, while the Indians, on the other hand, had lost eighteen or twenty killed and many wounded. The new long-range rifles had made the difference. The Indians had been chastised, but their resistance had not been broken.

Wright's official reports estimated the number of Indians engaged at Four Lakes at four to five hundred, and other officers gave even higher figures. Ord was amazed by these numbers and privately indicated that they were considerably exaggerated. "I was the only line officer with a spy glass," he wrote later, "[and I] took particular and frequent looks at the enemy before engaging them."[28]

Wright continued his advance on 5 September across a stretch of open prairie and discovered the Indians some three miles in front moving along the edge of a timbered area apparently bent upon intercepting his column. Three companies, Ord's, H. G. Gibson's and Tyler's, were deployed as skirmishers along the front and right. J.A. Hardie's company was thrown to the left, and the howitzers with infantry support were advanced to the line of skirmishers. The firing became brisk on both sides with the Indians attacking in front and on both flanks. Meanwhile, the Indians had set fire to the grass along the front and right flank. The fire nearly enveloped the soldiers and was threatening the pack train.[29] Ord passed his men through the flames at the least dangerous points, re-formed his skirmish line, and pushed ahead in the lead.[30] The other units advanced through the flames, and the pack train was moved to safety.

Again, Ord relied on his spyglass and carefully counted the enemy before he engaged them. In the general advance over rocks and through ravines, Ord's force was on the extreme left opposed by a large number of Indians. As the trail bore off to the right, Ord was soon separated from the main column and found his company entirely alone. He pressed the enemy over a distance of two miles. Notice was dispatched from the main column recalling Ord. Upon rejoining the main body, Ord's company was thrown forward in skirmish order to clear the way in front of the column. The action became lively over a distance of a mile and a half as Ord drove the Indians succes-sively from three high table rocks. Again, he was unaware that the main body had swung off to the right. A dragoon was dispatched to direct Ord to rejoin the column some two miles away. Ord later wrote that he would not have hesitated to take his company alone anywhere in the vicinity and felt no uneasi-ness at being two miles from the main body.[31]

The day's march had covered twenty-five miles, and the fight had been continuous for seven hours over fourteen of the twenty-five miles. The men were exhausted. But the Indians had been decisively defeated in the battle of Spokane Plains. Wright estimated the force of the enemy at five to seven hun-dred warriors, the three tribes of the battle of Four Lakes having been joined by the Pend d'Oreilles. Again, Ord privately took exception to these figures, but he hazarded none of his own. Though the balls flew through the ranks of the soldiers, amazingly only one man was slightly wounded. Colonel Wright was complimentary of the command in his report, and Captain Keyes reported, among others, Captain Ord and Company K as "particularly distinguished."

In the ensuing days, the hostiles came forward seeking terms of peace. Colonel Wright told the chiefs that they must come in with all of their people and with everything they had and to lay their arms at his feet. Meanwhile, he continued his march to the Coeur d'Alene Mission, relentlessly destroying animals and caches of food as he moved. Eventually he made treaties with the various tribes, and his terms were harsh. Among other things the Indians were required to deliver up individual transgressors, and, in pursuance of this demand, eleven accused murderers and thieves were summarily hanged.[32]

With the completion of the campaign Ord must have been pleased to learn that at last he was being transferred from "foreign service" in California to the Atlantic seaboard. In November 1858, Company K was broken up and its headquarters staff ordered to duty at Fort Monroe, Virginia.[33]

5

★★★★★

From Captain to General

ORD'S new station, Fort Monroe, was located on Old Point Comfort at the mouth of the James River and commanded the entrance to Hampton Roads. The Artillery School of Practice was here. This distinguished institution was the army's first postgraduate school, and all of the artillery companies, by rotation, were to pass through its regimen to enable both officers and men to sharpen their skills.

Ord's assignment was as Superintendent of Practical Instruction, a position which marked him as an officer of distinction among his fellow artillerists. He undertook his duties with a justifiable sense of pride. Indeed, the direction of affairs at the school was pretty much in his hands. He determined what drills the companies would go through and had full control of them. There was also classroom instruction in which he had a share. Here was an opportunity of which he took full advantage to polish his own knowledge and skills in the artillery way.[1]

At the time he entered upon his duties, Captain Ord was a mature officer, having just turned forty years of age. His experience was wide and varied. What was he like? What had shaped him? What were his views on military matters? What were his characteristics as a military officer? As to what shaped him militarily, it is quickly apparent that he shared with his

fellow officers the same molding influences, but he was superior to most in his ability to act upon the precepts of his
training.

Sylvanus Thayer, who became superintendent of the Military Academy in 1817 and left that position two years before
Ord entered West Point, embraced within the Academy's instruction the best military knowledge of the day. That knowledge was derived principally from French experience and more
particularly from the work of Henri, Baron de Jomini, who
wrote Napoleon's military biography. The Jomini influence was
carried on at the Academy by Dennis Hart Mahan, who had
begun his long career as Professor of Civil and Military Engineering three years before Ord entered West Point.

Ord's contemporary, Henry W. Halleck, published his
Elements of Military Art and Science in 1846, the same year he and
Ord sailed around the Horn to California. Halleck was influ-
enced by Jomini and emphasized many of the same ideas that
Mahan had set forth in the instruction at the Point. Few of
Halleck's ideas were original, but he summed up the thinking
current among Ord and his fellow officers. In the light of the
work of Mahan and Halleck, the views and characteristics of
Ord as an officer may be examined in some detail.[2]

Mahan stressed military history as the foundation of professional study in learning the art and science of war. Ord
absorbed this fundamental lesson well, for he mentioned from
time to time throughout his life reading military histories and
biographies. At a tense moment in the trouble with England
regarding the Oregon territory, he had enjoined one of his
brothers to "read Tacitus" and "the histories of our wars" in
preparation for future contingencies.

Professionalism was of prime importance to Ord. He was
one of a number of vigorous and ambitious young line officers
"glorying in the traditions of professionalism so dramatically
established on the battlefields of Mexico and striving to per-
petuate them in the dismal little forts of the West."[3] Each
regiment had its own distinctive character and sense of pride.
Ord's regiment, famous as the "Marching Third," usually
fought as infantry and was noted for its feats of endurance.[4] Professionalism meant discipline and the skill which comes from
training. Ord took particular pride in bringing his own company to the peak of efficiency. At Fort Vancouver, before his
last campaign in Washington Territory, his Company K had

bested all the other companies in dress, drill and target practice, and was judged by some at the fort to be the finest looking
company that had been there in years.[5]

Professional soldiers make war, and their concept of what
hostilities are or should be is of obvious significance. For Ord,
war was limited and not a matter of total devastation. So he
could write, during the Rogue River Indian War: "I never lose
sight of what is right and just, and even think how *little* harm I
can do the poor wretches we have to fight so as, at the same
time, to produce peace."[6] War was gentlemanly for Ord,
though no doubt some in his own day would account him
old-fashioned for holding such high principles.

In musing about war, Ord had defined it as "a state of
harm done to the human race . . . We are to do as little harm in
war and as much good in peace as possible. . .," he wrote in
his diary.[7] He pondered the possibility of reducing the inhu-
manity of the discipline of the military and naval service by
substituting machinery for men.

Ord believed the United States Army owed its existence to
what he called the "Spirit of Annexation," and this spirit, he
further believed, owed its existence to the "Spirit of the Army."
These views he expressed in an essay, or address, perhaps
intended for delivery before the officers at the Artillery School.
By annexation, he meant not only the addition of foreign territory, but also the continual deprivation of the Indian of his
lands. Here was nothing more than a restatement, with a
special emphasis, of the current idea of the Manifest Destiny of
the United States. According to this idea, Americans would
spread over the land—much land—and the territories and
peoples embraced would be greatly blessed by having the benefits of our democratic institutions. The special emphasis in
Ord's statement was upon the army as the agent of expansion,
while expansion in turn called for support of the army.[8]

As already seen, Ord's views on annexation had been
rather unsettled. His sensitivity enabled him to see American
selfishness and greed pitted against the rightful interests of
Mexicans and Indians. But the issue was not so simple; few
issues involving such diverse interests and people are simple.
For, at the same time, Ord also believed that, through annexation, civilization was advanced in backward and unoccupied
areas. Further, he thought that all people must be civilized and
Christianized sooner or later.[9] Thus, he fell in line with that

idealism and optimism prevalent in his day which was called Manifest Destiny, and he could see advantage in it for the army. Yet, he never completely lost his awareness that the juggernaut of progress may crush the innocent beneath its wheels.

In addition to such larger considerations as the nature of war, military professionalism and the use of an army in carrying out national policy, Ord held to a number of important principles, primarily tactical, all of which he had employed in one measure or another in the Indian fighting in Florida and on the West Coast. One he considered vital: Always have sufficient force to get the job done. There might be occasions when the force at hand was inadequate, he fully realized, but to overlook this principle in advance planning was to court disaster. Offensive, initiative, audacity were the key words to maxims dear to Ord's heart. He knew that operations properly conceived were to be based on fortifications and conducted with due regard to skillful maneuver, but, in action, Ord was prone to slam into the enemy head on. That he succeeded suggests that his advance preparations were well done. Timid commanders disgusted him. Speed was yet another very important principle which Ord took to heart, and this in an era of warfare when promptness was more the exception than the rule. Flexibility and practicality in adjusting to the realities of specific situations were other important qualities which he possessed. At the immediate tactical level, Ord did not neglect the appropriate use of advanced guards, outposts and reconnaissance.

In his address at the Artillery School, Ord gave further indication that his participation in the Indian wars had provided him with invaluable training. In fighting Indians, Ord said, continual watchfulness is necessary and becomes habitual, "and almost without knowing it one acquires some of the most important qualities of a good general: Coolness! Forethought! And above all precaution, and then, what Perseverance! What fertility of resources is learned by the officer compelled to make long marches in the wilderness!"[10] Ord noted that Indian war was the first school of Washington, Jackson and Taylor. Even Julius Caesar had a similar career, he continued, for was not the savage German of antiquity comparable to the savage Indian of modern times? To demonstrate the comparison, Ord paraphrased a passage from Tacitus, substituting Indians for Germans with remarkable effect.[11] Ord himself had amply demonstrated the qualities of good generalship which he had listed.

Ord possessed other qualities and talents which enhanced his military capabilities. He was observant; he had a feel for places and things. He was quite good at sketching and describing. He was a surveyor and cartographer. He was inventive. On the negative side, he was probably unduly careless of his own safety, but who is to draw the line between foolhardiness and that courageous example which a leader of men must show?

What sort of man was E.O.C. Ord in ways other than military? At age 40, he was energetic. Likenesses of the time portray him with a moustache and sometimes with sideburns. His dark hair had turned gray, prematurely so, for as early as age twenty-eight he had spoken of becoming as gray as a badger. He probably looked older than his actual years. He was a devoted family man. He was sociable, liked to meet people, and made frequent references to having called on friends. His interests were broad, for he read widely. His choices included *Blackwood's Magazine*, a British literary journal; a book of poems by Thomas Moore, popular Irish writer; and Dickens's works. He was an early reader of Herman Melville's writings. Not surprising is his interest in the histories of wars and his mention of his reading a life of Napoleon. He read the Bible, at least occasionally, and attended church from time to time. Along with reading, he did a good deal of writing in the years prior to the Civil War. He kept a diary fairly faithfully and wrote accounts of his experiences in the field which he sent to *Harper's Magazine*, the *New York Herald* and no doubt other publications. These elusive items were often published under pseudonyms.

Ord was honest. He did not attempt by sharp dealing to get ahead of his fellow men in the hectic gold-rush days in California. He was strong-minded, with his own ideas and his own ways. Yet, he was sensitive to the needs of others. He was restless to a fault, never satisfied for long in any one place, always on the lookout for a change. His views on various issues were not always consistent; he was changeable. So he had strengths and weaknesses; he acted and was acted upon. He was a man. But he arouses our curiosity, for he was no ordinary human being.

★★★★★

Without warning, Ord's routine at the Artillery School was interrupted on 17 October 1859 by the following order issued in

Washington at the express direction of Secretary of War John B. Floyd, a Virginian: "You will repair without delay to Harpers Ferry with the troops under your command and report to Brevet Colonel R.E. Lee, 2nd Cavalry."[12] Ord was handed this dispatch at Fort Monroe at 5:15 P.M., and, by 6:15, with a battalion of 11 officers and 142 enlisted men, he was on board a boat bound for Baltimore.[13]

On the night of 16 October, John Brown had startled the citizens of Harpers Ferry and vicinity by boldly crossing over from Maryland with eighteen men and seizing the United States military stores, the armory and rifle works, and terrorizing the citizens of the town and surrounding country. Brown's objective was the freeing of the slaves of the South, though his exact course of action to accomplish this was not clear. His coup was not followed by the insurrection of the slaves which he seemed to have expected. On the contrary, local citizens and militia came alive to the situation and moved against the invaders. On 17 October, Brown, with some of his followers and with hostages, was besieged in the engine house of the arsenal. The siege was soon joined by other militia companies from Virginia and Maryland. Since Brown's appearance in Harpers Ferry, several persons had been killed on both sides, some of them innocent citizens.

As intelligence began to filter out of the confusion at Harpers Ferry and reached President James Buchanan, the chief executive issued orders for the nearest available federal troops to move to the scene of the trouble. These were a detachment of marines from the Washington Navy Yard under Lieutenant Israel Green and the artillery from Fort Monroe under Ord. All were under the command of Colonel Robert E. Lee, who was accompanied by Lieutenant J.E.B. Stuart as aide. During the night of the seventeeth, Lee and the marines reached Harpers Ferry, while Ord and his troops reached Baltimore.

At daybreak on 18 October, Lee demanded Brown's surrender, which demand was refused. Lee then ordered the marines led by Green to assault the engine house. The attackers overwhelmed Brown's force with further bloodshed on both sides. Brown himself was wounded and taken prisoner with the handful of survivors of his band.[14]

In Baltimore, early on this same morning, Ord was marching his men to take the train for Harpers Ferry when he was handed a copy of a telegram from Lee to the adjutant general stating that his troops were not needed. Accordingly, the captain returned with his battalion to Fort Monroe.[15]

On 25 October, Brown was placed on trial at Charlestown, the county seat, eight miles from Harpers Ferry. He was charged by the Commonwealth of Virginia with treason, conspiracy with slaves to commit treason and murder. On 2 November, at the conclusion of the trial, he was sentenced to be executed at Charlestown on 2 December.

As the trial was in progress, and in the month following, feeling was very tense in the Charlestown-Harpers Ferry area. Governor Henry A. Wise of Virginia, responding to rumors of fresh outbreaks similar to Brown's and to rumored plans to rescue Brown from the Charlestown jail, ordered several companies of militia to the scene and promised to have a large force present on the day of the execution.[16] The governor was not in error in believing that an attempt at rescue might be made. Several plans were concocted by Brown's partisans in the North, but none was undertaken.[17]

Governor Wise called upon President Buchanan to send federal troops to the area as the day of execution approached. Under the president's direction, the secretary of war ordered four companies of artillery equipped as infantry from Fort Monroe to Harpers Ferry, "among them Ord's and Carlisle's companies."[18] The specific mention of Ord, who, as senior officer, would command the battalion totaling 240 men, was explained by the captain himself. Besides Colonel Justin Dimick, he said, there were three others who outranked him at Fort Monroe, but he was "the only one of the old officers at the place from South of Masons and Dixons [sic] line."[19] Once again, Colonel Robert E. Lee was assigned to overall command of United States troops at Harpers Ferry.

On 30 November, Lee, Ord and the artillery, aboard a Baltimore and Ohio Railroad train, proceeded to Harpers Ferry. Their approach to the town was by the same covered railroad bridge connecting Maryland and Virginia which Brown and his party had crossed on foot a scant six weeks before. Harpers Ferry lay on an uneven point of land where the Potomac receives the waters of the Shenandoah River. Just across the bridge was the railroad station and, beyond it, the arsenal buildings. To the right were shop buildings of the armory stretching for some distance along the Potomac.

Ord and his command were posted in one of the workshops of the arsenal where they remained quietly through the day of Brown's execution and for several days thereafter. The purpose of the expedition, Ord wrote, was "to please Wise and overawe Northern fillibusters [sic]—should they come."[20] The captain described the disgust of the people in and around Charlestown at being under the military restraints occasioned by Governor Wise's measures. "Most all are of opinion that Wise is almost as crazy as Old Brown and is rendering himself ridiculous."[21]

Ord's identification of himself as a Southerner raises questions about his views on slavery, abolition and related matters. Some of his Cresap relatives were slaveholders, though western Maryland was not by any means a heavily populated slave area, and his contacts with his kinsmen there were infrequent. Of course, he witnessed slaveholding at close quarters in the District of Columbia where he was brought up and in various places where he was stationed. "There is no doubt about it," he was to admit to his friend Sherman in 1863, "I was in 49 & until 54 a pro-slaveryman. . . ."[22] Apparently, the passage of the Kansas-Nebraska Act in 1854 opening those territories to the possibility of having slavery cooled his ardor. Nevertheless, he still had Southern sympathies and continued to have reservations about the capacity of the black people to assume responsibilities. His views along these lines cropped up in a number of instances during the 1850s.

On his journey from the East to California in 1850, Ord observed the dilapidated ruins of the once-splendid Spanish grandeur of Panama. The *conquistadores* were avaricious, he wrote in his diary, but they did build civilization. Their degenerate successors, Indian and Negro, now free from Spanish control, allowed everything to go to ruin. "If the present race continues to occupy the land," he wrote, "they must be conquered and made slaves ere any labor can be gotten out of them."[23] As his steamer proceeded up the west coast of Mexico, putting in at various ports, Ord gave expression to annexationist sentiments and added: "The degenerate race must yield to the barbarians from the north."[24] Back in southern California, he commented that Americans refused to work at field labor. The same condition existed in New Mexico. "Want slaves here much," was his comment.[25]

Shortly after he made these observations, the captain returned to the East and his unpleasant stay at Fort Independence in Boston harbor. On one of his visits to New York in

April 1851, he wrote to Pacificus: "The abolitionists are trying to raise a row in Boston & I am glad I am not there to mix in any such unpleasant and inglorious war."[26] The row was over Thomas Sims, a fugitive slave from Georgia, whom antislavery citizens were seeking to free in the face of Massachusetts officials' determination to enforce the Fugitive Slave Act.

In writing to one of his brothers in 1858, Ord, with obvious scorn, referred to his West Point classmate, Isaac I. Stevens, lately governor of Washington Territory, as having been a Douglas man. "If he isn't a black republican," Ord continued, "[he] will be."[27]

With his pro-Southern and proslavery slant, Ord wrote, in the aftermath of the John Brown raid, that the rabid abolitionists had set Brown on, and the Southern Democrats would be perfectly justified in electing their presidential candidate as a result of such folly. "So hurrah for their nominee. . . ," he said.[28]

Ord's cheer for the Southern Democrat was in vain, for, on 6 November 1860, Abraham Lincoln, Republican, was elected president. However, for the next four months affairs of state would continue under the direction of President Buchanan, who was faced with a rising secessionist sentiment in South Carolina and other Southern states. Buchanan was friendly to the South, in favor of compromise, and definitely opposed to any show of force which might precipitate secession or civil war. His stand was rather anomalous, for, while he denied the validity of secession, he did not believe the general government had the right to coerce a state. Efforts to conciliate the sectional differences were in progress, which inhibited any move likely to unsettle the South, even if the president had been disposed to take action.[29]

The crux of the conflict between the general government and South Carolina was the possession of three forts in Charleston harbor. Fort Moultrie, Fort Sumter and Castle Pinckney were under the command of Major Robert Anderson of the First Artillery. Anderson's position was a difficult one, perhaps with more political than military significance. He had force sufficient only to garrison one of the forts, and, at the outset of the critical period, had his troops in Fort Moultrie. The secession of South Carolina had not yet taken place in November 1860, but was impending. Major Anderson was thus in a delicate situation, and his actions were of considerable importance.[30]

Captain Ord had visited Charleston, was quite familiar with the layout of the forts there, and had a clear view of Anderson's military situation. On 26 November, he addressed a letter to the major at Fort Moultrie in which he touched upon several matters involved in the troubled state of affairs. The first was in the nature of a warning. He told Anderson that one of the best soldiers in his company had reported that a well-dressed stranger had been offering fifty and fifty-five dollars per month to the soldiers of his command to desert and take service in a Southern army. Ord's informant further said that many of the newly enlisted men were recent immigrants who thought secession almost certain and were ready to serve where they would get the highest pay. As Anderson's men at Fort Moultrie were even more accessible than Ord's, the latter thought it well to warn him of the danger. "You might mention to some of the prominent men, Major, in this secession move," he continued, "that any attempt to seduce our soldiers would tend to destroy such sympathy as southern U.S. Army officers might have for their grievances."[31] Anderson himself was a Kentuckian.

Ord relayed to Anderson a conversation he had had with Colonel René E. De Russy, chief engineer of the army, who was based at Fort Monroe. De Russy had told Ord that he thought it probable that Anderson had moved his force from the indefensible Moultrie to the inaccessible Sumter. "I shall be much gratified to hear from you, Major, and to learn that you are holding Fort Sumpter [sic] till the storm passes and men see to what they are drifting," Ord continued in his letter of 26 November.[32]

In making this statement, Ord was broadly hinting that Anderson should abandon Moultrie and move to Sumter, for the former was untenable in case of a landward attack, while the third fort, Castle Pinckney, was even less defensible. Furthermore, he was reinforcing his statement by making it appear that the chief engineer, Colonel De Russy, sanctioned such a move. In Ord's conversation with De Russy before the captain wrote his letter to Anderson, the colonel had agreed that Anderson should move to Sumter. "I knew that Col De Russy would not write it. . . ," Ord said a little later. "But I thought the weight of the Chief Engineers name—(then in the confidence of the Cabinet) would tell."[33] It is not known what Ord's influence was upon Anderson's course of action, but the captain's own stand in the crisis was made perfectly clear.

On 11 December, Anderson did receive authority from the secretary of war to move to Fort Sumter in case he should be attacked.[34] On 20 December, South Carolina seceded from the Union, and, on 26 December, Anderson, fearing hostile action, on his own initiative moved from Fort Moultrie to Fort Sumter. The move, whether well-advised or not, had the effect of further aggravating the South Carolinians, who promptly occupied Fort Moultrie and Castle Pinckney. The United States government was in an awkward position with a lone stronghold in a seceded state.

Ord chafed helplessly during January 1861 as the other states of the lower South seceded. By 1 February, seven states were out of the Union. Virginia still remained in the Union, but the captain was not optimistic that she would continue so.

In his characteristically aggressive fashion, Ord wanted action on the part of the authorities in Washington to uphold the flag of the United States. He determined to attempt to exert influence through political channels and, on 28 January, took pen in hand to write to Congressman John Sherman of Ohio. "Sir, this Fort wants a good commander," he bluntly began.[35] There might be a siege of it within a month, he continued, and there was not ammunition enough to last one day for the field or small arms. Fort Monroe was too important to be without the best commander available. Colonel Justin Dimick, the commanding officer, was a good old man, Ord went on, but lacking in energy. General Scott had expressed the same opinion to Ord, but the captain presumed that, in the great press of business, the general had overlooked the matter. Colonel De Russy he described as "a gallant but quite an old officer." He was a firm friend, Ord said, but perhaps both he and Colonel Dimick would be glad not to have to direct operations against Virginians.

The captain pressed on to indicate other measures of preparation which he believed necessary. The Navy Yard at Norfolk ought to be readied for defense. As it was, it invited attack and would fall easily before a hostile move. The vessels should be sent away or across to Old Point under the guns of Fort Monroe. "I am anxious, sir," wrote Ord to Sherman, "that the govt I serve should maintain itself with some honor and thats why I presume to trouble you with my suggestions."[36]

Ord was insistent that John Sherman should understand his motives. He simply wanted the best men where they were needed and did not want to deprive any officer of his position.

Conscience-stricken that his blunt statements might have injured Colonels Dimick and De Russy, Ord quickly dispatched a second letter reiterating his high regard for both officers and his desire not to disparage them in any way.[37]

Sherman passed the letters on to General Winfield Scott, who in point of fact, as early as 29 October 1860, had made recommendations that various forts in the South be strengthened and their commanders warned of possible attack. But Scott could name only five companies as available as possible reinforcements, obviously an insufficient number. Even more important, attempts at conciliation were in progress, and the United States could make no hostile move to embarrass these efforts or to precipitate a clash.[38] Ord's understandable zeal was overridden by these practical and political considerations.

★★★★★

Captain Ord had been lingering at Fort Monroe on borrowed time, for, in October 1860, he had been transferred to command Company C of the Third Artillery and ordered to Fort Vancouver, Washington Territory. He extended his stay in the East by securing permission from the secretary of war to experiment with firing round shot from rifled cannon. It well may be imagined that the captain was loath to leave the scene of action squarely in the middle of a national crisis to take position at one of the nation's more distant outposts. He probably left the East early in March 1861, for he assumed command of his new company on the last day of that month.[39]

★★★★★

Ord could only look on, and that from a great distance, as events unfolded in the East. On 4 March 1861, Abraham Lincoln was inaugurated president of the United States and upon him rested the responsibility of formulating a policy toward the seceded states. In February, these states had formed the Confederate States of America and established a provisional government. Lincoln's inaugural policy was one of firmness: he would "possess the property and places belonging to the government." Subsequently, he determined to maintain possession of Fort Sumter by dispatching a relief expedition to the beleaguered Anderson. His intent was made known to the governor of South Carolina, but the authorities of the Confederate government looked upon this action as a hostile move.

The order was given from Montgomery to reduce Fort Sumter. The bombardment of the fort on 12 and 13 April and its surrender on the thirteenth opened the hostilities between the North and the South. Both sides began preparations for battle, calling upon their citizens to rally to the colors.

★★★★★

Captain Ord, with his firm convictions and aggressive nature, was not likely to remain for very long away from the field of action. He would want to have a hand in putting down the rebellion of the South and working out the future of the nation. It may be assumed that he set out to move heaven and earth, if necessary, to secure a transfer to the East. In view of his ambition, he would make similar exertions to achieve a higher rank. The possibility of promotion to a generalcy in the rapidly expanding army was within reason. To secure a promotion would require strong influence, and Ord had long been aware that the weight of those highly placed was necessary in such matters. In the course of some twenty-five years in the service, he had made many friends (and a few enemies) among the officer corps. He was well-known at the highest echelon. Moreover, he was fully aware that politicians have much to say about military policy and military personnel. He made and kept current his political contacts. As an instance of this, at the time war was declared on Mexico in 1846, Ord had rushed to Washington, gone right to the House of Representatives, and called on his acquaintances to inquire about possibilities of promotion. He cultivated the members of Congress from the states of the regions in which he served, making a bipartisan approach and not just a Democratic one. Thus, he felt some "claim" to the support of legislators from the Pacific Coast. In addition, he established connections with political figures from his native state, Maryland, and from Michigan, where his parents had lived for many years. Ord would surely have shown some initiative in resorting to these people of power to secure advancement and transfer. Yet the records are unaccountably silent about these efforts.

In Washington, Montgomery Blair of Maryland, postmaster general in Lincoln's Cabinet, was an acquaintance, as was Senator Reverdy Johnson of that state. Senator James W. Nesmith of Oregon was an old associate. On the military side, Inspector General R.B. Marcy and Major General Henry W.

Halleck were in position to be helpful, and the same could be said of Quartermaster General Montgomery C. Meigs. Even the old generals Winfield Scott and John E. Wool were still on the scene, and both knew Ord quite well.

Yet, one well-placed friend, Major Julius P. Garesché, seems to have had the leading role in determining Ord's future at the start of the Civil War. Garesché was reared in Delaware, attended Georgetown College, entered West Point in 1837, and graduated two years after Ord. The two were together on various occasions in the course of their service, and a cordial friendship developed between them. Garesché was a devout Catholic, a man of high principle, whose personal qualities gained for him the highest respect of his associates. He became assistant adjutant general in Washington in 1855, and, in 1861, was senior assistant to Adjutant General Lorenzo Thomas. Garesché was in charge of the general business of the office and was relied upon so greatly by his chief that he became, in fact, acting adjutant general of the army.[40]

One of Major Garesché's principal functions was handling the mechanics of commissioning of officers, a strategic position and an influential one. Garesché suggested and advised that Ord be made a brigadier general of volunteers, and Lincoln issued the commission. Whatever the influence of others in the case, the greatest share of credit thus must go to Garesché for Ord's remarkable promotion from captain to general effective 14 September 1861.[41]

The impatient Ord in faraway San Francisco was elated by the news of his elevation. His preparations were swift, his departure sad, as he bid farewell to Molly Ord and their young children and embarked by steamer for the East.

6

★★★★★

A Tilt with McDowell

BRIGADIER General Ord arrived in Washington on 6 November. He put up at Willard's Hotel on Pennsylvania Avenue at Fourteenth Street. Willard's was the favorite meeting place of the notables of the city. Ord found the nation's capital orderly. Volunteers were pouring in and were promptly being taken to camps for training. Elaborate fortifications were under construction for the defense of the city. Washington was still a metropolis in the making. The few public buildings were widely scattered. The Capitol, yet under construction, its dome missing, lent an unfinished appearance to the scene.

Ord spent several days awaiting assignment and used the time to advantage to call on his friend Garesché, Postmaster General Montgomery Blair, Major General Henry W. Halleck, Adjutant General Seth Williams, Major Daniel H. Rucker, and, of course, upon "Little Mac" himself, Major General George B. McClellan, the General-in-Chief.[1] At length he received his appointment to a command in the field.

General Ord was assigned to command the Third Brigade of Brigadier General George A. McCall's division of Pennsylvania troops of the Army of the Potomac. The army was encamped in defense of Washington in a long line stretching from Langley to Alexandria along the south bank of the Potomac River. Ord found that McCall's division, made up of his own brigade and those of Brigadier Generals George G. Meade and John F. Reynolds, held the extreme right of the line at Camp Pierpoint near Langley.

The general moved into brigade headquarters in this elongated tent city. Colonel John S. McCalmont, one of his regimental commanders who had been temporarily in charge of the brigade, returned from leave to find himself superseded. Ord was tactful, and McCalmont described him as "frank, communicative, considerate."[2] The general set about to secure capable and faithful men for his staff. At the same time, he was not unmindful of political considerations. As aides, he chose Second Lieutenant Alexander B. Sharpe, a thirty-four-year-old lawyer from Carlisle, Pennsylvania, who was active in Republican politics, and First Lieutenant Samuel S. Seward, the young nephew of the secretary of state and erstwhile clerk in the San Francisco law office of Ord's brother-in-law, Samuel W. Holladay. After a time, Ord was joined in the field by his brother Placidus, for whom he had secured an appointment as assistant adjutant general of the brigade. "Placy" followed the fortunes of his brother through the entire war, and the general held him in the highest esteem and affection.

The general's mess included himself and his six staff officers. Meals were prepared and served by a talented Negro cook. The canvas mess tent boasted a rough table of pine, sans tablecloth, with legs stuck in the ground, camp stools and tin dishes. The tents of the general and his brother were connected. They had a board floor, a small box stove, cots, buffalo robes and blankets. "We manage to sleep quite comfortably," Placy reported.[3]

The Federal army, defeated and put to flight at Bull Run on 21 July 1861 and badly mauled in a relatively minor encounter at Ball's Bluff in October, had no precedent of victory to give it self-confidence as a fighting organization. The Army of the Potomac was pervaded with defeatism and timidity. The Confederates, on the other hand, inspired by two impressive victories, were in fine spirits. The men in gray facing toward Washington had not yet known defeat. They were confident that the South could whip the world.

After the July disaster at Manassas, Major General George B. McClellan had been called from West Virginia to save the capital. He busied himself with transforming a mob of citizens in uniform into a well-disciplined army, and he went at it with a flair. He was dashing and impressive in his manner, and he became very popular with the troops. Yet, for two months after the October defeat at Ball's Bluff, the Northern public, anxious for some sign of victory, heard nothing but the unsatisfactory news, "All quiet along the Potomac." Fewer than 100,000 Confederates at Centreville, about thirty miles away, held the nation's capital in a virtual state of siege, while the Army of the Potomac, numbering nearly 200,000, remained inactive. To add to the unrest, the weather was propitious for a move, despite the winter season, and the roads, hardened by a long dry period, were in better condition than in midsummer. McClellan was nothing if not deliberate.[4]

★★★★★

The inactivity and boredom of winter quarters were broken on both sides by foraging and scouting expeditions. The scene of these operations was that area of Fairfax County between Washington and Centreville, which became a sort of no-man's-land. The village of Dranesville lay about half way between the opposing camps.[5]

On the morning of 20 December, Ord rode westward at the head of his brigade out the Leesburg turnpike in the direction of Dranesville. He was under orders from McCall to drive back the Confederate pickets, which boldly had advanced to within four or five miles of the Federal lines, and to procure a supply of forage. McCall rather cautiously suggested to Ord the possibility of capturing the Confederate cavalry reserve of about one hundred men, supposed to be between Dranesville and the Potomac River. He gravely warned Ord to return before nightfall. The forage, said McCall, might be secured at some "rank secessionist's" of the neighborhood.[6]

Ord's column consisted of the Sixth, Ninth, Tenth and Twelfth Pennsylvania Infantry regiments, with the addition of the First Pennsylvania Reserve Rifles, known as the "Bucktails"; Captain Hezekiah Easton's battery of four pieces; two squadrons of cavalry; and thirty-eight forage wagons. His infantry totaled about 4,000 men.[7]

Learning enroute that the cavalry picket believed to be near the river had left and that there was a Confederate cavalry detachment at Dranesville, Ord dispatched his foragers to

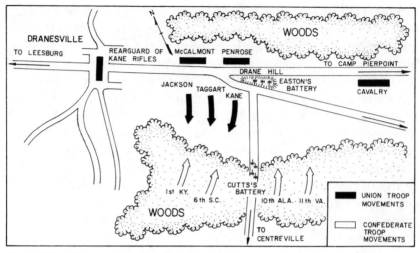

The Battle of Dranesville, 20 December 1861

Gunnell's farm between the pike and the river and proceeded to Dranesville to attempt to capture the enemy there. He entered the town with his artillery and cavalry and a small advance guard, flanked right and left by his two leading regiments, scattering the Confederate cavalry picket. He was eager for action, and, in his move into Dranesville, he was exceeding the letter of his instructions, as he very well knew.[8]

From the Confederate encampment at Centreville, Brigadier General J.E.B. Stuart rode forth toward Dranesville on the same morning, leading four regiments of infantry, totaling about 1,600 men—the Eleventh Virginia, Sixth South Carolina, Tenth Alabama, and First Kentucky—with 150 cavalry and Captain A.S. Cutts's Sumter Flying Artillery of four pieces. The purpose of his sortie was to cover an expedition of all the available wagons of the Confederate army in search of forage near Dranesville. Stuart sent his cavalry forward far in advance of the infantry to take possession of the Leesburg and Alexandria turnpikes which intersect just east of Dranesville on a commanding eminence known as Drane Hill. The Confederate cavalry, upon coming in sight of the intersection, found Ord's force already there and so reported to Stuart, who came forward at a gallop to reconnoiter. Stuart observed Ord's column passing along the Leesburg turnpike into Dranesville. He believed his forage wagons to be in great danger and dispatched his cavalry to notify the wagons to return to camp with all haste. He would attack Ord to enable his foragers to reach the haven of their own lines.[9]

Ord, in Dranesville, had posted his artillery on a small eminence and fronted toward Centreville. Learning that Stuart was to the south and east of Dranesville and moving up toward the turnpike, Ord expected an attack on both sides of the Leesburg turnpike along which the Federals had just come. Ord changed front eastward, that is, back in the direction from which he had come, posting Colonel John S. McCalmont's regiment to the left and Colonel Conrad F. Jackson's to the right of the pike. The Kane Rifles, or Bucktails, under Lieutenant Colonel Thomas L. Kane, remained in his rear to face any force in that quarter. Ord quickly realized the importance of the commanding position of Drane Hill on the top of which the two turnpikes intersected, and he hurried his entire force in that direction. He was in time. The Confederates had not yet reached there.[10]

Stuart knew the ground well, and it had been his intention to take position on the ridge now occupied by Ord, from which point, he later maintained, he could have held the entire Federal army at bay with his four regiments. But he was too late. His infantry and artillery had not yet come up. When they arrived, he deployed his troops on either side of the road. Cutts's battery was posted in the road some five or six hundred yards from the intersection of the turnpikes and behind a slight swell of ground, the muzzles of the guns just clearing the elevation. The Confederate infantry were well hidden by dense woods on either side of the road.[11]

Ord personally galloped ahead with the four pieces of Easton's battery toward a station he had selected for them on Drane Hill. His artillerymen ran past the selected point, capsizing one of their pieces. The general brought back the remaining three and told the captain where to post them. Meanwhile, Stuart's battery had opened fire on Ord's force. As Stuart's approach was from the south, it was necessary for Ord to swing his infantry around once again to confront the Confederates.[12]

After removing his exposed and useless cavalry from the road, Ord carefully observed the enemy's artillery fire and the situation of the Confederate battery and found that the Confederate guns were in a road which could be enfiladed. He ordered Captain Easton to right the capsized gun and bring it to a spot from which the road could be raked, and he removed two other guns to this location. Ord then personally gave the gunners the distance and the elevation and observed the result.

Finding after a round or two that the enemy's artillery fire slackened and the gunners were raking the road beautifully, unhampered by the enemy's fire, Ord told them "to keep at that," and galloped off to push his infantry forward.[13]

Stuart's artillery was in a precarious position, and there was no other place for it to go. Ord, "fresh from the Artillery School," as he later put it, had zeroed in on them precisely.[14] One shell exploded an ammunition wagon with terrible slaughter. Stuart himself reported that "every shot of the enemy was dealing destruction on either man, limber, or horse."[15]

Ord had difficulty with his green and dispirited infantry. He put three regiments in line, started them forward into the woods, inspiring and directing the men by his personal example and exertions and cheering them by encouraging remarks and by boldly leading the way. It required all his efforts and some little time to get them to show a bold front. He found much inclination to shirk and run away on the part of both officers and men. The Kane Rifles and Jackson's regiment were finally persuaded to charge. "I put them in the woods," said Ord, "pushed and exhorted them up the hill" in the direction of Stuart's battery.[16]

After the action had lasted about two hours, Stuart, outnumbered and with his battery in a vulnerable position, decided to withdraw from the field. He judged that he had given his wagons time enough to get out of the reach of his enemy.[17]

About the time Ord commenced his infantry charge, he was informed that McCall had arrived on the field. "As I was very busy urging the men forward," he later explained, "and as they required all my attention to keep them to their work, I did not at once report, but when we reached the ground occupied by the enemy's battery I reported to him."[18] At the spot lately held by Cutts's battery, Ord noted several dead around the exploded caisson, including three headless, blackened corpses. The road, in fact, "was strewed with men and horses; two caissons, one exploded; a limber; a gun carriage wheel; a quantity of artillery ammunition, small arms, and an immense quantity of heavy clothing, blankets, etc."[19]

Ord's losses were seven killed and sixty-one wounded. The Confederate losses under the circumstances were much heavier. Stuart reported forty-three killed, one hundred and forty-three wounded, and eight missing. Ord found twenty-one desperately wounded Confederates on the field whose wounds were dressed by his surgeons. They were carried to nearby houses, but nearly all were expected to die.[20]

A thrill went through the North as news of the first victory of the Army of the Potomac spread over the country. The relatively small importance of the affray was magnified and enjoyed to the fullest. The morale effect of the victory was immense. It served to exhilarate and nerve the dispirited Union ranks and gave the men some measure of confidence in themselves. It enabled McClellan to regain prestige lost as a result of the recent Ball's Bluff disaster. James Longstreet stated that the action so advanced McClellan's popularity as to lead someone to call him "the Young Napoleon." McClellan himself reported the affair as brilliant and issued a congratulatory order. The secretary of war, Simon Cameron, a Pennsylvanian, as well as Pennsylvania Governor A.G. Curtin, wrote letters full of praise to General McCall. The Dranesville victors were renowned throughout the country, and many citizens and Washington officials visited their camp to congratulate them.[21]

The battle of Dranesville was no great affair, but Ord had conducted it with boldness and skill. His standing in the army was greatly enhanced, though McCall's appearance at the close of the fight gave the division commander an opportunity, as Meade expressed it, "to carry off the lion's share of glory."[22] Ord now had a reputation as a fighting general—if, indeed, he did not have that reputation before. His fellow brigadier, John F. Reynolds, is said to have remarked upon hearing of the Dranesville battle: "Confound that fellow! I knew, if there was a fight to be scared up, Ord would find it."[23]

Ord gained the affection of the men of his brigade by sharing with them the perils of the battle line. Placidus Ord, joining the command just after the Dranesville action, termed the general "the idol of his men." Ord bore his prominence with becoming modesty; he would not think of having his picture taken. "His pride don't run that way," wrote Placy. The brother thought he could make a thousand dollars on the general's likeness, if he had it.[24]

In the spring of 1862, Ord was caught up in McClellan's plan for an overwhelming advance upon Richmond that was supposed to bring the war to an early conclusion. McClellan designed his operation as an amphibious invasion of the narrow peninsula lying between the York and the James rivers upon which Richmond is located. The navy would furnish transportation for more than 100,000 of his soldiers and provide an unassailable line of communication by water. The first of McClellan's troops embarked for the peninsula on 17 March. Ord's brigade was a part of Major General Irvin McDowell's corps, and this force was to march overland through Virginia to join McClellan on the peninsula. The brigade left its encampment in front of Washington in the middle of April and proceeded to Fredericksburg where McDowell's corps took position for its move against Richmond.

At this moment, Ord was rewarded for his action at Dranesville by a promotion to major general of volunteers, effective 2 May 1862.[25] "I think the promotion of Ord just and deserved," Meade wrote, "for if I had had the good luck to have been in command at Dranesville, I should have claimed the benefit of it."[26] Ord now had to leave his old "fighting brigade." This was a sorrowful parting, for the men had come to love their commander, and, for his part, Ord took pride in gaining the esteem of all in his command. "You would hardly believe how the boys were attached to him," wrote a sergeant of the Twelfth Pennsylvania.[27] Cheer after cheer resounded for the general in a leave-taking ceremony which, in the words of Placidus, was carried out "quite a la Mode."[28]

Major General Ord was assigned to command a newly created division in McDowell's corps composed of Brigadier General James B. Ricketts's and Brigadier General George L. Hartsuff's brigades of infantry and Brigadier General George D. Bayard's cavalry brigade. An order to Ord of 16 May directed him to organize his force immediately. Being now directly under McDowell was not a command position to Ord's liking. The latter had little respect for McDowell's military talents. He thought the loser at Bull Run was not fit to command. To make matters worse, McDowell's manner toward his subordinates was rough, and he did not hesitate to humiliate his officers in the presence of their men. Ord quickly had enough of this treatment, and, when the new Secretary of War Edwin M. Stanton had occasion to visit Fredericksburg, Ord sought a transfer. Meanwhile, he had to get along as best he could.[29]

McDowell's corps had an effective force of about 40,000 soldiers of all arms. McClellan, progressing but slowly on the peninsula, expected that they would be added to his command in the field. Indeed, it was the intention of Lincoln and Stanton that they should be. On 24 May, the Confederate cavalry under General Jeb Stuart in observation near Fredericksburg reported McDowell's troops starting southward.[30]

As Ord was working vigorously to organize his new division preparatory to its southward thrust, Major General Thomas J. "Stonewall" Jackson was in the Shenandoah Valley under orders to create a diversion by menacing Washington and thereby diverting reinforcements meant for McClellan on the peninsula. His force numbered about 16,000. Jackson struck the scattered Federal forces in the valley in turn, preventing them from uniting, and then moved northward down the valley to Harpers Ferry. So rapid were Jackson's movements, and so successful his whirlwind campaign, that he caused Northern newspapers to shriek, "Washington is in Danger."[31]

President Lincoln and Stanton acted without delay. On the very day that McDowell commenced his southward march from Fredericksburg (24 May), Lincoln ordered him to lay aside the move upon Richmond and to put twenty thousand men in motion for the Shenandoah to capture Jackson's forces. Major General James Shields's division was ordered to the valley, and Ord's division was directed to follow. The two divisions constituted about one-half of the entire corps. All was haste and confusion as the authorities, panic-stricken by the danger to Washington, urged the troops forward. Orders came from every direction—from McDowell, from Stanton, even from Secretary of the Treasury Salmon P. Chase.[32]

Ord's infantry brigades moved from Fredericksburg by water to Alexandria, then by rail to Manassas. For some reason McDowell ordered the artillery and cavalry to go by land to Alexandria, though their destination was also Manassas. Ord called the error to Stanton's attention, and they were ordered to go direct. On the morning of 28 May at Manassas, Ord received a dispatch from McDowell urging him to follow Shields at once. On this order, Ord made the laconic notation: "The Division not having a particle of transportation or rations."[33] The movement continued rather slowly toward Front Royal, and Ord reached Thoroughfare Gap on 30 May. The general reported faint sounds of artillery fire from the north. Jackson was still at work in the lower Shenandoah, as Shields's nearly 11,000 troops and Ord's 9,000 were headed toward the valley to cut off his line of escape. Major General John C. Frémont, with about 15,000 men, was pushing through from the west to close the trap at Strasburg.[34]

Early on the morning of 30 May, Ord left Thoroughfare Gap. McDowell, arriving at Piedmont about noon, was disappointed to find General Ord's division there, only five miles from its camp of the night before and in much confusion. McDowell reproached Ord severely for the disorganization and slowness of his command. "He pleaded sickness," said McDowell, "and that he had not been well for several days, and was now unable to hold a command, which he turned over to Brigadier-General Ricketts."[35] In a subsequent statement to the congressional Committee on the Conduct of the War, McDowell said: "He plead [sic] one excuse and then another, and finally said he was ill, and turned his division over to General Ricketts."[36] McDowell stated that the troops had been ordered away from Fredericksburg with only the supplies they had on their persons. When they finally dribbled into Front Royal on the morning of 31 May, by his own admission they were wet and very much exposed. Was Ord's "illness" utter disgust with McDowell's manner and with his failure to adequately provide transportation and supplies for his men?

In the meantime, while Ord languished, Jackson, eminently successful in accomplishing his goal, realized he must move rapidly to extricate his force from the trap closing upon him. The last of his troops, by a forced march, arrived in Strasburg on 1 June. Shields and Ricketts, the latter with Ord's division, left Front Royal for Strasburg on that day, but they were not in time to head off Jackson. Frémont was nearer. He reached Strasburg on 1 June, but, instead of disputing the passage of the Confederates, he took position on the heights nearby waiting for Jackson to attack. Jackson occupied the entrenched Federals by a few demonstrations, thus giving his long column ample time to escape. McDowell's corps, vital to McClellan's plans, had been detained and half the force sent on a fruitless chase after Jackson. Thus, Jackson's handful had held in check McDowell's 40,000 in addition to the troops in the valley under Frémont and Major General Nathaniel P. Banks. Furthermore, Jackson left the valley about 18 June and was able to add his force to Lee's in defense of Richmond.[37]

General Ord, on the face of it, did not show up well in the effort to catch Jackson. Illness hampered him, if it is granted

that his indisposition was a genuine sickness. Sufficiently recovered on 3 June, he resumed command of the division at
Front Royal and, at the same time, took pen in hand to address
a letter to the secretary of war asking to be relieved from
McDowell's corps. He reminded Stanton of his similar request
of a few days before at Fredericksburg. He told the secretary he
could not, without violating his self-respect, endure
McDowell's ungentlemanly manner. Ord went on to mention
orders "given in a rude, crude and insulting manner," which
had tended to demoralize his command. For more details, he
referred the secretary to the other officers of the division. "If no
alternative avails to relieve me of General McDowell's command," he wrote with finality, "I beg herewith to tender my
resignation as Major General of Volunteers."[38]

On 6 June, McDowell, who had also made his headquarters at Front Royal, departed for a visit to Washington. Before
leaving, he directed Colonel Ed Schriver, his chief of staff, to
inform Ord that he would be gone only a short time, and that,
in succeeding to the command in Front Royal, Ord was not to
give any instructions to McDowell's staff except to the chiefs of
the supplying departments, and to them "only when abso-
lutely necessary."[39] Ord reacted strongly to this show of no-
confidence. "I am the highest in rank here on duty. . . ," he
sternly reminded Schriver. "While I am the senior you will
obey my orders."[40] As for McDowell's order, Ord rescinded it
and directed all of McDowell's staff to report to him. Ord then
went over McDowell's head to the secretary of war and even to
the president. He explained the circumstances to Stanton and
said: "As the command of the staff is necessary to the efficient
command of the troops, I have, under the 62d article of war,
assumed command of the whole, and now ask if the President,
under that article of war, directs otherwise." He signed the
dispatch, "E. O. C. Ord, Major-General, Commanding at Front
Royal."[41] Ord then followed up by going to Washington to seek
relief in person. As he departed from Front Royal, McDowell's
staff wished him success when he bade them goodbye.[42]

In Washington, Ord thought it was his duty to state that
McDowell was not fit for his command. This was risky business, but Ord's determination and earnestness carried conviction with it. He did not believe that McDowell's people would
fight under him, and he himself was determined not to be with
any "bully-runners." "In my tilt with McDowell I *unseated*

him," Ord wrote.[43] McDowell was to have been the "big gun" of the abolitionist wing of the Republican party, he continued. In spite of his powerful backing, however, McDowell was transferred to Pope's new Army of Virginia and deprived of his departmental command.

A change was in the making for Ord also. He applied for a transfer to Halleck's army in the West. No doubt he had been making vigorous efforts for some time to escape from McDowell. His own prestige would have some bearing upon his success in this endeavor. Perhaps Garesché was helpful again. Unquestionably, Ord gained the assistance of powerful friends in the western theater of war. Halleck himself, overall commander in the West, was the key figure, but there was also Major General William T. Sherman, one of the principal participants in Major General Ulysses S. Grant's successful campaign. These men had brought the army victorious at Shiloh to a position deep in the interior of the Confederacy. On 8 June, Ord secured orders to report to Halleck in Corinth, Mississippi.[44]

7

★★★★★

Iuka and the Hatchie

G ENERAL Edward Ord reached Corinth, Mississippi, in the latter part of June 1862, and was pleased to find there and in the vicinity a number of his army associates from Pacific Coast days. In addition to Major General Henry W. Halleck, Major General William T. Sherman had a division in Major General Ulysses S. Grant's Army of the Tennessee, and Colonel Philip Sheridan held a cavalry command. Apparently, Ord and Grant had not met before. Ord reported to Grant as his immediate commander, and there began a relationship which would prove to be of the greatest importance to Ord. His assignment was to the Second Division of the Army of the Tennessee and the command of the garrison in Corinth. This assignment was more substantial than the one Ord previously had held in Virginia, and he wielded greater powers. Ord and his staff had their headquarters in a house only recently vacated by his old friend, now enemy, General Pierre G. T. Beauregard.[1]

Corinth was a well-situated town in the extreme northeastern corner of Mississippi at the junction of the Mobile and Ohio and Memphis and Charleston railroads. It contained a number of nice frame houses and a considerable business district. There were some disadvantages to the place. The water was hard and impure; there were no fresh vegetables, as the country for miles around had been stripped. "Here we have the hot sun, combined with Mississippi swamp air, which keeps us all under quinine and opium regimen, and our hospitals full," the general wrote.[2]

★★★★★

The Western area to which Ord was now assigned presented to the Union a much brighter aspect than did the East. After months of discouraging reverses to Northern arms, a series of successes was achieved in the West which led many to believe the end of the war was at hand. On 6 February 1862, Fort Henry on the Tennessee River had fallen to Grant. Ten days later, Fort Donelson on the Cumberland River surrendered to him. The loss of the forts was a severe blow to the Confederacy.

Grant soon was confronted with a new line of defense further south under the command of General Albert Sidney Johnston. The Confederate forces were ranged along the Memphis and Charleston Railroad with wings at Memphis and Chattanooga and the center at Corinth. Grant moved southward and, on 6 April, was encamped at Pittsburg Landing near Shiloh Church. Johnston assumed the offensive, attacking the unprepared Union forces on this date. The battle of Shiloh, as it came to be called, continued a second day and ended in the withdrawal of the Confederate forces to Corinth. The Confederacy suffered a severe loss in the death of General Johnston on the first day of battle. The command devolved upon Beauregard.

The pursuit of Beauregard was slow, and when the Union forces finally reached Corinth on 31 May, they found the town evacuated. The Confederates were subsequently forced to abandon Memphis and Fort Pillow, clearing the Mississippi River as far south as Vicksburg. Flag Officer David G. Farragut and Major General Benjamin F. Butler occupied New Orleans on 1 May. Halleck was credited with the successes in the West, and in July 1862, shortly after Ord's arrival, was made General-in-Chief of all the land forces of the United States and departed for Washington. Grant then assumed command of Federal forces in western Tennessee and northern Mississippi, with headquartered at Corinth. He had at his disposal about 46,000 troops. His line of defense stretched from Memphis across northern Mississippi to Corinth. Facing him were Confederates under Major General Earl Van Dorn and Major General Sterling Price, who were charged with operations in Mississippi, including the defense of Vicksburg.

Beauregard's successor, Major General Braxton Bragg, had taken his army to Chattanooga, from which point he would operate in east and middle Tennessee. Facing him was Major General Don Carlos Buell with the Army of the Ohio. One of Grant's main duties was to prevent any reinforcements of Bragg's troops.[3]

Early in September, Grant reorganized his line, and Ord was transferred to command the center in the Bolivar-Jackson area of Tennessee. Though he had been in Mississippi scarcely three months, Ord had attracted a following, for some of the most gallant generals and colonels applied to go with him to his new assignment. His force was the equivalent of an army corps, and its task was to guard the rail lines from Bethel to Humboldt and from Jackson to Bolivar. Grant's line now consisted of Sherman commanding the right at Memphis, Ord the center at Jackson, and William S. Rosecrans the left at Corinth.[4]

In the late summer and fall of 1862, a Confederate offensive was projected all along the line in both East and West. In the East, General Robert E. Lee, having checked Major General George B. McClellan on the peninsula and forced the Washington authorities to give up their effort to capture Richmond, moved out of the Confederate capital and up to the old Manassas battlefield where in August he and Jackson soundly thrashed Major General John Pope's Army of Virginia. Lee then crossed the Potomac into Maryland, and McClellan was sent to intercept him. Their armies met in the great battle of Antietam on 17 September. While Lee held his ground, his losses were severe, and he withdrew into Virginia. In the West, Generals Bragg and Edmund Kirby Smith invaded Kentucky in an attempt to menace Louisville and create alarm in the North. Buell cautiously watched them. Parts of Buell's and Bragg's armies met in an indecisive contest at Perryville, Kentucky, on 8 October, and the Confederates withdrew to eastern Tennessee.

As these actions were in progress, Van Dorn and Price launched an offensive against Grant's line. They not only desired to prevent Grant from sending reinforcements to Buell, but also courted the possibility of breaking through the Federal line into Tennessee and thence into Kentucky. They had an

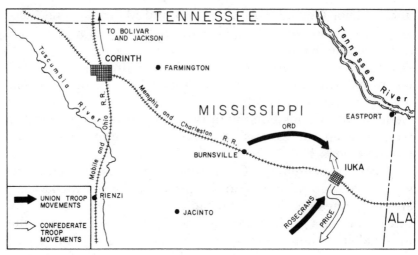

The Battle of Iuka, 19 September 1862

available force totaling about 40,000. On 11 September, Price, hearing that Major General William S. Rosecrans was at Iuka with only 10,000 men, moved against that position with about 17,000 troops. Grant withdrew the Iuka force to Corinth. On 14 September, Price entered Iuka.[5]

Ord was at once involved in a rather elaborate plan developed by Grant to destroy Price's force. Satisfied that Van Dorn could not reach Corinth in less than four days, Grant felt justified in leaving that place lightly guarded and throwing his force in the direction of Iuka to attack Price. The tactics involved a double-envelopment. Grant proposed to attack and hold his foe with one force and to strike him in the rear with another. The most efficient coordination was necessary in so complicated a maneuver; rapid communication was vital. Unfortunately, the terrain was not favorable for the plan. Stream, swamp and forest retarded movements and hampered communication between headquarters and field. So delicate a maneuver under such circumstances was, at best, uncertain.[6]

Rosecrans was ordered on 16 September to move south about twelve miles to Rienzi and Jacinto and turn eastward with his force of some 9,000 men until south of Iuka. He was then to move north and attack Price on both the Jacinto and Fulton roads leading into Iuka.[7]

On the same day, Grant issued verbal orders to Ord to prepare all the available forces in the Jackson-Bolivar command—the divisions of Brigadier General Thomas A. Davies,

Brigadier General Leonard F. Ross, and Brigadier General John McArthur—to form the left wing of the pincer. The combined forces were to move from Jackson and Bolivar via Corinth to Burnsville and, from there, north of the Memphis and Charleston Railroad on roads leading into Iuka from the north and west. After various detachments were made, Ord's force totaled only about 6,000. With rail transportation at hand, Ord had his troops in Corinth on 17 September within twenty-four hours after receiving his orders. On the morning of the eighteenth, he moved by rail to Burnsville, arriving about noon and finding Grant there. Grant remained in Burnsville to communicate with both wings by courier.[8]

Ord was ordered to get as near the enemy as possible during the remainder of the day, entrench his troops, and hold his position until the morning of the nineteenth. Rosecrans, it was learned, would be late, but he was expected to be near enough by the night of the eighteenth to enable Ord to press forward on the next morning, and bring on an engagement. Ord met Price's advance shortly after he left Burnsville, routing his pickets and capturing several prisoners. He took position about six miles from Iuka and was ready to attack on the morning of the nineteenth. Rosecrans had been further delayed.[9]

On 19 September, from nine o'clock in the morning until three in the afternoon, Ord made a careful reconnaissance of the Confederate front in preparation for the expected battle. By chance, General Dabney H. Maury, commanding the Confederate force fronting toward Burnsville, set his First Division on the march, intending to move nearer to the town where he knew the Federals were located. About 3 P.M. Ord's reconnaissance force advanced upon these Confederates. The reconnaissance was "handsomely conducted" and pushed with such boldness, Maury wrote, that he formed a battleline, expecting to receive an attack from Grant's entire army.[10]

While making his reconnaissance, Ord received from Grant further news of Rosecrans's slow progress and instructions from his chief not to attack until Rosecrans arrived or until he heard firing to the south of Iuka. About 4 P.M. Ord returned to Burnsville to consult with Grant, and both agreed that Rosecrans was too far to the south to make an attack that day. Grant instructed Ord to move his entire force forward to within four miles of Iuka and to await sounds of Rosecrans's attack before engaging the enemy. Ord issued orders for the advance.[11] At 6 P.M., he received the following dispatch, written at 4 P.M., from Brigadier General Ross: "For the last twenty minutes there has been a dense smoke arising from the direction of Iuka. I conclude that the enemy are evacuating and destroying the stores."[12]

At 8 A.M. on the twentieth, Ord heard firing in the direction of Iuka and moved rapidly into the town only to find that it had been evacuated during the night. The guns fired on the morning of the twentieth were the first heard by Ord, although on the afternoon of the nineteenth the head of Rosecrans's column had engaged Price just south of Iuka at about the time Ross reported the smoke. A brisk wind blowing in the direction of Iuka on the nineteenth had prevented the sounds of battle from reaching Ord.[13]

A courier from Rosecrans traveling by a circuitous route reached Grant on the morning of the twentieth with news of the battle of the preceding day. Hearing the guns on that morning, Grant thought the action was being renewed and ordered Ord to attack with all haste. The latter, however, had already entered Iuka in advance of the order.[14]

What of Rosecrans and his battle, and how had Price been able to slip so easily out of the trap? Rosecrans had been ordered to advance upon Iuka on both the Jacinto and Fulton roads, thus cutting off any southward avenue of escape for Price. Reluctant to split his force however, he had advanced only on the Jacinto road, making contact with Price on the nineteenth a mile and a half south of Iuka. A sharp struggle ensued in which severe losses were sustained by both sides. Nightfall brought an end to the contest which Rosecrans expected to renew at daybreak. During the night, however, Price determined to evacuate Iuka. He felt that his position between the two forces of Ord and Rosecrans was untenable, and so issued orders for a withdrawal. The wagon train of the Confederates was started during the night, and the troops were withdrawn from the field shortly before sunrise. With the Fulton road left open by Rosecrans, Price's escape was easily accomplished.[15]

Grant later stated his disappointment at the results of the battle of Iuka.[16] Rosecrans apparently allowed Price to escape from the trap by disregarding his chief's orders. As for Ord's part in the affair, Grant seemed to have been highly pleased

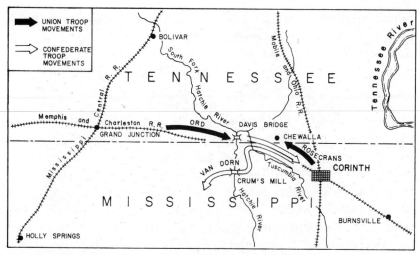

The Battles of Corinth and the Hatchie, 3–5 October 1862

with his promptness and willingness to fight. In one report Grant said: "On the night of the 18th the latter [Ord] was in position to bring on an engagement in one hour's march. The former [Rosecrans] . . . was 20 miles back."[17] Again, the Union commander reported: "General Ord's command showed untiring zeal, but the direction taken by the enemy prevented them taking the active part they desired."[18]

Van Dorn was still a threat to Corinth, and Grant directed Ord to move there at once with his force, less Colonel Marcellus M. Crocker's brigade which was left to garrison Iuka.[19] Ord subsequently returned with his command to the Jackson-Bolivar area.

At the time Ord was involved in the Iuka encounter, Bragg and Kirby Smith were well into Kentucky and menacing Louisville, while Buell was moving to defend that city. Van Dorn and Price, united after the Iuka affair, now determined to attack Corinth. Their aim was to prevent Grant from reinforcing Buell. Also, Corinth was an important railroad junction, and its capture might provide Van Dorn with an opening to penetrate into Tennessee and Kentucky.[20]

Van Dorn, with about 22,000 men, moved up to Pocahontas, turned east at this point, and crossed the Hatchie River on 2 October. This brought his army in upon Corinth from the north and west. Rosecrans, at Corinth proper, had about 15,000 troops within fortifications to withstand the Confederate assault. Ord, at Jackson and Bolivar, had about 8,000 troops which might be brought down to strike the Confederate flank or rear. Van Dorn fully realized that his blow would have to be delivered speedily, and, if unsuccessful, would require a rapid withdrawal from his position between Ord and Rosecrans.[21]

At the time the attack was imminent, Ord was far to the north on an inspection tour of his district. Grant ordered Major General Stephen A. Hurlbut, Ord's second-in-command, to come down from Bolivar, forty-four miles from Corinth, upon the enemy's rear. In addition, all possible troops which could be spared from guarding the railroad lines were withdrawn from that duty, making six additional regiments available. Four of these under Major General James B. McPherson were dispatched to Rosecrans in Corinth, and two were sent to Bolivar to reinforce Ord's command. Grant's plan, once the attack developed, was the same double-envelopment attempted unsuccessfully at Iuka. Rosecrans was to resist and hold, while Ord's force moved to attack upon flank or rear.[22]

Van Dorn's attack upon Corinth began on the morning of 3 October. There was hard fighting during the course of the day, and, by nightfall, the Confederates had succeeded in driving the Federals from their outer defensive positions. During the night, Rosecrans busied himself with defensive measures, while Van Dorn took position to deliver a decisive assault. A furious and bloody battle commenced on the morning of the fourth as Van Dorn made a supreme effort to take the town. The force of the Confederate charge carried some of the assailants into Corinth itself, but the Federals rallied to stem the tide. By 11 A.M. on the fourth, Van Dorn's repulse was complete, and a withdrawal was begun. McPherson with his four regiments reached Corinth just as the battle came to a close. Van Dorn lost 473 killed, 1,997 wounded and 1,763 missing, making a total of 4,233 casualties. Rosecrans suffered the loss of 355 killed, 1,841 wounded and 324 missing, totaling 2,520 casualties.[23]

Meanwhile, Hurlbut, with Ord's command, had left Bolivar for Corinth early on the morning of 4 October by way of Middleton and Pocahontas. At Middleton, his cavalry advance encountered a large body of Confederate cavalry and dismounted riflemen. Hurlbut ordered a battalion of cavalry to the front to drive the Confederate forces from the woods and to secure the crossing at the Big Muddy. The crossing was secured, but an attempt by cavalry to reach the Davis Bridge crossing over the Hatchie River before nightfall was in-effective.[24]

Van Dorn, retreating from Corinth, had anticipated that the Bolivar force would move down to dispute his passage across the Hatchie bridge and had rushed his forces in an attempt to secure the river crossing before the arrival of the Federal forces. He was advised by Colonel Wirt Adams of his advance force that he would be too late. Meanwhile, the victorious column of Rosecrans was expected to follow upon the Confederates' heels, making their situation precarious.[25]

Grant had informed Rosecrans of the movement of Ord's command under Hurlbut and ordered him to follow Van Dorn the moment the latter began to retreat. Rosecrans disregarded Grant's order and did not commence his pursuit until the next morning, 5 October, and then, being misinformed, took the road toward Chewalla instead of the State Line road further south by which the Confederates had moved.[26]

To make good his escape, Van Dorn had to cross the Hatchie River, the most important waterway in the region. The river-banks were bordered by woods and swamps, rendering the Hatchie a serious obstacle. The most important crossings were at Davis Bridge, some ten miles out of Corinth on the State Line road, and Crum's Mill, about six miles upstream, or south, on the road from Corinth to Holly Springs.[27]

Van Dorn pushed on toward Davis Bridge on the State Line road with the intention of engaging Hurlbut, while his wagon train and artillery hastened south on the Bone Yard road toward the crossing at Crum's Mill. He believed that he had no time to spare for a long battle at Davis Bridge, since Rosecrans was momentarily expected to strike his rear.[28]

On 4 October, news of fighting at Corinth reached Ord in Kentucky, and he immediately set out to overtake his command under Hurlbut. With his staff and headquarters guard, Ord reached Bolivar at 11 P.M., and, at 1 A.M. on the fifth, started out on horseback to overtake his column. On the way he encountered General Ross, one of his division commanders, who informed him that Hurlbut did not intend to do more than make a demonstration against the defeated Confederates. After an all-night ride, Ord overtook Hurlbut's column about 7 A.M., moving very slowly. This cautious movement of troops was not Ord's method of fighting, and, taking over the command from Hurlbut, he immediately "stirred them up."[29]

Ord's column moved toward Davis Bridge, some five or six miles in their front, but quickly found their advance disputed by Confederate cavalry, to which infantry and artillery were soon added. The road was narrow and winding, through swamps and dense woods, but the Confederates had no opportunity to make a stand under Ord's relentless pressure. They were driven at double-quick most of the distance to the Davis Bridge at the Hatchie. So rapid was Ord's advance that two Confederate batteries were overrun and captured.[30]

At the bridge, the Confederates endeavored to make a stand, but were scattered and driven across it. It was at this point that the bulk of the 420 prisoners taken by the Union forces were captured. The Confederates took position on a ridge across the river and some distance from it, from which they poured a galling fire into the Union ranks. Van Dorn's weary troops arrived in fragments, some of them to augment this holding force, while the bulk of his army was directed southward to the crossing at Crum's Mill.[31]

General Ord, on horseback, rode into the forefront of the fight at the bridge. He was dressed in rather remarkable fashion. Along with more conservative articles of attire, he wore a white coat, white socks and low-cut shoes! He was outstanding on the battlefield, to say the least, and quickly attracted the attention of both friend and foe. He had taken command of his own troops only a short time before and was relatively unknown to them. During the course of the fight, many of the men inquired who he was and, upon being told, made complimentary remarks about his being right at the bridge with his men where the action was hottest.[32]

Continuing his rush against the retreating Confederates, Ord ordered his infantry and artillery to cross the bridge. The charge was executed under a heavy fire of musketry and canister. Brigadier General James C. Veatch, commanding the Second Brigade, was ordered to cross the bridge and to form his regiments to the right and left of the road. Brigadier General Jacob G. Lauman of the First Brigade, constituting the reserve, reported to Ord at the bridge and was ordered to take position on the right. The brigade commanders executed their orders in the face of murderous fire. In this position, the troops were exposed en masse to a flanking fire of canister from a battery on their left, and here a considerable loss of men took place. Ord then ordered two sections of artillery to cross the bridge, which was done under a very heavy fire from the enemy's battery and infantry. Ord described his own losses, as the battle continued, as probably greater than the enemy's.[33]

About midday, after the action had been in progress for some four hours, Ord began to feel that his own position was precarious. His force amounted to only six regiments of infantry and one of cavalry, about 5,000 strong.[34] He dispatched a report to Grant telling of the action: "The enemy has four batteries playing upon us and a large body of infantry, and . . . [I am] apprehensive we will have to fall back unless we are speedily reenforced."[35]

At this moment, while Ord was directing one of his batteries to take a new forward position and scolding General Hurlbut for not showing some vim, a bullet slammed into his leg above the ankle. "Hurt like the devil," he later said.[36] Thinking that his foot was shattered, Ord turned command over to Hurlbut and rode off the battlefield with an aide to the nearest place for wounded. There it was found that the ball had passed between the bones and had to be cut out from the side opposite its point of entry.[37]

The action continued for some time under the new commander. At 2:10 P.M., from a hospital near the bridge, Ord dispatched a communication through Grant to Rosecrans, who was then moving ineffectually down the Chewalla road, begging him to create a diversion if he could possibly do so. Eventually Hurlbut crossed the bridge, extended his line rapidly to the left, and crowned the hill from which the Confederates had poured their shot and shell. The fight ended at about 3:30 P.M., at which time the Confederates made a strong demonstration on the right of General Lauman's brigade. Under cover of this attack, they hauled off a crippled battery, leaving the caissons, and retired from the field. Hurlbut claimed credit for driving the Confederates from the field. Van Dorn, on the other hand, reported that they held their position on the ridge overlooking the Hatchie under the command of General Price until orders were given to take up their line of march on the Bone Yard road behind the Confederate train.[38]

No pursuit was attempted on the fifth by the troops under Hurlbut. The infantry, which had started at Bolivar at 3 A.M. on the fourth, had marched twenty-six miles on that day and, on the fifth, had fought their way over five miles of difficult country and had been under fire at close range for seven hours. They were too tired to pursue.[39]

Figures of the losses for the participants in the action over the Hatchie reveal the Confederate loss in matériel as two batteries (previously mentioned) and about nine hundred small arms. In manpower, the Federal army suffered more severely, losing 46 killed, 493 wounded, and 31 missing. The Confederate losses, not so accurately determined, were fixed at 32 killed (as this number were buried on the field) and an estimated 153 wounded. The principal Confederate loss was in prisoners, the number being 420.[40]

The battle of Corinth and the associated action at the Hatchie were of great strategic importance. They paved the way for a Federal offensive in the West which was to lead to the success at Vicksburg and the complete opening of the Mississippi River. Grant, though victorious, was keenly disappointed at the outcome. He excused Rosecrans's failure in his report of the battle, but it was clear that he had hoped for greater results.[41]

At both Iuka and the Hatchie, Ord fulfilled his part with promptness and efficiency. Moreover, he had demonstrated remarkable courage. These qualities were not lost upon Grant. In a special order he paid high tribute to his wounded lieutenant: "In parting with General Ord the commanding general of the district regrets losing the services of so gallant an officer and so able a commander, and wishes to express the desire, in all sincerity, not only that he may be speedily restored to duty, but that he may be restored to the same field he is now being relieved from. Especially would this be desirable to the commanding general so long as it is his good fortune to command his present armies."[42]

Words of praise of this nature from Grant were not to be taken lightly. He had the capacity to select able subordinate military commanders. Ord was now a "Grant man,"[43] a member of a military clique which included such men as Sherman, McPherson and John A. Rawlins. These men had proved themselves in the Western campaigns and were destined to rise to high position in Grant's train as he won further successes and ultimately became the general-in-chief of all United States forces.

Ord himself was pleased with the fight at Davis Bridge and called it a "pretty battle." "The highest compliment that I have received," he continued, "is that the enemy estimated my force at 20,000." The newspapers apparently gave the most publicity to Rosecrans and Hurlbut. Of the former Ord wrote: "I am senior to Rosecrans, but I don't keep correspondents around my hd quarters, besides I don't care for their puffs. I make the Army puff me. The soldiers know who does the fighting."[44]

Ord had a high opinion of his troops. They behaved well. He had won their hearts at the Hatchie, and was sorry to be parted from them so soon. The Western men, he thought, were better fighters than the Eastern. Congratulations came to Ord from his friend Garesché in Washington, who noted with pleasure that Ord was as popular with his Western troops as he had been with those in the East.[45]

General Ord spent the night after the battle in a field hospital near Davis Bridge. "Had sad time with dead and dying around me," he wrote.[46] The next day, he accepted the offer of one of his staff, Captain Alexander B. Sharpe, to go to his home in Carlisle, Pennsylvania, to recuperate. This journey in itself was something of an ordeal: by rail from Jackson, Tennessee, to Columbus, Kentucky; by steamer to Cairo; by rail to Chicago, and thence to Carlisle. At the frequent stops, the general had to be carried in a man's arms from car to car or be placed on a cot and carried to a house or hotel.[47]

While recuperating at Captain Sharpe's, General Ord received a visit from Major William Painter, one of his former staff officers from Dranesville days. The major was full of the disastrous military operations in Virginia and Maryland, and told Ord that he and a number of the general's former officers wanted to follow him to his next command. What that next assignment would be Ord did not know, but he had a preference: "Genl. Grant had just given me an Army Corps and the largest District in his command; and I shall go back to that country if I can, as soon as I am well."[48]

8

★★★★★

A Tale of Two Sieges

DURING the months of October and November 1862, Ord was convalescing from his wound received at Davis Bridge. By 10 November, he could walk a little on crutches, and, by the seventeenth, the wound began to close and the discharge to cease.[1] Late in November, he was sufficiently recovered to serve with four other generals on the military commission appointed to investigate the operations of the army under Major General Don Carlos Buell in Kentucky and Tennessee. The commission held hearings in Cincinnati, Louisville and Nashville. Buell, it will be recalled, had been opposed to Bragg in this area but had not pressed matters as his Washington superiors thought he should. He was relieved of command, and an investigation was ordered.[2]

According to Major General Lew Wallace, president of the commission, Major Donn Piatt, judge advocate at the hearing, gave the five generals word from above that the commission had been "organized to convict"—Edwin M. Stanton and Henry W. Halleck wanted to get rid of Buell. The members of the commission did not believe this, according to Wallace's recollection, and Piatt became an object of contempt for suggesting that the commission would condemn an officer regardless of evidence.[3] Ord apparently gave Piatt a severe tongue-lashing for such presumption and made an enemy of him. However, Ord did believe Piatt as to Stanton's intentions:

"It is pretty certain that Stanton packed the court that tried Fitz John Porter," he wrote, "& I know that he packed the Milty Commission that tried D. Carlos Buell, for I was on it and Don Piatt our judge advocate told me so—ie, that Dana & I (the minority) *'were put on as lame ducks.'"*[4] Presumably, the three generals of the "majority," Lew Wallace, Brigadier General Albin Schoepf and Brigadier General Daniel Tyler, as partisans of the Radical Republicans, were supposed to vote to convict Buell, a conservative Democrat. Ord and Brigadier General Napoleon J. T. Dana as conservative Democrats were expected to favor acquittal. The Buell Commission was still holding hearings in March 1863 when General Ord was relieved for active service in the field.

★★★★★

During Ord's convalescence late in 1862 and in the early months of 1863, the Union cause was set back by one disaster after another. Only the Western theater showed a glimmer of promise. In the East, McClellan was sacked by President Lincoln for failing to follow up and destroy General Robert E. Lee's army after Antietam. Major General Ambrose E. Burnside was put in his place, and, at Fredericksburg in December 1862, threw the flower of the Army of the Potomac upon Lee's entrenchments and was repulsed in a sickening slaughter. Major General Joseph Hooker was next in line, and, though his force was far superior in numbers, Lee and Jackson whipped him soundly at Chancellorsville in May 1863.

In the West, toward the end of 1862, William S. Rosecrans, successor to Buell, was at Nashville facing Braxton Bragg at Murfreesboro. The Union commander moved against the Confederate and there ensued a bloody encounter at Murfreesboro (Stone's River). The contest was a Union victory, though indecisive. It did result in Bragg's withdrawal into northern Georgia.

Vicksburg was the prize in the West much sought by the Union. After the capture of New Orleans by Flag Officer David G. Farragut and General Benjamin F. Butler in May 1862, portions of Butler's army ascended the river and made two ineffectual attempts to capture the city. After Corinth, General Ulysses S. Grant struck out into Mississippi toward the same objective, but he did not get very far. Major General Earl Van Dorn made a surprise raid upon the Federal supply depot at Holly Springs and destroyed the military stores essential for the expedition. At the same time, Grant had sent General William T. Sherman directly down the Mississippi River upon the river city. Sherman's effort also failed when he was repulsed at Chickasaw Bluffs near Vicksburg in December 1862. Grant took personal command on the Mississippi River in January 1863, and, by May, had invested Vicksburg and commenced the siege of the river city. Thus matters stood when Ord again took the field.

★★★★★

Ord very much wanted to serve again under Grant, but this seemed unlikely, as all of Grant's corps commands were filled. Ord was ordered to take charge of a detachment of the Seventh Corps at West Point, Virginia, at the head of the York River. To Ord, this was but little better than being shelved. He thought that he deserved a larger command, and he applied directly to Halleck for one, saying that both Grant and Sherman had written for him to come to the West and that he might get a corps if he did so. His remonstrance was successful, for, on 25 May, he was ordered to report in person immediately to Grant at Vicksburg.[5]

★★★★★

At this time, Molly Ord and the children arrived from California via the Isthmus. Ord met them in New York, but had only three or four days to spend with them, hardly sufficient for the younger of the five children to get reacquainted with their father, and then he was off to join General Grant.[6]

★★★★★

Grant had launched an audacious campaign in the spring of 1863 to reduce Vicksburg. He marched his troops overland on the Louisiana side of the river to a point below the Mississippi city, while Admiral David D. Porter ran past the Vicksburg batteries at night with transport facilities. The troops were transferred to the Mississippi side and began an advance northeasterly. Grant had about 50,000 troops in the Vicksburg vicinity, while Lieutenant General John C. Pemberton, commanding the Confederate forces in the area, could concentrate 30,000 to 40,000. After an encounter at Port Gibson, Grant pushed on, drove the Confederates out of Raymond and approached Jackson. Pemberton, meanwhile, was faced with con-

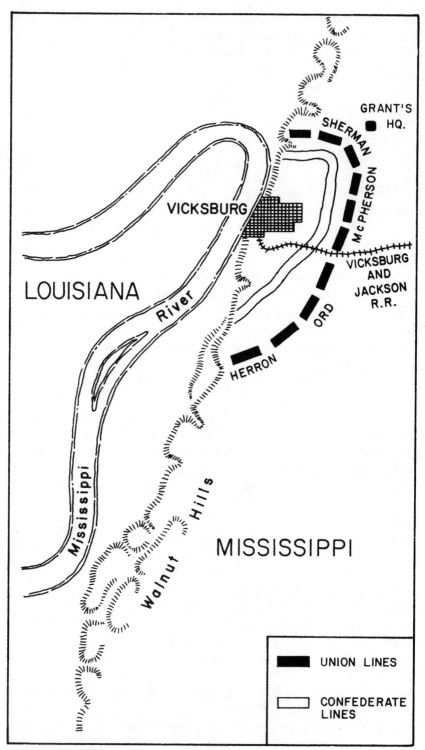

The Siege of Vicksburg, 18 May–4 July 1863

flicting orders from President Jefferson Davis and General Joseph E. Johnston, overall commander of Confederate forces in the West. Davis ordered Pemberton to hold Vicksburg at all costs, while Johnston ordered him to unite forces with his own to oppose Grant. Pemberton vacillated, as Grant moved to Jackson and forced Johnston out of that city and northward to Canton. The Union commander then turned upon Pemberton and defeated him at Champion's Hill. The Confederate withdrew into the defenses of Vicksburg, and Grant reached the city on 18 May.[7]

With Johnston at his rear, Grant desired to take the city as soon as possible. An assault on 19 May failed, as did a second attempt three days later. Grant then realized he must resort to siege operations. A line of circumvallation was constructed from Haines's Bluff on the north to Warrenton on the south, while a line of countervallation from the Yazoo River to the Big Black River was held by Sherman to ward off any attempt of General Johnston to raise the siege. The latter now had an army of about 25,000 troops. Grant's own forces were heavily reinforced, and, by late June, the Federal army numbered over 71,000 troops and had 248 guns. The efforts of the besiegers were directed toward contracting their lines by forward approaches, or saps, closer and closer to the Confederate line of defense.[8]

Ord arrived before Vicksburg on 18 June. He found on the right of Grant's line Sherman's Fifteenth Corps, temporarily under Major General Frederick Steele, and McPherson's Seventeenth Corps; on the left Major General John A. McClernand's Thirteenth Corps, and, to the left of that, the divisions of Jacob G. Lauman and Francis J. Herron. It was Grant's intention to place the divisions of Lauman and Herron, plus reinforcements which had arrived from General Burnside's command in the East, under Ord. This arrangement was not made, for, on the day of Ord's arrival, a major shake-up occurred in Grant's command. On 18 June, Grant relieved McClernand of his command of the Thirteenth Corps, and Ord was appointed to succeed him, subject to the approval of the president. The immediate occasion for McClernand's removal was a congratulatory address to the Thirteenth Corps in which he assumed for himself most of the credit for the Vicksburg campaign and charged the other corps commanders with failure to support him properly in the unsuccessful assault on the city on 22 May. The real cause for the removal, as Charles A. Dana, special agent of the secretary of war, then observing at Vicksburg, explained to Stanton, went much deeper than the congratulatory order: "That cause, as I understand it is his [McClernand's] repeated disobedience of important orders, his general insubordinate disposition, and his palpable incompetence for the duties of the position."[9] Grant privately confided to Dana also that McClernand's relations with the other corps commanders made it imperative that the command of the army should not devolve upon him, as it would in case Grant should be disabled.[10]

McClernand was a "political general," one of that variety of general officer who possessed high rank through political influence. He was not a trained soldier, and it was apparent that his presence at Vicksburg was a menace to the Federal cause. The removal seemed to give general satisfaction to the army itself, "the Thirteenth Army Corps sharing, perhaps, equally in the feeling with other corps of the army," wrote Grant to Halleck a few days later.[11]

President Lincoln's confidence in Grant and in his choice of Ord as McClernand's successor was affirmed on 10 July by an order approving the appointment. Grant spoke of Ord's assuming command of the corps as a very great relief. "The change is better than 10,000 reinforcements," he wrote.[12]

Ord took hold of his new task with a will. He now commanded one of the largest corps in the West, as the Thirteenth Corps consisted of the five divisions of Brigadier General Peter J. Osterhaus, Brigadier General Andrew J. Smith, Brigadier General Alvin P. Hovey, Brigadier General Eugene A. Carr and Brigadier General Jacob G. Lauman (the last-named temporarily attached). Ord's task was compounded by McClernand's incompetence, for the latter, with little conception of siege methods, was slow to push forward his approaches, and his connecting trenches were too narrow for effective use. Thus, the quality of the siege works and forward approaches on McClernand's front was poor, and the forward progress of his approaches lagged behind that of Sherman and McPherson. The best approaches were selected only after Ord's arrival, by which time the siege was nearly half over.[13]

"Ord is working very hard to bring up the lines where McClernand left them behind, but it will take some time to remedy the disorder which that incompetent commander produced in every part of the corps he has left," wrote Dana to

Stanton on 22 June. Again, he wrote: "Ord reports that it will require about ten days to bring the siege works in his front to the same general efficiency and safety as those of McPherson and Sherman."[14]

Ord found that McClernand's trenches were mere rifle pits only three or four feet wide, through which no artillery could pass and in which only a few troops could assemble. Their arrangement was not systematic for defense and support. Further, he found that the batteries still remained in the position which they had occupied at the beginning of the siege. By 25 June, only a week after his arrival, a great deal had been accomplished by Ord in widening the trenches, connecting them and making it possible to move men and artillery through them.[15]

Nightly sorties were made upon Ord's working parties, usually with slight loss. As the line of the besiegers tightened, the working parties were soon near enough to be assailed by hand grenades from the Confederate entrenchments. Eventually, the lines were even closer. Once on Ord's front, when the pickets were being posted, they became mixed with the Confederates'. There was a discussion between the opposing picket officers in which they agreed to arrange their lines by compromise. In some places, the men were about ten yards apart. Under such conditions, there was naturally a great amount of fraternizing and exchanging of social amenities. Considerable Confederate desertion to the Union lines also took place throughout the siege.[16]

A Union mine was exploded on McPherson's front on 25 June. The crater was secured, but there was no further result. Very little advancement was made in the siege after the explosion of the mine. For this, there were at least two good reasons. The unmerciful summer heat of Mississippi produced a pervasive feeling of listlessness among the besiegers. At the same time there was a conviction based on reports from within the city that the place would soon fall from starvation.[17]

Ord acquired information about the scarcity of food in the besieged city from two prisoners and a Negro boy captured by his cavalry near the mouth of the Big Black on 1 July. Letters in possession of the prisoners, as well as their statements, revealed the dire shortage. Wrote Ord to Grant: "If the statements in the letters of the amount of rations (and the black boy says it has been but one-quarter pound of bacon and meal each for ten days past) can be relied on, the information is valuable. It is strongly corroborated by the statements of deserters for some days past."[18] The Confederate ration described by the boy was exactly the ration commenced on 18 June in the city. There were other privations as well. Water was scarce, and the unwholesome water of the Mississippi River was brought in barrels for the use of the Confederate troops. The 3,500 civilians, many of them refugees, were exposed day and night to the constant shelling from the Federal fleet on the river and from the land batteries. Caves were dug inside the city for protection. Hospitals overflowed with diseased and wounded. Food prices skyrocketed. Remarkably, the *Vicksburg Citizen* managed to publish a few issues during the siege.[19]

Grant planned a final assault for 6 July, but it did not materialize. On the night of 2 July, Pemberton had a conference with his division and brigade commanders, and they advised arrangement of terms of surrender. In the morning of 3 July, Major General J. S. Bowen of the Confederate army met General A. J. Smith of Ord's corps with a proposal for an armistice for the purpose of arranging terms of capitulation. A meeting between Pemberton and Grant was arranged to take place the same afternoon between the lines. Grant was attended by his staff and Generals Ord, McPherson, Logan and A. J. Smith. Pemberton was accompanied by General Bowen and Colonel L. M. Montgomery.[20]

Ord later recalled his impressions of the occasion. The meeting took place in front of McPherson's corps a few yards from the Confederate redoubts, which were lined with soldiers. A truce was in force while the conversations were in progress, but Ord seemed for some reason to have suspected treachery on the part of the Confederates. The scene of the meeting placed nearly every officer of high rank of the Federal army under short rifle range of the Confederates. Ord suspected a plot to fire on the party and kill all of the rank of the Union side. He mentioned the ugly appearance of things to McPherson and advised that the troops be kept on the alert. Ord soon became satisfied from Grant's coolness and the manner of Pemberton that his concern was unfounded.[21]

Pemberton insisted upon conditions of parole for his army which Grant would not agree to, but it was decided that Grant would submit his own proposals in writing that night. Before formulating his conditions, Grant called his corps and division commanders to his headquarters for a "council of war." According to Ord's account, Grant told the officers that Pemberton would surrender, provided his officers and men were not sent North but were paroled, and "that they had a great horror" of Northern prisons. Pemberton had further declared that, unless he got these terms, he and his troops would cut their way out if not sooner relieved by Johnston.

As the senior officer present, Ord spoke up first. He said that as General Lee had invaded Pennsylvania and a great battle was probably being fought, the demand for troops would be great, and an order was very likely on the way to take part of Grant's command from him. Should this happen, the siege would have to be abandoned. Ord went on to say that the effect of the siege was beginning to tell on the men, that another assault would be costly and doubtful of result, that the nation anxiously awaited the surrender, and that paroling 30,000 "disgusted rebels" would damage their cause at home. "Every officer present I think was of my opinion as to the importance of a prompt termination of the siege and the advantage of these terms," Ord later commented.[22] Only one other officer spoke up, said Ord. General Steele "in his blunt way said he didn't think the rebels would be such d——d fools as to surrender on those terms."[23]

The terms of parole favored by Ord were the terms decided upon by Grant. In a dispatch to Admiral Porter, Grant stated that his own feelings were against the terms of parole, but that all of his officers favored them. Pemberton accepted them with minor reservations, which concluded the negotiations of terms of capitulation. The time of surrender was set at 10 A.M. on 4 July.[24]

The fourth of July was a day of relaxation. Ord directed that the working parties should rest and clean up and that the men be given half a gill of whiskey all around. There should be no noise along the lines at the surrender hour. Toward evening, the relaxation tended to get out of hand. Ord telegraphed to Grant that there were no guards along the Confederate works to keep either side from crossing. The town was full of plundering Yankees, and the Rebels were straggling out unchecked. The occupation force in Vicksburg should put a stop to this, he said.[25]

The fall of Vicksburg was a severe blow to the Confederacy. Over 31,000 dejected and disillusioned Confederates were paroled to spread a feeling of disaffection and defeatism throughout the South. In addition to the lost army, 172 cannon, about 60,000 muskets and a large quantity of ammunition fell into Union hands. Moreover, with the fall of Port Hudson to Major General N. P. Banks on 9 July, the Mississippi River was under Federal control throughout its length. The fate of the Confederacy was sealed, said Grant, by the fall of Vicksburg. From this time forward, the Union cause was in the ascendancy.[26]

★★★★★

Ord and his corps, without being permitted to set foot in the captured city, made preparations to leave the Vicksburg trenches immediately. Joe Johnston was at their backs, and Grant designated Sherman to command an expedition to move against him. Sherman requested his own corps (the Fifteenth, then under Steele), Ord's Thirteenth, and Parke's Ninth, about two-thirds of the investing army. Ord was greatly pleased to be under the immediate command of his old friend Sherman. Ord was notified on 3 July to be prepared to move the moment Vicksburg fell. Sherman sent troops immediately to secure the crossings at the Big Black River. The Fifteenth Corps was ordered to cross the Big Black at Messinger's Ferry, Ord's Thirteenth at the railroad bridge and the Ninth at Birdsong's Ferry, the whole to concentrate near Bolton and move from there against Johnston.[27]

Ord's corps was a mighty force in itself, composed of 14,400 infantry, 440 cavalry and 63 pieces of artillery. Each soldier was equipped with 150 rounds of ammunition and not less than five days' rations of hard bread, salt, coffee and sugar. On the morning of 5 July, Ord moved out the bulk of the corps toward the Big Black River bridge. The following day was consumed in rebuilding the bridge and making the crossing. The route was new to Ord but not new to his troops who were now retracing their steps toward Jackson by way of the bridge, Edwards's Station, Champion's Hill, Bolton and Clinton. Ord described the four-day march as "hot and exhausting," and, indeed, the men suffered considerably as they toiled forward under the hot July sun. So intense was the heat that a number of cases of sunstroke occurred; night marches were finally used. Besides the disabling heat, chills and fever took their toll, and surgeons complained that they had no quinine to give the men. Dust and lack of water added to the discomfort.[28]

Ord's lead division under Osterhaus was continually engaged in skirmishing with Confederate cavalry and artillery, as Johnston's force of 20,000 infantry and artillery and 2,000 cavalry began falling back toward Jackson. As Ord pushed along, he encountered Confederate breastworks of cotton bales thrown up along the route, as the Southerners harassed the advancing men in blue. Ord's soldiers broke open the bales and slept on the soft cotton, which would have brought one dollar a pound on the New York market.[29] He observed parties of paroled Confederates from Vicksburg going eastward. They were "ragged, sallow, emaciated, and seemed depressed and disconsolate."[30]

On 10 July, the three corps arrived before Jackson on three converging roads, Parke to the north, Steele in the center and Ord to the south. Sherman reported that the entrenchments found at Jackson in May had been strengthened and extended to the Pearl River on the flanks and heavy guns mounted on the salients. Johnston's army within the city was not well-equipped for battle, lacking in matériel and horses. The Confederate commander believed that lack of water would force Sherman to make an assault, but, should he not do so, Johnston himself would have to attack Sherman or abandon the place. To add to his difficulties, the Confederate was handicapped by desertion of his troops in large numbers.[31]

Ord moved his corps into position before the breastworks of the city and gained ground to the front whenever possible. There was brisk skirmishing in the process and some loss of life. Lines of trenches were dug, and bales of cotton were used for parapets.

Ord was directed to send strong forces to Pearl River on the extreme right for the purpose of securing a point from which to attack the railroad across the river. In pursuance of this direction Ord ordered General Lauman commanding the division on the extreme right of the corps to circle around to the right and to strike the Jackson-New Orleans railroad about three miles from the Confederate lines. Lauman was to proceed with caution up the railroad toward the Confederate lines and to report if any considerable force of the enemy were met. Lauman was further instructed to send a party to examine the

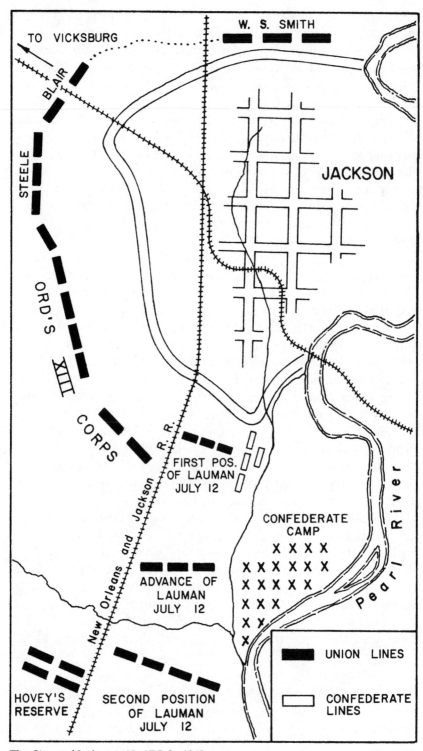

The Siege of Jackson, 10–17 July 1863

river. Ord was particularly concerned that the move should be made with caution, and only thirty minutes after his first orders, he sent a dispatch to Lauman with minute instructions for the advance.[32]

On the night of 11 July, Lauman reported to Ord that his division was in position on the railroad. On the morning of the twelfth, in executing Ord's order that he send a party to examine the river, Lauman sent a substantial force eastward to strike the river at a point below the city. He was unaware of the disposition of the Confederate line at this point, which took a southeasterly direction toward the river. Dense woods prevented his readily determining the nature of the ground. He made no reconnaissance and had no skirmishers out to cover his force. In his eastward march he ran squarely into the main Confederate line, and, mistaking it for advanced entrenchments, ordered an attack.[33]

Lauman's force consisted of Colonel Isaac C. Pugh's brigade plus another regiment, totaling about 1,000 men, with a battery and another regiment following. This force charged squarely into Breckinridge's division and Captain Robert Cobb's and Captain C. H. Slocomb's batteries, receiving a deadly cross fire from both muskets and artillery. Of the 800 men in Pugh's brigade, 465 were listed as killed, wounded or missing. The men and horses of an artillery section were nearly all lost, and an infantry regiment brought off the gun by hand. Three stands of colors went down. In the hasty retreat, all of the dead and wounded were left under the enemy's guns.[34]

General Ord was greatly angered by Lauman's disobedience and carelessness. Ord stated that the attack had been delivered without notice and without support of other division commanders. The point of the attack, he further noted, was defended by several thousand Confederates and was open to artillery fire from front and flank for 600 yards in front of their works. Ord knew nothing of the attack until Captain James C. McCoy of Sherman's staff reported to him and "stated that General Lauman told him to say to General Ord, 'I am cut all to pieces.'"[35] Ord hurried to Lauman's division immediately. He found the men scattered and ordered Lauman to gather the remnants and call the rolls. He did not know how to do it, Ord reported. Fearing that the enemy might follow up his advantage, Ord relieved Lauman and placed Brigadier General A. P. Hovey in command of the division. The right end of the line was reinforced and made secure.[36]

Ord directed a general advance on the front of the Thirteenth Corps. As Ord's entrenchments neared those of the besieged, Confederate skirmishers bitterly contested the ground and sallies were repeatedly made along the front. Ord pushed a reconnaissance in force to Pearl River on the right on 15 July. The Confederates on the opposite bank withdrew, and a line of works was constructed in that direction on the sixteenth.[37]

As the siege progressed, Ord was involved in the destruction of the railroads in the vicinity of Jackson. Grant had explicitly directed Sherman to see to this task. Sherman was determined to so effectually destroy the railroads that they could not be repaired again during the war. Under orders of 10 July, Ord sent all his available cavalry southward to destroy at least one mile of track and all bridges for at least fifteen miles from Jackson. Another force was directed northward to Canton and beyond for the same purpose. Ord and Parke each kept one brigade busy breaking up railroad track, burning the ties, and bending the iron to render it useless. Under orders of 15 July, Ord directed a second expedition of his cavalry to the south. The force was directed to proceed fifteen to twenty miles, and, with tools to be carried in wagons, to tear up about a mile of track. After a rest, the force was to move toward Gallman and repeat the performance, giving attention also to bridges, cars and depots. The party would go on to Brookhaven, where it was expected that locomotives, cars, station houses, etc., would be found, all of which were to be destroyed. The commanding general was solicitous for the success of the expedition, directing that, upon his return, the officer in charge should make a minute report of all that he had done. He "should be careful to make his work so good that it will not require another trip."[38] The expedition was eminently successful. Ord reported the destruction of four locomotives; fifty-two cars; a number of bridges; the depots at Byram, Bahala, Crystal Springs, Gallatin and Hazlehurst; one mill and a large quantity of lumber; seventy hogsheads of sugar. All this was in addition to the track destroyed. It would require years to rebuild this ravaged countryside.[39]

The extension of Ord's line to Pearl River previously mentioned was a grave threat to the Confederate left flank and rear, and no doubt brought home to Johnston the precariousness of his situation. Another powerful influence upon the Confederates was the Federal artillery which commanded the entire city.

A supply of artillery shells for a general cannonade was expected from Vicksburg, but, meanwhile, a galling fire was to be maintained to encourage a desired sortie from Johnston. In time, the Union artillery fire slackened by reason of the shortage of ammunition. The expected ammunition train did not arrive until the night of the sixteenth.[40]

General Johnston, finding that Sherman's siege operations were successful and that the Federal ammunition train had arrived, made preparations to evacuate Jackson. The withdrawal was skillfully accomplished during the night of 16 July. On the seventeenth, Sherman moved into the city and notified Grant that Johnston was retreating east with 30,000 men "who will perish by heat, thirst, and disappointment." Some 400 Confederates had been taken as prisoners and others were being picked up. No extended pursuit was attempted.[41]

Ord's troops and others continued the work of destruction of the railroads. Ord's men alone destroyed in the usual fashion an additional ten and one-half miles of track south of Jackson. Several hundred bales of cotton on the city's entrenchments and within the city were burned. The city itself did not escape. "The enemy burned great part of Jackson," reported Sherman to Grant, "and we have done some in that line. The place is ruined."[42] "It was a sight truly heart rending to see such destruction. . . ," wrote Placy Ord.[43]

Ord was ordered to move his corps back to Vicksburg. With the return of the various parties from their expeditions of demolition, the corps moved out on the Raymond road on 21 July. The return was greatly complicated by the large number of sick and wounded. Ord had his ambulances make two trips from Vicksburg. In addition, he transported 3,200 sick men by wagon back to the river city.[44]

Ord had participated in an important campaign which had cost the Union 1,122 in killed, wounded and missing, with the Thirteenth Corps suffering the heaviest loss (751), principally as a result of Lauman's attack. Confederate prisoners taken numbered 764.[45] Personnel losses, however, were negligible insofar as the war efforts of the opposing armies were concerned. The important features of the campaign were the loss to the Confederacy of an important railroad junction and the effective destruction of the railroads for a considerable distance from the city.

Ord's corps and the rest of Grant's victorious army were now available for further service. For Ord, there were various possibilities. Grant offered him the command of an expedition against Sterling Price in Arkansas, but left the matter to Ord's discretion. For reasons not apparent, Ord chose not to go. His corps was posted to Natchez, but this turned out to be a very brief assignment. On 7 August, Halleck ordered Grant to send an army corps of from 10,000 to 12,000 men to General N. P. Banks, commanding the Department of the Gulf in New Orleans. Ord's corps was designated to go.[46]

★★★★★

New Orleans, Ord found upon reaching his new post, was "quiet, clean, healthy, tolerably cool, & if the present condition of things lasts will go to ruin in a few years."[47] Placy Ord reported that one store in ten was closed and prices were very high. "Only think of having to pay 35 cents a pound for beefsteak and a dollar apiece for chickens," he wrote.[48]

Ord did not relish the idea of a command under a politician. Banks, like McClernand, was a political general. Ord wrote in a letter to Sherman that he had seen Generals William B. Franklin, William H. Emory and Charles P. Stone. Stone, Banks's chief of staff, handled the military, he noted, while Banks "takes care of the ladies and signs the important docs."[49] Banks was very polite to Ord, insisted that he bring Mrs. Ord to New Orleans, and was accommodating in many ways. Ord himself fit in very nicely with his new associates. "The Genl. is a great favorite among his brother Generals," Placidus wrote.[50]

There was urgency in the military situation in the Department of the Gulf. Orders for a move of the New Orleans forces into Texas seem to have come from the highest civilian authority, the president and the secretary of state, with political as well as military considerations in mind. The French invasion of Mexico for the purpose of making that country a French dependency constituted a serious menace to the Union cause. Should France gain control of Mexico and then espouse the cause of the Confederacy, Napoleon III would have an open avenue through Texas to aid the Confederacy with matériel or troops. To prevent this eventuality, the government of the United States desired to establish itself in force in Texas.

Under orders, Ord began dispatching the troops of the Thirteenth Corps to Berwick Bay, from which point they were to follow Franklin's Nineteenth Corps up Bayou Têche to Vermilionville. Elaborate preparations had been made for a lengthy land campaign. Banks had assembled an immense supply train, a large artillery force, and other impedimenta for a long expedition of conquest and occupation. After dispatching his last division from New Orleans, Ord hastened to the Têche country. He arrived on the banks of Vermilion Bayou in the evening of 10 October. On the following day, Banks left the field, and Ord, as senior major general, assumed command. He made his headquarters in the town of Vermilionville.[51]

On 12 October, Ord reported to Banks' chief of staff: "I am quite indisposed today; feel feverish, etc., and will send all applications and other matters of importance which my staff cannot properly attend to to you for action."[52] On the seventeenth, Banks directed Ord to advance a force against the Confederates in the vicinity and to make examination of the westward route. Franklin notified Banks that, on the sixteenth, Ord was too ill to attend to duty. Finally, after eight days of illness, Ord was relieved of command on 20 October, and Major General C. C. Washburn succeeded him as temporary commander of the Thirteenth Corps with Franklin taking command of all the forces in the field.[53]

Though Ord's removal from the scene was not the occasion for the action, Banks proceeded to abandon his land expedition. There were ample reasons for the abandonment: ahead of the troops was a 300-mile march across a barren country. Fall and winter rains promised floods and difficult roads. The enemy would be on flank and rear, and, at the end of the march, there would be another enemy force to reckon with.[54]

While Ord was ill, Banks hit upon a plan of invasion of Texas by sea. Vessels were concentrated at New Orleans, and the Thirteenth Corps under its temporary commander, Major General Napoleon Jackson Tecumseh Dana, was selected to comprise the expedition. Under convoy of three naval vessels, the corps sailed from New Orleans on 26 October. Troops were landed at Brazos Santiago, at the mouth of the Rio Grande; Brownsville, up the Rio Grande about thirty miles; Port Isabel; Corpus Christi; Mustang Island; and Fort Esperanza, at the entrance to Matagorda Bay. No further operations were attempted, since the troops were insufficient in numbers to do more than hold the various points occupied.[55]

General Ord, ill with a severe respiratory infection, had spent the month of November with his family in Louisville. They had a difficult time of it, for, not only was the general ill, but his children were also, the malady resulting in the death of one of them. Ord was much improved by the end of the month, and wrote a request to Halleck for an assignment to a dry climate. He pleaded not to be put under a politician. "For one Banks is a nice gentleman," he conceded.[56]

Ord realized that his chances for a move to a drier climate were not the best, for Halleck was not inclined to grant every request, especially of officers who had asked to be changed as often as Ord had. The request was not granted, and, in January 1864, Ord returned to New Orleans to resume command of the Thirteenth Corps, establishing his headquarters in that city. Dana remained in command of the occupation force in the field.

The supply problem for the Texas command was a serious and at times exasperating one for General Ord. There were acute shortages of clothing, shoes, forage, horses and that very necessary adjunct of military life, the soldier's pay; while, by some quirk of the quartermaster, there was an oversupply of greatcoats, camp kettles and mess pans. One regiment was reported to be four months in arrears in pay. Horses were in bad condition from lack of forage resulting from a drought in Texas and Mexico. Finally, Ord wrote one of his division commanders with apparent exasperation: "I cannot give orders which will fatten the horses, pay or clothe the men, but I will send the general commanding a copy of Colonel [Edmund J.] Davis' report, so that if possible he may correct some of the evils—supply some of the necessities reported."[57]

Dana was eager for action in Texas, believing that the defeat of General John B. Magruder, the Confederate commander opposing him there, would revolutionize Texas and lead to the dissolution of the Confederate army. Banks, however, made it clear that Dana was not to embark upon offensive operations and ordered Ord to visit Texas for the purpose of determining the minimum number of troops necessary to hold the points occupied. Ord spent several days early in February inspecting the Texas posts.[58]

Back in New Orleans there was bad news in store for Ord. Upon his return on 16 February, he was informed by Banks that President Lincoln had authorized the reinstatement of McClernand in command of the Thirteenth Corps. Political considerations, of course, prompted Lincoln's action, and perhaps the chief executive had his eye on the presidential election not many months away. From Texas, there came a plaintive cry for help from Dana to Ord: "My dear fellow you got me here in your kindness of heart, but it will be a most cruel unkindness if you leave me in McClernand's hands." Ord in New Orleans needed help too. Queried Dana: "What the deuce is going to become of you now?"[59]

Ord took the initiative by writing to President Lincoln that he was sure that reasons existed, though unknown to him, which were sufficient for the change. He therefore resigned command of the corps. Ord continued his letter by requesting duty in another department. "This application is made," he wrote, "to conform with your wishes and my duty. . . . I remain sir (I think) without fear or resentment the Obedient Servant of the President: E. O. C. Ord, Major Gen'l, Volunteers."[60] The matter was referred by the president to the secretary of war. General Ord was directed to go to Louisville, Kentucky, and to report by letter to the War Department for a new assignment.[61]

9

★★★★★

The Crater and Fort Harrison

A S he journeyed northward, General Edward O.C. Ord had ample time to reflect upon his situation. No doubt he was stung by the loss of his command and mortified at Major General John A. McClernand's reinstatement. The Thirteenth Corps was one of the largest in the Army, and its commander occupied a very respectable position. Ord expected to be compensated for its loss by assignment to a post of equal eminence. In whatever field he served, his seniority as a major general of volunteers would place him near the top in the hierarchy of command.

Upon arriving in Louisville, Ord reported to the secretary of war by letter dated 10 March 1864, in which he expressed the hope that he would be assigned to duty at once.[1] By rather fortuitous coincidence so far as Ord was concerned, on the day before in Washington, D.C., Ulysses S. Grant was commissioned lieutenant general and given command of all Union forces. This development certainly augured well for Ord's future.[2]

Grant immediately set about organizing his forces preparatory to a concerted move against the Confederacy. The way had been prepared for him, at least in part, by the great Union victory at Gettysburg in 1863. After General Robert E. Lee's loss there, the Confederates had returned to Virginia to await the next Federal move. In the West, the Southerners had gained the upper hand at Chickamauga in the fall of 1863, but Grant had redeemed that defeat by relieving the siege of Chattanooga and pushing the Confederates back into northern Georgia. Now, in the spring of 1864, Grant's plans called for General William T. Sherman's army of some 100,000, poised at Chattanooga, to begin its push in the direction of Atlanta. Joe Johnston faced Sherman's host with about 50,000. General George G. Meade's Army of the Potomac, numbering about 115,000, which Grant would accompany in person, would move against Lee's army of about 60,000 then occupying the region below the Rapidan. Lee was supported by Pierre G.T. Beauregard's approximately 30,000 in the Richmond-Petersburg area. The Army of the James, about 30,000 men, under General Benjamin F. Butler would move from Fort Monroe toward Richmond and Petersburg, making a Union diversion in Lee's rear.

Grant planned one other diversion in Virginia, and it was in this operation that Ord was to have a part. The Shenandoah Valley, a source of supplies for the Confederate forces and so often used by the Southerners as an avenue of invasion of or threat of invasion to the North, was still in Confederate possession. Grant would have two forces from Major General Franz Sigel's Department of West Virginia move into the valley. A cavalry column under Major General George Crook would start from Charleston, move south to Saltville, destroy the East Tennessee and Virginia Railroad, and move northeasterly in the valley to join the second force. This latter was to be under Ord's command and would consist of about 10,000 men of all arms. It would move out from Beverly toward Lynchburg, destroying anything the enemy might use to prolong the war. Grant did not expect much to result from the West Virginia expeditions.[3]

Sigel had difficulties, as he found that he could gather only about 6,500 troops for Ord's expedition, and incessant rains prevented his concentrating the required supplies. The magnitude of the force had greatly diminished. Eventually Ord recommended that his expedition be abandoned, basing his views on reports of his principal subordinates in the field that a force with an infantry train and artillery could do no good in the difficult country to be traversed; he suggested that a cavalry expedition be sent instead. He felt that, if carried through, his expedition faced almost certain defeat. Subsequent events proved these views correct. On 19 April, Grant relieved Ord from duty in Sigel's department.[4]

★★★★★

In this interim, Ord's loyalty to the Union cause was called into question. This was a recurring phenomenon which had started in 1862 when newspaper rumors began to be circulated questioning the general's devotion to the cause of the North. In all probability, the Radical abolitionists whom Ord had displeased in his affair with McDowell were responsible for the stories.

Ord was one of a number of conservative Democrats appointed by Lincoln to high command. Democrats, in fact, dominated the military, a condition causing great discomfort to the Radicals. The latter embarked upon a program of persecution to drive the Democratic generals from power. Ord was merely one intended victim among many. The Committee on the Conduct of the War was the chief instrument of the Radicals in their effort to purge the army of Democratic and conservative influence. The committee resorted to all sorts of underhanded practices to achieve its objectives—courts-martial, investigations, dismissals and "smear campaigns" in the press. Ord appears to have been a victim of the last-named technique.[5]

The Radicals had considerable material to shape into propaganda where Ord was concerned. In the first place, he was born south of the Mason-Dixon line and considered himself a Southerner. He had definitely been a proslavery man in the early 1850s. At the outbreak of the war, he had intimated that he had some sympathy for the South. Though he would fight for the Union, he was not by any means an abolitionist. To complicate matter further, his wife was a Virginian, closely related to highly placed Southern officers, while several of his brothers had openly lent their sympathy to the South. The general was vulnerable, to say the least.[6]

Ord was sensitive to the newspaper stories which had appeared in the summer of 1862, but he felt sure that he enjoyed the confidence of the president, the Cabinet (including, of course, the secretary of war), and both Generals Grant and Halleck. In addition, and best of all, he had confidence in himself.[7]

The general's Virginian wife, still in California at the time, came forward with moral support, declaring her loyalty to her husband. She wrote to him that he "must fight his prettiest" for Uncle Sam to whom he owed so much. She thought that some of the stories questioning his loyalty might be due to his

Southern connections, and she wanted her share of those connections set right.[8]

In the spring of 1863, while he waited for assignment to duty following his recovery from the wound received at the Hatchie, Ord was impelled to sit down and write to Halleck on the subject of his loyalty: "General [Daniel] Tyler has written a denial of ever having heard me use disloyal sentiments," he said.[9] Though the circumstances are not clear, statements that Ord had expressed disloyal sentiments had arisen out of random conversations at the time of the Buell hearings. They had become sufficiently noticeable to call forth Ord's letter to the General-in-Chief. Ord had gone on, shortly thereafter, to his Vicksburg assignment, but even here his past began to catch up with him in a most remarkable way.

On the march from Vicksburg to Jackson in July, soldiers of the Ninth Army Corps ransacked a house near Clinton, the property of one Cox, a former steward of Jefferson Davis. Secreted in the attic of the house were the books and papers of the Confederate president, which had been taken from the Davis plantation home near Vicksburg and stored there for safekeeping. The contents of the several boxes found were dumped on the floor, and the soldiers proceeded to help themselves to souvenirs.[10] In time, what was left of the collection fell into the hands of Sherman, commanding the Jackson expedition, who appears to have processed the papers before transmitting them to Washington. Newspapers in the North made a great stir about a forthcoming exposé which would prove quite embarrassing to many prominent Northern men who had written to Davis. "There is nothing concealed that shall not be made known," announced the *New York Times*.[11] Except for those letters which fell into the hands of the soldiers, however, the collection seems to have been carefully guarded. The incident was soon forgotten.

Ord very narrowly missed becoming involved in the matter, for he had corresponded with Davis. But for Sherman's sharp eye, he might have been seriously embarrassed. Sherman lifted from the collection and sent to Ord several of his letters written to Davis when the latter was senator from Mississippi. Ord was grateful to Sherman and expressed pleasure that the correspondence had not fallen into the hands of newspapermen. "The apparently pro slavery sentiment in one letter might have attracted attention," he wrote to Sherman. "There is no doubt about it, I was in 49 & until 54, a pro slavery man, and I am not quite such a radical now as to think we can turn all these black people loose among the whites, any more than we could so many tame Indians, with advantage to either race."[12] Conservative views such as these Ord could express privately to Sherman, but, had they become current among the already aroused Radicals, they could have laid the general open to further harassment.

As a matter of fact, Ord continued to be dogged by suspicions regarding his loyalty and under a rather unusual set of circumstances. Molly had come East with the children in 1863, and, in the period of about a year which followed, had in fact become a source of embarrassment to the general. "My enemies have made much use of the fact that my wife is a secessionist and related to their officers," he wrote to Placidus. "She could not resist the temptation of associating with those of similar ideas, and all I could say only made her the more persistent." Women's views help to "make men cut each others throats both practically and politically," he concluded.[13]

Molly Ord's ties to Southern officers were of a sort not likely to be overlooked. Her brother was Colonel James Thompson of the Confederate service, and her stepmother's brother was Lieutenant General Jubal A. Early, C.S.A. With the Ords consorting with the sister of one of the highest ranking Confederate generals, and with that lady being closely associated with them by marriage, it is no wonder that the general's enemies, including those of the Radical abolitionist persuasion, should seize upon these circumstances and make the most of them. There were newspaper rumors that Ord had been mustered out of service, and at least one highly placed Union officer, General Robert E. Schenck, was reported to have said that Ord ought to be mustered out. Ord was beset from the distaff side as well: "I have had this fact of my wife's family politics thrown in my teeth by Generals wives—my seniors. . . ," he wrote to Placidus.[14]

On top of all this, Sigel had been badly beaten at Newmarket by Breckinridge, and Ord was in the unhappy position of having asked to be relieved before a battle. He was prompted to write both Secretary of State William H. Seward and Secretary of War Edwin M. Stanton explaining that his request to be relieved from duty under Sigel just before the battle was not due to a lack of courage or of interest in the Union cause. He proceeded to tell of his difficulties with Sigel and the inadequacy of the expedition organized by him. Ord concluded his letter to Seward by saying that he would be pleased if President Lincoln should learn its contents.[15]

Ord came very near resigning his volunteer commission, concluding that he was no longer useful, if he was to be bandied about in subordinate places on account of his family ties. He was referring apparently to his assignment to Sigel, and there is no doubt but that he was greatly vexed at being placed in a minor command under Sigel, who was essentially a political general. Ord privately told Placidus that he would not ask for duty again unless some disaster should make his services necessary.[16]

On 4 May, Grant crossed the Rapidan with the Army of the Potomac. There followed six weeks of heavy fighting and maneuvering as Grant pressed relentlessly in the direction of Petersburg and Richmond. The blood and fire of the Wilderness were followed by the terrible carnage of Spotsylvania, and the casualty lists of both Grant and Lee mounted dreadfully. Grant's diversionary force under Butler proceeded to get itself bottled up at Bermuda Hundred. In the valley, Sigel, with the command lately under Ord, was routed at Newmarket by Breckinridge and retreated to a position near Strasburg. Sigel was then reduced to command of a division, being superseded in his department command by General David Hunter.

Grant maneuvered his way to Cold Harbor near Richmond, where furious assaults upon Lee's entrenchments resulted in sickening slaughter of the attackers. Disengaging, the Union commander sent the Eighteenth Corps down upon Petersburg, but assaults by the Northern forces failed to break Lee's line. The bluecoats then resorted to siege methods against Lee's army defending that city.

In the Shenandoah Valley, Sigel's successor, Hunter, captured Staunton. He then moved to Lynchburg in an effort to capture that place. Lee dispatched Early with his corps to the valley, just as in 1862 he had sent "Stonewall" Jackson. Hunter timidly withdrew his force from Lynchburg and moved back into West Virginia, leaving the valley open.

★★★★★

Toward the end of June, Ord wrote to Placidus that he wanted to leave for the front on 1 July. The old war horse was becoming restless for action.[17] The general had earlier stated that he would not ask for duty again unless some disaster should make his services necessary. Actually, a disaster of sorts was impending, and Ord's departure for Grant's headquarters at City Point near Petersburg could not have happened at a more opportune moment. In the early days of July, Jubal Early swept down the Shenandoah Valley, crossed the Potomac at Harpers Ferry on 5 and 6 July, and, on 9 July passed through Frederick, Maryland, taking the road to Washington, D.C. This was the old "Stonewall" Jackson game pushed with vigor by an able and tough West Pointer, and it created a panic in the Washington-Baltimore area.

There was an urgent need of a firm hand to take charge of the defense of Washington, and, late on the night of 7 July, Halleck conferred with Grant about this matter: "Of Couch, Ord, and Gillmore, I think the latter the best and have sent for him tonight."[18] To which Grant replied on 8 July: "I would feel much greater confidence where Ord commanded than where Gillmore did. The former I know to be skillful in the management of troops, and brave and prompt. The latter I do not know so much about."[19] No orders came for Ord, and, on 9 July, Grant directed him to proceed to Washington and to report to Halleck for orders. In notifying Halleck of this action, Grant wrote of Ord in the following terms: "I would give more for him as a commander in the field than most of the generals now in Maryland."[20] The lieutenant general suggested that Ord might be sent to Baltimore to take charge of that city's defenses.

Early's force consisted of about 10,000 infantry and 4,000 cavalry and artillery. From the vicinity of Frederick, the Confederate leader dispatched Bradley Johnson's cavalry brigade toward Baltimore to cut the Northern Central Railroad and the Philadelphia and Baltimore Railroad. Meanwhile, the Southern infantry pushed out of Frederick to Monocacy River. Here they were met by a hastily gathered force of about 4,000 infantry and one battery under General Lew Wallace, commanding the Middle Department with headquarters in Baltimore. With superior numbers Early crossed the Monocacy and routed Wallace's force, though the delay caused by Wallace probably had important bearing upon the sort of reception accorded the Confederates when they reached Washington on 11 July.[21]

Ord at last got into the action. On the afternoon of 11 July, as Early arrived before the defenses of Washington, President

Lincoln relieved Lew Wallace of the responsibilities of command in Baltimore and assigned Ord to the command of the Eighth Army Corps and all the troops in the Middle Department.[22] This action was taken because Wallace had lost the confidence of Grant and of the authorities in Washington, his fight at Monocacy being accounted a disaster rather than an important delaying action. Actually, the delay of Early had given Grant time to send up the hardy veterans of the Sixth Corps who filed into the Washington defensive works just in time to check Early's advance.

Ord reached Baltimore on the night of 11 July. He found the city still much excited and, as a first duty, had to calm the fears of the populace. The general conferred with Mayor J. Lee Chapman, who then issued a statement of Ord's views. Ord did not approve the stores being closed and would not issue any orders suspending business. He had no objection if the mayor desired to enroll the citizens, but he believed that a sufficient number had already volunteered. He did not believe the city to be in any imminent danger.[23]

On the morning of 12 July, Ord quickly began to get the feel of the Baltimore situation. Wallace had drawn all his troops into the city except for a guard at the Relay House, some five miles in the direction of Washington. The roads out of the city were patrolled for a few miles. Within the city, Ord had Brigadier General James Ricketts's division of the Sixth Corps, numbering about 2,500, between 2,000 and 3,000 hundred-days men and armed citizens, 200 sailors and 500 Negroes. After consultation with Governor Augustus W. Bradford, Ord asked him to issue a proclamation calling out the militia of Baltimore to the number of 10,000 for the purpose of completing and manning the works about the city. The general sent to Grant for two or three batteries of siege howitzers, as there were few guns in the city. A great handicap was the lack of cavalry which prevented him from sending out for information. The strengthening of the fortifications was pushed with great energy under Ord's direction.[24] A 13 July dispatch to the *New York Herald* stated that "the entrusting of the safety of the city to General Ord has given the greatest satisfaction, and the excitement of the people is now materially allayed."[25]

Reliable reports of Bradley Johnson's cavalry began to trickle in on 12 July. Having skirted Baltimore, the Confederates started southeasterly in a daring strike at Point Lookout to release the several thousand Confederate prisoners confined there. But, at this juncture, Jubal Early determined that the Sixth Corps was too much for him at Washington and that he would return with all possible haste to the valley of Virginia. He recalled Johnson, disengaged his infantry, and began to withdraw toward Rockville.[26]

Ord joined in the pursuit. Leaving a small force with Wallace, he departed for Washington with about 5,000 men to join the Sixth Corps which had left the Washington trenches and was closely pressing the Confederates. The nimble Early eluded his pursuers, and got across the Potomac and back to the valley, where he was to be heard from again.

Ord himself was detained at Washington by a dispatch from Halleck informing him that Grant had asked that he be sent to him for assignment to duty. Ord reported to City Point, and, on 21 July, Grant appointed him to the command of the Eighteenth Corps in Butler's Army of the James which was approved by the president a week later.[27]

N.P. Banks, Franz Sigel, and now Benjamin Butler! Was there no end to the political generals? Actually, Butler was the last of the lot to command a department and army in an area where important operations were in progress. His incompetence had been amply demonstrated, and yet he was a force to be reckoned with politically. Grant had inherited him and could not remove him—at least for the present.

Benjamin Franklin Butler was a Massachusetts lawyer, politician and industrialist. Once a Democrat, he was now a Radical. Very early in the war, Lincoln had commissioned him a major general of volunteers, and he was one of several Democrats so honored. His greatest fame had been achieved at New Orleans, where, early in 1862, he commanded the troops which occupied that city in cooperation with the naval forces of Flag Officer David G. Farragut. Butler's regime in New Orleans was characterized by excesses. While his brother, Andrew Jackson Butler, made a fortune trading in cotton with the "Rebels," Ben Butler hanged a citizen for tearing down the Union flag, insulted the women of New Orleans in official orders, and was proclaimed an outlaw by President Jefferson Davis. Though eventually removed, Butler turned up next as commander of the Department of Virginia and North Carolina and of the Army of the James. "Beast" Butler, as he was called in the South, had proceeded to get himself bottled up at Bermuda

Hundred and was uncorked by the arrival of Grant's army in the Richmond-Petersburg area. Butler's great crime lay in his presumptuous disposal of the lives of his soldiers in military operations which he lacked the competence to direct.

Butler was not without talent. His personality was extraordinary. He had a certain strength of mind which impressed many with whom he came in contact. Positive and domineering, he gave the impression that he knew exactly what needed to be done. He was an able administrator. Withal, he surrounded himself with cronies, many of them with him since New Orleans days, and, as they were his beneficiaries, they accorded him a loyalty most remarkable in the face of his many blunders.[28]

Butler's army consisted of the Tenth and Eighteenth Corps hitherto commanded by Generals Quincy A. Gillmore and W.F. ("Baldy") Smith. Butler had quarreled with both and they with one another, until now both corps had new commanders. The Tenth Corps fell to Major General David Bell Birney, son of the famous abolitionist. Ord's Eighteenth Corps was an impressive command with more than 11,000 men present for duty. These were veterans tested in the fire of the bloody fight at Cold Harbor and of the June assaults upon Petersburg.

Ord's corps was on the extreme right of the line before Petersburg, with the corps right resting at the Appomattox River. The Tenth Corps was to the north, with its line stretching between the Appomattox and the James River at Bermuda Hundred. To Ord's left was Meade's Army of the Potomac, composed of Ambrose E. Burnside's Ninth Corps, Gouverneur K. Warren's Fifth Corps, Winfield Scott Hancock's Second Corps, and Philip H. Sheridan's Cavalry Corps. The way to Richmond, twenty-three miles to the north, lay through Petersburg, the hub of a railroad network which supplied the Confederate capital.

★★★★★

Union and Confederate entrenchments faced one another for miles in front of Petersburg, but they came closest together on Burnside's front where, at one point, they were less than 400 feet apart. At this point, the line was held by the Forty-eighth Pennsylvania Infantry Regiment which had a goodly contingent of coal miners among its number and was commanded by Lieutenant Colonel Henry Pleasants, a mining engineer. From a chance remark of an enlisted man, Colonel

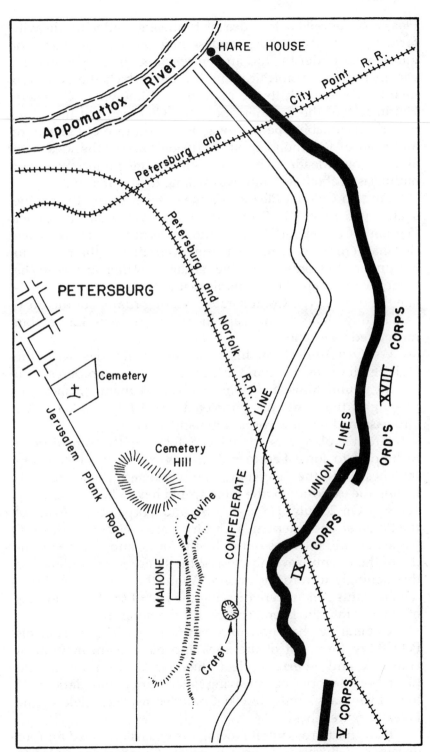

The Battle of the Crater, 30 July 1864

Pleasants conceived the idea of tunneling under the heavily fortified Confederate line, and setting off a huge charge of gunpowder under the fort and entrenchments, thus blowing a gap in the enemy fortifications through which the Northern infantry could push to the high ground known as Cemetery Hill in rear of the Southern position. Command of this ridge would presumably open the way to the capture of Petersburg and then of Richmond itself. Burnside took to the idea with alacrity, but Meade, while not vetoing the project, was not enthusiastic about it. Grant was willing to give it a try.

And so Colonel Pleasants's men began to dig their mine shaft on 25 June. By 17 July, the miners were directly under Pegram's Confederate battery and were nearly 511 feet from the shaft entrance. Lateral galleries were dug to the right and left under the Confederate line, adding another 75 feet to the length of the shaft. An ingenious method was devised to ventilate the tunnel. The Confederates, hearing rumors of the excavation, dug shafts to intercept the Northern mine tunnel, but misjudged its location.

As Ord undertook his new responsibilities with the Eighteenth Corps, he found these preparations in progress and quickly found himself deeply involved in them. In fact, the digging of the shaft was completed on 23 July, the day after Ord assumed his new corps command.

Grant's plan was to make a feint in the direction of Richmond to force Lee to pull troops out of the Petersburg trenches. With the Petersburg line weakened, the assault following the explosion of the mine would have a better chance of success. On 26 July, Hancock's Second Corps of the Army of the Potomac and Sheridan's Cavalry Corps set out northward, passed behind the lines of the Tenth Corps, and, on the morning of the twenty-seventh crossed the James River and moved threateningly toward Richmond. About this same time, Colonel Pleasants's men were carrying the last of the 8,000 pounds of powder into the lateral galleries of the mine shaft.

General Lee had no choice but to pull a large part of his Petersburg force out of the lines and place them in front of Hancock and Sheridan, lest they walk unhindered into Richmond. Troops began leaving Petersburg before dark on 27 July. Eventually, only 18,000 Confederates were left in the Petersburg trenches.

Plans for the assault following the explosion called for four divisions of Burnside's corps to go in. Grant ordered Ord to report to Meade for orders for the impending attack. Under Meade's orders, the Eighteenth Corps was pulled out of the line on the night of 29 July, being relieved by General Gershom Mott's division of the Second Corps. Two of Ord's divisions relieved Burnside's troops in the trenches so that the latter could be massed for the assault. The Second Division of the Tenth Corps under Brigadier General J. W. Turner and the Second Division of the Eighteenth Corps of Brigadier General Adelbert Ames were placed behind Burnside's divisions under Ord's direction as reserve supports to be sent forward as needed. A terrific artillery bombardment from 110 guns and 54 mortars was to commence with the explosion of the mine. The blast was to be set off on the morning of 30 July at 3:30 A.M.

At the appointed hour, Ord joined Burnside at the latter's field headquarters in the trenches behind one of the batteries about one-third to one-half mile to the rear of the point of assault. As Burnside was the senior major general of the two, Ord told him that he would obey any instructions that he might give. The entire attack was thus to be made under Burnside's direction.

At 3:30 A.M., all waited tensely for the blast. No explosion. At 4:30 A.M., they were still waiting. In the mine shaft, Pleasants's men found that the fuse had burned out at a splice. They relighted it. At about 4:45 A.M., the ground trembled and then rose with an ear-splitting blast. Men, guns and fortifications were thrown skyward, then tumbled grotesquely back to earth. At the same moment, the artillery opened up a mighty bombardment, and it seemed as though the noise of the mine explosion never really ended. Dust filled the air and was reinforced by smoke from the firing of the artillery shells. Noise, wild confusion and poor visibility made it difficult to tell what was really going on. The blast killed or injured nearly 300 Confederates and disabled two of the four guns of Pegram's battery. The crater torn in the earth by the explosion was approximately 170 feet long, 60 to 80 feet wide, and 30 feet deep.

After recovering from the shock of the explosion, Burnside's lead division, commanded by General James H. Ledlie, which had moved down a covered way to the front line of Union trenches, debouched from this narrow passage only to discover that the parapet in front of the Union lines had not been removed, though orders had been issued for its removal. Valuable time was lost getting out of the front line trench and over the breastwork for the charge toward the Southerners' line. The Union troops dribbled out a few at a time and occupied the crater, and, as more came, they filed into the Confederate trenches to the right and left of the great hole. For a time, there was practically no resistance from the stunned Confederates.

At 5:40 A.M., Meade telegraphed Burnside that he had learned that the Ninth Corps troops had stopped at the crater and adjacent works, and he directed Burnside to push them on toward the crest of Cemetery Hill and to call upon Ord to move his troops forward. Burnside relayed these instructions to Ord, who sent word to his division commanders to move out from the Union lines and support Burnside's troops on the right. By this time, the Confederates were beginning to come to life, opening up with rifle fire upon the crater and adjacent line.

Turner reported to Ord toward 7 A.M. that he was unable to move, as Burnside's troops in front of him jammed the covered way. Meanwhile, Meade had telegraphed directly to Ord to move his troops upon Cemetery Hill without reference to Burnside's troops. This order Ord sent to Turner and Ames. Turner responded that the move was not possible, as the only way out of the Union lines was the covered way opposite the crater which was still full of Burnside's troops. When the way should open, he would have to go in by head of column and develop to the right.[29]

Ord fretted and paced back and forth, irritated that things were going so badly, and finally left the headquarters battery, "saying that he was going into the crater."[30] At 7:20 A.M., perhaps about the time Ord set out, the youthful Brigadier General Adelbert Ames pencilled a dispatch to him: "Would it be convenient for you to come down to the covered way to our own advance works? I think nothing will be done unless you do. Your judgement would decide all doubts."[31]

When Ord reached the front line about 8 A.M., he went out in front of the Union trenches into the open area between the trenches and the crater. He saw white troops in groups of two or three moving across the open space about seventy-five yards to the crater, and, after these, black troops of Ferrero's division, the last of Burnside's corps, moving toward the same destination. This entire area was swept by enemy fire, and Confederate artillery was beginning to throw shells into the disorganized Federal ranks which now numbered many thousands. The Federals in the crater and nearby trenches were useless and virtually helpless. At about this hour, Confederate Major General William Mahone's division took position in a ravine between the crater and Cemetery Hill. A scattering of Federal troops moved beyond the line of the crater toward this ravine.

Ord directed Turner not to put his men in the crater or the trench to the right already filled with men, but to make a charge to the right where Confederates were massing. Over the parapet they went and moved toward the enemy's trench. Ord returned to Burnside's headquarters, where he soon received a dispatch from Turner reporting that Colonel Louis Bell's brigade of his division had been met by a heavy fire resulting in the stampede of a Negro regiment which had deployed to the right ahead of them. The black troops had done good fighting up to this point, but, when they ran into Mahone's withering fire, they broke and ran, carrying Bell's brigade with them back into the Union lines.

At 9 A.M., Ord rode back to where Meade was. At this same hour, Burnside suggested to Meade that the Fifth Corps be put into the fight. It is very likely that Ord was responsible for Meade's telegraphing to Burnside at 9:30 A.M. that he had heard the attack had been repulsed and that if, in Burnside's judgment, nothing more could be done, the troops should be withdrawn to the Union line. Ord returned to Burnside, and then the two of them went to see Meade. Grant was also present. Burnside wanted to persist in the attack, but Ord said very positively that Cemetery Hill could not be taken. Grant, with Meade's concurrence, ordered a withdrawal. Burnside, however, delayed the transmission of this order until after noon.

Meanwhile, the Confederate mortar shells were slamming into the crater resulting in an unbelievable slaughter of the closely packed Federals. Under the hot sun, without food or water, and without hope, they repulsed one Southern attack in midmorning, but a final charge by Mahone's men after 1 P.M., eventuating in hand-to-hand combat in the crater, overwhelmed the survivors. So ended the battle of the Crater.

The Union losses were about 4,400, of which 458 were killed, 1,982 wounded and 1,960 missing. Nearly 4,000 of the total were in Burnside's corps and nearly 400 in Ord's divisions. The Second and Fifth Corps suffered slight losses. The Confederate casualties were only 1,500.[32]

"Who is responsible?" queried a *New York Times* correspondent writing from Washington. The same newspaper noted a feeling of despondency in the capital city following the failure at the Crater and said there was much anxiety there to fix responsibility for the wholesale slaughter. Meade thought Burnside was in great measure responsible, as he asked Grant to relieve the Ninth Corps commander and preferred formal charges against him.[33] Burnside was sent North, his unfortunate military career ended, though he was never court-martialed.

Ord was one of the leading witnesses before a special court of inquiry with Major General Winfield Scott Hancock as president. Ord expressed his opinion that the first cause of failure was that the troops were not well disciplined. "They probably had not had time to become soldiers," he stated. This judgement would bear upon the disorder among the troops at the crater and the stampede of others back to the Union lines. A second cause, he said, was the limited access to the point of attack provided by the covered way. The judgment of the court was that, though Burnside believed his measures would lead to success, he disobeyed Meade's orders in forming his assault column and made inadequate preparations for the passage of troops. Three of Burnside's division commanders were censured, two for remaining in rear in a bombproof shelter and the third for failure to carry out orders with energy. One brigade commander was cited for failure to go forward.[34]

★★★★★

Ord's corps resumed its previous position on the right of the line before Petersburg. On 12 August, Grant telegraphed to Butler that the black and white troops of the Tenth Corps might be used to man the Petersburg fortifications and Ord's "Eighteenth Corps might be got foot loose to rest and fit up for other service, which I will make known to you."[35] Butler directed the Tenth and Eighteenth Corps to exchange positions. This removed Ord's force from the Petersburg front and placed it in a healthy location between the Appomattox and James Rivers, with headquarters at Hatcher's farm near Bermuda Hundred.[36]

Grant's plan for other service was some time in the making, but, wrote a *New York Times* correspondent, "portents of a coming *something* were unmistakable." At Butler's headquarters, on the afternoon and night of 28 September, Ord and other high officers and their staffs came and went briskly.

There was a certain tenseness in their manner, and an air of excitement pervaded the place in spite of efforts to be casual. But no question was asked by the journalist and nothing was volunteered about the mystery. "In all my experience I never knew a plan to be kept so profoundly secret," he wrote.[37]

On this day, the two corps commanders, Generals Ord and D.B. Birney, and General August V. Kautz, commander of the cavalry division of the Army of the James, met with Butler to receive orders for a movement north of the James against Richmond. Each of the generals had a copy of the orders, which covered sixteen pages of letter paper copied by a manifold letter writer. Butler read the orders, which were divided under several headings with elaborate explanations of each point. Opportunity was given for the generals to ask for clarification of any matter not clear.

The plan was to pull away from the front most of the Army of the James, the Tenth and Eighteenth Corps with the cavalry corps; move this force across the James River and then upon Richmond with a view to capturing the city; or, if capture could not be effected, to pull reinforcements from the Petersburg front to permit the Army of the Potomac to cut further the rail and other lines of communication of that city. It was estimated that in the long Confederate line stretching north of the James River to Richmond there were no more than 3,000 men to impede the Union movement. Butler offered promotions and six months' extra pay to the officers and men of the leading division, brigade or regiment which first entered Richmond. The entire operation was to be carried out in secrecy. Ord was to cross the river with two divisions and strike the right end of the enemy's line near the river. Birney with the Tenth Corps and one division of Ord's corps, a force totaling 10,000, would cross at Deep Bottom, move up to the New Market road, and take that road toward Richmond. Kautz's cavalry, about 1,700 men, would follow Birney up the New Market road and then cross over to the Darbytown road toward Richmond.[38]

Ord issued no written orders and did not give verbal orders to the troops until after dark on 28 September. About 9 P.M., he drew 4,000 men from the trenches from General George J. Stannard's and General Charles A. Heckman's divisions and marched them to the river opposite Aiken's Landing. Between 9 P.M. and midnight, a pontoon bridge was thrown over the James. At midnight, the troops began crossing the

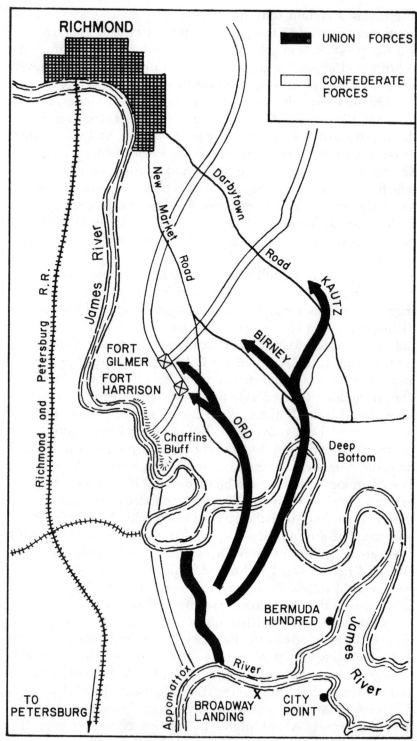

The Advance upon Richmond, 29 September 1864

river, and, by dawn, about 4:30 A.M., were in formation and moving against the Confederate skirmish line. For three miles or so, they moved steadily up hill and down and through the woods until about 7:30 A.M., when they reached the open ground in front of Fort Harrison, the strongest bastion on the Richmond front.[39]

Fort Harrison was a six-sided earthwork, slightly more than a quarter of a mile on a side. It stood on high ground and was supported by smaller works. Several heavy guns were mounted in the fort, and these began to boom out as Ord's force approached. Ord took a few minutes to make a hasty reconnaissance and then quickly formed for an assault. Stannard's division, with Burnham's brigade in the lead, covered by the Ninety-sixth New York Regiment commanded by twenty-year-old Colonel Edgar M. Cullen, moved forward over the open ground against the southern face of the fort. General Heckman was directed to move his division along the edge of a wooded area to the east of the fort and, when directly opposite, to attack from the east, but he went too far into the woods, got his brigades scattered, and was not in the right place at the right time to aid in the attack. The burden of the assault fell entirely upon Stannard's division.[40]

Across the open field, 2,000 men charged at quick time. The Confederate defenders poured out upon them a severe fire of musketry and artillery, and many began to fall. When they reached the base of the hill, the Union line wavered a bit. If they stopped, the attack would be ended. Ord ordered all of his staff officers forward at a gallop to keep the men moving, and the general himself was among the first to plunge into the melee. Up the hill they went, now at double-quick, and jumped into the ditch just under the enemy's parapet. Behind them on the hillside were scattered the sprawled figures of many dead and wounded, but there was no time for a backward look.

Ord and a number of officers and men followed the ditch around to the far side of the fort in order to cut off the route of escape of the defenders. They helped each other over the parapet and entered the salient. Ord ordered the guns of this bastion seized and turned them upon the adjacent parts of the fort and drove out the Confederates. He next tried to gather a group of his men with the idea of swinging around within the fort to drive out the defenders from the inside, but the men were so scattered he could not rally enough of them to undertake this operation. There was great confusion within the fort, and the smoke of battle obscured much of the action. Ord discovered that nearby all of the people with him were company officers. Gathering them together, he set out within the fort in a westerly direction toward the James River to size up the situation and to examine the possibility of seizing the enemy's pontoon bridge by which reinforcements might come to the relief of the Confederates.

Just as this movement was under way, Ord was wounded in the upper part of the right leg. By great good fortune, again the general escaped the real horror of a minié ball wound, for the bullet had damaged the fleshy part of the thigh inside without touching the bone. Ord staunched the wound with an improvised tourniquet and continued in command until a surgeon came up to him and entreated him to retire. Ord then sent for General Heckman, whose troops had still not engaged the enemy, and turned over the command to him. The capture of Fort Harrison was by this time complete with some 20 guns and 300 prisoners in hand.[41]

Heckman attempted to take Fort Gilmer, next important field work in the direction of Richmond, by a frontal assault, but was repulsed with heavy losses. Ord remained in Fort Harrison as this action was in progress, and, upon hearing of Heckman's repulse, began to become concerned about the situation. It was now about 10 A.M. The Confederates continued to control both banks of the river; they had a pontoon bridge by which they could cross reinforcements and possibly cut Ord's line of communication with his own pontoon bridge. As a harassment, Confederate gunboats on the river below were lobbing shells into Fort Harrison. Yet another very important consideration was that Ord's force had exhausted its ammunition. Butler had limited the ammunition to sixty rounds per man, and had ordered that no reserve ammunition wagon should cross the pontoon bridge without specific orders from him.

Ord sent staff officers to Deep Bottom, where both Grant and Butler were supposed to be, to request that ammunition, artillery and troops be forwarded and that a new commander be sent to take charge. Hearing nothing from either general, Ord was put in an ambulance which he insisted should also carry some of the wounded soldiers, and set out for Deep

Bottom to communicate with his superiors. He was unable to contact either man, but afterward learned that Grant had reached Fort Harrison just after his departure.[42]

Grant was highly pleased "at the handsome manner in which the fort had been carried."[43] He went into the fort on foot, where he found the ground blasted by shot and shell and so covered with killed and wounded that he had to feel his way with care. He climbed up to have a look over the north parapet at the city of Richmond, easily visible in the distance. This was his closest look so far at the Confederate capital.[44]

The assault upon Fort Harrison was a remarkable victory. It has been estimated that fewer than one out of every eight assaults in the war resulted in success. This attack, it is true, had not the magnitude of Cold Harbor or the June attempts upon Petersburg, but it was an intense action. Ord had the element of surprise on his side, and Fort Harrison was rather lightly defended. Yet, these defenders fought desperately behind their breastworks and had about twenty pieces of artillery to aid them. Of Stannard's division, 2,000 charged up the hill to Fort Harrison and some got inside the fort, but, when the noise died away and the smoke lifted, about 600 of them lay dead or wounded on the hill and within the earthworks, or were missing or prisoners. A thirty percent casualty rate is not inconsiderable.[45]

The judgment of an eminent British military historian, Major General J.F.C. Fuller, on the capture of Fort Harrison provides an unbiased expert opinion of the assault: "The capture of Fort Harrison deserves more than a passing mention, for it clearly shows that as late as the autumn of 1864, when the art of field fortification was of high order, well led troops could still carry out successful though costly frontal attacks. The lesson that the capture of this fort teaches us is that had Ord been in command of the Eighteenth Corps on June 15, Petersburg would most certainly have fallen."[46]

To the north of Fort Harrison, Birney had advanced on the New Market road as far as Spring Hill, where strong earthworks were carried by assault. Field fortifications and concentrated resistance by the Confederates halted his advance about six miles from Richmond. His casualties were less than 1,000. The line established by Ord and Birney in the action of 29 September so threatened Richmond that Grant determined to hold it. Accordingly, this position north of the James was held by Butler's two corps extending from Fort Brady on the James to Fort Harrison and thence northerly across the New Market road.[47]

Within Richmond, panic seized the populace as Fort Harrison fell and Union forces advanced upon the city. An eyewitness in the Confederate capital called the excitement the greatest he had known there. All of the local defense organizations were called out and squads were sent into the streets to press all able-bodied men into service. Even two members of the Cabinet were temporarily detained by zealous recruiters. For hours, the tocsin rang in the city at the instance of Governor William Smith, "frightening some of the women."[48]

General Lee was quite sensitive to the danger posed by the new Union position, particularly at Fort Harrison. The fort threatened the rear of neighboring works at Chaffin's Bluff and thus made his Richmond defenses vulnerable. On 30 September, Lee massed two divisions and a brigade supported by artillery and made vigorous assaults upon Fort Harrison in an effort to retake it. The Union forces were there in strength to receive these attacks, which were repulsed with very heavy losses to the Confederates.[49]

The Union was making significant progress in several battle areas in the latter weeks of the year 1864. Even as Ord was attacking Fort Harrison, Meade was extending his line below Petersburg. Sheridan with his cavalry and the Sixth Corps was soon to engage in operations which would result in the sound defeat of Jubal Early and the devastation of the beautiful Shenandoah Valley. Sherman had captured Atlanta and was about to begin his famous march to the sea. Thomas and Schofield were seeing to the defenses of middle Tennessee and at Franklin and Nashville would decisively crush General John B. Hood as he attempted a final desperate offensive in the West.

★★★★★

Ord took leave of his staff at Eighteenth Corps headquarters at the moment Lee's veterans were throwing themselves upon Fort Harrison in their vain effort to recapture that stronghold. The general was accompanied northward by his personal aide, Major S.S. Seward. At Baltimore, a *New York Times* correspondent found Ord at Barnum's Hotel, and the general told him he hoped "to be up and at it again in a few weeks."[50] Ord's destination was Bellaire, Ohio, were Molly Ord and the children were living. He was anxious to be with his family again and especially to greet his newest daughter, Mary Mercer, who was less than a week old.[51]

Ord spent two months with his family while convalescing. He returned to duty with his corps in the lines before Richmond on 1 December. His return was "received with great satisfaction by the army," according to a *New York Herald* correspondent writing from Butler's headquarters.[52]

Apparently, Butler had been awaiting this moment to effect a reorganization of the Army of the James. By orders of 3 December, the Eighteenth and Tenth Corps ceased to exist, and, in their places, were created the Twenty-fourth Corps to be composed of all of the white troops of the old organizations with Ord as commander and the Twenty-fifth Corps made up entirely of the Negro troops with Major General Godfrey Weitzel as commander.[53] This segregation policy was apparently designed by Butler to give the black troops a chance for glory as a unit.

In announcing his corps staff, Ord designated as chief of staff a thirty-year-old Indianan, Brigadier General Robert S. Foster. One of his assistant adjutant generals was Major Theodore Read, a very capable soldier from Illinois. The youthful Lieutenant Thomas G. Welles, acting aide-de-camp, was the son of the secretary of the navy. His presence on the staff along with young Major S.S. Seward, nephew of the secretary of state, gave Ord two powerful friends at court.[54] The general busied himself with the organization of his new command in preparation for the military demands of the new year that lay ahead.

CHAPTER

10

★★★★★

Army of the James

EDWARD Ord, while holding the temporary rank of major
general of volunteers, wanted very much to be made a
brigadier general in the regular army. Others were achieving
this grade, but, in spite of his outstanding service, no promotion was forthcoming for him.[1] The general had gained a number of military laurels, the most noteworthy being, of course,
the capture of Fort Harrison. Placidus wrote that the "grand
attraction of all visitors" to the front was Fort Harrison, and
that all marvelled that Ord was able to capture that powerful
fortification. Yet, Placidus continued, "he is not promoted in
the Regular army for that work yet—being only a Lt. Col. of
Artillery in the regular service in rank. His time will come,
however."[2]

Ord attempted to hasten the time. He had acquired many
influential friends in Washington and throughout the army. In
the very early days of 1865, he betook himself to the nation's
capital during a brief leave of absence and there marshaled the
support of some of these political friends. Eleven senators and
representatives from the states of Pacific slope informed the
secretary of war of their desire to have Ord appointed to the
first vacancy in the rank of brigadier general. Supreme Court
Justice Stephen J. Field, a Californian, joined in the request.
Ord asked Senator James W. Nesmith of Oregon, whom he had
known when Nesmith was colonel of Oregon volunteers in the

Indian war of 1855, to take charge of the petition. The general wrote to Nesmith that Senators J.M. Howard and Zachariah Chandler of Michigan, John A.J. Creswell and Reverdy Johnson of Maryland and Edgar Cowan of Pennsylvania had all promised to see the president or the secretary of war on his behalf and Secretary of the Navy Gideon Welles and Judge Loving of the Court of Claims would do what they could on notice.[3] There was no immediate result from this effort.

★★★★★

Ord returned from his political foray on 8 January 1865 just in time to hear the news that Benjamin F. Butler had been removed from the command of the Army of the James and of the Department of Virginia and North Carolina and that he, Ord, had been appointed to succeed Butler temporarily. How unexpected by Ord the news may have been is a matter of conjecture.

Grant had taken the initiative on 4 January to terminate Butler's military career. The lieutenant general pointed out to Edwin M. Stanton that, in his own absence, Butler succeeded to the command of both armies, and there was a lack of confidence in his ability to direct so large a force. "His administration of the affairs of his Department is also objectionable," Grant stated.[4] Learning on 6 January that the secretary of war was not in Washington, Grant promptly telegraphed to President Lincoln asking immediate action on the matter. Lincoln relieved Butler.[5]

The order removing Butler was transmitted to the headquarters of the Army of the James on the morning of 8 January. The announcement startled the officers and men of the command generally and created special commotion among the staff. By midafternoon, Butler had vacated his headquarters. Ord accompanied his predecessor to City Point for a brief conference with Grant, returning to headquarters that night.[6]

This was indeed a moment of triumph for Ord in his steady climb to prominence. He now commanded an important army which, with auxiliaries, numbered approximately 50,000 officers and men present for duty. He had under his sway a military department which may safely be termed the most important area of operations in the war. Moreover, he stood third in rank in the military hierarchy on the Richmond-Petersburg front, for only Grant and Meade ranked him. As

Ord's steamer conveyed him up the James toward Aiken's Landing after his conference with Grant, one cannot help but wonder whether his thoughts may have gone back to those days many campaigns ago in the winter of 1861 when McCall's three brigadiers had their troops ranged along the Potomac. Ord, George G. Meade and John F. Reynolds! Reynolds, it was reported, had been offered command of the Army of the Potomac, but had refused it. Meade had eventually succeeded to that command and had directed the army successfully at Gettysburg. Reynolds, second-in-command to Meade, had fallen on the first day of the Gettysburg holocaust. Meade's Gettysburg laurels were sufficient to continue him in command of the army. Now Ord, too, had reached a great height.

Butler's downfall, in the view of many, was a result of the failure of his Fort Fisher expedition. In December, Butler and Godfrey Weitzel, in cooperation with naval forces, attempted to capture Fort Fisher at the mouth of the Cape Fear River. The fort guarded the approach to Wilmington, North Carolina, the last open port of the Confederacy on the Atlantic Ocean. The expedition was a miserable failure—another inglorious moment for the much mishandled Army of the James. The fiasco was highlighted when a second Fort Fisher expedition under General Alfred H. Terry captured the fort on 15 January 1865. On 22 January, the combined forces of Terry and Major General John M. Schofield captured Wilmington. In addition, the *New York Herald* spoke of great dissatisfaction with Butler's high-handed arrests, imprisonments and punishments in connection with the administration of civil affairs in the department. The same journal noted that the indiscretions of several of Butler's selfish and irresponsible subordinates contributed much to his removal.[7]

On 4 February, Grant requested that Ord be permanently assigned to the Department of Virginia. North Carolina had been previously detached to form a separate command under Schofield. Ord was permanently assigned on 6 February.[8]

★★★★★

Ord was forty-six years of age at the time of his elevation to army and departmental command. He probably looked older, as noted before. A "common soldier" left an interesting description of the general as he appeared on the return march to Burnsville following the Iuka affair. "All that day," wrote the young man, "I marched pretty close to the tail of the horse that Gen. Ord was riding, and with boyish curiosity, I scanned the old general closely . . . . He looked old to me, but really he was, at this time, only about forty-four years of age. He certainly was indifferent to his personal appearance, as his garb was even plainer, and more careless than Grant's. He wore an old battered felt hat, with a flapping brim, and his coat was one of the old-fashioned, long-tailed oil-cloth 'wrap rascals' then in vogue. It was all splattered with mud, with several big torn places in it. There was not a thing about him, that I could see, to indicate his rank."[9] Another wartime observer described Ord as "that spare man with iron gray hair and moustache," his eyes "bluish-gray and kindly."[10] Just after the war, Ord encountered Confederate Colonel Christopher Q. Tompkins, the same who had been captain of Company F on that long-ago voyage around the Horn. Wrote Tompkins of Ord after this eighteen-year interval: "He retains his individuality in all respects." And then he continued: "Time has whitened his raven locks and furrowed his smooth features."[11] Brady photographs of Ord made at this time are varied in their representations. One close-up study of his face shows a no-nonsense look of hardness and determination, and others are, in similar vein, sternly military. However, one view in particular of Ord and his staff shows the general in a relaxed, rather unmilitary, hands-in-pockets pose.

Ord's strong personal qualities and military capabilities had clearly demonstrated his fitness for high command. Few officers "did more constant hard service" than Ord, wrote General E.D. Keyes.[12] After the battle at the Hatchie, Grant had spoken of him as a "gallant officer" and "able commander," and, at the time of Early's Washington raid, had described him as "brave," "prompt" and "skillful in the management of troops." General John F.C. Fuller praised his aggressive leadership at Fort Harrison. Indeed, the terms fearless, aggressive and skillful well describe his behavior at Dranesville, Iuka, the Hatchie, Fort Harrison and in other fields.

Ord's personal courage was so remarkably demonstrated as to require special notice. Never lacking in self-confidence, he seemed to have acquired an extra measure of daring, as if inspired. Early in the war, he had written his brother-in-law, Samuel Holladay, that, if he should live, he expected to have an active hand in working out the salvation of the nation. "I don't know whether God has instilled any extra wisdom into my mind," he continued, "but this I feel, that he has stirred my heart, cleared my head, and given me courage to meet considerable danger in the cause."[13]

Just after his return to duty following his recovery from the Fort Harrison wound, Ord sat down to write Secretary of War Stanton a letter remonstrating against an order permitting officers to dispense with badges of rank in the field. This in spite of his unmarked appearance after Iuka! He thought this order would do much harm. The example of their officers he considered the greatest stimulus for the privates in battle. "The officer should be conspicuous, his badges discernable afar," Ord wrote.[14] Napoleon's generals and other officers were "gaily dressed" and were at the forefront whenever the men needed encouragement. When the French Emperor presented badges of honor, they were conspicuous, and it was understood that they were to be worn in battle. Ord noted that there were instances told in history of a general or king, conspicuously dressed, falling in battle, and a substitute dressed like the fallen leader being put forward to lead the men to victory. The general cited his own practice used at Fort Harrison of sending his mounted staff into the thick of a fight to keep the men in the ranks at their work. Sherman also used this technique. "If we could dress our field officers in scarlet capes, and make it worth their while to *lead* their regiments while so dressed and mounted," Ord continued, "we would have but few failures to follow in the men. There would be less colonels but more victories."[15] This old-fashioned, chivalric ideal of warfare was an ideal dying but not quite dead. Such a statement might be taken with a smile, but, coming from a man who wore a white coat as he sat astride his horse directing a hot fight on the banks of the Hatchie, it must be taken seriously.

Proficiency in the movement of troops, noted by Grant, was not the only tactical skill possessed by Ord. He was skilled in reconnaissance in force with infantry, he was fully aware of the importance of keeping flanks covered, he knew the value of cavalry for reconnaissance, he was expert in the firing of artillery, he was proficient in the emplacement of artillery with due regard for the safety of the gunners and the avoidance of an enfilade, and he was skilled in siege operations. It was a maxim with Ord always to have sufficient force to accomplish the task at hand. He appreciated the use of psychological warfare and was aware of the bearing of the political situation upon military policy.

Ord was one of the best, and possibly the best, assault leaders of the Union army and one of the most skillful in the handling of troops in a variety of situations. Perhaps he worked best under Grant's overall direction. Nevertheless, he exercised independent command on specific occasions and did so admirably, taking the initiative where required.

Ord's personality was complex, but major features emerge in clear outline. As one of his brothers remarked, he had no ordinary mind. By this he probably meant that Ord's mind was quick and active, and that he had certain capacities for learning that were extraordinary. But there was also the "eccentricity" so often remarked upon. In what did it consist, besides those peculiarities of dress and appearance? Mainly, it consisted of unusual ideas, original ideas. His imagination was quite active. For instance, throughout his life, he toyed with inventions; among these were a signaling device and a quick-release buckle. But more important were his ideas in the realm of human relations and even in affairs of state touching governmental policy at the highest level. He could propose that field officers wear scarlet capes into battle. He could—and did—propose (as will appear) that the killing in this war should stop and he staked his considerable position upon this proposal. These are only examples of his unconventional thinking. There were others of consequence. They were not all practical.

What can be said of Ord the eccentric? First, he was a real person. As Tompkins said, "he retains his individuality in all respects." He had the courage to be himself, a sign of genius. He was not ordinary. He was the kind of person needed to keep the human race from dull conformity. His unusual ideas represent vision, a forecast of "the possible," a commentary on human potentiality. As his eccentricity was combined with honesty, he could advance constructive alternatives. Mankind has not produced enough "genuine persons" of the kind represented by Ord.

★★★★★

Ord's new headquarters were to the north of the James River three miles from Aiken's Landing. Here, he had a snug log house which boasted three large rooms with carpeted floors and comfortable beds for himself and Placidus. The Army of the James continued to occupy the line won in the operations of 29 and 30 September 1864, extending from the Darbytown road on the right to Dutch Gap on the left and, in addition, held the defenses of Bermuda Hundred between the James and the Appomattox.[16]

Ord took hold of his new duties convinced that much was wrong with both army and department. How could it be otherwise with the recent commander a politician and one about whom an air of venality seemed to cling? Butler was gone, but he had left behind him at headquarters and throughout the department and army a faithful swarm of Butlerites. With his usual slashing vigor, Ord tore into them. He would stir them up and change them about. Removals and transfers became the order of the day in both army and department.

Chosen to be Ord's successor in command of the Twenty-fourth Corps was Major General John Gibbon, an able soldier and, like Ord, an artillerist. The appointment "enlarged my sphere of duty under a commander (Ord) for whom I had great respect and regard," Gibbon wrote.[17] As he ranked Major General Weitzel, Gibbon's move to the corps made him second-in-command in the army and department.

Godfrey Weitzel, commander of the Negro Twenty-fifth Corps, had been Butler's protégé. He had been a first lieutenant in 1860 at the age of twenty-five; at twenty-seven, a brigadier general and now, at twenty-nine, major general of volunteers. His rise had begun at New Orleans where he served as chief engineer of Butler's expedition of 1862 and as assistant military commandant of New Orleans after the occupation of that city. Weitzel was devoted to Butler and despised Ord. He feared for his own future. "To serve under *Ord* is bad enough," he wrote to Butler.[18]

The cavalry division of the Army of the James was commanded by Major General August V. Kautz, no stranger to Ord, as the two had been together on various occasions during the Indian wars in Washington and Oregon territories in the 1850s. Kautz rose steadily in rank during the war, being especially favored by Butler. He was strongly attached to Butler, did not get along with Ord, and thought the latter treated him unjustly. In commenting on Ord's permanent assignment to the army and department, Kautz wrote: "This was not very satisfactory to the loyal friends of Genl. Butler. The service of the staff at headquarters was much more harassing under Ord than under the former commander. Ord was too eccentric and erratic and the mental strength of Butler was something with which Ord could not hope to compete, and there was more or less discontent at this time at headquarters."[19]

As chief of staff, Ord inherited able Brigadier General John W. Turner, a West Pointer of Weitzel's class of 1855. He had been Butler's chief commissary at New Orleans in 1862, and later was made chief of staff of the Army of the James. "I am very much discouraged since you left," he wrote to Butler, "and have but little heart for anything." Later, he wrote of the "great and radical changes" in the department.[20]

Brigadier General Charles K. Graham was a one-time navy man. He had served in several campaigns. Butler assigned him to the command of the naval brigade and a flotilla of army gunboats. Graham wrote to Butler asking him to use his influence to have him transferred to Sherman's army. "For many reasons I desire to leave the Department, feeling convinced that a very narrow course is going to be adopted towards all your friends," he said.[21]

Others of lesser note gave their former commander various reports, all adding up to great gloom among the Butlerites. Captain Fred Martin, commissary of musters of the department, wrote: "I do not expect you will hear much more from the Army of the James."[22] From Major William P. Webster, serving as provost judge in Norfolk under Butler's appointment: "The Army of the James is extinct."[23]

The civil affairs of the Department of Virginia required that Ord make many trips by steamer down the James from Aiken's Landing to Fort Monroe, Norfolk, and other points, with routine stops at Grant's City Point headquarters. This "civil front" was a substantial part of Ord's command, and there were several important areas of administration which absorbed a good deal of his attention during the course of the winter. They included the relationship of the military to the civil government in Virginia, the administration of Negro affairs, and investigation of a large illicit trade out of Norfolk into the Confederate lines which supplied many of the necessities of General Robert E. Lee's army. Each of these will be dealt with in turn. It should be noted that many aspects of the overhauling of the department originated in Grant's headquarters, with Ord responsible for the actual changes made.

When Butler became commander of the Department of Virginia and North Carolina in November 1863, he suppressed civil government in those portions of eastern Virginia under his control. He established a provost court in Norfolk to sit in lieu of civil courts. As provost judge, he appointed Major William P. Webster, who happened also to be his brother-in-law. Fees and fines derived from the court proceedings went into the Civil Fund. However, these revenues were only a small part of the fund, for the general had other sources. He levied a 1 percent tax on items imported into the department. He taxed vessels and oyster men, and required merchants to purchase licenses at army headquarters. In the issuance of permits for trade, Butler first called in all outstanding licenses, then issued new ones to a favored few who reaped large profits from their preferential position. In particular, the liquor traffic was the privilege of certain Massachusetts companies who were in Butler's good graces. Those who complained about Butler's taxes had their property confiscated, and some were banished from the department. Others were jailed for alleged disloyalty. Such highhandedness delighted the Radicals, but it was a repetition of the excesses of New Orleans.

Butler realized the value of controlling public information. Early in 1864, he established a newspaper in Norfolk called the *New Regime*. It styled itself the official journal of the department, but was, in effect, a personal organ. The printing establishment was confiscated by Butler with questionable justice. The same duo which had produced the *New Orleans Delta* for Butler in 1862 had charge of the *New Regime*. John Clark, one-time editor of the *Boston Courier*, was editor, and Lieutenant Colonel E.M. Brown, publisher. The office of the paper was manned with soldier labor, and yet the journal printed much advertising along with Butler's official orders. While Butler harassed the citizens, the *New Regime* extolled his virtues.[24]

The civil authority ousted by Butler in eastern Virginia was a part of the "restored" government of Virginia which had its seat in Alexandria. Its leader was Francis H. Pierpont (sometimes Pierpoint). The Pierpont government was important, for upon this foundation Lincoln and Johnson would reconstruct Virginia. Now that Butler no longer commanded, the Alexandria government quickly moved to send a delegation to confer with General Ord about the sustaining of civil government in the department. To strengthen his cause, Governor Pierpont presented to President Lincoln a petition by sixty-three citizens of Norfolk complaining that their civil government had been suppressed by the military. Lincoln's endorsement, dated 28 January 1865, read: "Submitted to Major General Ord, asking in connection, a respectfull hearing for Gov. Pierpoint."[25] The governor proceeded to Grant's headquarters and then to Ord's on 11 February. The results of his consultations with the generals were soon apparent.

On the evening of 16 February, Governor Pierpont addressed a mass meeting of the citizens of Norfolk and Portsmouth in Mechanics Hall in Norfolk.[26] To a "large and enthusiastic" throng, the governor announced the restoration of civil government. The civil courts would open and municipal officials would resume their functions in the matter of sanitary regulations, repairing of streets, etc. As there would continue to be large numbers of soldiers in both Norfolk and Portsmouth, it was agreed that the military should continue to have charge of the police. Special attention was given by the governor to the condition of the Negroes in the new order of affairs. "I concurred with the military authorities in their decision to take charge of Sambo," Pierpont said, "and thus he is disposed of for the present to the satisfaction of all parties, including, as I hope, Sambo himself."

The governor referred to Ord and his officers as "earnest, *fighting* men" who "desire to have nothing to do with the civil fund." Pierpont struck a backhanded blow at Butler and his ilk by denouncing those who would take advantage of the revolutionary times to appropriate to themselves the property of others. He enjoined all to support the military in their work, but especially with regard to the suppression of the large illicit trade through Norfolk by which General Lee was able to maintain his army in Petersburg and Richmond. General Ord had determined that this flow of goods should be cut off and had forbidden any more permits to trade beyond the picket line.

At this point in his speech, the governor was interrupted by Major R.S. Davis, a Bostonian who had been with Butler in New Orleans and had served until recently on the general's staff in Virginia. Davis inquired if Pierpont was charging General Butler or Butler's commander until recently in the Norfolk area, General George F. Shepley, with complicity in the trade. The governor cited the military commission then sitting in Norfolk under Ord's orders inquiring into the matter as well as a committee of Congress which had recently sat with the commission. He then flatly charged that the supplies for Lee's army "were furnished with the connivance of some of the late military authorities here." Lieutenant Colonel O.L. Mann, provost marshal of Norfolk under Ord's appointment, intervened to enable the governor to continue, but the latter stated that his speech was ended. Colonel Mann then asked Major Davis if he wished to speak, but he declined to do so.

It was about the time of this Norfolk meeting that Ord drafted a letter to President Lincoln reporting a personal inspection which he had made of the Eastern Shore of Virginia. "I found them all loyal," he said of the people there, "where they are taxed and ruled as if disloyal, where the civil government under my orders will soon be in unobstructed operation with the tax necessary for its maintenance. . . ." He went on to describe the oppressive military rule imposed by Butler. Turning to the situation of the Negroes, he reported that both whites and blacks wanted the military to continue to care for them. "Each of the races for the present desires to be protected from the other, not having had time to discover that their interests are the same," he told the president.[27]

A few days after Butler was relieved, Ord repaired to Fort Monroe for an interview with him regarding the fiscal affairs of the department. In a meeting which Butler described as "very pleasant," the books of the department were surveyed and explained in detail. Butler turned over to Ord the astounding sum of $258,000 and accounted for an additional quarter of a million dollars already spent. Butler said Ord reported to Grant that he was satisfied with his accounting.[28]

There were actually three funds under Ord's control as turned over by Butler. A fund of about $68,000 had been raised by Butler by retaining one-third of the state bounty paid to Negro soldiers. This was intended to support the families of soldiers. Butler had invested this money as the capital for a savings bank for the Negroes in Norfolk. Ord made no expenditures from this fund and turned it over to the Freedmen's Bureau. A Norfolk City Fund had been established by a tax imposed by Butler for the support of white schools in that city. Finally, there was the much-mentioned Civil Fund which Ord placed in the custody of the trusted Major S.S. Seward.

The Civil Fund was in the amount of $129,659.23, which had been accumulated by the collection of court fees, taxes,

licenses to trade and rents of buildings on government property. Of the total, more than $31,000 consisted of Confederate
notes, Southern state railroad bonds and Southern state bank
notes. During the nearly six months in which Ord commanded
the department, an additional $66,000 was collected. Dis-
bursements during the same period came to more than $94,000.
Ord turned over to his successor a little over $101,000.[29]

The decline of the Civil Fund may be readily accounted for.
On 2 February, in an order to Lieutenant Colonel John
Coughlin, provost marshal general of the department, Ord
stated his desire to gradually remit the various license fees,
taxes and rents, explaining that his object was to reduce the
prices at which goods were sold to soldiers. He intended, he
said, to set up a board of officers to fix the tariff on all items sold
by traders. The general directed Coughlin to ascertain fully the
sources of revenue which made up the fund. In reference to the
obnoxious monopolies and special privileges granted to traders
by the Butler regime, Ord directed that these should cease at
once, that Coughlin should issue a public circular to his provost
marshals to positively prohibit them, and that any found to
exist should be reported.[30]

One of the main expenditures from the Civil Fund was for
salaries and rations of missionary teachers sent from the North
to instruct the Negroes. In addition, there were numerous
disbursements for debts incurred under Butler. Butler's perver-
sity extended to waging war by confiscation, and Ord ordered
the return of $10,000 in gold seized by Butler from Jewish
refugees from the South upon their giving proof of loyalty.
Ord found on hand a large quantity of silverware, watches and
jewelry which were also returned insofar as possible to those
who claimed them.[31]

With regard to the arbitrary arrests allegedly made under
Butler's orders, Grant ordered Ord to undertake an investigation of all prisons and of the circumstances of confinement of all
prisoners in the department and to discharge all persons not
properly confined. Over the next several weeks a number of
soldiers being punished for minor offenses were released by
order of Ord, and directions were given for the correction of
improper prison conditions. Still another examination of the
case of each prisoner was ordered in March with provision that
civilian prisoners with certain exceptions be released on parole
or bond.[32] From this limited evidence it is not possible to judge

Butler's actions in the matter, but in *Butler's Book* the general convicted himself by his own hand. He said of his arrests that they "were all arbitrary" and admitted that a number of persons were arrested by him and confined without charges "for the good of the service."[33]

★★★★★

In the latter part of 1863, Butler established an organization to see after the Negroes in his department. He appointed a superintendent of Negro affairs with assistant superintendents who were charged with the task of finding employment for the blacks, protecting them from fraud, supervising their relations with their employers, seeing to it that they had the necessities of life and medical care, and assisting the freedmen's aid societies in their charitable endeavors.[34]

Ord was interested in determining whether the Negro affairs were being administered honestly and economically. Lieutenant Colonel Horace Porter, a young West Pointer who was aide-de-camp to Grant, was made Ord's special investigator. Ord directed Porter's attention to the farms and schools established for blacks, the issuance of rations which he wanted kept at a minimum, the disposition of large quantities of clothing coming from the North for the Negroes, and the operation of the savings bank of Norfolk which Butler had established for Negroes.[35]

As Porter launched his inquiry, one of the matters which occupied his attention was the issuance of rations to the missionary teachers in the black schools. These had been supplied under Butler's orders, but Ord was informed that the Washington authorities would no longer allow the issue, and he had it stopped. Porter recommended that the rations be issued and paid for out of the Civil Fund. He pointed out to Ord that the passage of the Freedmen's Bureau bill by the Congress was imminent, and this would relieve the department of the question. "Until this occurs, I think it would be a wise policy to prevent as far as possible the impression that Butler is evidently endeavoring to create in the North. . . ," Porter wrote to Ord, "that since he has turned his back on the negro in this Dept. all support has been withdrawn from him."[36]

One of the persons apparently influenced by Butler's views was Massachusetts Senator Henry Wilson, who was vitally interested in the welfare of the Negroes. General Ord got wind of the senator's displeasure and wrote to him that he had heard that Wilson believed that he, Ord, was "undoing all that General Butler did for the colored people" in the department and that he had "refused to issue rations to the teachers of colored children." The general proceeded to explain in detail that the rations were being issued and paid for with department funds. Ord went on to say that he was very much pleased with the work of the benevolent people of the North in educating Negro children and in providing for the relief of the poor of both races. "General Butler will inform you that I heartily endorse his proceedings as far as they had gone into operation in so humane a cause," he said.

Ord gave Senator Wilson a homely description of the plight of the Negro and revealed in it a good deal of his own attitude toward the freedmen: "I hope you will remember that the poor blacks in my Department are now like unto a simple hearted youth from the country, arrived in town with his patrimony. A stranger is the youth, and cannot tell a friend from a sharper, and you know that in cities there are some of the latter class who would insist upon their right to care for and protect such strangers."[37]

The issue of rations still troubled Ord. In the latter part of March, he again ordered a thorough investigation of the schools at Norfolk and Fort Monroe with particular attention to the number of missionary teachers fed at public expense and how many of them might be dispensed with. "Some certainly must," he said. He also asked that a plan be devised to levy a tax to pay the government for their rations.[38]

Probably as a result of Colonel Porter's work, three assistant superintendents of Negro affairs were replaced, and one was arrested, apparently for alleged malfeasance. The greatest shake-up occurred in the District of the Peninsula where Lieutenant Colonel John Coughlin, provost marshal general of the department, was placed in charge of the freedmen. He was directed to take a census of the blacks and to form a police force of able-bodied men to be paid as soldiers. All other able-bodied men were to find employment within a week or would be mustered into the army. Wives and families of Negro soldiers were to be protected and supported, but in such families where there were no dependents, the wives must find employment or be provided with employment. These orders went on to encourage the cultivation of the land by Negroes, whether on their own account or under the direction of the department's Bureau of Negro Affairs.[39]

To protect further the agricultural efforts of the Negroes, Ord ordered that lands used by the Bureau of Negro Affairs not be sold for taxes. He directed that 500 condemned cavalry horses, wagons and other implements be provided for the farms. Upon the suggestion of General George H. Gordon that the entire sale of land for taxes scheduled for 15 March in Norfolk be postponed so that the lands might be used by freedmen and for other purposes, Ord made direct application to the secretary of war for a delay. By direction of the president, the sale was deferred for thirty days, during which period the new Freedmen's Bureau could select such land as it might require.[40]

Porter mentioned early in his investigation that gentlemen from the missionary and freedmen's aid societies were in Norfolk investigating. "They find nothing wrong," he noted. He said of his own inquiry that he had found little dishonesty.[41]

About a week after Ord succeeded Butler, the War Department telegraphed to Grant that reports had reached Washington of a large-scale trade through Norfolk by which Lee's army was being supplied. One estimate placed the value of the items sent into the Confederate lines at $100,000 per day. Similar traffic was reported from the Western area of operations. Butler, just arrived in Washington, blamed the Treasury Department, since, under the law, that department could appoint agents to purchase products of the Confederate states, allowing one-fourth of the value to go back in supplies. There were indications of flagrant abuses of the law. Assistant Secretary of War Charles A. Dana asked Grant to investigate the Norfolk situation and report what action was needed on military grounds.[42]

Grant asked Ord to suggest what might be done to get at the facts. The latter replied in a private letter that he proposed setting up a military commission with power to summon witnesses and call for papers, and, after thorough investigation, to try and sentence persons found guilty of illegal actions. He proposed for chairman of the commission General George H. Gordon of Massachusetts whom he described as "shrewd and fond of such hunting." A West Pointer who had resigned from the army in the 1850s, Gordon had attended Harvard Law

School and entered upon a legal career. His Civil War service had been distinguished. As members of the commission, Ord suggested Colonel J.H. Potter of the Twelfth New Hampshire and Major Theodore Read, departmental assistant adjutant general. Grant thought well of Ord's commission, and the general proceeded with the appointments. The commission carried on its probe in Norfolk from 21 January to 20 March, at which time it reported.[43]

"If we can fasten the matter upon either Treasury or Benjamin F.'s agents, clap them in the guard house, . . . the politicians will find they have started the wrong rabbit with a bushy tail. . . ," Ord wrote to Grant.[44] Ord's mentioning Butler was certainly germane to the matter, for Butler had had much to say about trade in the department. Indeed Butler's New Orleans administration had had an unsavory odor of corruption through precisely the same kind of speculative commerce now alleged to be thriving in Norfolk. It is clear that Butler's deceased brother had made a fortune in Louisiana through trade with the Confederates. Was Butler himself involved? Always, the wily Ben was just beyond reach, and nothing could be pinned on him.[45]

Even as the machinery for investigation was established, measures were taken to close the gates upon the commerce. Eventually, Grant suspended all trade operations based on permits of any kind in Virginia except the Eastern Shore Peninsula. A thorough overhauling of the military police force was undertaken, for upon this body depended the internal security of the department and the proper movement of goods and people. Lieutenant Colonel John Coughlin was named by Ord as provost marshal general of the department, and seven provost marshals for the principal cities and districts of Virginia were replaced within a week's time, and their books and papers closely examined.[46]

Brother-in-law Webster kept Butler informed of developments in the new state of affairs. There were two cordons of pickets around Norfolk and a guard on the boats, he reported. A new regiment of white troops was assigned to provost duty, while additional Negro regiments were on picket duty. There was a soldier on duty for every hundred feet. Those persons riding out into the country had their passes closely scrutinized and vehicles examined. "One would think that Lee's army was in the immediate vicinity. . . ,"[47] Webster wrote. The restrictions and control measures imposed by Ord and Grant were apparently successful, for intelligence reports gathered from Confederate deserters indicated that the large export of cotton through the lines in exchange for provisions had virtually ceased.[48]

Meanwhile, the Gordon commission, described by Webster as "the dreaded tribunal," got under way with a vigorous investigation. Nearly a dozen cotton traders were lodged in jail, and suspicion came to rest upon General George F. Shepley, commanding the District of Eastern Virginia. Shepley, a Maine lawyer, had been with Butler in Louisiana and had been appointed by the latter to be commandant of New Orleans and later military governor of Louisiana. Webster reported to Butler that Shepley was saying that all permits for the establishment of stores and for trade were issued under express orders from Butler. "Many think he is ready to implicate you to save himself," Webster continued.[49]

Gordon believed that testimony was being withheld through fear and that an attempt had been made to intimidate witnesses. He recommended to Ord that the removal of Shepley and Provost Judge Webster would likely bring out truth now held back. Ord promptly relieved Shepley and ordered him to report to Weitzel for orders. Gordon was appointed district commander in his place. At the same time, Ord wrote Webster saying that the validity of the acts of the provost court had been called into question by the judge advocate general of the army and that it would probably be necessary to discontinue the court. Noting that Webster had already indicated a desire to resign, Ord suggested that the judge would not want to await the end of the tribunal. Webster resigned.[50]

After examining fifty witnesses and accumulating 1,096 pages of testimony, the Gordon commission prepared a report which was forwarded by Grant to the War Department on 20 March.[51] It showed that, by permission of Butler and Shepley, several stores were established in 1864 at Elizabeth City, South Mills, Coinjock, Ballyhack, Washington Ditch and Hamburg in Virginia and North Carolina to trade in the products of the Confederate states. In September 1864, through Assistant Adjutant General George H. Johnston, Butler had appointed a military commission to try Logan Hurst, Charles Whitlock, one

Richmond, and Ezra Baker, who, without proper authorization, were supplying the Confederates with provisions in exchange for cotton. They were found guilty, fined $1,000 each, and sentenced to prison. After he was relieved, Butler confirmed the fine, but remitted the imprisonment in each case. The trial was good instruction in how to conduct such business. Captain Johnston soon resigned his commission and, with Shepley's permission, established a store at Coinjock, North Carolina. Johnston then secured permits from Shepley totaling more than $300,000 which he sold to traders who carried the goods into the Confederate lines.

Another central figure in the trade was Fisher A. Hildreth, Butler's brother-in-law. He perceived good business talent among the four whom Butler had arrested and tried for illicit trading. Hildreth induced Whitlock to enter into a partnership with him and J. M. Renshaw. The latter had been Hildreth's clerk in New Orleans, where Hildreth had been in business when Butler commanded there. Eventually, Hildreth came to be the center of a network of partnerships and arrangements for trade which included Logan Hurst and Ezra Baker, defendants along with Whitlock before Butler's commission, and other traders named Sherman, Riddle, McKay and George W. Lane. In most of his deals, Hildreth invested little or no capital, but brought to the enterprises his influence with General Butler. Hildreth's partner Lane purchased more than 500 bales of cotton, said to have been worth more than $300,000.

Bankers in Norfolk disclosed that Hildreth had made many sealed deposits, that Renshaw deposited a total of more than $54,000, that Captain Johnston deposited nearly $33,000, that Whitlock deposited more than $92,000, besides special sealed deposits. Such pelf was not inconsiderable, but there was more. Once the cotton was procured and brought into Norfolk, it had to pass through the hands of DeWitt C. Farrington of Massachusetts, technically a Treasury agent, but actually Butler's personal agent. Farrington bought all the cotton he could on his own account, borrowing from the Civil Fund the necessary money for his initial purchase! He marketed other cotton in the North, charging a 5 percent commission for his services. He kept no records.

The Gordon commission pointed out that the large scale trade carried on in Virginia and North Carolina was known to Generals Butler and Shepley, and, in fact, was carried on with their permission. They must have known that great quantities of provisions were reaching Lee's army through this traffic. The Gordon commission recommended that Johnston, Hildreth and others be brought to trial, and that Butler and Shepley be dealt with as might seem best for the public good. Ord approved this report, and in forwarding it, recommended that those named be tried as soon as practicable.

On 30 April, after the fighting was over in Virginia, Ord inquired of the War Department what action was contemplated and was told by Stanton that the cases were before the judge advocate general for report. On 9 May, the judge advocate general reported that the press of business had made it impossible to examine the voluminous proceedings of the Gordon commission and suggested that Gordon dispose of the matter as he might see fit. It was Ord's belief that the men should be tried by the military or not at all. As it appeared that higher authority would not act, on 8 June, Ord ordered Gordon to release all persons held for trial for trading with the enemy.[52] As early as March, Butler had predicted that the matter would never come to trial. It remained for Webster to confirm the general's uncanny judgment and to write a valediction on 22 June: "Every one arrested has been released, and all charges dismissed and Generals Ord and Gordon gone."[53]

11

★★★★★

Ord and Longstreet: A Coup for Peace

E DWARD Ord was a keen reader of the Southern press, particularly of the Richmond papers but of others as well. On 16 December 1864, he wrote Secretary of State William Henry Seward enclosing copies of two Richmond papers, the *Sentinel* and the *Enquirer*, and calling the secretary's attention to certain editorials in them. The Richmond papers supported the proposition of arming the slaves, an action favored by President Jefferson Davis and by General Robert E. Lee. Indeed, Lee had proposed the immediate liberation of slave soldiers and the emancipation of the families of those who served faithfully to the end of the war. On the other hand, the papers revealed a strong opposition to this idea in South Carolina, for, if such a policy were carried out, it would very likely mark the end of slavery in the South. Ord pointed out to the secretary that bitter dissensions had arisen in the Confederacy and that the interests of Virginia were in conflict with those of the cotton states to the south. Virginia was being ruined by the war and now contemplated arming her slaves, or, as Ord explained it to Seward, to continue the war "she is willing to give up slavery for the remote prospect of obtaining what she calls her independence." The general proposed to increase the discord in the South by having the United States offer to withdraw her armies from Virginia on condition that she free her slaves. "This offer . . . might be accompanied by an acknowledgement of her right to arrange her own state affairs," Ord continued. The result would be that Virginia would return to the Union a free state and, along with her, North Carolina.[1]

On the following day, Ord wrote Seward another rather long letter on the subject of arming the slaves, stressing his conviction that the Confederate states now in desperate condition should not be allowed renewed strength for the struggle by arming their slaves and sending them against the North. He believed that the armed slaves when subjected to Union fire would have no alternative but to use their weapons in return. Richmond newspapers expressed confidence that the blacks would fight for the Confederacy. Adverting to his earlier suggestion about withdrawal of Union troops from Virginia, Ord noted that, as a matter of course, the withdrawal would be southward. Ord could see much value in the truce or suspension of hostilities which might result from the suggested offer to Virginia. It would bring about communication between the soldiers of both sides and produce a disposition on the part of the Rebels to give up the fight and go home. This phenomenon had been observed by Ord after the fall of Vicksburg. Ord quoted Ulysses S. Grant, who was not at the moment present at the front, as saying that such a truce " 'would in six weeks cause half the rebel army to desert.' "[2] What Seward thought of Ord's unusual ideas does not appear.

Here, undoubtedly, was one of Ord's eccentricities. His ideas were extravagant, and he himself referred to them as "crude." On the other hand, it should be noted that nobody could say when the bloody war would end or how much more killing and destruction lay ahead. Moreover, Ord was not by any means the only person thinking of peace and ways to achieve it short of fighting to the bitter end.

A few weeks later, on 25 January 1865, Grant telegraphed Ord, then at Fort Monroe, that he would leave the following day for an extended absence and that Ord should return to his headquarters in the field to take charge of both armies. General George Gordon Meade was absent, and General John G. Parke, who had the Army of the Potomac temporarily, was ordered to report to Ord.[3] To command this mighty force for a time even in a period of inactivity was a great responsibility.

On the afternoon of 29 January, a Confederate flag of truce approached the Ninth Corps front at Petersburg; there was communication with Ninth Corps headquarters out of which came a dispatch from General O.B. Wilcox, temporary corps commander, which began as follows: "Alexander H. Stephens, R.M.T. Hunter, and J.A. Campbell desire to cross my lines, in accordance with an understanding claimed to exist with Lieutenant-General Grant, on their way to Washington as peace commissioners."[4] Alexander H. Stephens of Georgia was vice-president of the Confederate States, R.M.T. Hunter of Virginia was a senator and former Confederate secretary of state, and John A. Campbell of Alabama, once a member of the United States Supreme Court, was Confederate assistant secretary of war.

The message went from Wilcox to Parke to Ord, who referred it to the Washington authorities. From Edwin M. Stanton came word to Ord that the War Department had no information about any understanding about peace commissioners. "You will therefore allow no one to come into your lines under such character or profession until you receive the President's instructions, to whom your telegram will be submitted for his directions."[5]

On the morning of 30 January, Lincoln instructed Ord to inform the three commissioners that he was dispatching a messenger to them. The messenger, Major T. T. Eckert, was directed by Lincoln to proceed to General Ord and, with his assistance, procure an interview with the three. He was to determine whether or not they were willing to come for an informal conference on the basis of a letter from Lincoln dated 8 January 1865 to Francis P. Blair, Sr., which required that they enter into discussion "with a view to securing peace to our common country." Blair had gone to Richmond early in January to attempt to arrange for peace, though his mission was unofficial. Ord was directed to provide protection and comfortable accommodations for the commissioners, but their presence was not to affect any of his military movements or plans.[6]

On 31 January, Grant was again at his headquarters and proceeded to have the three men brought through the lines. There was great cheering on both sides as they came through. They spent the night of 31 January at City Point. While there, they talked with Grant and apparently tried to persuade him that the quickest way to end the war was through a military convention, or armistice, between himself and Lee.[7] They also talked to Meade in a similar vein. Stephens proposed to the latter that the fighting be stopped and expressed his belief that the slavery question could then be settled. The commissioners pressed their views on this point. "They then said they thought it a pity this matter could not be left to the generals on each side, and taken out of the hands of politicians," Meade wrote.[8] Meade responded to the three realistically that any proposals to suspend hostilities, unless permanently, would be rejected, and that, while he believed the generals could settle the slavery question more speedily, he did not think it possible for it to be done in this way. While he prayed for some result from the peace effort, he did not think there was much likelihood of any.[9]

On 3 February, Stephens, Hunter and Campbell conferred with Lincoln and Seward aboard the *River Queen* at Hampton Roads. Stephens proposed to the president that there be a military convention, or armistice, pointing out to Lincoln that, as Commander-in-Chief, his power to make such an agreement was undoubted, and that, once hostilities were suspended, other matters could be taken up. Lincoln agreed that he had the power, but thought a mere armistice not an adequate basis on which to settle all questions. He was later asked, presumably in the course of conversation aboard the *River Queen*, to reconsider the matter. He did so, but determined it could not be done.[10]

Lincoln stood firm on three conditions: reunion, emancipation and no cessation of hostilities short of an end to the war and the disbanding of all forces hostile to the United States. Lincoln did express a personal willingness to consider compensated emancipation, but the Confederates were noncommittal. The conference ended without apparent result, though Stephens afterwards said he thought Lincoln might make a bid for an armistice through the military.[11]

Ord was not entirely clear of the matter, for, on 3 February, Grant requested him to send a spring wagon and ambulance to Aiken's Landing on the following morning to convey the commissioners back through the lines. At the landing, the three were quartered for a time aboard the United States flag-of-truce steamer *New York*. Here Ord called on them and remained aboard in conversation with them for more than half an hour, after which the three returned to the Confederate side. What was said was not recorded, but it would be reasonable to assume that the Confederates stated to Ord pretty much the same views they had expressed to Grant and Meade and may possibly have revealed something of their conversations with Lincoln and Seward.[12]

On 5 February, close on the heels of the Hampton Roads conference, Lincoln placed before his Cabinet a message which he proposed to send to Congress asking that the two houses should resolve that the president pay $400 million as compensation for the emancipation of slaves in those states of the South which ceased their resistance to the United States by 1 April. The president contemplated preparing a proclamation to be issued in connection with the resolutions in which he would offer pardon and restitution to those in rebellion. As none of the Cabinet members supported Lincoln's plan, the matter ended there—or so it seemed.[13]

★★★★★

The dull days of winter along the Richmond battle front challenged the ingenuity of bored young soldiers, both Reb and Yank. There was much fraternizing. Newspapers and tobacco were exchanged at some points along the line, and more venturesome combatants contended with one another in foot races.[14] These activities were harmless enough, to be sure, but they attracted the attention of military authority at a very high level.

At noon on 25 February, under a flag of truce, Ord, with part of his staff and in company with John Gibbon, proceeded up the New Market road past the Union line toward Richmond. At the Confederate line, the cavalcade was met by Lieutenant General James Longstreet and several attendants. This meeting resulted from a note sent by Ord to Longstreet, who commanded the Confederate First Army Corps on the Richmond front opposite the Army of the James. In the note, Ord stated that bartering between the troops along the picket line should be stopped and asked for an interview to arrange the matter. Longstreet quickly perceived that this was a pretext to provide an opportunity for the discussion of some other subject, and arrangements were made for a meeting.[15]

This was an occasion for the renewal of an old friendship, for Ord and Longstreet had been together at West Point and had encountered one another many times in the course of their service in the old army. After the two generals had discussed the matter of bartering, Ord asked to talk to Longstreet alone.

The two went aside, and Ord began to speak of things political and military. Regarding the recent Hampton Roads conference between Lincoln and the three Confederate peace commissioners, he noted that politicians in the North were afraid to deal with the matter of peace, and that the only way to broach the subject was through officers of the armies. Ord went on to say that on the Union side they thought that the struggle had lasted long enough, and that, as old friends, they should get together to talk. Ord suggested to Longstreet that the fighting should be suspended by agreement between Grant and Lee, that Generals Grant and Lee should meet for a talk, and that Mrs. Longstreet, a girlhood friend of Mrs. Grant, should go into the Union lines accompanied by Confederate officers and pay a social call. Then Mrs. Grant, escorted by Union officers, would return the call and visit Richmond. While more cordial feeling was developing between the two armies, negotiations would proceed until terms of settlement honorable to both sides could be found.[16]

Longstreet replied that he was not authorized to discuss the subject raised by Ord, but he would report to General Lee and other Confederate officials and would send word to Ord if it were found possible to follow up on the matter. On Sunday night, 26 February, General Lee came from his Petersburg headquarters to the president's mansion in Richmond at the request of the Confederate executive. Besides Davis and Lee, Secretary of War John C. Breckinridge and General Longstreet were present. President Davis assumed that Ord's overture for a military convention or compact between Grant and Lee suspending hostilities was in pursuance of Lincoln's discussion of the matter with the three Confederate commissioners at the Hampton Roads conference. Several hours were spent in discussing the Ord proposal, and it was finally decided to arrange another meeting with General Ord and to give a favorable response to his suggestion. "Secretary Breckinridge expressed especial approval of the part assigned for the ladies." A telegram was dispatched to Mrs. Longstreet summoning her from Lynchburg to Richmond.[17]

On the following day, Longstreet requested an interview with Ord to be held on 28 February at the same place where they had met before. Longstreet asked for the meeting "for the purpose of arranging more definitely the exchange of political prisoners." The Confederate said he "would be pleased to meet

Lieutenant-General Grant at the same time and place on the same subject,"[18] but Grant did not come. In this second meeting, Longstreet reiterated Ord's earlier proposition that the fighting must stop and a convention be made based upon a desire for peace that would be "equally honorable to both parties." To this, Ord readily agreed. "He [Ord] says that General Grant has the authority to meet you," Longstreet reported to Lee, "if you have authority to appoint a military convention, and proposes that you should indicate your desire to meet General Grant, if you feel authorized to do so."[19]

Longstreet had gone to the meeting with the intention of proposing to Ord that Grant should write to Lee and express a desire for an interview. He went on to explain to Lee that Ord had made his suggestion first to the effect that Lee should make known to Grant his desire for a meeting looking toward a military convention. Since Ord had initiated the entire business, Longstreet felt that he should accede to this suggestion. "If you think it worth your time to invite General Grant to an interview it might be upon some other as the ostensible grounds, and this matter might be brought up incidentally," Longstreet wrote to Lee. He further stated his presumption that Grant would first suggest a convention on the basis of reunion, "but if I have not misunderstood General Ord's conversation," he continued, "General Grant will agree to take the matter up without requiring any principle as a basis further than the general principle of desiring to make peace upon terms that are equally honorable to both sides."[20] Grant was prepared to receive Lee's letter, Ord said.

Ord went on further to say that Lincoln desired to put into operation a scheme to pay for the emancipated slaves and that this might be a part of the terms of the military convention "and relieve the matter of political bearing." This last was in the nature of a "remote probability" to be dealt with in the advanced stages of the discussion of the settlement.[21]

President Davis wrote Lee that the point as to whether he or Grant should issue the invitation to a meeting was "not worth discussing." He left it to Lee's judgment to determine whether a conference would be useful, and, at the same time, granted him full authority "to enter into such an arrangement as will cause at least a temporary suspension of hostilities."[22]

Longstreet endeavored to have Lee name a matter other than the military convention as the topic of the meeting to which he would invite Grant and then to bring up the subject of cessation of hostilities in the course of the discussion. Lee preferred to be straightforward in his invitation of 2 March, but he did dispatch a second letter to Grant under the same date in which he expressed the hope that, in the proposed meeting, they could settle certain details relating to the exchange of political prisoners, which Ord and Longstreet had discussed. Lee stated to Grant that he desired "to leave nothing untried which may put an end to the calamities of war," and proposed the interview to explore the practicability of a convention.[23]

Grant forwarded Lee's dispatch to Stanton on the night of 3 March. He explained that Ord had met Longstreet at the request of the latter to discuss the question of political prisoners, and that a general discussion had followed which had led to Lee's proposal. This was true, but made no mention of the first Ord-Longstreet meeting initiated by the former. Grant went on to ask for instructions.[24]

In Washington, on the night of 3 March, President Lincoln and several members of the Cabinet, including Secretary of War Stanton, were at the Capitol until a late hour considering bills passed in the closing moments of the Thirty-eighth Congress. A messenger from the War Department delivered Grant's dispatch to Secretary Stanton who read it and handed it to President Lincoln. Others read the missive, which included Lee's bid for a cessation of hostilities, and a fairly general enthusiasm seized the group. In the words of Ward H. Lamon, who was present, "Mr. Lincoln's spirits rose to a height rarely witnessed since the outbreak of the war," and he began to express his willingness to grant "the most lenient and generous terms to a defeated foe."[25]

Stanton, who had remained silent amid this scene of celebration, now turned upon Lincoln in a great rage and addressed him forcefully. He told the president that he was overlooking the most important question: "How and by whom is this war to be closed?" He reminded Lincoln that tomorrow was inauguration day, and chided him, saying that he was not fit to be president unless he presided over "an obedient, loyal, and united people. . . . If any other authority than your own be for a moment recognized; or if terms of peace be agreed upon that do not emanate from yourself, and do not imply that you are the supreme head of the nation—you are not needed."[26] Stanton went on to say to Lincoln that his work was already achieved except for reconstruction and that he should not be a party to aiding others to acquire the fame which rightfully belonged to himself.[27]

Upon hearing this tirade, Lincoln fell into deep thought for several minutes and then addressed his war minister: "Stanton, you are right; this dispatch did not at first sight strike me as I now consider it."[28] Whereupon he wrote out a telegram to Grant which was sent over Stanton's signature at midnight: "The President directs me to say to you that he wishes you to have no conference with General Lee, unless it be for the capitulation of General Lee's army. . . ." Grant was further enjoined from deciding or conferring upon any political question. "Such questions the President holds in his own hands, and will submit them to no military conferences or conventions." Grant was urged to "press to the utmost" his military advantages.[29] In a second dispatch to Grant sent at the same time, Stanton said very pointedly that "General Ord's conduct in holding intercourse with General Longstreet upon political questions not committed to his charge is not approved."[30]

The following day, Grant telegraphed to Stanton that he would obey the directions given and pointed out that, because he had no authority to act upon Lee's proposal, he had applied for instructions. To General Lee, he sent a dispatch with the following statement: "General Ord could only have meant that I would not refuse an interview on any subject on which I have a right to act, which, of course, would be such as are purely of a military character. . . ."[31]

What was Ord's thinking as he moved through this episode of contrivance, endeavoring to influence men and events in matters of high state policy? It is quite credible that in the meeting aboard the *New York* at Aiken's Landing, Stephens, Hunter and Campbell had impressed upon Ord the idea that the initiative for peace must come from the generals. Their view that the questions relating to peace, such as slavery, could be settled if taken out of the hands of politicians would certainly be well received by Ord, for he always despised the place-seeker. Did the three also persuade Ord that Lincoln would welcome an opportunity to respond to a bid for peace from the military? Lincoln's plan for compensated emancipation was long known. Did Ord get wind of the president's renewal of this idea in his proposal to the Cabinet of 5 February? These questions cannot be answered, but it seems essential to the logic of the situation that Ord felt that Lincoln would be glad to be "forced" to consider the question of peace if presented by the military. Lincoln's initial reaction when he read Lee's overture at the Capitol on inauguration eve would seem to bear out this view. Ord's scheme almost worked!

What was Grant's place in this affair? One can only speculate upon this point. Ord may have said: "General, we must take the initiative and open negotiations with General Lee." To which Grant might have responded: "No, we have no authority to do so." Ord could have rejoined: "But I feel sure President Lincoln would welcome a move on your part to break the ice." The stolid Grant remained unresponsive; the impetuous Ord said he was not afraid to try it. "You'll get your fingers burned." Grant might have warned. But Ord was insistent, and the meeting with Longstreet followed.

How was it that Ord could say, "General Grant has the authority to meet you," as reported by Longstreet to Lee? This question cannot be answered either. Ord was not ordinarily given to the use of guile to attain his ends, but it is not impossible that he would consider the present object so important that a bit of subterfuge was in order. Very likely, he did not expect Longstreet to take his suggestions literally. That is, he may have been saying: "Have General Lee invite General Grant to a meeting on a military matter, then the question of a military convention could be raised in the course of their discussion." Ord no doubt thought that all things were possible where well-intentioned officers and gentlemen set themselves to the task of working out their differences.[32]

Yet another puzzling aspect of the matter lies in the Confederate motives in the case. President Davis seemed anxious for a truce, if only a temporary one. However, there is no evidence of a willingness on his part to give up the struggle. Even so, there are disquieting indications that, if Ord's plan had been tried, it might have produced major results. On the day after Lee's surrender at Appomattox, Lee and Grant had a private conversation lasting nearly an hour. The correspondent Sylvanus Cadwallader wrote: "During this conference Lee stated that if Grant had assented to a meeting which he had proposed some weeks before, peace would undoubtedly have resulted therefrom."[33] Two days after this conference, Assistant Secretary of War Charles A. Dana, who was accompanying Grant, dispatched to Stanton: "If General Grant had agreed to the interview he [Lee] had asked for some time ago they would certainly have agreed on terms of peace, as he was prepared to treat for the surrender of all the Confederate armies."[34] This is uncorroborated. Nevertheless, the nagging feeling remains that, if Ord's plan had been tried, it might well have developed into a peaceful settlement of the conflict.

Ord's suggestion as to the part to be played by the ladies added an ingenious touch to his plan. These hard-bitten men of war had been battering one another for nearly four years, and there would be uneasiness and awkwardness about their meetings. The presence of ladies would give warmth to the encounters, add an air of politeness and gentility, and make for an atmosphere of good feeling in which agreement might be possible. Mrs. Grant was heartily in favor of participating in Ord's plan, but quoted her husband as saying: "It is simply absurd. The men have fought this war and the men will finish it."[35]

It might be argued that Ord's peace effort was silly, unrealistic and very likely impractical, even if accepted by Lincoln. Moreover, the war was nearly at an end anyhow, and the time had passed when a negotiated peace was in order. Perhaps so. But the fact remains that, at some risk to his own future, Ord tried his best to stop the flow of blood and avoid some of the bitterness of a fight to the death. Stanton was not quite correct when he told Lincoln on 3 March that his work was done except for reconstruction, for it did not take into account the severe fighting which yet remained and the hundreds of lives of Confederate and Union soldiers which would be sacrificed before the end of the war. Ord would have saved those lives.

General Ord had attempted a coup and had failed. He was under no illusions about his future. "He don't think he will be long in this Department or in command of it," Placidus Ord wrote to his wife on 10 March. He went on to say that the general had reserved a house for himself at Fort Monroe in case he should be removed from command of the department.[36] However, he was not removed, and at least two related reasons may be adduced in explanation: first, he could fight; and second, he still enjoyed Grant's confidence.

★★★★★

The month of March 1865 was a period of preparation on the battle front for the impending spring operations, but there was still time to indulge in the glorification of the soldier's life, in the deceptively enticing appeal of military pomp. About the middle of the month, Secretary of War Stanton visited the front of the Army of the James and was accorded the customary review of the troops. There was yet one other dignitary to entertain. On 26 March, came President Abraham Lincoln and a large retinue, including Mrs. Lincoln, General Grant, Mrs. Grant, Admiral Porter and Mrs. Ord. The presidential party came up the James aboard the *River Queen* and were met at Aiken's Landing by Generals Ord, Gibbon and Godfrey Weitzel and their respective staffs.[37]

It was three or four miles to the parade ground of the Army of the James, and most of the visitors mounted horses to cover this distance. In the group was Captain John S. Barnes, U.S. Navy, who had served as special escort to Mrs. Lincoln aboard the *River Queen*. As the party left the landing, General Ord presented the captain to Mrs. Ord, who was also on horseback. The general made suitable remarks about the horsemanship of sailors, saying, "Captain, I put Mrs. Ord in charge of the navy." Many years later, Captain Barnes recalled that Molly Ord "was a remarkably handsome woman, and a most accomplished equestrienne, riding with extreme grace a spirited bay horse."[38] Mrs. Lincoln and Mrs. Grant rode in an ambulance escorted by Lieutenant Colonel Horace Porter and Lieutenant Colonel Adam Badeau of Grant's staff. At the head of the cavalcade rode President Lincoln who chatted with Grant and Ord as he jogged along.[39]

The presidential group arrived late; the troops had been in review formation for several hours, and they had had no noon meal. There were hasty consultations between the troop commander and General Ord and between Ord and Grant, and the latter presented the situation to the president with the question as to whether the review should await the arrival of the ambulance in which Mrs. Lincoln was riding, which had for some reason been delayed. Lincoln indicated that the review should begin at once. The president, with Grant and Ord, proceeded down the line in front of the troops, receiving their "present arms" as bands played and colors streamed in the March breeze.[40]

Mrs. Ord asked Captain Barnes if she should join the entourage behind the president. The naval officer referred the matter to an army staff officer who gave assurance that it would be proper. They joined the reviewing column. Shortly after, and as the review was still in progress, the ambulance belatedly drove on the field.[41] When Mrs. Lincoln discovered that Mrs. Ord was with the presidential party and had even ridden beside the president for a brief interval after leaving the landing, she fell into a great rage: "What does the woman mean by riding by the side of the President and ahead of me? Does she suppose that *he* wants *her* by the side of *him*?" She was in a frenzy of excitement. Mrs. Grant tried to quiet her, but this enraged her even more. At the risk of arousing greater ire, Mrs. Grant defended her friend, Molly Ord, against the irrational accusations.[42]

As the ambulance appeared on the field, Mrs. Ord said to Captain Barnes: "There come Mrs. Lincoln and Mrs. Grant; I think I had better join them." They left the reviewing party and galloped across the field to the ambulance.[43] The reception of Molly Ord was blistering: "Then Mrs. Lincoln positively insulted her," Badeau wrote, "called her vile names in the presence of a crowd of officers, and asked what she meant by following up the President." Molly Ord burst into tears and tried to find out what great crime she had committed. Mrs. Lincoln raved, Mrs. Grant continued to defend Mrs. Ord, and the officers present were "shocked and horrified." The president's wife carried on her unreasoning tirade until she was exhausted.[44]

General and Mrs. Grant and the general's staff were the guests of President and Mrs. Lincoln at dinner in the evening. Before the assembled company "Mrs. Lincoln berated General Ord to the president," Colonel Badeau wrote, "and urged that he should be removed. He was unfit for his place, she said, to say nothing of his wife." Grant defended Ord vigorously.[45]

Mrs. Lincoln's behavior was not governed by reason, and she was indeed an object of pity. Her conduct must have been quite mortifying to the president, who had to bear an added weight of sorrow and trouble along with the many tribulations of his office.

★★★★★

Ord figured prominently in Grant's plans in January and February of 1865 as the lieutenant general gave constant consideration to the possibility of taking the offensive. Not only did these plans indicate Grant's aggressiveness, but also his reliance upon Ord to lead the contemplated attacks. No doubt, the weather and the state of the roads had much to do with this matter. On 9 January, Grant asked Ord to examine his Bermuda Hundred front between the Appomattox and the James Rivers to determine whether he could go through "by a surprise and by massing." "I could give you an additional corps to hold what you got, and would give up all north of the James, except two or three important points, if it could be done."[46] Again, on 31 January, Grant, who had just returned to his headquarters from several days' absence, ordered Ord to prepare all of his forces for a move. At this moment, Grant apparently did not know that the three peace commissioners were waiting at the front lines to come through. Ord explained their presence and inquired: "Will this affect your order to move?"[47]

Again, on 2 February, Grant asked Ord to investigate the prospects for a move around the Confederate left on the railroads running north from Richmond. If the weather continued good, the lieutenant general thought of making a move in that direction, in which case he would reinforce Ord with one corps from the Army of the Potomac and hold a second corps in readiness to join him, if needed. The Bermuda front was again considered by Grant on 24 February when he asked Ord to examine the line between the Appomattox and the James to see if a hole might be made in the Confederate defenses.[48] Nothing came of any of these plans, as rain, snow and possibly other factors prevented.

Even though the winter months were a period of relative inactivity, they brought a steady stream of deserters into the Union lines, testifying to the declining fortunes of the Confederacy. Ord encouraged this in every possible way. "Scatter the newspapers containing the President's report of the peace conference on your picket line, so as to have it thrown across to the rebels," he telegraphed Gibbon a few days after the return of Stephens, Hunter and Campbell.[49] Ord reported thirty-eight deserters on 17 February, forty-three on 18 February, and forty-two on 20 February. Grant noted that desertion had been on the increase on Ord's front since the return of the peace commissioners and that the crossover was more prevalent on his front than on Meade's. In March, Grant issued an order promising to pay Confederates for arms and horses brought over. Ord ingeniously conveyed these orders to the Confederate side with kites, bows and arrows.[50]

The *New York Herald* correspondent reported that he had listened attentively to the interrogation of deserters at the office of Colonel Manning, provost marshal general of the Army of the James. The deserters all told a sad story of conditions inside the Confederate capital and expressed the view that the Southern cause was lost.[51] To some extent, desertion worked in the other direction, and Ord was energetic in his efforts to suppress it. "General Ord's army is no place for bounty jumpers or deserters. . . ," a newspaper correspondent wrote. A soldier convicted by court-martial of desertion on one day was shot the next.[52] In March, Ord offered a reward of $100 and three months' leave or furlough to any soldier or officer who shot or brought in a deserter caught in the act of going over to the enemy.[53]

★★★★★

In the four or five weeks preceding the opening of the spring campaign, Ord continued the reorganization of the Army of the James with the aim of eliminating the last vestiges of Butlerism, or at any rate to put the remaining Butlerites where he wanted them. At headquarters, the general completed a rather thorough shake-up in the staff organization. Ord's favorite, Lieutenant Colonel Theodore Read, succeeded Colonel Ed. W. Smith as department assistant adjutant general. On 20 March, Read was advanced to chief of staff, and Brigadier General John W. Turner was assigned to command an Independent Division of the Twenty-fourth Corps.[54] Turner summed it up when he wrote to Butler that "all of the old staff have now left the Headquarters except Martin and Manning, both of whom stand well in Ord's estimation."[55] In addition to assigning Turner to Gibbon, Ord designated Major General George L. Hartsuff to command the defenses of Bermuda Hundred, relieving Brigadier General C.K. Graham. He had Brigadier Generals Charles A. Heckman and Edward A. Wild transferred out of the Twenty-fifth Corps. General August V. Kautz was shifted by Ord from the command of the cavalry division to succeed Wild in command of one of the black divisions. Kautz was highly displeased with this change and was convinced that Ord expected him to refuse the command because of race prejudice.[56]

Ord's selection of Brigadier General Ranald Slidell Mackenzie to succeed Kautz in command of the cavalry division brought to the fore one of the most remarkable officers to serve in the Civil War on either side. Mackenzie was the nephew of John Slidell, Confederate commissioner to France. He was still a West Point cadet in 1862 when Grant fought at Shiloh and George B. McClellan began his advance on the peninsula. Graduating in that year as the top man in his class, Mackenzie took part in most of the important battles in the East and was several times wounded and brevetted. His ability and courage were remarkable. At twenty-four years of age, he was a brigadier general of volunteers and commanded a division of more than two thousand mounted men.

By the time Ord had Mackenzie, Theodore Read and John W. Turner in their new places, the days of preparation had come to an end. It was late March, and these men of Ord's army would now try themselves against the tough foe defending Richmond and Petersburg.

12

★★★★★

In Pursuit of Lee

ULYSSES S. Grant's attack order of 24 March 1865 ener-
gized the gigantic Union war machine and moved it
against the embattled Confederates. Edward Ord's army was to
have a prominent part in the Federal spring offensive. Ord
himself was to be in the forefront of the operations. That Grant
would place him there is a significant commentary on Ord's
military talents and Grant's judgment of them.

Grant's order directed a move to the Union left below
Petersburg to turn the Confederates out of that place and to
enable Philip H. Sheridan to cut the Southside and the Danville
railroads. Sheridan's cavalry was to spearhead the offensive,
moving westerly to Dinwiddie Court House and thence northerly to sever the two rail lines out of Petersburg and Richmond.
G. K. Warren's Fifth Corps and Andrew A. Humphreys'
Second Corps of George G. Meade's Army of the Potomac
were to follow Sheridan toward Dinwiddie. H. G. Wright's
Sixth Corps in its position on the left south of Petersburg
would be prepared to move, while Major General John G.
Parke's Ninth Corps would be the holding force to occupy
the lines of the Army of the Potomac before Petersburg extending from the Appomattox River and sweeping below the
city to cross the Weldon Railroad.[1]

Ord was ordered to detach three divisions from the Army
of the James on the Richmond front, two white and one black,

and march them down below Petersburg to join the Army of the Potomac and Sheridan's cavalry in the operations. Mackenzie, with most of Ord's cavalry, would take part in the movement. General Godfrey Weitzel would remain in command of the troops of Ord's army in the lines before Richmond and between the Appomattox and the James. Weitzel at Richmond and Parke at Petersburg were to attack without waiting for orders if they should observe a weakening of the Confederate defenses on their respective fronts, a development which would suggest that the cities were being evacuated.[2]

Coordinated with the spring campaign in Virginia were operations in all of the other theaters of war. Grant's grand strategy was to make a concerted drive against the Confederacy on all fronts. Across the Mississippi River, John Pope was preparing to move against Edmund Kirby Smith and Sterling Price; E.R.S. Canby, opposed by Confederate Richard Taylor, was pushing in the direction of Mobile; George H. Thomas was sending out two cavalry expeditions, one under James H. Wilson into Alabama, the other under George Stoneman from East Tennessee toward Lynchburg; Winfield Scott Hancock was concentrating a force at Winchester, Virginia, for use as needed; and, finally, William T. Sherman's powerful army, linked up with the forces of John M. Schofield and Alfred H. Terry at Goldsboro, North Carolina, on 22 and 23 March, was only 120 miles from Petersburg.[3]

Ord selected from the lines before Richmond Robert S. Foster's and John W. Turner's divisions of John Gibbon's Twenty-fourth Corps and William Birney's Negro division of Weitzel's Twenty-fifth Corps. He prepared them for a long hike southward to join the striking force below Petersburg. As the success of this move depended to a great extent upon secrecy, the ever resourceful Ord took great pains to prevent the Confederates from observing his maneuver. A few days before their departure, he quietly withdrew from the line of works most of the troops who were to go, made a demonstration on the right with them, and placed them in the rear where they were out of sight. The remainder of his command he kept in motion with frequent changes of camps. For several nights, pickets were detailed only from the regiments which were to remain. On the night of the departure of the three divisions, the camps vacated by them were kept lighted with tents standing. Bands played the calls as usual. For some days afterward, this same appearance was kept up.[4]

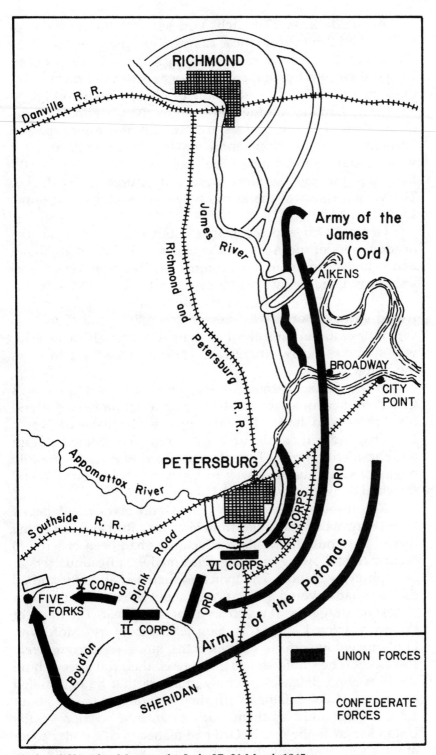

Ord and Sheridan Move to the Left, 27–31 March 1865

About dark on 27 March, Ord sent off the divisions of Gibbon and Birney from these camps. They marched briskly to the James River at Aiken's Landing, crossed the pontoon bridge there, and pushed steadily across the Bermuda Hundred peninsula in the direction of the pontoon bridge at Broadway Landing on the Appomattox. Not overlooking any detail, Ord had the bridges over which the troops passed covered with moist straw and compost. An all-night march it was through the darkness. The roads were in terrible condition, but the foot soldiers were not appreciably delayed. The wagon trains of the army, however, were slowed down somewhat.[5]

General Ord and most of his staff rode away from the headquarters of the Army of the James at 3 A.M. on 28 March and followed up the moving column. At 7:40 A.M., Ord was at Broadway Landing and sent a dispatch to Grant to report his men all across the bridge there. Both Gibbon and Ord had issued stringent orders to prevent straggling, and there was very little of it. Turner's division, marching strongly in the lead, was six miles below Broadway. The trains had yet to cross the bridge.[6]

In the course of the morning, Ord went over to Grant's City Point headquarters and there paid a call on his old friend Sherman, who had left his armies at Goldsboro, North Carolina, and had dashed up to City Point to confer with Grant and President Lincoln. This pleasant interlude was necessarily brief, for Ord must get back to his weary soldiers, who still marched doggedly southward.[7]

At sunset, Ord's column halted and bivouacked below Petersburg about four miles from Hatcher's Run and just to the rear of the front line position which they had been ordered to occupy the following morning. Ord made his headquarters at Humphreys's Station. The men had marched all night and all day and had covered a distance of about thirty-six miles with almost no stragglers. It was truly an amazing feat. The trains of the army arrived almost as soon as the infantry. Moreover, Ord's ingenious efforts to screen the move were completely successful. The Confederates maintained their full force behind the Richmond defenses, entirely unaware that he had pulled out about 14,000 infantry with their wagon trains and about 1,800 cavalry and had them ready to go into position on the Union left far to the south. Ord had managed this under cover of darkness even though his own lines were but a rifle shot away from the Southern lines, and he had crossed two bridges under their surveillance.[8]

On the morning of 29 March, Ord's force moved into the position recently occupied by Humphreys's Second Corps near Burgess's Mill. At the close of this day Grant's entire force was poised to strike exactly as scheduled. To Ord's immediate left was Humphreys's Second Corps and to the left of it, Warren's Fifth Corps. To Ord's right was Wright's Sixth Corps and to its right Parke's Ninth Corps. Sheridan's cavalry was at Dinwiddie Court House about six miles from the extreme left of the infantry line.[9]

On 30 March, Ord advanced to make better connection with Humphreys and Wright. This movement involved considerable skirmishing, with Ord reporting strong resistance. Early on the thirty-first, Ord pushed forward Turner's and Foster's divisions under instructions from Grant to keep the enemy busy and to go through if it appeared possible. The men advanced in a blinding shower of rain and overran the Confederate picket line, capturing nearly 200 prisoners and driving the remnant back into their main works. This established Ord's position within 400 yards of the principal line of work of the enemy. Ord kept up a blizzard of fire upon the line and heavy guns of the Southerners, greatly reducing their return fire. On the following day, 1 April, there was additional skirmishing, and Ord continued to establish batteries and to carry out a reconnaissance in anticipation of further action.[10]

Lee sought to counter Grant's moves by extending his own thin infantry line westward. On 30 March, Pickett's division and Fitz Lee's cavalry occupied Five Forks, and, on the following day, were joined by the cavalry of Rooney Lee and Tom Rosser. On the morning of 1 April, Sheridan, having Warren's Fifth Corps ordered to him, moved against Pickett at Five Forks. Mackenzie's cavalry, now operating under Sheridan's orders, struck between Pickett's force and the main Confederate line to the east, cutting off the embattled Southerners. While Sheridan's cavalry slashed at Pickett's front, portions of the Fifty Corps fell upon his left flank. The Confederates were completely routed, hundreds being made prisoners. Only certain cavalry units and a remnant of infantry made good their escape. The Southside Railroad was now within easy reach of Sheridan's force.[11]

Grant thought it probable that Lee might throw all his available troops against Sheridan. The Confederate command-

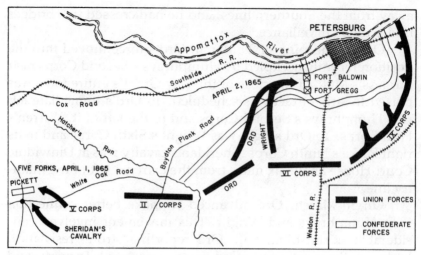

The Breakthrough at Petersburg, 2 April 1865

er did order three brigades of Bushrod Johnson's force to evacuate the three miles of line to the west of Burgess's Mill and to go to the support of the cavalry in defense of the Southside Railroad. In addition, on the afternoon of 1 April, Major General Charles W. Field's division of about 4,600 men was ordered from Richmond to aid in saving the road. These were the first Confederate forces to leave the front of the Army of the James since Ord had slipped away five days before, and, even then, the Confederates had no positive information of Ord's absence from the Richmond front.[12] So much for Ord's skillful deception!

On the night of 1 April, Grant dispatched to Ord: "Get your men up and feel the enemy and push him if he shows signs of giving way."[13] Ord reported back with evident disappointment that he had just discovered a morass on his front which would make forward progress difficult and wished that Grant would let someone else take that portion of the line and put his men in the open where they could give a better account of themselves. To this, Grant responded that he did not want Ord to fight his way "over difficult barriers against defended lines" and that Ord should draw a reserve out of his line to throw in where someone else might penetrate. As General Wright had expressed confidence that the Sixth Corps could go through, the General-in-Chief ordered Ord to put his reserve on the right to help the Sixth Corps or to go through on their own front, should Ord find it practical to do so.[14]

Grant ordered an assault all along the line for the following morning, and Ord gave directions through Gibbon to his division commanders to make preparations for the attack. "Have an issue of liquor given your men early tomorrow morning," his dispatch concluded.[15] At the appointed time, a terrific artillery bombardment opened up, after which Wright sent forward his Sixth Corps; the time was shortly after 4 A.M. His assault shattered the Confederate line held by Henry Heth's and Cadmus Wilcox's divisions of A.P. Hill's corps. Upon hearing of Wright's success, Grant directed Ord to go to his assistance. The Sixth Corps commander, as early as 5:20 A.M., had asked Ord if he could either attack or send troops to support his further movements. Ord ordered Gibbon to send all available force to support the Sixth Corps. All of Foster's division and two of Turner's brigades were ordered to the right to Fort Welch, the point of the Sixth Corps breakthrough, though they were apparently not engaged there. Shortly afterwards, Harris's brigade of Turner's division, left on Ord's front, was pushing forward, and, after encountering slight resistance, carried the Confederate works, capturing guns, battle flags and prisoners. Birney's division of black troops moved forward and found the lines in their front abandoned. Parke's Ninth Corps had advanced on its broad front facing the city of Petersburg itself and carried the main line held by Gordon's corps but was unable to break the Confederates' second line.[16]

Hundreds of Confederate prisoners were herded to the rear. Ord telegraphed to City Point that he had about 1,000 prisoners at his headquarters at Humphreys's Station and only a handful of men to guard them. There was also a large quantity of ammunition and supplies left exposed by the movement of the troops against the Southerners. Five hundred marines were sent and returned with 3,000 prisoners, which probably included those captured by Wright.[17]

Later in the day, Miles's division overtook the remnants of Heth's and Wilcox's divisions at Sutherland Station, and a severe engagement took place. The approach of Sheridan's cavalry from Ford's Station and a division sent by Meade from the Petersburg front caused the Southerners to withdraw in haste, leaving guns and many prisoners.[18]

Ord chafed impatiently at headquarters as all the action was taking place. He dared not leave Humphreys's Station without orders. At 10 A.M., Ord asked Grant if Humphreys would cover this rear while he moved this force and Wright's toward Petersburg. To this, there was apparently no reply. Ord then showed proper initiative in the absence of orders by directing his command to move upon Petersburg. At 10:40 A.M., the general dispatched to Grant that his command was moving upon the city from the west in conjunction with Wright's, as indicated in his previous dispatch. The general wanted to move his headquarters with his troops. At noon, Ord was still at his headquarters impatiently awaiting orders from Grant as to the further disposition of forces, but he had learned that the lieutenant general had gone toward Petersburg to look into matters at first hand and was momentarily beyond reach.[19]

Meanwhile, under Ord's orders, the three divisions of the Army of the James under Gibbon, along with the three divisions of the Sixth Corps, pressed on to Petersburg. Their progress was checked by a strong double line of forts protecting the western front of the city, extending from the Appomattox River to the main Confederate line and perpendicular to it. Forts Gregg and Baldwin were the principal works blocking the way. If these forts could be taken, there would remain only one Confederate line on the western side of Petersburg. The defenders of the city would be in considerable danger, and any subsequent withdrawal would be precarious. With Gibbon in command, the men of Ord's army were ordered forward at about one o'clock in the afternoon, though Ord was apparently not present. Foster's division, supported by two brigades of Turner's, moved upon Fort Gregg, while Harris's brigade of Turner's division pushed forward against Fort Baldwin. Fort Gregg was the focal point of Confederate resistance. The Southerners felt this line must be held, and the fragments of Cadmus Wilcox's division and N.H. Harris's brigade of Mahone's division, totaling about 500, were ordered to hold it. The Federals moved steadily to the attack under a heavy fire of artillery and musketry. Upon reaching Fort Gregg, they found it surrounded by a deep ditch of considerable width, partially filled with water and covered by flanking fire from right and left. They surged across the ditch and up to the parapet. Within the fort, the vastly outnumbered Southerners fought tenaciously, pouring out a murderous fire into the ranks of the attackers. Finally, the wave of blue surged over the parapet and poured into Fort Gregg engulfing the last of its gallant defenders. Within the fort, 55 Confederate dead were found heaped upon one another, and about 200 prisoners, most of them wounded, were taken. Fort Baldwin soon fell to Harris's men, who captured 60 prisoners. It was a costly victory. Gibbon had lost in the day's operations 10 officers and 112 men killed, and 27 officers and 565 men wounded, most of them at Fort Gregg. Ord was high in praise of his own men but could not forbear paying tribute to the stubborn defense of the Southerners, as he spoke of their "desperate courage worthy a better cause."[20]

The forces of Ord and Wright now confronted Lee's last defensive line, but no immediate effort was made to carry it. Grant issued orders for an attack all along the Petersburg line for the following morning, 3 April. Once Lee was sure that Grant would not press him on the afternoon of 2 April, he issued orders for Petersburg and Richmond to be evacuated during the night, the Petersburg force to move north of the Appomattox, and the whole army to move westerly toward Amelia Court House with a view to uniting with Johnston in North Carolina.[21]

Ord's headquarters were alive before daylight on 3 April. At 4:30 A.M., Ord learned from a prisoner just taken that the Petersburg defenders were packed and ready to evacuate, and he so dispatched to Grant. Ten minutes later, Meade reported that the Ninth Corps had occupied a large part of the enemy works in its front and that no enemy was in sight. It was quickly apparent that the Confederates had abandoned the city. It is not entirely clear which troops were the first to enter Petersburg, but, at 5:30 A.M., Ord dispatched to Grant that "General Birney reported his division as having gone into town at 4:30 A.M.," indicating that the Negro troops of Ord's army were the first to go in.[22]

Ord was directed to pursue the fleeing Confederates promptly, moving his command southwesterly on the Cox road which followed along the line of the Southside Railroad. His force was under way by 8 A.M. and was the left wing of the pursuing bluecoats. The Ninth Corps followed Ord. The bulk of the Army of the Potomac, the Sixth, Fifth and Second Corps, took the River road to the north and roughly parallel to Ord's route. Sheridan with his cavalry was on both roads in advance of the infantry. Lee's scattered forces from Petersburg and Richmond were converging upon crossings of the Appomattox which would bring them to the south bank of that stream near Amelia Court House.[23]

Ord reached Sutherland Station about thirteen miles from Petersburg in the course of the afternoon, where Grant and his

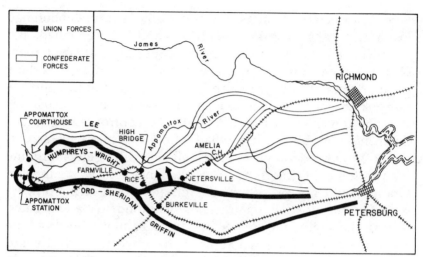

From Petersburg to Appomattox, 3–9 April 1865

staff caught up with his column. Here the tardily reported
news arrived from Weitzel that Richmond had fallen to that
part of Ord's army under his command. There was great cheering among the soldiers of the Twenty-fourth Corps as news of
the success of their comrades-in-arms spread through the
bivouac at Sutherland Station.[24]

Ord had directed Weitzel on 1 April to open an artillery
barrage on the Richmond front to determine the Confederate
strength by their return fire. The enemy was found to be
present in force. On 2 April, an attack by Major General George
L. Hartsuff on the Bermuda front proved the Southerners were
still there. In the early hours of the morning of 3 April, there
were explosions followed by fires in Richmond. At about 3
A.M., it was apparent to Weitzel that the Richmond front was
being abandoned, and he ordered an advance at daylight.
Before leaving his headquarters on 27 March, Ord had sent a
dispatch to Weitzel warning him of torpedoes (land mines) and
directing that, in event of evacuation, Weitzel keep his advancing columns in woods and bypaths and send cattle and old
horses up the roads first.[25]

Some reports indicated that the first infantry unit to enter
Richmond was the Negro brigade of Brevet Brigadier General
Alonzo G. Draper of Kautz's division, though the white troops
of Brevet Brigadier General Edward Hastings Ripley's brigade
of Charles Devens's division were the first infantry to go to the
heart of the city. The bluecoats passed several lines of strong

fortifications lately held by their enemies but now silent and abandoned. A choking pall of smoke hung over the city, and flames leaped up at various places. The meaning of the early morning explosions was clear: the Confederates had set fire to Richmond as a military measure. As the troops passed into the city, thousands of Negroes crowded the streets to cheer with special enthusiasm their brothers of the Twenty-fifth Corps and Colonel Charles Francis Adams's Negro cavalry. Many of the white citizens were annoyed and concerned that so many Negro troops had been brought in.[26] Weitzel rode ahead and entered the city hall where he received the surrender at 8:15 A.M. He reported "the greatest confusion, pillaging, and disorder reigning, and the city on fire in several places."[27] General Shepley, who had raised the first United States flag over the state capitol, was appointed by Weitzel to be military governor of Richmond with orders to restore order and put out the fire. With the aid of citizens, the fire was contained by 2 P.M., but the business district of Richmond, about twenty blocks, lay in ruins, and the bridges over the James River had been destroyed.[28]

Ord's army had performed very creditably under Weitzel's direction. The troops were well behaved, and their work had been well done. They could count as part of their capture 500 cannon, 5,000 muskets and much matériel, more than 1,000 straggling Confederates and 5,000 wounded Southerners in hospitals.[29]

"I congratulate you that the Army of the James and not the Army of the Potomac were the first to enter Richmond," brother-in-law William P. Webster in Norfolk wrote to Benjamin F. Butler, though it was not quite clear just what Butler had to do with it.[30]

In Washington, Secretary Stanton was disturbed by the possibility of a lingering Butler influence and expressed his concern to Grant: "I would greatly prefer some other person than Shepley for military governor. Please remove him immediately and appoint some good man of your own selection, who has not been connected with Butler's administration. Had not Weitzel better have duty elsewhere than in Richmond?"[31] Grant was too much occupied with his pursuit of Lee to give immediate attention to the matter.

At Sutherland Station, Ord in consultation with Grant prepared instructions for Weitzel. Weitzel was named governor of Richmond and told to be his own treasury agent. He was directed to act as commander of the department in matters requiring immediate attention. He was to seize tobacco and sell it to feed the poor. Food and other necessities were to come into the city. The white men were to be registered, a military commission appointed for the punishment of offenses against law and order, a police force organized, and gas and water companies started. Those who came forward to take the oath of allegiance were to be protected in their property. "By property, persons are not meant." No taxes were to be imposed or rents paid other than to recognize ownership of loyal landlords. "Allow loyal men to open hotels, but not grog-shops," Ord's order concluded.[32] In a subsequent dispatch, Ord directed Weitzel to keep as few troops in the city as possible and to place the divisions of Devens and Kautz in camps out of town ready for field service.[33]

★★★★★

Ord's troops were up early on the morning of 4 April to continue their march on the Cox road. After steady progress of fifteen miles, they reached Wilson's Station where they bivouacked for the night. As Ord's movement was in progress, a few miles to the north, Lee's column was advancing upon Amelia Court House. Lee himself was at Amelia. The hard-pressed Confederates had expected to be rationed at this point, but, through a miscarriage of plans, there were no supplies. Such lead as the Confederates had over their pursuers was lost, as the army remained at Amelia awaiting the meager provisions their foraging parties might secure in the vicinity.[34]

Sheridan with his cavalry was pressing Lee closely. He reached the Richmond and Danville Railroad near Jetersville during the day where he learned definitely of Lee's presence at nearby Amelia Court House. His cavalry force was no match for Lee's army, and he entrenched to await the arrival of Meade's infantry. The Fifth Corps reached him late in the afternoon.[35]

Grant, who continued with Ord's column, directed Ord to push two of his divisions as far as possible toward the vital railroad junction at Burkeville, where the rail lines out of Richmond and Petersburg crossed. On the morning of 5 April, Ord's men began a forced march in an effort to reach Burkeville. If they could do so, they would be squarely across the Richmond and Danville Railroad and could block Lee's principal route of escape to the southwest should the Confederates manage to get through or around Sheridan and Meade. Birney's division was left at Black and White's to guard the railroad.[36]

Ord led the march through a beautiful rolling countryside, one of the richest counties of Virginia. Aristocratic mansions stood abandoned along the way, but there were few of the wealthy to witness the passing of the blue column. Ordinary whites received the soldiers "sensibly" and in some cases "joyously." The Negroes were elated and crowded up to Ord's column in large numbers to catch a glimpse of General Grant.[37]

About 2 P.M., Ord's men reached Nottoway Court House, having marched about twenty miles since early morning. Dispatches from Sheridan at Jetersville awaited Grant, and the news they conveyed was good. Lee's entire force, out of rations or nearly so, lay between Amelia Court House and Jetersville. "We can capture the Army of Northern Virginia, if force enough can be thrown to this point, and then advance upon it," Sheridan stated.[38] In a subsequent dispatch, the cavalry commander said that he was preparing to attack the Confederate infantry. "Everything should be hurried forward with the utmost speed," Sheridan urged. "If General Ord can be put in below it will probably use them up."[39]

Sheridan's dispatches were read to Ord's weary soldiers, and they were sharply excited. They clamored to march all night, giving earnest of their intentions by starting off briskly, cheering and yelling wildly. Grant received tremendous cheers as he rode along the column. As one division exhausted itself, another would pick up the noise, and the shouting was continuous for miles along the road.[40]

To the northward, only a dozen miles from Ord's column at about 1 P.M., Lee pushed his force past Jetersville on the Richmond and Danville Railroad but quickly encountered Sheridan's entrenchments. Believing the Union line too strong to be carried, Lee determined to break away from Sheridan, press as rapidly as possible for Farmville some fifteen miles westward on the Southside Railroad, supply the army with supplies sent from Lynchburg, and then turn southward. In order to be successful, this maneuver had to regain for the Confederates the time lost in Amelia. Thus, they set out upon a seemingly endless march day and night, while straggling reduced their numbers and made them vulnerable to attack.[41]

About 11 P.M., Ord's force reached Burkeville after a march

of nearly thirty miles. This was soldiering with a vengeance! The men were too tired to build fires and cook supper, but simply threw themselves to the ground and were instantly asleep.[42]

Grant had left Ord's column about 7:30 P.M. on this day, 5 April, borrowing most of the mounted orderlies of Ord and Gibbon as escort in order to visit Sheridan at Jetersville. He reached there about 10 P.M. He found that Humphreys's Second Corps and Wright's Sixth Corps had joined the Fifth Corps and Sheridan's cavalry. As Lee's movements were not yet clear, Grant dispatched to Meade that, if the Confederates still remained at Amelia in the morning, they would be attacked, but the lieutenant general believed that Lee would withdraw and that he should be vigorously pursued. Grant dispatched in similar vein to Ord at Burkeville, saying further that Ord should move west at eight in the morning and watch all roads running south between Burkeville and Farmville. The spy hurrying toward Burkeville with Grant's dispatch to Ord was captured by the Confederates. Thus, Ord was left at Burkeville without orders. For Lee, the intelligence revealed by the captured dispatch was ominous, for it showed that Ord was ahead of the Confederates in the race westward. Lee knew, too, that only greater speed or a battle might overcome his disadvantage. Moreover, the captured dispatch was the first *certain* news that Ord's army had left the Richmond front.[43]

Before daylight on 6 April, Ord dispatched a small force from Burkeville to destroy High Bridge near Farmville which spanned the Appomattox with a railroad bridge overhead and a wagon crossing underneath. Apparently, orders to do this were given verbally by Grant to Ord before the lieutenant general left Ord's column on the evening of 5 April. "As Lee appeared to be aiming for either Danville or Lynchburg," Ord said, "Lieutenant General Grant directed me to cut the bridges in his front, and wait orders at Burkeville, which it was important to hold."[44] The force sent consisted of two small regiments of infantry from Turner's division, totaling about 500, and Ord's headquarters escort of 80 troopers of the Fourth Massachusetts Cavalry under Colonel Francis Washburn. Their orders were to move as rapidly as possible, make a reconnaissance when near the bridge, and, if it were not too well guarded, to burn it, and then to return with great caution. The little detachment moved up the road to High Bridge some ten miles northwesterly, probably without much vigor, for they had had only about four or five hours of rest since their nearly thirty-mile hike of the day before.[45]

Ord notified Grant that he had sent the bridge-burning force and further informed him that he was tearing up one rail of each of the railroads toward Danville and Lynchburg. A line of rifle pits was being thrown up for protection against cavalry. Nearly all of Ord's supply trains were at Burkeville.[46]

Sometime about 9 or 10 A.M., Ord became apprehensive for the safety of Colonel Washburn's detachment, as Lee's cavalry might be operating as far west as High Bridge. He sent his chief of staff, Brevet Brigadier General Theodore Read, to take charge of the party with instructions to reconnoitre well before moving up to the bridge. After Read's departure Ord received a dispatch from Sheridan informing him that Lee's supply trains were west of Amelia Court House moving through Deatonsville in the direction of Burkeville. Ord entrenched the divisions of Turner and Foster at Burkeville, assuming that Lee's entire army was headed toward him. He sent the best staff officer at hand to warn Read that Lee's army was in his rear and that he must cross the Appomattox and return by making a wide swing around through Prince Edward Court House, but this last courier was driven back by Lee's cavalry.[47]

General Read overtook the bridge-burning detachment of Ord's force, detoured to take the cavalry into Farmville on reconnaissance, returned to the infantry, and headed for High Bridge about two miles in front. In the meantime, the van of Lee's army under James Longstreet had reached Rice only two or three miles to the rear of Read's force and between High Bridge and Burkeville. Longstreet, of course, knew of Ord's presence in Burkeville, and, expecting attack, entrenched his force. He also knew of Read's bridge-burning party and realized that, if Lee's force had to cross to the north side of the Appomattox again, High Bridge as well as two bridges at Farmville might be vital. Longstreet dispatched Tom Rosser with a small cavalry division in pursuit of Read. Thomas T. Munford with Fitzhugh Lee's division of cavalry and M.W. Gary with his brigade of cavalry were sent in support. Rosser overtook Read about noon near the bridge.[48]

Read, no ordinary soldier, had been cited by Ord for gallantry at the capture of Fort Harrison, and had risen steadily to his position as chief of staff of the Army of the James. Though greatly outnumbered, he was determined to fight. He "drew up his little band of 80 cavalry and 500 infantry, rode along the front of his ranks, inspired them with all his own daring, and began the battle with an army in his front." The Federal cavalry charged boldly, and the fighting became quite severe. General Read fell mortally wounded, as did Colonel Francis Washburn. Eventually, all of the officers of the cavalry detachment were either killed or wounded. After stout resistance, the surrounded Federals surrendered. The victory was dearly bought by the Confederates, for dead were Brigadier General James Dearing, Colonel Reuben B. Boston, and Major James W. Thomson.[49]

The tragedy at High Bridge resulted from an error in judgment on the part of Grant or Ord. The error lay in their failure to realize that Lee's army could march as rapidly as their own. If Grant's verbal order to Ord to destroy the bridge was clear and positive, then the error was Grant's. The lieutenant general notified Sheridan during the course of the day that Ord had sent two regiments on an errand of bridge destruction, but he indicated no particular concern for their safety. If, on the other hand, Ord had wide latitude in the matter of bridge destruction, then the responsibility for sending the force was his. Why had not Sheridan sent the "highly essential" cavalry to Ord which Grant had directed him to do on 4 April? Perhaps there was belated compliance, for, on 6 April, as Read and his band were marching to disaster, Mackenzie's cavalry division was on its way to join Ord.[50]

The idea of destroying High Bridge was well conceived, for, as it turned out, the bridge proved to be quite important to Lee's army. Besides this, Read's action, according to Grant, probably slowed the Confederate advance sufficiently for the Federals to secure their wagon trains on the following day.[51]

Ord, at Burkeville, was without orders on this day of disaster at High Bridge. During the morning, he took steps to determine the exact direction the Confederate column was taking. He learned that the Southerners were moving westerly with a view to getting around him and swinging southward. This placed the Confederates at Rice between Ord and Read's party, a development described above, though Read's fate was not known to Ord until sometime in the afternoon. At about 11 A.M., Ord moved without orders: "I left Burkeville for Farmville as soon as I found the direction which the rebels were taking, orders to that effect having been sent me," Ord said, "but I had done it when they reached me, with the intention of intercepting them in front or striking them on their flank."[52]

Ord moved Foster's and Turner's divisions up to Rice where Longstreet was entrenched. Forming line of battle, the bluecoats advanced and found the enemy in strong position. Ord prepared to attack, but night fell before he could carry out his intention. Reviewing the events of the day, it becomes clear that it was Read's bridge-burning party which distracted and delayed Longstreet at Rice, and it was Ord's presence at Burkeville which stopped the Confederate advance. It was Ord's move to Rice to confront Longstreet that pinned down the head of Lee's westward thrusting column. It is not surprising that Grant was pleased with Ord's movements, noting that they contributed greatly to the day's successes.[53]

It was, indeed, a day of successes for the Union, for, elsewhere on 6 April, Lee's army suffered disastrous losses. Behind Longstreet stretched a long column of weary infantry and a cumbersome wagon and artillery train pulled by starving horses. Sheridan's cavalry and the Second, Sixth and Fifth Corps of the Army of the Potomac were upon their flank and rear. The cavalry raked the left flank of the column unmercifully, capturing wagons and artillery and impeding the progress of the infantry. The Sixth Corps fell upon the broken column at Little Sayler's Creek and captured about 6,000 men, including Generals Richard S. Ewell and G. W. C. Lee. John B. Gordon's command, Lee's rear guard, strayed from the main Confederate column and was beset by Humphreys's Second Corps at the crossing of Sayler's Creek with casualties numbering about 1,700. The Confederates sustained total losses for the day of about 8,000 casualties.[54]

Following the successes of Sheridan and Meade, Grant dispatched to Ord that Lee's army was almost in a rout and expressed the belief that the Confederates would cross the Appomattox at Ligonton and Stony Point bridges. He directed Ord to send his two divisions to Farmville to hold the crossing there. The lieutenant general apparently was not aware that at this moment Longstreet's force was between Ord and Farmville. It was probably well after nightfall when Ord received Grant's dispatch, and Ord's next action, of necessity, would be to deal with Longstreet on the following day.[55]

After the losses of 6 April, Lee realized the necessity of

transferring his broken army to the protection of the north bank of the Appomattox. Also, the all-important rations brought by rail from Lynchburg awaited the hungry Confederates at Farmville. After witnessing some of the disastrous actions of the day, Lee went to Rice after dark and ordered Longstreet to disengage his troops from Ord's force and proceed to Farmville to the rail and wagon crossings there. The commands of Mahone and Gordon would cross at High Bridge and move up the railroad to Farmville. The river crossings would be burned, and Lee's army might then gain some advantage in their effort to elude Grant.[56]

During the night, Longstreet's men toiled up the muddy road to Farmville, followed by the wagon train and the cavalry. At High Bridge, Gordon's troops passed over the wagon crossing followed by Mahone's division. The engineers of the latter division were to fire both the railroad and wagon bridges. Moving up to High Bridge close behind the Confederates on the morning of 7 April, Humphreys's Second Corps found several spans of the railroad bridge destroyed, but the wagon bridge was only slightly damaged. The Confederate engineers had received belated orders to apply the torch, and the Federals were upon them before they could complete their task. The fire at the wagon bridge was quickly extinguished, and the confident bluecoats crossed to the north bank of the Appomattox and pushed up the railroad toward Farmville close behind the Confederates.[57]

In the meantime, Grant had moved his headquarters to Burkeville, from which point he directed the Fifth Corps and Mackenzie's cavalry to proceed westward to Prince Edward Court House. They would be in position to block the way, should Lee attempt a direct thrust from Farmville to Danville. The Sixth Corps and Ord's divisions were directed to converge upon Farmville. Ord discovered Longstreet's withdrawal early in the morning and pressed on toward Farmville. The pursuit was close, for at times Ord's men had to drive Confederate skirmishers before them.[58]

With Ord and Wright to the south of the Appomattox and Humphreys to the north pressing hard upon Farmville, Lee must extricate his army quickly. As the hungry Confederates marched into Farmville, they found the issue of rations suspended and the trains sent back down the line to Appomattox Station. After the Confederate infantry and wagon trains had crossed the river, the railroad and wagon bridges at Farmville were burned. With such safety as this afforded, Lee must now push along the main road westward until it intersected the railroad again. The rail line was south of the river all the way, and there was no access to the Confederate supply trains nearer than Appomattox Station.[59]

Ord and Gibbon rode into Farmville, the former making his headquarters in the Methodist Church and the latter in a nearby home. Grant came up from Burkeville and established himself at a hotel. That afternoon, Ord and Gibbon visited the lieutenant general at the hotel, and there ensued a free discussion of the military situation. Grant told the two generals that he intended calling upon Lee to surrender. He had spoken in a similar vein to General Wright.[60] Accordingly, a letter timed at 5 P.M. on 7 April was dispatched under flag of truce to Confederate headquarters north of the river and was received there sometime after 9 P.M. After pointing out the "hopelessness of further resistance" on Lee's part, Grant stated that he felt it his duty to shift from himself "the responsibility of any further effusion of blood" by asking for the surrender of the Army of Northern Virginia.[61]

Lee's reply of the same date was delivered to Grant in Farmville early the next morning, 8 April. The Confederate commander did not agree that further resistance was hopeless. He reciprocated Grant's desire "to avoid useless effusion of blood," but, before considering the surrender proposal, asked Grant to state the terms he would offer.[62] Grant's reply was immediate: "Peace being my great desire, there is but one condition I would insist upon, viz, that the men and officers surrendered shall be disqualified for taking up arms again against the Government of the United States until properly exchanged."[63] The Union leader offered to meet Lee or to appoint officers to meet Lee's officers anywhere to work out the terms of surrender.

Under orders given on the night of 7 April, the pursuit of Lee continued on the morning of the eighth. Sheridan's cavalry, including Mackenzie's command, rode westward through Prince Edward Court House and on to Appomattox Station to attempt the capture of the Confederate supply trains and to head off the retreating Southerners. Wright's Sixth Corps crossed the Appomattox at Farmville on Ord's pontoon bridge and joined the Second Corps following directly upon Lee's rear. Meade was with these two corps.[64]

Grant expected to receive a reply to his second note to Lee

and wanted to stay in position to communicate readily with the Confederate commander. Accordingly, after dispatching to Stanton on 8 April that he was confident of receiving Lee's surrender the next day, he crossed the Appomattox and joined Meade and his two corps.[65]

Ord's command marched up the railroad toward Lynchburg at daylight. Before leaving Farmville early on 8 April, Ord issued an order relieving General William Birney of his command of the Negro division and directing him to report to City Point for duty. Ulysses Doubleday's brigade was assigned to Foster's division and W.W. Woodward's to Turner's division. James Shaw's brigade had been left behind to guard the railroad and was not mentioned in the order.[66]

By Grant's special direction, Meade was ordered to have Charles Griffin's Fifth Corps, then at Prince Edward Court House, to follow Ord's force up the road toward Lynchburg. As Ord put it, Grant gave him directions "to pick up Griffin's corps" and follow "on the heels of Sheridan" to intercept Lee's army.[67] In making this disposition, it seems clear that Grant wanted Sheridan to harass the fleeing Confederates and to impede their progress, but cavalry would not be enough. It seems equally clear that Grant wanted an infantry commander whom he could trust to move the troops and to fight. Ord was the man. With Grant's departure to join Meade, Ord was now the ranking officer of the Union column south of the Appomattox which included his own infantry, the Fifth Corps and Sheridan's cavalry.

CHAPTER

13

★★★★★

To Appomattox

EDWARD Ord rode out of Farmville at the head of his
column with most favorable portents for the march ahead.
The weather was fine and the roads in excellent condition. The
troops were wildly enthusiastic. They had discarded all unnecessary impedimenta in anticipation of a long hard march. The
soldiers well understood their task and the importance of head-
ing off the fleeing Confederates. With John W. Turner's division in the advance, followed by Robert S. Foster's, they
marched steadily westward.[1]

About noon at Prospect Station, Ord found Major General
Charles Griffin's Fifth Corps waiting to fall in behind the Army
of the James. The general was met in the road by a party of Fifth
Corps officers who were now under his command. He greeted
these men of the Army of the Potomac courteously, and they
reciprocated heartily. Among the officers was Brigadier General Joshua L. Chamberlain of Maine who commanded two
brigades. Chamberlain, one-time Bowdoin professor and
winner of the Congressional Medal of Honor, thought the
preference given to Ord's troops on the road was proper,
considering the general's rank. But he and the other officers of
the Fifth Corps wondered if there were reasons other than
military that Ord's army "should be sent around to the extreme
left to cooperate with Philip Sheridan, while the Army of the

Potomac was dismembered and divided right and left."² One can only speculate on this point, but, as already noted, Ulysses S. Grant knew the capabilities of Ord and Sheridan and wanted them in the forefront of the campaign; he either did not trust George G. Meade or did not want him to get in position to carry off a lion's share of glory.

The forward movement continued, and Ord's men doggedly kept on, passing Walker's Church as the afternoon began to wane. Ord rode along the column observing the progress of his men on this tiring march. He sternly restrained one of his staff officers who was ordering the infantry from the road to expedite his passing. The general took the roadside himself rather than inconvenience his weary foot soldiers.³

At one point, heavy firing was heard toward the front in the direction Sheridan's cavalry had taken, and the tired men were inspirited by the prospect of engaging the hard-pressed Confederates. However, after a time, the firing ceased, and Ord sent orders to his subordinate commanders to bivouac for the night. Just as the troops were marching to their campsites, a dispatch was handed to Ord from Sheridan at Appomattox Station reporting that he had captured the four trains of cars loaded with rations which the desperate Southerners were trying to reach, along with a hospital train and twenty-five pieces of artillery. The cavalry commander begged for infantry support. Ord did not hesitate. He dashed to the head of his column, quickly countermanded his order to encamp, and directed that the march continue. The nearly exhausted men responded with a renewed effort as the news of Sheridan's success spread at once, and the need to get assistance up for the morrow was fully realized. They kept going beyond the dusk and into the night. About midnight, a halt was called a few miles from the hamlet called Appomattox Court House. Few attempted to make coffee; most simply fell to the ground to sleep.⁴

Only three or four miles to the north of Ord, the head of the Confederate column under General John B. Gordon wearily approached Appomattox Court House late in the afternoon of 8 April and encamped. The rear guard, which had been closely pressed all day long by Andrew A. Humphreys's Second Corps, was about six miles from the Court House. Robert

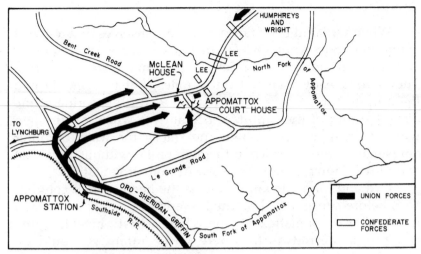

Appomattox Court House, 9 April 1865

E. Lee made his headquarters about two miles from the village. The Confederates must move westerly in the morning on the Lynchburg road. This would take them through Appomattox Court House and past Appomattox Station about three miles away. On this Lynchburg road and on either side of it near the Court House, Sheridan had planted his cavalry. Lee expected to push through them.[5]

Grant was with Meade's army close upon Lee's rear. About midnight on 8 April, he received Lee's reply to his note of early morning. The Southern leader stated that he had not intended to propose the surrender of his army, but rather to determine Grant's terms which might lead to peace. He offered to meet Grant between the lines on the following morning at 10 A.M. to negotiate.[6] At an early hour of the morning of 9 April, Grant responded to Lee that he had no authority to treat on the subject of peace and that the proposed meeting would be to no avail. He affirmed his own desire and the desire of the North for peace, saying that the terms on which peace could be secured were well known. "By the South laying down their arms they will hasten that most desirable event. . . ," he wrote.[7] Having dispatched this answer to Lee, Grant left Meade's column just west of New Store, crossed the Appomattox, and passed through Walker's Church to the road on which Ord's force was moving.[8]

★★★★★

When Ord and his infantry threw themselves down to rest at midnight on 8 April, Ord felt that he could not afford himself and his men more than a brief respite. They were bone tired. They had already marched thirty miles, but the general had them up in three hours. At 3 A.M. on 9 April, cheering at the distant sound of the captured locomotives which cavalrymen were running up and down the tracks for want of other amusement, they hurried into their ranks without breakfast and moved down the road toward Appomattox Station.[9]

Ord and John Gibbon rode past the head of their column, and, before sunrise, had reached Sheridan's headquarters at a house near Appomattox Station. Over a hasty breakfast, the generals conferred as to where Ord's infantry should be placed.[10] As the senior officer, Ord had the final word and bore ultimate responsibility for the disposition of the forces at Appomattox Station. He did, in fact, command all of this mighty force of infantry and cavalry.

Ord's infantry was near at hand, for the Twenty-fourth Corps had halted about 4 A.M. near Sheridan's headquarters and massed in a large open field where they stacked arms. The men occupied themselves preparing breakfast and catching up on their sleep. The Fifth Corps was close behind, moving from their camp at 4 A.M. and nearing Sheridan's headquarters about 6 A.M.[11]

As Ord's infantrymen were moving up to Appomattox Station, the remnant of Gordon's corps of the Southern army numbering about 1,600, supported on the right by the 2,400 cavalrymen of Fitzhugh Lee, moved down the Lynchburg road about 5 A.M. to clear the way for the Confederate wagon train and for Longstreet's corps. The Rebel yell, the crack of musket and carbine, and the booming of artillery signaled the onslaught of the Confederates upon the Union cavalry line. Ord's men had to make a final surge to check this thrust. Under orders from Ord, Gibbon directed the Twenty-fourth Corps to continue its movement to the west in order to get across the Appomattox to Lynchburg road. Then the corps would be in position to swing back on that road and to press in upon Appomattox Court House from the south and west, meeting the Confederates head on. At the same time, Ord directed Griffin's Fifth Corps to be deployed in line and faced directly toward Appomattox Court House. On its left, it would join the

Twenty-fourth Corps and the general direction of its movement would be from the south and southeast. The terrain was rolling and wooded with now and then an open field.[12] Much depends on Ord's disposition of forces, for, if the troops could be placed in time, the two corps would block the entire valley in which Lee's escape route lay.

Ord's men approached the Appomattox-Lynchburg road about 6 A.M. Firing became heavier in front of them, and Foster's division in the lead covered the last half-mile at double-quick. Retreating bodies of Sheridan's cavalry showed that the Confederates were making a determined effort to break through and that the horsemen were not able to hold the ground. Foster's division was formed across the Lynchburg road, fronted toward Appomattox Court House and just in time. Immediately before them, the cavalry was desperately trying to stem the tide. As Colonel Thomas O. Osborn's brigade of Foster's command deployed, the cavalrymen holding the horses for their dismounted cohorts became demoralized and rode through the infantry line in several places. Horses frightened and unattended also broke through the ranks of the foot soldiers.Osborn's battle line was broken up three times before the troops were rallied. They were formed without a moment to spare, for a force of Confederate infantry came out of the woods in hot pursuit of the fleeing cavalry. A volley from the blue ranks checked the shouting Confederates and sent them scurrying back in confusion. As it chanced, Ord's troops were coming to the aid of their own, for Ranald Mackenzie's cavalry division had been placed immediately on the Lynchburg road about a mile and a half from Appomattox Station. Confederate infantry attacked their front, and cavalry, their left flank. The arrival of Ord's force extricated his command from a dangerous position, Mackenzie reported.[13]

Osborn's men advanced with great enthusiasm even though both of their flanks were exposed. In time, Colonel George B. Dandy's brigade was placed on the left of Osborn and Colonel W.W. Woodward's Negro brigade on the extreme left. Colonel Harrison S. Fairchild's brigade was en echelon in support. Two batteries were brought up to take part in the forward movement, and a strong skirmish line was thrown to the front.[14]

Ulysses Doubleday's brigade of black troops was on the Lynchburg road immediately in rear of Foster at the moment

Sheridan's cavalry was being routed. Cavalry skirmishers and their supports "pressed in a panic-stricken mob along my line, through which they vainly tried to break," Doubleday said.[15] Confederate infantry pushed the cavalry so closely that Sheridan, who was on the field at this point, ordered Doubleday to break out of the infantry column, form a line of battle on the right, and push the enemy back. Upon encountering Doubleday's line the Southerners fell back in disorder and were pushed for half a mile by the Union skirmish line. The Confederate pressure on the right of the road which caused the diversion of Doubleday also caused Gibbon to throw Turner's division into the woods to the right. Making connection with Foster on his left, Turner pushed the Confederate infantry before him in the general advance upon the Court House.[16]

After seeing to the placement and progress of the Twenty-fourth Corps, Ord rode to Griffin's Fifth Corps to see to its place in line beside the Twenty-fourth. The corps made connection with the Twenty-fourth on the right of Turner's division, and encountered much the same situation in its advance as the Twenty-fourth. General Romeyn B. Ayres's division of the Fifth Corps was hurried forward at double-quick and deployed in two lines of battle with David L. Stanton's brigade on the left, Joseph Hayes's on the right, and James Gwynn's in support of Stanton. The lines were formed barely in time to rescue the retreating cavalry and to check the vigorous charge of the Confederate infantry. Joseph J. Bartlett's division was formed in two lines of battle to the right of Ayres. Edgar M. Gregory's brigade was on the left of the division, Alfred L. Pearson's in the center, and Joshua Chamberlain's on the right. With a strong skirmish line to the front, the Fifth Corps pressed forward. Following orders from Sheridan, the cavalry moved off to the right as the foot soldiers came to their relief.[17] Thus, under Ord's direction, his infantry command of two corps relieved Sheridan's cavalry and converged upon the little hamlet of Appomattox Court House.

★★★★★

General John B. Gordon, commanding the Confederates facing Ord's two corps, was forced to report to General Lee about 8 A.M. that he could do no more without help from Longstreet. Lee sent for Longstreet, and the latter, as well as General Mahone, advised surrender. The Confederate commander sadly determined to go to Grant and surrender his army on terms laid down in Grant's note of 8 April providing for parole of the surrendered troops. Lee mounted about 8 A.M. and rode to the rear, as he supposed Grant was with Meade's army pressing closely upon the Southern column. At Meade's skirmish line, Lee was met by Lieutenant Colonel Charles A. Whittier, assistant adjutant general to General Andrew A. Humphreys who commanded the Second Corps of Meade's army. Whittier delivered Grant's note to Lee of early morning, sent before he left Meade's column, in which the Union commander had stated that he had no authority to treat for peace. Lee immediately responded with a note requesting an interview to arrange for the surrender of his army on terms indicated in Grant's letter of the day before. This communication was dispatched through Colonel Whittier about 9 A.M. Lee realized that he had not notified Gordon of his intention to surrender, nor had he authorized Longstreet to send out a flag of truce. He dispatched a courier with this intelligence.[18] The time was about 9:30 A.M.

★★★★★

On the Lynchburg road, Ord's infantry and artillery steadily advanced upon Appomattox Court House, and the Confederates so recently on the offensive were routed and forced to flee in a confused mass. Over the rolling country, the retreating Southerners would appear on the crest of a hill and then be completely lost to sight, only to reappear on the next slope. The Federal skirmish line pressed them hard, the men forgetting their long night march, their short rations and their lack of sleep.[19]

Foster received intelligence that the enemy was moving to his left, which held the possibility that they might swing around his left flank. To prevent this, he brought up Fairchild's brigade from its supporting position, put it on that flank, and then gradually moved with his entire force to the left until he reached the Bent Creek road. This road from the northwest intersected the Lynchburg road about a half-mile from the Court House. Doubleday's Negro brigade rejoined Foster's command at this point. Turner's division meanwhile had pressed on through the woods and fields until their battle line approached open ground upon a crest overlooking the Court House.[20]

In the advance of the Fifth Corps, General Charles Griffin rode with his staff and colors between the skirmish line and the first line of battle. His division commanders, Joseph J. Bartlett and Romeyn B. Ayres, with their staffs and colors, were conspicuous as they rode with the skirmish line on the extreme front. It was a majestic sight as the great formation emerged from woods and swept relentlessly across the open fields. From the crest of hills ahead, Confederate artillery fired at the approaching Federals, but their aim was too high, and they did little damage. Soon the Southern artillery was caught up in the retreat of the gray infantry and all pushed pell-mell back to Appomattox Court House.[21]

Ord established his headquarters near Appomattox Court House in a residence conveniently located between the Army of the James and Fifth Corps, a central position from which he might direct operations. From this point, the general and staff swept across the Fifth Corps front on reconnaissance, reaching the extreme right of its battle line as it neared the town.. He issued precautionary orders to Chamberlain commanding the brigade on the extreme right, warning him that enemy artillery was massed to rake the crest of a ridge directly ahead. They pushed on in spite of the danger and reached the top of the rise. In the valley below "as in an amphitheater" was what remained of Lee's army, infantry massed, artillery parked or standing in column, cavalry moving here and there. A courthouse and a few houses constituted the town.[22] Some of the Fifth Corps skirmish line entered the town itself and "there was a strange mingling of blue and gray uniforms in the streets."[23] The Union skirmishers began to pick up prisoners. With Ord's two corps of infantry bearing down upon them and Sheridan's cavalry reforming on the right and preparing to charge in, the Confederates were in a precarious position. Suddenly a white flag appeared borne by a mounted Confederate officer. The time was about 10 A.M.

The flag of truce met General Ord at the Fifth Corps front.[24] There was more than one flag of truce, and it cannot be determined with certainty which one reached Ord. Colonel Green Peyton of Gordon's staff was sent by his commander to seek out General Ord and request a truce. Peyton encountered George Armstrong Custer of the cavalry who sent word to Sheridan that the Confederates wanted to surrender. Custer then rode into the Confederate lines and successively encountered Gordon and Longstreet and demanded that the Confederates surrender to him, but, in each instance, was rebuffed.

Another flag of truce was borne by Captain R.M. Sims of Longstreet's staff. He, too, encountered Custer, but was given an escort to go to other parts of the Union line.[25] Perhaps it was his flag seen by Brevet Brigadier General Charles S. Wainwright, chief of artillery of the Fifth Corps, who was placing some guns at a point where the Army of the James and Fifth Corps joined. As he was unlimbering his guns, "a flag of truce came galloping up to the house in front of which Ord had his headquarters, when all firing was immediately stopped."[26]

Ord, knowing that a surrender had been called for and terms asked for by Lee and set forth in response by Grant, realized that the flag of truce meant acceptance by Lee of Grant's terms. He did not hesitate to order that the buglers sound the cease fire.[27] The general was exultant in this moment of triumph, not only for the success of his own efforts, but also for the thousands of men under his command who had made the victory possible. Chamberlain dramatically pictured "the gallant, gray-haired Ord, galloping up cap in hand" and shouting "your legs have done it, my men."[28]

Meanwhile, Sheridan had ridden to the Court House with his staff and escort where he met Generals John B. Gordon and Cadmus M. Wilcox. Gordon requested a truce until Lee and Grant could confer. Sheridan was not inclined to grant a suspension of hostilities unless he had some assurance of surrender, pointing out that so far as he knew nothing had been settled in the correspondence between Grant and Lee and that the recent attack on his line had been made by the Confederates with a view to escape under the impression that the Union force was only cavalry. Gordon assured Sheridan that Lee's army was to be surrendered. The two agreed to meet again at the Court House in half an hour with their respective senior officers—Ord with Sheridan, and Longstreet with Gordon.[29]

As Ord with his staff and escort rode down from the ridge toward the Court House, the scene about him was indeed remarkable. The two armies were in plain view of one another, the Federals on the crest of hills overlooking the village, the Confederates along woods on the other side of town. Through an opening in the trees the wagon trains of the Southerners could be discerned. There were perhaps two dozen houses in the village scattered along two streets, and, at the center, rising above the other buildings, was the two-story brick courthouse, plain and square and with a dome-like roof. This scene was a noisy one, for the Union soldiers were shouting and cheering exultantly, while up and down the line bands were blaring with abandon.[30]

On the outskirts of the village, General Ord left most of his staff and escort and advanced with a few general officers including Sheridan and certain staff members to the courthouse. Longstreet approached and there followed handshaking and introductions. Among those present in this strange encounter of Blue and Gray were Union Generals Gibbon and Griffin, who commanded Ord's two infantry corps; Wesley Merritt and George Crook of Sheridan's command; Ayres, Bartlett and Chamberlain of the Fifth Corps. Confederates present besides Longstreet and Gordon were Generals Henry Heth and Cadmus M. Wilcox and Colonel Charles Fairfax. In the course of the fraternizing at the courthouse steps, flasks of whiskey were produced by the participants. Enemy drank the health of enemy in this incongruous period of peace, where only moments before they had been fighting to the death. Some of the conferees sat on the steps of the courthouse, others stood in the street, and still others sat on a nearby fence and chatted.[31]

Sheridan did not like Ord's armistice, and, according to Chamberlain, did not make any effort to hide his views. "He is for unconditional surrender, and thinks we should have banged right on and settled all questions without asking them." All of the Confederate officers "assure him of their good faith and that the game is up for them."[32] Indeed, Longstreet had brought with him a dispatch, a duplicate of the one sent by Lee through Meade's line earlier in the morning, in which the Southern commander asked for an interview to arrange for the surrender of his army. This dispatch was sent by Ord to Grant with Colonel F.C. Newhall of Sheridan's staff as the bearer.[33]

Ord and Longstreet retired from the group at the courthouse steps and engaged in a lengthy private conversation. It was strange that these two men who, only a scant two months before, had met under a flag of truce—at Ord's solicitation—in an effort to bring about peace should now meet again with the same object in view. There is no full account of what the generals said, but Ord did tacitly consent to the cessation of hostilities proposed by Lee to Grant, and it was understood between Ord and Longstreet that there would be no troop movements on either side. The conference lasted approximately an hour and a half, during which time it was expected that Grant would arrive. By noon, the lieutenant general had still not appeared, and Ord and his party rode back to the Union lines.[34]

For the time, General Ord had the power to dispose of matters as they involved the armies at Appomattox Court House. He had at his command some 30,000 seasoned campaigners poised to strike at the old enemy. It was a decisive moment in a great civil war. But he withheld the blow. Without hesitation, he assumed the responsibility of an armistice, and thereby saved the lives of many good men in blue and gray. He had chosen the way of peace. Perhaps it was the Sheridan view reflected in a *New York Times* dispatch stating that the suspension of hostilities "was caused by an agreement made by General Ord consenting to a cessation of firing so as to communicate with General Grant, and was done, it is said, without proper authority."[35]

★★★★★

General Lee remained on Meade's front after sending his first note of the morning to Grant at about 9 A.M. In spite of the note, the troops of Humphreys's Second Corps began to press forward to attack. Repeated requests were made by the Confederates that the advance be suspended, but Humphreys was under direct orders not to allow the negotiations to interfere with his operations. He pressed on. Lee himself was personally force to withdraw.[36]

Lee's note to Grant of 9 A.M. reached Meade at about 10 A.M. It was read by him and then sent on to the lieutenant general. Meade himself went forward to his front, arriving just in time to suspend an attack upon the Confederate rear. Shortly after 11 A.M., Meade sent a note to Lee agreeing to an informal truce for one hour. Lee received this message between 11 A.M. and noon.[37] At this time, Ord's truce had been in effect for approximately an hour.

Lieutenant Charles E. Pease, the bearer of Lee's dispatch to Grant, overtook the Union commander at 11:50 A.M. about four miles west of Walker's Church. Grant immediately wrote out a reply in which he stated that he would push forward to the front to meet Lee and that Lee might send word to him on the

Farmville-Lynchburg road as to where their meeting to arrange the surrender might take place. Grant sent Lieutenant Colonel Orville Babcock of his staff with this dispatch and with orders to take the most direct route to Lee. Grant and his retinue proceeded on in the direction of Appomattox.[38]

★★★★★

Ord and Longstreet were ending their lengthy interview at the courthouse about the time Babcock rode off to find Lee. Either at the conclusion or shortly before the conclusion of the interview, Sheridan sent his chief of staff, Brigadier General James W. Forsyth, through the Confederate lines to consult with Meade. Forsyth told Colonel Walter H. Taylor, Lee's assistant adjutant general, that Sheridan doubted his authority to recognize the truce agreed to by himself and General Gordon. By implication, this would cover the truce made by Ord and Longstreet. Forsyth was to confer with Meade about the matter.[39]

At the moment of Forsyth's arrival on Meade's front about noon, Meade was writing a dispatch to Lee apparently in response to a letter just received from the Confederate. Meade stated to Lee that he had no authority to suspend hostilities unless it was with the clear understanding that Lee was prepared to surrender on the terms already advanced by Grant. He would forward Lee's letter to Grant, but suggested that the Southern leader might more readily communicate with Grant through other parts of the Union line. "I am now advised by General Forsyth," Meade continued, "that a cessation of hostilities has been agreed upon between your command and General Ord."[40] In view of this existing truce and to enable Forsyth to report his action, Meade agreed to an armistice until 2 P.M., which he said he would prolong upon hearing of Lee's agreeing to Grant's terms.[41]

★★★★★

An uneasy period of waiting followed Ord's parting from Longstreet and his return to the Union lines. At 12:25 P.M., Ord sent a firmly worded dispatch to Lee in which he stated that a movement of trains or troops seemed to be in progress from Lee's army toward the west and that it had gone on for some time. "I have ordered as part of the suspension of hostilities a cessation of all movements," he wrote to Lee. "I expect the same order on your part."[42]

It was probably about 1 P.M. that Ord received the second note from Lee to Grant to pass through his hands. The first had been sent on by Colonel Newhall; the second was written by Lee in pursuance of Meade's suggestion that Lee attempt to communicate with Grant through some other part of the Union line. The note contained the same request for an interview.[43]

At 1:10 P.M., Ord sent a dispatch to Meade, no doubt in view of the impending expiration of the truce on Meade's front, which had less than an hour to run. He asked Meade to extend the truce. Ord noted that he had received the two notes from Lee to Grant asking for an interview to arrange for the surrender of Lee's army. The appearance of the troops and trains of Lee's army indicated no preparations for battle. "In my personal interview with General Longstreet I tacitly assented to the proposed cessation of hostilities, made in the letter to General Grant. . . . I am quite sure that General Grant if present would grant the cessation asked for," he continued, "and hence agreed to it and hope you will do the same on the assurance of General Lee that no move will be made by his troops or others cooperating therewith."[44]

Ord's position became increasingly difficult as the afternoon began to wear away. By 2 P.M., Grant had still not arrived, and the tense period of waiting had reached a critical point. Ord addressed a dispatch to Grant in which he recapitulated the events of the day including the forced march with his two corps, his blocking Lee's effort to break through Sheridan's cavalry "which could not hold the ground," his driving the Confederates back in the direction of Meade until Lee's request of 10 A.M. for a cessation of hostilities to confer with Grant, and his transmitting Lee's two notes asking for an interview to arrange for the surrender. "I am about to write to him [Lee] a joint note with General Sheridan that unless he surrenders on the terms you offered we must renew the fight."[45]

Ord had not hesitated to assume full responsibility for the armistice and for decisions made on his front. There is no reason to assume that he now sought to share that burden with Sheridan by the "joint note." Properly, Sheridan's force was an independent command, and the cavalry commander reported directly to Grant as did Ord and Meade. Ord was technically the overall commander on his front and would make ultimate decisions under the circumstances, but it is not unreasonable that he and Sheridan should arrive at a common judgment and express their views jointly.

Colonel Orville Babcock left Grant four miles west of Walker's Church at noon to go to Lee to arrange for the meeting of the generals. He was ordered to take the most direct route. There is no evidence to indicate that either Ord or Sheridan knew of his passing through the lines. It is quite apparent from Ord's dispatch of 2 P.M. that he had not seen Babcock and did not know of Grant's note to Lee borne by Babcock. It must be assumed that Babcock went through the lines under a flag of truce at some point other than Appomattox Court House. It is reasonable to assume further that it would require Babcock an hour or so to reach General Lee, who was a half-mile from the courthouse, and that he did reach the Southern commander about 1 P.M. or soon thereafter. Babcock delivered the note from Grant to Lee in which the former stated that he was on the way to the front to see Lee. The Southerner was anxious that the temporary truce be continued meanwhile and asked Babcock to inform Meade of the latest development in the negotiations. Babcock wrote a dispatch to Meade in Grant's name instructing him to continue the truce, and Meade reported receiving such instructions at 2 P.M. when his own temporary truce had expired.[46]

Lee, with his aide, Colonel Charles C. Marshall, and his orderly, Sergeant G.W. Tucker, in company with Babcock, went to the village of Appomattox Court House to find a place for the meeting with Grant. Marshall was sent on ahead to find a suitable room, while Lee and Babcock waited. Eventually, Marshall returned and conducted the party a short distance past the courthouse building to a brick house on the left of the Lynchburg road owned by Major Wilmer McLean.[47] It was about two o'clock, and it may be supposed that, shortly thereafter, word reached Ord and Sheridan that Lee was awaiting Grant at the McLean house. Grant arrived after 2 P.M., having required more than two hours to come by a circuitous route from the neighborhood of Walker's Church to Appomattox.[48] The long wait was over.

Ord, Sheridan and others met the Union commander in the road near the village. After greetings were exchanged, Grant was informed that Lee was waiting in the McLean house. Grant, Ord and Sheridan, along with Grant's staff and a few other officers, rode to the house. All dismounted, and Grant alone went inside to meet Lee. After a brief interval, Colonel Babcock came to the door and motioned for the waiting officers to come in. Ord and those with him entered quietly and ranged themselves about the room, Grant, plainly dressed, was seated in an old office chair in the center of the parlor. Lee, resplendent in full uniform, was across the room near the front window, seated in an arm chair beside a square marble-topped table.[49]

Lee seemed anxious to get on with the business at hand, and, after some casual conversation, suggested that Grant write out the terms of surrender. The Union commander had a small wooden table brought to him and proceeded to address a note to Lee in which he set forth the conditions as follows: that duplicate rolls of the surrendered officers and men be prepared; that officers give individual paroles not to take up arms again until exchanged and officers to sign paroles for their men; that arms, artillery and public property be turned over to officers designated by Grant, but not including the side arms, private horses or baggage of officers; that each officer and man might then return to his home. Lee expressed the hope that Grant might permit Confederate artillerymen and cavalrymen in the ranks who owned their own horses and mules to take these home with them. Grant magnanimously consented. Lee then had Colonel Marshall write out a brief note of acceptance which the Confederate commander placed on the marble-topped table and signed. Lee observed, in further conversation with Grant, that his men were out of rations. Grant offered to send 25,000 rations, judging the remnant of the Confederate army to be about this figure. The Southern commander was manifestly grateful for the consideration shown by Grant.[50]

While the terms of surrender and the acceptance were being copied, General Grant presented Ord, Sheridan and other general officers as well as his staff members to General Lee.[51] As Ord greeted Lee, he may well have recalled their last cooperative encounter at Harpers Ferry in 1859 in a well-remembered moment of the past. Now another, even more momentous, historical occasion was at hand in the great civil war which John Brown had helped to forge. In this moment, Ord, with great skill and energy, had outmarched Lee's army, had confronted the Confederate line with massive force, and had brought the gray giant to a standstill. He could well feel satisfaction, but a satisfaction tempered with compassion.

The formalities were over. Lee took his leave at about 3:30 P.M. Grant and his officers came out as the Confederate mounted. The Northern commander took off his hat in salute, and the other Union officers made the same courteous gesture.

Lee raised his hat in acknowledgment, and then rode away toward his own lines.[52]

★★★★★

General Ord was aware that the actions at Appomattox in which he was a principal participant were of great importance in the life of the nation. He quickly perceived the historical significance of the furnishings of the McLean house parlor, and paid Major McLean forty dollars for the marble-topped table at which Lee had sat and on which he had signed his acceptance of Grant's terms. Sheridan purchased the small table on which Grant had written the terms of surrender, paying McLean twenty dollars in gold. Other items were bargained for, but apparently some mementos were carried away without being paid for. The souvenir hunters were so insistent that McLean had to sell or see his possessions taken away without receiving payment for them.[53]

★★★★★

"Lee's army surrendered today," Ord telegraphed to Molly, anxiously waiting at Fort Monroe for news from the front. "Army of the James did first rate."[54] Indeed, the forced march of the Army of the James and of the Fifth Corps under Ord was an amazing performance—one of the most remarkable feats of the entire war, especially when the result produced is taken into account. The march began at Farmville at daylight on 8 April and ended at Appomattox Court House at 10 A.M. on 9 April, interrupted by only three hours of rest. The men of Gibbon and Griffin had marched for about twenty-six hours, and the units under Ord's command, which had reached the extreme left of the Union line at the Bent Creek road, had covered approximately forty miles. There was almost no straggling, and Ord wrote that he did not think the troops could have behaved better. There was amazement at Ord's feat in another quarter on that morning of 9 April: "General Lee would not believe General [John B.] Gordon when the latter told him that Ord's army was in his front. . .," so Gordon told Ord after the surrender.[55] Others in position to judge Ord's work pronounced it good. Grant had said that Ord was "skillful in the management of troops, and brave and prompt." So he had proved to be. No less a military authority than William Tecumseh Sherman, who knew something about marching, wrote of Ord: "I have always understood that his skillful, hard march the night before was one of the chief causes of Lee's surrender."[56]

★★★★★

Ord's command continued quite active as Grant designated the Twenty-fourth and the Fifth Corps to remain at Appomattox under Gibbon's command to carry out the surrender agreement. Gibbon, Griffin and General Wesley Merritt, second in command to Sheridan in the cavalry, were appointed commissioners to work out the details of the surrender with Confederate commissioners. Colonel Michael P. Small, chief commissary of Ord's army, was assigned the task of supplying the promised 25,000 rations to Lee's army. Ord's acting chief quartermaster, A.B. Lawrence, was ordered to take charge of all captured and surrendered property and stores. Mackenzie's cavalry and Turner's division were sent to receive the surrender of Lynchburg. They captured large quantities of guns and supplies and paroled hundreds of Confederates.[57]

★★★★★

The final campaign in Virginia from 29 March through 9 April had cost the Union 1,316 killed, 7,750 wounded and 1,714 captured or missing.[58] The Confederacy had lost its most important army and its general-in-chief. That the cause of the South could be kept alive in the face of the accomplishment of Ord and his fellow Union combatants seemed now a remote possibility.

General Ord probably accompanied Grant to his second interview with Lee which occurred on the morning of 10 April. About noon on that day, Ord left Appomattox in company with Grant. Their small party rode to Burkeville on horseback and there entrained for City Point. Frequent breakdowns on the hastily rebuilt railroad delayed their arrival until an early hour on 12 April.[59] Grant's ultimate destination was Washington; Ord's was Richmond, where the immediate problems of that war-scarred city and of the entire Department of Virginia would occupy his attention in the weeks ahead. Ord approached his difficult task in the same spirit of conciliation which had marked his effort to bring the fighting to an end at Appomattox. This "spirit of Appomattox" he quite felicitously expressed in his report of the surrender: "The rebels laid down *our* arms that night—it is to be hoped never to take them up again except in defense of our common country."[60]

CHAPTER

14

★★★★★

In Vanquished Richmond

EDWARD Ord's first action at City Point was to telegraph to Molly Ord, waiting in Richmond with two of their children, that he would come up by steamer in the course of the morning. Then his telegram continued: "Send word to Mrs. General Lee that her husband and sons are quite well, are paroled, not prisoners, but the general is going to Danville on business and will soon be with her. She can telegraph to him now through General Gibbon at Appomattox Court House."[1] This thoughtful concern for the invalid Mrs. Robert E. Lee was an indication of the conciliatory direction Ord's policies in Richmond would take. Actually, the general's reputation had preceded his coming, for even as the pursuit of Lee was in progress and word spread of the occupation of Richmond by Ord's army, the *Danville Register* stated that people in that city acquainted with General Ord had reason to hope that his treatment of the people of Richmond would not be "so hard, and cruel and inhuman" as that accorded the citizens of some other captured places.[2]

On the morning of 12 April, Ord took leave of Ulysses S. Grant at City Point and boarded a steamer which conveyed him up the James River to Richmond. Following the winding waterway, Ord passed Aiken's Landing near his old headquarters, then through what had been his own lines for so many months and through the Confederate defenses now stark and abandoned. The course of the James was in the rear of and parallel to the Confederate defensive lines extending northward to the fallen Confederate capital. How strange to be on the enemy side of Chaffin's Bluff and in the rear of Fort Harrison, which he had wrested from Robert E. Lee's firm grasp! As Ord approached the landing, Richmond lay before him, substantially in ruins. The bridges over the James were charred or mangled wrecks, while a large part of the business district was a blackened mass of brick walls, chimneys and heaps of rubble.

Ord made his headquarters in the mansion recently vacated by President Jefferson Davis. To this already famous place came Mathew Brady, photographer, to make a pictorial record of scenes and personalities of the historical phenomenon that was the American Civil War. Brady made plates of General Ord and staff on the steps of the Davis Mansion, in one of which the general stood in a quite unmilitary, hands-in-pockets pose. Several other pictures featured the surrender table, Ord's trophy of war from the Wilmer McLean house. The table was in the background as General and Mrs. Ord and nine-year-old Bertie, their oldest child, posed on the porch of the mansion. The two ladies in the picture were fashionably dressed, attractive Molly Ord, thirty-four years of age, in a demure pose. The general at this time was forty-six years of age and distinguished in appearance. He was of average build, his posture military, his well-defined features firmly set. An unruly shock of gray hair crowned his head, and, in that bewhiskered age, he was clean-shaven save for a moustache.[3]

Ord found the attitude of the citizens of Richmond cordial and cooperative. The people of the city had apparently expected a general pillage of the place, but, when they realized they were not to be harshly treated, they reached out hospitably to the occupying force. Placidus Ord, who had entered with Godfrey Weitzel's troops, remarked that the cordial reception was quite in contrast with the bitter feeling he had encountered previously in New Orleans.[4] The paroled officers and men of Lee's army in Richmond expressed to General Ord their trust in the United States and sought to merit confidence in return. The general was able to report within a week after his arrival: "Generals W.H.F. Lee, Heth, Pickett, Alexander, and others, and many prominent and formerly wealthy citizens, are asking me what they shall do to make their bread, expressing their great desire to co-operate with this Government if they

General Ord and the surrender table. U. S. Signal Corps photo No. B-1753. *(Brady Collection) National Archives.*

General and Mrs. Ord and daughter Roberta. U. S. Signal Corps photo No. B-5091. *(Brady Collection) National Archives.*

General Ord and Staff. U. S. Signal Corps photo No. B-167. *(Brady Collection)* *National Archives.*

can have peace and protection."[5] This was certainly an auspicious beginning for Ord's policy of conciliation.

★★★★★

Ord's first official act of consequence on the day of his arrival in Richmond was to order Weitzel and his entire Negro corps from Richmond to a position south of Petersburg. This removed Shepley from his position as military governor. It will be recalled that Secretary of War Edwin M. Stanton had already expressed to Grant a desire that Shepley be removed. The decision to order the black troops out was made by Grant before he and Ord parted company at City Point on 12 April.[6]

Ord's handling of the Negro corps had already excited adverse comment. At Farmville, on 8 April, he had broken up the division of black troops of the Twenty-fifth Corps and had sent its commander, General William Birney, to the rear to a nominal command. The exact cause of Ord's action is not known, but there were a number of indications that Birney's work was not satisfactory.[7] Birney himself had other ideas as to why he was relieved, and he unburdened himself to his old chief, General Benjamin F. Butler. He was removed, he wrote, for the same cause that had led to the displacement of a host of functionaries of the Butler regime and to efforts to unseat Weitzel. "After you left," continued his missive to Butler, "it was understood that to be a 'Butler man' was to be damned.

. . ." Ord's discrimination against the Negro troops on the final campaign, Birney said, was "so marked as to attract general attention." He threw them to the rear, to the flank, gave them the hardest work, encamped them where there was no water, separated them without cause from their supply train, and "kept them back from the front whenever he could." Continued Birney: "He was much chagrined at my getting into Petersburg first and censured me for it—although I should have been severely censured if I had permitted the town to fall into the hands of pillagers."[8] The same thought was relayed by Weitzel to Butler: "The 25th Corps not only entered Richmond first, but Petersburg also. Birney thinks he was shelved because his *'niggers'* were most wide awake and discovered the evacuation and went in first at Petersburg."[9]

Ord's management of the black troops was in keeping with his previous attitudes on matters racial and political. In the words of young Colonel S.S. Seward, the general was "very conservative." This convervatism meant that Ord was willing to forgive rebellious Southerners and forget their sin of secession if they would but return to the Union. Further, it meant that the black people should be free, but, as they were unprepared to assume responsibilities, they would have to be looked after. These views stand in contrast with those of Birney, a self-styled Radical, with those of Butler, and with those of many others that the Southerners must be punished and their ex-slaves elevated. Ord probably thought of the war as an unfortunate encounter between gentlemen brought on by unscrupulous politicians. It may well be that if he had had his way, there would have been no Negro soldiers enlisted in the Union army. It seems clear that he looked upon Birney's division as auxiliary to the white troops, though it must be said that they had come under fire on the Appomattox campaign and had acquitted themselves well.

In the light of Ord's attitude toward the Negro corps, it seems likely that he wanted the black soldiers out of Richmond, at least in part, because their presence would be offensive to the white citizens there. Weitzel, at any rate, thought so. "But you know the niggers had to leave there," he wrote to Butler. "The smell was offensive to the F.F.V.'s."[10]

The matter was not yet at rest, for Ord was determined to have the entire corps removed from Virginia. The conduct of the Negro soldiers gave rise to complaints, and, though Weitzel defended them, Ord's wishes prevailed. All of the black troops in the department were assigned to the Twenty-fifth Corps, and the whole ordered to Texas.[11]

R.M.T. Hunter and Judge J.A. Campbell appeared at Ord's headquarters on the morning of 14 April and earnestly pressed the general for permission to go to Washington to confer with President Lincoln. It may be surmised that they desired to influence the president to bring about an armistice and to restore the Union along the lines already advanced by Campbell in conversation with Lincoln at the time of the president's visit to the fallen Confederate capital. Their plea elicited from Ord a telegram timed at 11 A.M. and addressed to President Lincoln, stating that the two Southerners desired a permit to visit him in Washington, "I think with important communication."[12]

The dispatch was apparently delayed in transmission for it was marked "Received 9:30 P.M." at the War Department. A messenger promptly conveyed the communication to the White House. As President and Mrs. Lincoln had gone to Ford's Theater for an evening of entertainment, S.P. Hanscom, editor of the *National Republican*, offered to serve as bearer. Hanscom proceeded to the theater, entering the presidential box sometime after 10 P.M. and handing the telegram to the president. This was the last dispatch of this long and bloody war to be read by Abraham Lincoln.[13]

About 10:30 P.M., another figure furtively entered the presidential box and approached the president from the rear, pistol in hand.

In the very early morning hours of 15 April Ord received a telegram timed about midnight which began: "The President was assassinated at Ford's Theater at 10:30 to-night and cannot live. The wound is a pistol-shot through the head."[14] After lingering for nearly nine hours, Lincoln was pronounced dead at 7:22 A.M. on 15 April.

General and Mrs. Grant had been invited to accompany President and Mrs. Lincoln to Ford's Theater on the evening of the fourteenth, but the general and his wife were anxious to visit their children who were in school in Burlington, New Jersey, and had left Washington early in the evening. Word of the assassination reached them en route, and the general returned to Washington on 15 April. At 4 P.M., Grant sent a telegram to Ord which must be read not only in light of the assassination but also in view of the fact that a state of war continued to exist and that armies were yet operating in various places throughout the South:

> Arrest J.A. Campbell, Mayor Mayo, and the members of the old council of Richmond, who have not yet taken the oath of allegiance, and put them in Libby Prison. Hold them guarded beyond the possibility of escape until further orders. Also arrest all paroled officers and surgeons until they can be sent beyond our lines, unless they take the oath of allegiance. The oath need not be received from any one who you have not good reason to believe will observe it, and from none who are excluded by the President's proclamation, without authority of the President to do so. Extreme rigor will have to be observed whilst assassination remains the order of the day with the rebels. [15]

The assassination of Lincoln was a terrible crime, producing a great shock all across the North. The usually stolid Grant was caught up in the angry revulsion of feeling which seized the people. The "rebels" were held responsible and there was a demand for retaliation, for punishment, especially of Confederate leaders believed to be parties to an assassination conspiracy.

Grant's dispatch placed Ord in an agonizing position. To obey orders was a requisite of his position and a habit of a lifetime. But to obey this order would destroy the fragile structure of good will he was so carefully building in Richmond. Ord replied:

> Cipher directing certain parties to be arrested is received. The two citizens I have seen. They are old, nearly helpless, and I think incapable of harm. Lee and staff are in town among the paroled prisoners. Should I arrest them under the circumstances I think the rebellion here would be reopened. I will risk my life that the present paroles will be kept, and if you will allow me to do so trust the people here who, I believe, are ignorant of the assassination, done, I think, by some insane Brutus with but few accomplices. Mr. Hunter and Campbell pressed me earnestly yesterday to send them to Washington to see the President. Would they have done so if guilty? Please answer. [16]

Ord's calm response contrasts sharply with the excitement in Grant's directive. It required courage on Ord's part to balk in the face of direct orders from higher authority. But the stakes were too high in this instance for blind, unthinking obedience. He would risk his life that Lee and his officers and soldiers were honorable men and would keep their word and that the citizens of Richmond were worthy of trust. Ord had sized up the assassination with uncanny judgment: done by an "insane Brutus with but few accomplices."

Twelve hours after the death of the president, General Grant had recovered a measure of stability:

> *On reflection I will withdraw my dispatch of this date directing the arrest of Campbell, Mayo, and others so far as it may be regarded as an order, and leave it in the light of a suggestion, to be executed only so far as you may judge the good of the service demands.* [17]

The assassination of Lincoln interrupted another effort at conciliation in which Ord was involved. On 14 or 15 April, Congressman Elihu B. Washburne of Grant's Illinois district arrived in Richmond. Washburne had come directly from Appomattox Court House whither he had gone in the wake of Grant's pursuing force and where he had witnessed the laying down of Confederate arms. Washburne conferred with Ord in Richmond, and their views were in agreement. At noon on 15 April, the congressman dispatched to the president: "I do trust you will not deem it necessary to call an extra session of Congress. I believe it would lead only to evil." Of the Confederate army at Appomattox, he said: "I talked with a large number of their general officers, and found a much better spirit than I had anticipated."[18] Ord sent an accompanying communication: "I heartily indorse Mr. Washburne's telegraph. The change in sentiment here, after contrasting the past tyranny with the present unexpected good order and freedom, makes me think your proclamation of emancipation will be supported by a majority in Virginia."[19]

Which president was addressed? Abraham Lincoln had expired four and one-half hours before the timing of these telegrams. In the confusion and uncertainty of the moment, perhaps the death of the president was not yet verified in Richmond. From the context, it would seem that Abraham Lincoln was the intended recipient, but it might be that the senders hoped to produce an effect upon the policies of Lincoln's successor. Apparently, Washburne and Ord hoped that the adjournment of Congress until December would deprive the vindictive Radical Republicans of a forum in which to express their harsh views toward the South and thereby spoil efforts at conciliation and reunion.

General Ord's interference in political matters was probably uncalled for in view of his presumably nonpolitical position as a soldier. But here was another instance, so far as he was concerned, where extraordinary measures were called for to advance the significant interests involved. There is no known response to the Washburne-Ord effort, though, for various reasons, President Andrew Johnson did not call a special session of Congress. There was a response to Ord's earlier communication handed to President Lincoln in his box at Ford's Theater. The reply was from President Johnson, conveyed through General Grant: "The President does not desire to see Messrs. Hunter and Campbell, or either of them, at Washington. . . ." There then followed a mild reproof from the lieutenant general: "You are reminded in this connection of the impropriety of addressing the President direct, and requested to address your communications to the lieutenant-general or the Secretary of War."[20]

Ord's work of reconciliation would go on, but the assassination had thrown a dark pall over his efforts. His task would be much more difficult in the weeks ahead.

★★★★★

Two days after his arrival in Richmond, Ord reported his earliest actions to Secretary Stanton: "I am (where I can do so consistent with the interest of the service) kind to the submissive, and I am trying to make the military rule acceptable."[21] To citizens, he granted passes to return to their homes on the same terms that Grant gave to Lee's army—that is, free transportation on government carriers. Five days later, which happened to be the day of Lincoln's funeral, 19 April, Ord sent another lengthy dispatch to the secretary of war in which he described the unsettled conditions in Richmond and recounted the measures he had taken to cope with them. Several thousand men of the Army of Northern Virginia had arrived in Richmond, some of them residents of the city, others en route. Every day, two or three hundred additional Confederates arrived, gave themselves up, laid down their arms, and were paroled under Ord's orders on the same terms as Lee's army. All of these were on the verge of starvation and without money. There were about 25,000 women and children "of all colors" in the city in the same condition. "Labor and bread these people must have," Ord wrote. The destitute were encouraged to leave the city. To expedite the readjustment, canal, railroad and milling companies had been authorized to resume operation. Employment had been provided for all of the black men, and sewing shops were to be opened for the black women. Thousands of Negroes were flocking into town and roaming the countryside. "They should be set to work. We cannot afford to feed them in idleness," the general continued.[22] In reply, Stanton approved Ord's measures to provide employment. He acknowledged that temporary subsistence would have to be supplied, but under a carefully limited policy.[23]

Shortly after Ord's exchange with Stanton, Colonel Adam Badeau reported to the general on the work of the relief commission for Richmond of which he was president by Ord's appointment. Since the capture of the city, 128,132 rations had been issued to about 15,000 people. This was nearly one-third of the population of Richmond. Of those relieved, 500 were paroled Confederate officers and soldiers who received the "destitute ration" from the commission at Ord's direction. Coal and wood were also issued to white and black needy.[24]

In Washington, there was an obvious lack of coordination of views between Stanton and Grant regarding occupation policy, probably occasioned by the unsettled conditions produced by the assassination. Even as Stanton was giving cautious approval to Ord's actions, Grant came down hard on Ord to check his lenient policy toward paroled Confederate soldiers. On 18 April, Grant directed Ord not to issue any more forage or subsistence to parolees and ordered that the accumulation of some 3,000 of them at Fort Monroe awaiting water transportation be turned back and forced to make their way home through the country. The strong reaction to the assassination was still apparent in Grant's stern language. In another message of the same date, the lieutenant general directed Ord to forbid his provost marshal general to issue any more passes for parolees to go to Washington or to the loyal states.[25]

Ord protested to Grant that the railroad and canal routes had been destroyed; there were no horses, mules or carriages; the money of the Confederates was worthless; they could not get work; they had no food. "It would be absurd to expect them, with the bridges through the country burnt, to foot it away. . . ," he said. Indeed, some whose lands had been confiscated for freedmen's farms had no homes. Many had wives and children with them. "If I am not authorized either to feed them or send them away by the most expeditious routes I cannot be responsible for the consequences," Ord concluded.[26]

Grant had just come from the funeral of President Lincoln when he composed his reply: "We cannot undertake to bear all the hardships brought on individuals by their treason and rebellion," he began. "It was no part of the agreement that we should furnish homes, subsistence, or transportation to Lee's army after the surrender."[27]

Grant's dispatch concluded with the information that General Henry W. Halleck would start for Richmond the next day and would "take up and settle all present difficulties." Halleck was to command the newly created Military Division of the James to include the Department of Virginia, part of North Carolina, and the Army of the Potomac. Thus, the former chief of staff was placed over both George G. Meade and Ord.[28]

Ord issued an order in the latter part of April providing for free transportation to Halifax for paroled officers if they wished to go abroad. Stanton revoked the order.[29] On 1 May, Ord was authorized by Halleck to provide transportation without charge for paroled prisoners and their families to Atlantic and Gulf Coast cities as far as New Orleans. Suddenly, the authorization was withdrawn by higher authority. "These people can't get home except by turning highway robbers on the road. . . ," Ord expostulated to Grant.[30] Finally, Grant authorized Halleck to transport all parolees at Fort Monroe to their homes.[31] Ord won that struggle after all.

A distasteful task fell to Ord during May and early June when he was directed to arrest and imprison several former Confederate officials, some of whom had held high positions. These included James A. Seddon, former secretary of war; R.M.T. Hunter; John A. Campbell; and Robert Ould, former commissioner for the exchange of prisoners.[32]

Ord found a more agreeable task in expediting General Lee's application to President Johnson for amnesty as offered in the president's proclamation of 29 May 1865. By this executive pronouncement, Johnson had required that high civil and military officers of the Confederacy should make special individual application to him in order to have their civil rights restored.[33]

Lee determined to set an example for the South by making application. In the meantime, Federal Judge John C. Underwood had asked a grand jury at Norfolk to indict Lee for treason.[34] Nevertheless, Lee persisted in his desire to make application and undoubtedly conferred with Ord who sought to pave the way for favorable action in Washington. Ord worked quietly through Brigadier General Rufus Ingalls, chief quartermaster of the army. Ingalls, one of Grant's classmates at West Point, was, like Ord, interested in promoting reconciliation. The lieutenant general being absent from Washington, Ingalls went to see General John A. Rawlins, Grant's chief of staff, who assured him that, if Lee would take the oath and ask for pardon, "General Grant will cheerfully advise the President to grant it." Ingalls then consulted a number of men presumably close to President Johnson who assured him that the president would give full pardon. All of this information Ingalls sent to Ord in a confidential letter, advising that Lee should forward his papers through Ord to Grant right away. "If successful there will be great benefits following to all concerned," Ingalls concluded.[35]

On 13 June, Lee wrote to Grant and enclosed his application for pardon. Grant endorsed the letter by condemning Judge Underwood's effort to secure the indictment of Lee, since the latter was a paroled prisoner of war. This, Grant sent to the secretary of war. At the same time, he forwarded Lee's application to President Johnson with an "earnest recommendation" that the president extend pardon to Lee. Grant noted that the oath of allegiance required by recent order of the president to accompany the application was not found, and he was informed by Ord that the order requiring it had not reached Richmond at the time Lee's papers were forwarded.[36]

As it turned out, the matter proved to be disappointing to Ord. Several weeks later, on 2 October 1865, the very day on which Lee was inaugurated as president of Washington College, he went before a notary public and took the amnesty oath. The document was sent to Washington. Under mysterious circumstances, the oath became lost among State Department records, and President Johnson took no action on Lee's application. The Confederate commander died in 1870 without having his citizenship rights restored.[37]

The Department of Virginia eventually was divided by Ord into districts and subdistricts with commanders charged with duties of military occupation, including the superintending of Negro affairs within their respective jurisdictions. Toward the latter part of May, this organization embraced more than fifty counties with principal occupation forces at Petersburg, Fort Monroe, Norfolk, Lynchburg, Fredericksburg, Charlottesville and Williamsburg. The restoration of civil government was begun with the arrival of Governor Francis Pierpont in Richmond on 26 May.[38]

The commanders in all parts of the state reported to Ord that the people were cooperative and that they desired to take the oath of allegiance to the United States. Local officials were often among the first to come forward to renew their loyalty. All who applied were permitted to take the oath. Confederate soldiers continued to trickle in to the various cities to be paroled, and many of them also renewed their allegiance.[39]

Relief to those at the point of starvation was a first requisite. The issuance of rations to the poor in Richmond continued. By Ord's order relief committees were established in Petersburg and Manchester to supervise the issue to the destitute there. In Lynchburg, abandoned Confederate property was issued to the poor. Colonel E.V. Sumner, Jr., reported to Ord in the middle of May that he was issuing 700 rations daily in Fredericksburg and vicinity. Generally speaking, in the rural areas there was food enough, though there were specific instances of distribution ordered by Ord.[40]

More important in the long run were those actions taken by the occupation authorities to reopen trade, encourage industry and business, and enable farmers to put in a crop.

Shortly after Lee's surrender, Grant had issued an order lifting restrictions upon trade in Virginia and other areas. This did not meet the problem, for such trade as was carried on was done by permit from agents of the Treasury Department. Halleck and Ord sought to have these trade permits revoked. Though Stanton made strong representations to President Johnson in the matter, the Treasury Department continued its control.[41]

Ord had initiated a policy carried forward by Halleck of returning railroads and canals to the corporations which shared ownership of them jointly with the Commonwealth of Virginia. Quartermaster General Montgomery Meigs objected to the plan, saying that the facilities should be placed under the Board of Public Works of Virginia, which generally controlled three-fifths of their stock. This was adopted, though the state then turned over the facilities to the companies for operation.[42]

Early in the occupation, Ord requested that the superintendent of mails for the army establish post offices in the towns of the department "in order that the citizens may have facilities for resuming and carrying on their business." In addition, on 14 May, Ord called to Halleck's attention the fact that all of the telegraph lines were military lines and suggested that they be opened to private business transactions. Halleck so recommended, and the Washington authorities approved. In general, Ord believed that all who had taken the oath could resume their business "and military authorities will render them all assistance in their power."[43]

The recovery of agriculture was much complicated. Aside from the problems associated with the unsettled condition of Negro labor, there were many difficulties arising from the devastation of war. From all parts of Virginia, reports came in to Ord of the scarcity of animals. Also in short supply were seeds, implements and harness. Those areas which had been in the paths of the armies were hardest hit. In a number of instances, Ord ordered the distribution of captured Confederate supplies and unclaimed property for the use of poor farmers. More generally helpful was the sale to farmers of condemned government horses and mules.[44] In some places, citizens were reportedly not able to buy necessary equipment to make a crop, but there is practically no evidence of issue to them gratis by the military in these early days of occupation.

General Ord had inherited from Butler an organization to look after displaced and unemployed Negroes in that portion of Virginia behind the Union siege line at Richmond and Petersburg. Butler had expanded upon work began earlier in the war by Charles B. Wilder of the American Missionary Association, who was later commissioned a captain and placed in charge of Negro affairs. Under the already existing wartime arrangement, work had been provided for the black people; farms were established for the employment and support of those not otherwise gainfully occupied; and schools were opened for black children.[45] With the pacification of Virginia, many more thousands of Negroes had to be looked after over a vast area embracing most of the state. As already observed, many flocked into towns and cities without food and without any means to earn their keep.

Colonel E.V. Sumner, Jr., at Fredericksburg, reported to
Ord that Negroes displaced from that area during the war were
returning "possessed in some cases with an idea that they are
to be the owners of the Plantations where they were former
slaves."[46] They were roaming about unwilling to work and
expecting to be fed. In the Petersburg command, General
George L. Hartsuff reported the same condition.[47] On the other
hand, General J. Irvin Gregg stated that the Lynchburg area
was quiet. "Negroes are orderly and disposed to remain on the
plantations and work," he wrote.[48] Colonel Samuel B.M.
Young, commanding a brigade of cavalry near the same place,
reported that few planters wanted to pay the Negroes for
working, but wanted them to work as before, or leave. General
Alvin C. Voris at Louisa Court House made a similar report to
Ord, noting the "very creditable efforts" of the freedmen and
absence of vagrancy among them.[49]

Repeatedly, orders were issued by Ord requiring that all of
the freedmen should work. No rations were to be issued to
those capable of work. Where possible, they might be recon-
ciled to their former masters, but they were not to be forced to
work for them. They could make their own bargains. In
Petersburg, a regular employment bureau was established to
serve as a clearing house for the placing of labor, the work
agreements to be made under the supervision of the officer in
charge of the bureau.[50]

Where it was possible to control the movements of the
Negroes to keep them from becoming a burden, Ord instructed
that this be done. Women and children were furnished free
transportation out of Richmond if they could support themselves in the country, thus relieving the terrible congestion of
the Virginia capital. Stringent orders were issued to subordinate commanders everywhere to keep the black people from
coming into the towns.[51]

In the unsettled conditions prevailing in Virginia, it was
not possible for individual enterprise either in the country or in
towns to provide employment for the thousands of displaced
and destitute freedmen. The United States government had
to provide.

In Richmond, Ord attacked the employment problem by
appropriating money from the Civil Fund and establishing a
clothing bureau. Negro women were set to work making clothing for destitute members of their race. They used captured and

condemned tents, wagon covers, and, eventually, raw wool and cotton which they made up into cloth. Ord later reported that, at the time he was relieved from command in June, 17,000 suits were almost finished and about 100,000 yards of cloth were on hand.[52]

Ord directed the superintendents of Negro affairs in the Norfolk area to gather the unemployed women and hire them out. Should there be no demand for their labor, they were to be set to work as nurses, to make clothing or to wash for prisoners or for other Negroes, or to be detailed as laundresses and sent to the companies of the Twenty-fifth Corps in which they claimed to have husbands. If all else failed, they were to be gathered into buildings in which would be opened "a grand *general* washing establishment for the City, where clothing of anyone will be washed gratis." Hard work and restriction, Ord believed, would cause them to seek employment, and the "ultra philanthropists" would not be shocked.[53]

The most comprehensive effort by far to provide for the Negroes was in the establishment of farms for them on abandoned or confiscated land. They were furnished with seed, implements and condemned cavalry and artillery animals to enable them to make a crop. Farms were established in all parts of the state, in some instances for abandoned women and children whose husbands and fathers had wandered away. Labor contracts were to be made with able-bodied freedmen on the government farms. Ord notified his subordinate commanders that the wage paid to Negro laborers should be the same as the soldiers' pay with deduction for rations. Ord reported to Stanton that he would provide funds to operate various mills, apparently in connection with the farms. "Think I can make the Department of Negro Affairs self-sustaining," the general stated to the war minister.[54]

General J. Irvin Gregg at Lynchburg posed a question to Ord about the subsistence of abandoned women and children on plantations where the owners were unable to support them. Gregg reported numerous cases of this sort, and, from other indications, the problem seemed widespread. The farmers were "disposed to do right," Gregg thought, but had not the means to support the nonproducers until a crop was made. The Lynchburg commander suggested that he be authorized to issue rations which could be paid for in kind. He further stressed the necessity for the husbands and fathers of the deserted freedmen to return to look after their kin. Ord approved the issue until the farmers could sell anything to pay for the rations. Tobacco might be taken in payment. Ord enjoined Gregg to issue on these terms only when the planter was willing to keep families together. "You will do all in your power to prevent the able-bodied men from deserting the women and children and old persons, and when practicable send them back," Ord advised.[55] Two days later, the general sought information from his district and subdistrict commanders regarding the need for implements so that they might be issued to farmers who were "unable yet willing to support the helpless members of families of laborers necessary to cultivate their lands."[56]

The task confronting Ord and his command in Virginia was staggering. As early as 11 May, the general estimated that about 100,000 Negroes were "under the direction of government agents and dependent upon them for labor, food, and clothing."[57] The recently established Freedmen's Bureau then about to be organized within the War Department would soon take over the work among the Negroes in a comprehensive and systematic fashion.

★★★★★

Ord's pronounced concern for the welfare of Confederates in Virginia and his stern regulation of the freedmen caused the Radicals to take notice. One Burnham Wardwell, an acquaintance of General Butler, wrote to the latter of the freedom and privileges enjoyed by the Confederate officers and soldiers in Richmond. "Vile murderers walk our streets at will," he said. "We want Butler back."[58] After elections were held in Richmond, Wardwell wrote Butler that all important offices were filled by "violent secessionists" and that the latter were "looking quite as independent as they did when receiving the smiles of Major General E.O.C. Ord who was all smiles to violent and wealthy *Traitors.*"[59] General William Birney, stationed at Wilson's Landing, wrote Butler in exasperation: "I cannot believe that the War Dept. is aware of what has been going on in this Dept. since you left it."[60] U.H. Painter, correspondent of the *Philadelphia Inquirer*, wrote in the issue of 19 April of the privileges enjoyed by Confederate officers in

Richmond and was critical of Ord's policies. Ord was sufficiently provoked that he asked the inspector general of the
army to investigate and took occasion to detail the restrictive
regulations he had placed on the Confederates.[61]

Ord's departmental provost marshal general, General
Marsena R. Patrick, noted in his diary under date of 7 June 1865
that a number of Ord's orders had been revoked by higher
authority and that he himself was having trouble carrying out
orders in relation to Negroes because of the interference of
Northern people. Patrick blamed a (New York?) *Tribune* correspondent for sending material to his paper apparently critical
of the Ord regime which had provoked an investigation by
Washington authorities. Halleck was sent for to give a report
in person.[62]

Just what part Ord's conservatism played in the termination of his command in Virginia cannot be precisely determined. It is reasonable to assume that it was a significant factor
and possibly the deciding one. Certainly his policies had become controversial, and neither Stanton nor Grant, from the
tenor of their responses to Ord, were inclined to go along
sympathetically with his leniency toward the "rebels" and his
handling of the blacks. Halleck, in spite of a reputation for
Radicalism, fell in with a number of Ord's policies and seemed
actually to have been influenced in several important matters
by Ord. Though he may have had a hand in Ord's transfer, it is
not apparent that he was responsible for it.

Sallie A. Putnam, who experienced the Richmond occupation, cited Ord by name along with others of the Federal military for their kindness. "They softened greatly the first bitter
experience of our subjugation," she wrote.[63] Ord had done
what he could to heal the wounds of war, but his course in
Virginia had been run. On 14 June, he was directed to report to
the adjutant general for orders. On 15 June, he departed from
Richmond.[64]

CHAPTER

15

★★★★★

King Otho I
(of Mississippi and Arkansas)

EDWARD Ord's new command was the Department of the Ohio embracing the states of the Old Northwest with headquarters in Detroit. This placed him in William T. Sherman's division. Sherman had had enough of war, and the division commander wrote Ord that he proposed "to let things subside to a chronic state of peace."[1] However, there were for Ord some exciting events from time to time to absorb his energies and to provide that action he found so necessary as an antidote to his restlessness. Striking iron miners at Negaunee, Michigan, interfered with trains and mail, and Ord sent troops to protect lives and property. Race riots at Cairo, Illinois, prompted the general to suggest that the Negroes there be distributed by families where their labor was needed. The Fenians, Irish revolutionaries, threatened invasion of Canada from bases in Ord's department.

The condition of peace required that a reorganized military establishment be crystallized out of the vast Union army of the Civil War. In this new hierarchy, Ord was given a prominent place. In August 1866, he received the coveted commission as brigadier general of the regular army along with appointment as brevet major general. The powerful influence of General Grant no doubt counted heavily, but it was imperative also that senators recommend to President Johnson that he appoint Ord. The petition on Ord's behalf bore the names of twenty-one senators of both parties, including such notables as J.W. Nes-mith, John Sherman, Reverdy Johnson, S.C. Pomeroy and T.A. Hendricks. Under the new army organization, Ulysses S. Grant was listed as general, Sherman as lieutenant general, five division commanders as major generals, and ten depart-ment commanders including Ord as brigadier generals.[2]

Ord passed a little over a year in Detroit in what, for him, were relatively calm circumstances. His tenure in the Old Northwest was terminated by an order of 6 August 1866 assign-ing him to the Department of the Arkansas, including the state of Arkansas and the Indian Territory to the west with head-quarters in Little Rock. He proceeded promptly to his new post.

Ord found the Arkansas capital hardly more than a frontier village. Little Rock was the largest place in the state, and, before the displacements of war, had counted all of 3,727 inhab-itants. Cholera and other maladies were ravaging the populace at the time of Ord's arrival. The soldiers of the garrison were very hard hit, about one-third of them being ill. Food items when obtainable were extravagantly priced.[3]

Ord's new command was actually a frontier in process of development—perhaps arrested development in view of the disruption of war. Arkansas had been a state only thirty years. Her population had been 435,450 in 1860 with 111,115, about 25 percent, being slaves. The slaves were located principally in the eastern and southern parts of the state in the rich valleys of the Mississippi, Arkansas, White and Ouachita Rivers. In the up-country to the north and west, there were small farms. The census had indicated substantial numbers classified as "farm laborers" and "laborers," giving rise to the possibility of a rather unusual competition between free white labor and slave labor.[4] The undeveloped frontier character of the country was further seen in the fact that only about one-fourth of the land was included in farms, and, of this, only about one-sixth was improved land. Incident to the frontier were lawlessness in remote areas, a high rate of illiteracy, deficient or nonexistent schools, very little manufacturing, and rather primitive trans-portation facilities.[5]

To accomplish his many tasks, Ord had 1,041 men, none of them mounted. To effectively keep order, he needed mounted troops. "I might as well send snails to catch antelopes as send Infantry . . . to arrest violators of law in Arkansas," the general complained.[6] Most of the troops were required in the Indian

Territory. Fortunately for Ord, the Indian problem was not serious, though wild Indians made occasional forays on the frontier to steal horses. As the Indians of the plains had all the best horses and he had none of any description, the general could do little to apprehend these raiders. "About one footman to sixty Indians" was Ord's estimate of the odds against him.[7]

★★★★★

By the time Ord came into this Arkansas command among his recent enemies, significant political events in the line of reconstruction had already taken place. Lincoln had established or accepted Union governments in Arkansas, Louisiana, Tennessee and Virginia. The government in Arkansas, established in 1864, was endorsed by President Andrew Johnson in 1865. Governor Isaac Murphy, a Unionist, held the executive authority in this regime, but, in elections held about the time of Ord's arrival, Conservatives, mainly ex-Confederates, gained overwhelming control of important state offices and of the legislature. Unionists and ex-Confederates began a feud with political and economic implications. There were complaints of violence, including murders of freedmen. Ord was impelled to issue a general order instructing his local commanders to arrest persons (regardless of color) who might be charged with crimes where civil authorities were unable or unwilling to apprehend them. Those arrested were to be held until a proper judicial tribunal was ready to try them.[8]

This was the unpromising condition when, on 26 October 1866, in addition to his other duties, Ord was appointed assistant commissioner of the Freedmen's Bureau for Arkansas. The Bureau of Refugees, Freedmen, and Abandoned Lands, to use its full title, had been created in the War Department under an act of Congress of 3 March 1865. The bureau was under the direction of Commissioner Oliver Otis Howard with an assistant commissioner in each Southern state. The agency had supervision over the objects named in its title and was specifically authorized to issue relief supplies and to settle freedmen on abandoned lands. A second act, passed over President Andrew Johnson's veto on 16 July 1866, extended the life of the bureau for two years and considerably enlarged its powers. The agency was to cooperate with private benevolent organizations interested in the welfare of freedmen and might lease buildings for schools for the Negroes, with teachers to be provided by the charitable groups. The Freedmen's Bureau was to have judicial powers to secure the civil rights of all. This provided for the establishment of bureau courts to adjudicate where the civil rights of freedmen were involved.[9]

Arkansas's Negro population was estimated at 110,000 in 1865, with more than 42,000 of these located in nine counties, principally in the rich valleys. Labor was in demand on the cotton plantations,[10] which meant that there were few refugees, and the bureau issued few rations, though the agency did maintain hospitals for indigent freedmen.

Shortly after his appointment as assistant commissioner, Ord wrote to Commissioner Howard challenging a report of his predecessor that freedmen's rights were being neglected and that murders of freedmen were numerous. The disposition of the educated and intelligent people of Arkansas was to treat Negroes well, Ord said. The legislature had just considered a civil rights bill which was certain to be passed at its next session.[11] As for the killing of Negroes, the general cited cases in which civil authorities had apprehended and punished murderers of freedmen and loyal whites. The ignorant and passionate do commit murders, and "in the remote regions, [where] forests and swamps abound, and population is very scant, it is difficult for Civil authority to arrest or confine the guilty, but the murders are not confined to any color or side in politics." There are always two sides to every question, Ord wrote to Howard. "Bullies and blackguards are alike, North and South."[12]

Yet, as time went on, Ord received regular reports from bureau agents that whites were murdering Negroes or committing outrages upon their persons or property. Ord cracked down on lawless elements with Circular Order No. 30 of 14 December 1866. He noted the attacks on freedmen and pointed out that civil authorities frequently refused to take cognizance of them. He authorized bureau agents who observed such negligence to make use of United States marshals to arrest offenders, and to call upon nearby military posts for assistance. Ashley County was particularly troublesome. Negroes were so maltreated there that Ord threatened to remove all of the freed people for their safety. Of course, he had no authority to make such wholesale removals, but the threat had the desired effect. Outrages upon freedmen dropped dramatically.[13]

The general believed the trouble was a matter of economics as well as race. There were in the state, he wrote to Howard,

"many poor and laboring white men who feel themselves ag-
grieved and degraded at having to compete with negroes as
tenants or laborers, especially where the negroes underbid
them. . . ."[14] They would be glad to have the Negroes driven
out. Where these white people had Negroes among them, they
would disregard laws for the protection of freedmen or elect
only such officials as would not punish outrages upon them.
This prejudice or caste feeling was violently manifested in any
instance where a Negro sought to protest an injury or redress a
wrong, "then," said Ord, "the pistol, worn by almost every
white man in Arkansas, settles the dispute. . . . As the negro is
servile, ignorant and unused to firearms, one white man can
dictate to a hundred negroes."[15] In this very realistic appraisal,
the general stressed that the prejudice he described was characteristic of all whites, not just ex-Confederates.

Agents of the bureau were sometimes defied, insulted and
even assaulted, and Ord firmly defended them. At the same
time, he sought to educate the landlords to a more tolerant
view of the agency. He enjoined agents to "carefully and courteously" impress upon the landowners that the bureau's purpose was to protect the only agricultural labor available to
them, and that, if necessary, the freedmen could find other
lands on which to subsist. Once "intelligent gentlemen" were
convinced of the mutual benefits resulting from cooperation
with sensible agents of the bureau, prejudice against agents
would cease, "except among the ignorant and unreflecting."[16]

To further complicate relations between the races, the cotton crop harvested in the fall and winter of 1866-67 was poor.
In addition, the exorbitant federal tax on cotton further reduced
profits. Ord protested to Howard that the tax ought to be
removed. In the pinched circumstances, there were reports
from local agents at Camden and Monticello that Negroes were
driven off the plantations by their employers at the time the
crop was "laid by" to avoid awarding the freedmen their
share. Ord sent troops to Helena in January 1867 to hold planters to the terms of their contracts with freedmen, as the conclusion of cotton picking was the time of settlement between the
parties concerned.[17]

The planters were not entirely at fault. There were complaints by agents in Jacksonport and Camden that freedmen
did not live up to the terms of their contracts. Early in March
1867, the general issued a circular order directing agents to hold
freedmen strictly to the terms of their contracts and to have

them returned to the plantations from which they had wandered off, unless abuse had caused their departure. Agents were to cooperate fully with civil authorities in execution of laws where freedmen were concerned.[18]

General Ord pursued an even-handed course in the matter of racial adjustment. His actions were responsible in some measure for improved conditions. More than one local bureau agent noted that his Circular Order No. 30 had produced results in better treatment of Negroes.

★★★★★

Under Ord's administration in Arkansas, the judicial functions of the Freedmen's Bureau were only slightly developed. President Johnson refused to support the provision for bureau courts, and Howard was forced to tell his assistant commissioners to use their own judgment about what matters they would adjudicate and how they would interpret their judicial powers. Ord chose to make very limited use of bureau courts. He directed that local bureau agents should cease their judicial functions except in certain specified minor matters and let civil courts adjudicate where they were operating without hindrance. One of the matters Ord placed under the jurisdiction of agents was enforcement of work contracts.[19]

★★★★★

Education of the Negroes was an important function of the Freedmen's Bureau, and General Ord supported and encouraged the effort in Arkansas. The bureau leased school buildings; missionary and charitable groups in the North provided and supported the teachers.[20]

Leading whites in Arkansas were aware of the benefits to be derived from educating the freedmen, but they feared that bureau supervision of Negro education would encourage social equality. Most ordinary whites were opposed to Negro schools and had a lordly contempt for the missionary teachers who came from the North to instruct the largely illiterate black population. The Negroes themselves were eager for schooling and made some effort to help pay the costs.[21]

In March 1867, when a change of assignment for Ord removed the bureau work from his immediate supervision, there were 23 schools, 24 white and 3 black teachers, and 1,091 pupils with 771 in average attendance. A few of the school buildings were owned by freedmen. The sum of $320.80 was paid in tuition by 453 pupils. Total support from all sources during the month was only a little more than $1,000.[22]

Ord took the initiative in increasing the educational offering by polling his agents to determine whether new schools might be established on plantations and what encouragement planters were inclined to give them. The response was favorable. In addition, plans for a graded or model school at Little Rock were being perfected toward the latter part of Ord's tenure as assistant commissioner.[23]

Ord nearly doubled the number of schools for freedmen and substantially increased the number of pupils, but it is clear that the bureau's effort in Arkansas was quite small. Even so, the work should not be entirely discounted. Through the bureau's pioneering endeavor, the Negroes became aware of the meaning of public education; whites became accustomed to the idea of Negro education; teachers were recruited; school property was passed along to later state authorities; and much valuable information relating to the problems of schooling for freedmen was in hand. Subsequent state efforts based on this foundation came to involve much larger numbers of Negro children.[24]

★★★★★

General Ord, along with Commissioner Howard and others in the North, was interested in making the freedmen independent farmers. The Southern Homestead Act, passed by the Congress on 21 June 1866, was supposed to contribute in an important way to the achievement of this worthy objective. It provided that government lands in Alabama, Arkansas, Florida, Louisiana and Mississippi were to be available to freedmen in eighty-acre homesteads, and that former Confederates might not take advantage of homesteading prior to 1 January 1867. The Homestead Act was poorly executed, as Ord discovered. Little provision had been made for surveys. Moreover, the Negroes had no ready means to supply themselves with implements or to support themselves while getting established on the free land. In February 1867, Ord was able to report to Howard that a colony of freedmen had been settled near Fort Smith under the new law, but actually few homesteads were taken up in Arkansas in 1867 and 1868.[25]

Ord's tenure as assistant commissioner of the Freedmen's

Bureau in Arkansas was scarcely of five months' duration. In this brief period, he took a firm stand for order in the face of partisan and racial conflicts. He placed the blame for trouble on both sides. He wanted to trust the educated and intelligent citizens and appealed to their best intentions. At the same time, he found much prejudice and violence expressed toward blacks by whites of all sorts. He undertook to defend impartially the contractual interests of both planters and laborers. He used the judicial power of the bureau sparingly, while advancing the educational and homesteading functions as strongly as he could. In summary, he made positive steps though surrounded by difficult and unsettled circumstances.

Even as Ord was wrestling with the problems of postwar Virginia and Arkansas, the Reconstruction of the Union was proceeding, but upon a troubled path. As already noted, Lincoln had accomplished wartime Reconstruction in four substantially occupied states of the South—Arkansas, Louisiana, Tennessee and Virginia. Upon his accession to the presidency at the close of the war, Andrew Johnson had endorsed the governments in these states and had set forth by proclamation the conditions under which the remaining states of the old Confederacy might resume their customary places in the Union. Johnson's conditions were generous. Wayward Southerners would be pardoned by the president upon their taking an oath of loyalty to the United States. The highest ranking civil and military officials of the Confederacy and the wealthiest citizens must make special application to the president for pardon. Under a Unionist provisional governor appointed by Johnson for each state, the voters were to elect a convention which was to rescind the state's ordinance of secession, acknowledge the end of slavery, and repudiate the Confederate debt. Johnson suggested, but did not require, that qualified blacks be extended the suffrage. Under this lenient plan, all of the former Confederate states but Texas had established governments by December 1865, and, in that month, their senators and representatives sought admission to the Congress. None of the states provided suffrage for blacks. The Congress, though not of one mind, refused to seat the Southerners. Moderate Republicans wanted to prevent ex-Confederate leaders from resuming their powers politically, and they wanted protection for the freedmen. The small but increasingly influential Radical Republican faction would place political disabilities upon ex-

Confederates, confiscate their property and divide it among their former slaves, and enfranchise the blacks to assure Republican ascendancy.

The president and the Congress became locked in a struggle for control of the reconstruction process. In April 1866, the Congress passed a Civil Rights Act defining citizenship so as to embrace the black people and placing civil rights under Federal jurisdiction. Johnson vetoed the bill, thereby driving most of the moderate Republicans into the Radical ranks. The act was readily passed over the president's veto. In similar fashion, the previously mentioned bill extending the life of the Freedmen's Bureau and enlarging its powers became law. Of greater significance in Reconstruction was a constitutional amendment to be known as the Fourteenth Amendment which defined citizenship to include the black people; restrained the states from interfering with the rights of a citizen; limited a state's representation in Congress in proportion to its denial to its citizens of the right to vote; and disqualified from office-holding those who had taken an oath to support the Constitution of the United States when entering upon an office civil or military and then had engaged in insurrection or rebellion against the United States or given aid or comfort to its enemies, though the disability was removable by a two-thirds vote of the two houses of Congress. The amendment also affirmed the validity of the debt of the United States and the invalidity of the Confederate debt. While Negro suffrage was not explicitly mentioned, it was obviously implicit in the congressional proposal. The amendment passed the Congress on 13 June 1866, and was sent to the states to be ratified by the necessary three-fourths of their number.[26]

Ord, while yet in Detroit, observed the struggle over Reconstruction with keen interest and, in view of his conservatism, was greatly concerned over the possibility of Negro suffrage then being proposed by leading Radicals. In January 1866, he wrote to Sherman urging him, Philip H. Sheridan and George H. Thomas to talk to William P. Fessenden, Justin S. Morrill and other leading members of Congress to influence the shape of legislation for the South. Grant, Ord said, was no talker. Ord wanted Sherman to impress upon the political leaders that "only danger lies in the agitation" of the Negro suffrage question. He believed that Negro suffrage was not necessary to the Republican party's retaining power. "You *know* that our soldiers came back from the war more prejudiced against admitting blacks to an equal share of political privileges than they ever were before. I think they will vote almost to a man against such proceeding. . . ." After further comment, Ord said: "The whole subject is a dangerous one, and men who have lived only at the north can not be expected to see the dangers."[27]

In June, just after the Fourteenth Amendment had been proposed by the Congress, Ord wrote to Secretary of State William H. Seward noting that he had read in the newspapers that President Johnson, Secretary Seward and others would visit Chicago soon. Ord expressed the hope that the party would pass through Detroit. "You will find many friends and admirers here," Ord told the secretary.[28] Scarcely a month later Ord wrote again to the secretary of state, commenting on Seward's moderate views and hoping that such words could be spoken in Chicago and in other places in the "growing and powerful country on the upper Mississippi, and on the Missouri." Ord went on to score the Radicals for openly asserting that the president intended ignoring the North and getting up "a sort of southern Congress." Such efforts were designed "to rekindle and maintain the animosities of a state of war." The intent of the Radicals, Ord went on, was to array the people on their side as the only security for the North on the one hand against the president and the South as the combined enemy of the North on the other. "What a rebuke to such nonsense," Ord wrote, if the president surrounded by his Cabinet, his generals and admirals, such as Grant, Sherman, Thomas and David G. Farragut, would visit the heart of the country and address the people.[29] There was no doubt about Ord's stand in the matter of Reconstruction.

In August, about the time Ord set out for his new assignment in Arkansas, President Johnson began his famous "swing around the circle," in which he visited Chicago and many other important cities. Though surrounded by his Cabinet, his generals and admirals, his speaking tour was a political disaster. Heckled and ridiculed, Johnson lashed back intemperately, losing dignity and bringing his office into contempt. In the congressional elections which followed in November 1866, Johnson suffered a great defeat. Nothing stood in the way of the Congress seizing control of Reconstruction.

★★★★★

The Congress did indeed move, and in a manner which was to affect Ord very directly. On 2 March 1867, the national legislature passed the Reconstruction Act dividing the Southern states into five military districts for reconstruction purposes and setting forth the congressional terms by which the former Confederate states might be readjusted to the Union. By direction of President Andrew Johnson on 11 March 1867, Ord was assigned to the command of the Fourth Military District, comprising the states of Mississippi and Arkansas with headquarters in Vicksburg.[30] His task was to carry out the will of Congress in the execution of its Reconstruction terms.

The Reconstruction Act began with the assertion that no legal state governments or adequate protection of life and property existed in ten of the Southern states. The district commanders were to protect all persons and punish all criminals, allowing local civil courts to try offenders, or, when necessary, to organize military commissions or tribunals to take jurisdiction. All interference by state authority with military power under the law was declared to be null and void.

The Reconstruction law went on to prescribe the conditions under which the states might be restored to their places in the Union under the direction of the district commanders. They were to form constitutions in agreement with the Constitution of the United States. The constitutions were to be made by conventions elected by voters regardless of "race, color, or previous condition," who had been residents of the state for at least a year prior to the election of the convention delegates. The constitutions must provide that those qualified to vote henceforth should meet these same conditions as to race, color, etc. The constitutions were to be ratified by a majority of the registered voters and submitted to the Congress for approval. The legislatures elected in the states under these constitutions were to ratify the proposed amendment to the Constitution commonly referred to as Article Fourteen, and, when this article had become a part of the Constitution of the United States, the states were entitled to representation in Congress, and the military rule would cease. Those disqualified from holding office under the proposed Fourteenth Amendment to the Constitution of the United States might not be delegates to the state conventions, nor could they vote for delegates. Thus, the white Southerners disfranchised under the Reconstruction Act were those who had previously taken an oath to support the Constitution of the United States when entering upon an office civil or military, state or Federal, and then had engaged in insurrection or rebellion or gave aid or comfort to the enemies of the United States.[31]

"The power thus given to the commanding officer over all the people of each district is that of an absolute monarch," President Johnson remonstrated in a vigorous but vain veto message.[32]

Ord, whose usual inclination was to restlessly seek change, in this instance found himself in a position unsought and unwanted. He wrote to Senator Henry Wilson of Massachusetts that he was opposed to the congressional plan "in toto." His similar expressions to Grant caused the acting secretary of war to say of the district commanders in an allusion to Ord that they would execute the law " 'faithfully without bias from any judgement of their own as to merit or demerit of the law.' "[33] This was certainly not an auspicious beginning for Ord. His pronounced conservatism would render his new assignment distasteful, to say the least. "I think I can manage the Indians better than I can the whites," he wrote to Sherman upon learning of the possibility that the Indian Territory would be removed from his command and Mississippi put in its place. "I wish I could get out of this military governor business and out of the South,"[34] A few days later: "Grant won't let me go on to Washington for fear I will beg off, I suppose, but I have determined to stick it out. . . . In the mean time, my dear General, I shall write you from time to time perhaps to ask advice, perhaps to get consolation."[35]

The *Little Rock Daily Arkansas Gazette*, leading Conservative Democratic journal, expressed pleasure upon Ord's appointment. The universal sentiment of the people of the community was, as the *Gazette* expressed it, "that his course toward them had been that of a patriotic soldier and liberal-minded gentleman, and if military rule they must endure, they have no preference for any other officer in the service as district commander."[36]

Ord proceeded to his new headquarters in Vicksburg in the latter part of March and shortly journeyed on to Jackson. This same route he had known under other circumstances in 1863. The general observed the terrible marks of wartime devastation still evident in the Mississippi capital. Once a flourishing town of 3,199 people, Jackson had been subjected to wanton destruction. Ord himself had had a hand in tearing up the railroads, but that was simply the more polite aspect of the matter. The torch had been applied to the business district and to many residences. Soldiers had ransacked the town taking what they wanted and vandalizing what remained. Sherman himself had described the city in 1863 as "one mass of charred ruins," and in his report had deplored the "tendency to plunder and pillage."[37]

In Jackson, Ord would deal with the state government created under Andrew Johnson's plan of Reconstruction. The president had appointed William L. Sharkey, Mississippi Unionist and former Whig, to be provisional governor. Under Sharkey's general direction, an election had been held in October 1865, and General Benjamin Grubb Humphreys, an old Whig and one-time Confederate brigadier, unpardoned by the president, was elected governor. The judges of the High Court of Errors and Appeals who were elected were all members of the "secessionist" party. The congressmen were all old-line Whigs except for one Union Democrat. The legislature promptly passed a Black Code restricting the civil rights of Negroes and denying them political rights. The body refused to ratify the Thirteenth and Fourteenth Amendments.[38] This was the government with which Ord had to work and which, though declared illegal by Congress, like the Murphy regime in Arkansas would function on a stand-by basis while the general performed his work of reconstruction.

In Jackson, Ord was the guest of Governor Humphreys. Humphreys later recalled that Ord called upon him at the governor's office, and that they had a "long and pleasant interview." Of their conversation, the governor wrote:

> He frankly admitted the delicacy of his task, and so often used the expression, "I hope, Governor, we may so cooperate as to make our task easy." I asked him to explain what he understood by my "cooperation." He replied that as his education was entirely military and having spent his life on the frontier or in camp, he knew but little about civil affairs, and hoped that I would so administer the civil affairs of Mississippi as not to become an impediment to the reconstruction he was obliged to enforce.[39]

On this visit to the Mississippi capital, Ord made a favorable impression. The *Jackson Daily Clarion* noted that, since the end of the fighting, the general had shown "a spirit of magnanimity and justice" toward the people of the districts in his command. The *Clarion* editor, Ethelbert Barksdale, took pains to point out that Ord was the officer who had conferred with General Longstreet about Grant's willingness to negotiate with Lee following the failure of the Hampton Roads conference early in 1865. The journalist believed that Ord would administer the Reconstruction Act with fairness.[40]

★★★★★

The Mississippi of old was a far cry from the Mississippi over which Ord ruled. The agricultural economy of cotton and slavery had been bountiful. Peerless Natchez, pearl of the plantation domain, had once been the wealthiest city per capita in the United States. The population of the state in 1860 had been just under a million. Blacks outnumbered whites 436,631 to 353,901 and constituted 55.2 percent of the total. The cotton crop of 1859 had been more than 1,200,000 bales, making Mississippi the leading cotton producer in the nation. The plantations were in the river counties of the fertile Mississippi Delta and the black prairie lands of the northeast and of the Delta fringe areas of the west central part of the state. Farms, as distinguished from plantations, were in all parts of the state, but especially in the hill country of the northeast and the pine barrens of the south. More than three-fourths of Mississippi farmers were yeomen owning small acreage and few or no slaves and bringing some diversification to agriculture. The yeomen were loyal to the slave system.[41]

★★★★★

The first general order issued by Ord called upon civil officers of the district to arrest and punish all offenders against the laws so as to obviate as far as possible the exercise of military power. In response, the leading newspapers of Mississippi and Arkansas expressed gratification that Ord would not interfere with the civil government and affirmed their belief that the people would give him their full cooperation.[42] Governor Humphreys issued a proclamation to the people of Mississippi enjoining officials to carry out their duties, asking the citizens to support civil powers and not to resist military authorities. Said the governor: "Military power may become intollerable [sic] only when it is placed in the hands of the vicious and the unjust, which, happily is not the case in Mississippi."[43]

General Ord, as super-governor over two states, possessed executive, legislative, and judicial powers which he might exercise through existing civil authority or directly upon the people. The record of civil affairs of the Fourth Military District is replete with evidence that Ord was called upon to deal with an avalanche of civil problems. Letters received in his office dealt with such matters as these: "stole a mule from me in 1866;" "is defrauding his hands of their share;" "stole some cotton from me in 1865;" "has borrowed $3000 from me and won't repay it." There was also the merchant who wanted his return from the crop before the division between the laborer and planter; and the poor widow with a large family who called upon the general for help. Not to be overlooked was the proposal of one W. Hunt, an enterprising gentleman of Hamburg, Arkansas, who wanted Ord to go in with him in working one of his plantations, Ord to furnish twenty good mules. Added to these should be the numerous complaints of outrages upon freedmen and Union men. No doubt many trivial matters were ignored, but the records show that any complaint of any consequence and any problems worthy of notice were attended to. Altogether this was a remarkable administrative performance, testifying to the systematic attention to detail in Ord's headquarters and to the general's vigorous conduct of civil affairs.

Ord was fortunate in having effective subordinate commanders for each of the states under his control. Brevet Major General Alvan C. Gillem commanded the subdistrict of Mississippi, and Brevet Brigadier General Charles H. Smith the subdistrict of Arkansas.

In addition to filling vacancies in civil offices occasioned by deaths, resignations and expiration of terms, Ord had the power to remove officials and to appoint their successors. This power was described fully in the Third Reconstruction Act of 19 July 1867. Appointees to any vacancy were to take the so-called "iron-clad" test oath previously specified by Congress, and thus all were to be Union men. On 29 July 1867, Ord notified all state and local officials that any attempt on their part to obstruct the carrying out of the Reconstruction laws by speeches or demonstrations in public meetings would be considered as cause for removal.[44]

Ord's appointments and removals were remarkably few. In Mississippi, he did not remove any state officials, as distinguished from county and municipal officers. In Arkansas, he removed only one at the state level. Out of several hundred local officials in Mississippi, only about twenty-four were removed, and the total of appointments made by Ord numbered approximately one hundred. In Arkansas, about nineteen were removed and some thirty-five appointed.[45]

Ord sought the advice of Governor Humphreys in matters of appointment in Mississippi, and the governor was quite cooperative. The general also relied heavily upon Federal District Judge Robert A. Hill who appears to have been one of his principal confidants in Mississippi matters. One appointment made by Ord evoked more than ordinary comment. On 18 September 1867, the general named Benjamin T. Montgomery to be justice of the peace for Davis Bend near Vicksburg in Warren County. Montgomery was a talented Negro who had been the slave of Joseph E. Davis, brother of Jefferson Davis, and had served the elder Davis as plantation manager. It is likely that all or almost all the people in Davis Bend were Negroes. This twelve-mile long peninsula jutting into the Mississippi River contained six plantations, including the famous "Hurricane" and "Briarfield" of the Davis brothers.[46]

General Ord went to Little Rock early in April to attend to matters relating to the finances of that state. The treasury was in good condition, and the treasurer, L. B. Cunningham, as Ord assured him later, had committed no irregularity. Nevertheless, the general removed Cunningham from his office and ordered Colonel Henry Page to succeed him. This was the first instance of the removal of an official in Arkansas by Ord, and as the official was highly placed, the action created something of a stir as far away as Washington. Secretary of War Stanton directed an inquiry to the general about the matter. Ord responded that he believed the treasurer would be called upon to receive as state funds scrip or warrants, issued by the assumed state authority during the rebellion, which the state Supreme Court had recently declared receivable. The general went on to say that he believed that Cunningham would improperly dispose of state funds and that the First Reconstruction Act made it his duty to protect the community from this injury. Privately to Sherman, Ord confided that had he not taken charge of the Arkansas funds, there would have been nothing in the treasury at the end of the year. He anticipated having some $300,000 in United States bonds after paying all state expenses. In addition, Ord expected soon to begin paying interest on the state debt which, he said, had not been paid for twenty years.[47]

Colonel Page found the treasury in good condition, as the Murphy government had been honest and economical. There was approximately $72,000 in the general fund on 25 April 1867. More money came in. Ord ordered Page to invest $100,000 in United States Treasury bonds. By 1 October 1867, the treasury balance on hand was more than $200,000.[48]

Ord's removals and appointments in Arkansas were few, though it must be said that the general was fully encouraged by the Radicals to be active in this matter. Ord's refusal to make wholesale removals caused the Radical press to denounce him and to demand his replacement.[49] On the other hand, the general's moderation did not place him with the Democrats. Said John S. Dunham of the Conservative *Van Buren Press*: "Arkansas is very fortunate in her commander, but it is very plain that he did not consult southern men in his appointments."[50]

★★★★★

Just as Ord was super-governor over Mississippi and Arkansas, so also was he super-legislator. Any order issued by him was a law. His relationship to the legislatures of the two states and his handling of specific laws passed by them had considerable significance as they related to his task of implementing the acts of Congress.

In Mississippi, the legislature was in session at the outset of Ord's rule. The general did not interfere with the meeting, but those laws or portions of laws which in his judgment were not in agreement with acts of Congress or which impeded his making these acts effective were set aside or not allowed to be enforced. Ord's "legislation" by order related principally to the maintenance of law and order, protection of labor, and rights of the freedmen.[51] These will be dealt with as separate matters.

In Arkansas, by a communication of 15 April 1867, Ord directed Governor Murphy to inform the members of the Arkansas legislature, then temporarily adjourned, that their reconvening would be incompatible with the First Reconstruction Act and that they were not to reassemble. This directive was issued at about the same time Ord removed the state treasurer, and as previously stated, the general was called upon by the secretary of war to give an accounting of his actions. Ord explained to Stanton that the legislature was in recess until July when it would undertake the trial of two of the state's judges, one of whom was a loyal man who was to be tried because he had, in pursuance of his judicial duty, attempted to protect loyal men from being tried by disloyal ones. Ord said he believed the third section of the First Reconstruction Act imposed upon him the duty of protecting all persons in their rights and of punishing criminals.[52] On the other hand, to his friend Sherman, the general gave a different reason: "I have taken charge of the funds in this state," he wrote, "dissolved the legislature composed of late rebs of an extravagant turn of mind."[53] What then was the general's motive in proroguing the Arkansas legislature—justice or economy, or perhaps both?

The legislature terminated by Ord had begun its deliberations late in 1866 and had continued to meet up to 23 March 1867. Ex-Confederates controlled the body and bent their efforts toward undoing the work of the Unionist legislature of 1864–65. They sought to return the state to prewar conditions. The Conservative lawmakers undertook to purge the state judiciary of some of the more objectionable Unionist judges.[54]

The charge that the legislature was extravagant may be readily evaluated. As in Mississippi, Ord set aside such laws as were in his view discriminatory or obstructive and to this might be added in the case of Arkansas, laws providing for extraordinary expenditures of money. The ex-Confederate lawmakers had passed a pension law "for the relief of the destitute, wounded, or disabled soldiers, not otherwise provided for by the United States" and for the relief of widows and children of deceased Confederates. Ten thousand dollars of the first year's appropriation was to purchase artificial limbs for soldiers. Governor Murphy vetoed the measure as an obvious reward to those who had been enemies of the United States, but the bill was promptly and overwhelmingly passed over his veto. By an order of 7 October, Ord forbade any state or county officers to pay to the families of Confederate soldiers any money not allowed on the same terms to the families of Union soldiers regardless of race. The provision of artificial limbs was not affected by Ord's order. By an act of 18 March 1867, the Arkansas legislature made another generous gesture in authorizing the loan of the bonds of the state to the Little Rock and Memphis Railroad. Ord quickly quashed this offer of state aid.[55]

★★★★★

The state courts of Mississippi and Arkansas came in for some interference by Ord's orders. Judgments of courts were set aside in a few cases. Certain court proceedings were interdicted. Courts were required to bring their practices into conformity with the Civil Rights Act of 1866. Special tribunals were set up for specified types of cases. Pressure was brought to bear upon Ord to issue an order in the form of a stay law to postpone the collection of debts, and he did so. Also, the general ordered that no fine, penalty, or rule of evidence not applicable to white men might be applied to Negroes.[56]

In Arkansas, the Conservative Supreme Court had rendered a decision in December 1866 in the case of *Filkins* v. *Hawkins* providing that acts of civil officials of the state during the rebellion were valid. This affirmation of legitimacy of the late secessionist government of Arkansas caused Ord to direct General Smith to issue an order providing that no payments in money or scrip on account of services rendered during the rebellion would be allowed by virtue of the court's ruling. Ord deemed the decision to be hostile to the laws of the United States.[57]

Special tribunals were set up by Ord to adjudicate certain matters. Disputes between landlords and tenants over partition of the crop were to be settled by boards of arbitration composed of three members, one selected by each party and a third to be selected by these two. The general stated that, since the state courts of Mississippi and Arkansas were not open to persons too poor to give bond, such boards were necessary. Ord explained to Grant that the boards were designed to protect the freedmen from their landlords who, as the crop was small, were taking it all.[58]

The First Reconstruction Act had provided that district commanders might establish military commissions to try criminals or disturbers of the public peace. A military commission was composed of a panel of officers and was not bound by any particular rules of procedure. During the period of his command in the Fourth Military District, Ord issued several general orders describing the kinds of offenses which might subject persons to trial by military commissions. Horse stealing was a great nuisance, and the general prescribed that horse thieves be tried by commission. In August, Ord said that he had been informed that some landholders had been driving off their laborers on "frivolous pretexts" in order to avoid paying them their wages or share of the crop. Freedmen's Bureau agents were directed to investigate so that offenders might be brought to trial before a military commission. Complaints were made by Union men of Choctaw County, Mississippi, and Independence County, Arkansas, and probably by men from other places, that they could not secure justice in the "rebel"-controlled courts of their respective counties. Ord directed that the way be opened for such persons to have their cases tried by military commissions. All criminal cases involving white and black in which there was loss of life or assault with intent to kill were to be tried by military commissions. All persons not authorized to do so were prohibited from carrying concealed weapons under penalty of forfeiture of the arms and trial by commission. There was much stealing and selling of country produce at night, and the general decreed that such night sales were illegal and that both civil officials as well as military commissions would enforce this regulation.[59]

In summary, there were fifty-six cases decided by military commissions during Ord's tenure. Forty-one of these were in Mississippi, involving forty-eight defendants. Of these forty-eight, there were thirty-three whites and fifteen Negroes. In Arkansas, there were fifteen cases, twelve of the defendants being white and three black. In the great majority of cases, the principals were accused of stealing horses or mules. There were thirty-nine in this category. Theft of various items was charged in three other cases. Two cases concerned the buying of government property from a soldier. There were seven cases of assault of one kind or another, in four of which Negroes were the victims. There were two cases of murder, in both of which whites were charged with killing Negroes. One case of attempted rape with subornation of perjury involved whites. In some sixteen cases, with white defendants in some and blacks in others, the verdict was "not guilty." General Ord remitted or reduced the punishment of nine individuals. The heaviest sentence was life imprisonment for a white man who murdered a Negro in Arkansas. Only two cases had any political implications, and they were of no significance.[60] The famous McCardle case in Mississippi began before a military commission, but was not brought to a conclusion by the military. It will be discussed in another connection.

In conclusion, General Ord threatened to use military commissions a good deal more than he actually resorted to them. In instances where he did use them, he seemed to be mainly concerned with safeguarding lives and property. While commissions were certainly arbitrary, there is no evidence to indicate that he abused the extraordinary judicial powers vested in him.

★★★★★

General Ord had under his purview a substantial Negro population surrounded by unusual circumstances and having particular needs for protection and guidance. The condition of the Negroes was unsettled and uncertain. It was Ord's task to formulate and implement policies with regard to the black people within the broad scope of the laws he had been charged with executing.

The Negroes of Mississippi and Arkansas, along with their brothers and sisters in the other Southern states, in many instances had been physically dislocated by the war. Out of the turmoil, they had achieved freedom, a priceless condition, but it had come to them at a moment when they were economically and socially uprooted. Hardly recovered from the shocks of displacement, the freedmen then had thrust upon them by acts of Congress the responsibilities of citizenship. In addition, they were expected to adjust to their new status and bear their responsibilities with the stigma upon them of servility and an alleged racial inferiority. Most were not prepared either by training or experience for their new duties. About 90 percent of the adults among them were illiterate. Too much was expected of them too soon.

General Ord had advice for the black people, and he embraced his counsel in one of his earlier official pronouncements. His General Order No. 5 of 15 April 1867 contained this admonition:

> The most important duty devolving upon freedmen in their new condition is that of providing by their own labor for the support of themselves and families. They now have a common interest in the general prosperity. This prosperity does not depend so much on how men vote, as upon how well each member of

society labors and keeps his contracts. Freedmen are therefore urged not to neglect their business to engage in political discussions but continue to comply with their contracts and provide for themselves and families, for unless they do so, a famine may come and they will have no food. [61]

The general assured the freedmen that, when the time should come for them to register and vote, all would be given the opportunity. Quite naturally, the order was warmly received by Conservatives in both Arkansas and Mississippi. [62]

A few reports came to Ord's headquarters that the Negroes would not work. Yet it is remarkable that there were so few complaints, and it must be presumed that there were many thousands of freedmen who did work well and elicited no comment. It was General Ord's judgment that the Negroes were willing to work. [63]

In August, as the cotton-picking season got under way, disputes arose between landlords and tenants over the settlement of the contract terms, and, as already noted, Ord took steps to protect the freedmen by both military commissions and boards of arbitration. The general took pains to point out that complaints of laborers being defrauded were made against a low class of men. He called upon all gentlemen planters "to aid him in punishing and bringing into contempt all persons whose treatment of their hands reflects discredit upon their class." [64]

In both Mississippi and Arkansas, local governments were inclined to deny to freedmen the benefits of the poor laws. In the latter part of 1867, as crop failures brought increasing hardship, Ord issued an order requiring the benefits and protection of the laws for the Negroes of both states. As the black people bore their share of taxes, he pointed out, they should be fully benefitted by the poor laws. Failure to provide for pauper freedmen would be considered dereliction of duty by local officials and a violation of the spirit of the Civil Rights Act of 1866. [65]

The Mississippi Black Code, which had become law on 24 November 1865, had authorized counties to levy a poll tax not to exceed one dollar per head on all freedmen between the ages of eighteen and sixty for the support of the paupers of their race. General Ord declared the tax to be a violation of the Civil Rights Act of 1866 and ordered that no official might collect the tax upon Negroes as a class, but only such taxes as were levied regardless of color. Of other taxes there were complaints from some that Negroes paid too much and from others that taxes due from Negroes could not be collected. When the mayor of Aberdeen reported that Negroes refused to pay street, road and poll taxes, Ord sternly charged him to enforce the laws on all alike as regards both money and work regardless of race.[66]

There was remarkably little lawlessness against Negroes in both Mississippi and Arkansas. A few complaints from both states were made to headquarters. In his annual report of 27 September 1867, Ord stated that civil authority in Arkansas had shown they would not act in cases of an aggravated nature against freedmen, and he had just issued orders to try such cases by military commission.[67] Not to be overlooked in assessing the situation was the fact that the general had scattered detachments of troops over his district to keep order and protect the freedmen.

There were considerably more Negroes in Mississippi than in Arkansas, which probably accounts in part for the more varied problems relating to freedmen arising in the former state. The domestic relations of Negroes raised questions which were propounded to Ord as the arbiter of all things in the Fourth Military District. The Black Code of Mississippi of December 1865 had forbidden the intermarriage of whites and blacks, the offense being classified as a felony with conviction bringing a sentence of life imprisonment in the state penitentiary. A citizen of Enterprise, Mississippi, presumably a white man, wrote to Ord that the marriage contract was ignored by freedmen as well as by many white men and yellow girls. He asked Ord to moderate the state law to allow intermarriage between parties having a real affection for one another. The probate clerk of Sunflower County, Mississippi, asked Ord if he should issue a marriage license to a Negro man to intermarry with a white woman. A justice of the peace in North Mount Pleasant, Mississippi, reported that he had received complaints of freedmen deserting the women with whom they had lived for many years and taking up with other women. What should he do in such cases? A citizen of Macon, Mississippi, asked Ord to intervene to prevent the prosecution of certain white men for holding illicit intercourse with Negro women. To this last request the general responded that he did not deem it his duty to interfere in the matter. As this is the only response of Ord on record, it would indicate that the general probably allowed the state law to prevail in all cases.[68]

In April, May, and June of 1867, a number of applications for relief were made to Ord in behalf of destitute citizens in Mississippi. Both blacks and whites were in need. The Freedmen's Bureau had been charged by the War Department with the task of issuing rations to the destitute of both races. Ord directed Gillem to carry out this order. However, it does not appear that there were large numbers of needy.[69]

Requests were directed to Ord for assistance in providing schools for freedmen in Mississippi. Ord referred such petitions to Gillem as assistant commissioner of the bureau. The effort to provide schools for black children, while better than nothing, was still quite feeble. Just as in Arkansas, relatively few of the Negro children were touched by the bureau's provision. In 1870, less than 3,500 were enrolled in Mississippi and many of them did not attend regularly.[70]

As in Arkansas there was some defiance of bureau agents. Where people resisted summonses, Ord directed Gillem to send troops to make some arrests and bring offenders to Vicksburg for trial. The effect, he believed, would be salutary. Agents should summon persons only once, the general said. Thus, Ord supported bureau agents, but, at the same time, he protected citizens against arbitrary and unlawful actions. A responsible citizen came to headquarters and verbally accused the bureau agent in Panola County, Mississippi, of gross corruption and of "maintaining a reign of terror" in the county. Ord ordered an investigation which bore out the truth of the charges. The agent was court-martialed for accepting bribes and violating orders and was sentenced to a year in prison.[71]

On 30 July 1867, Grant telegraphed Ord that charges had been made "of the very partial manner in which justice is administered by General Gillem between laborers & ex-rebel employers." Radical partisans were responsible for the charges. The General-in-Chief directed Ord to look into the matter, and, if he found the charges just, to "apply such remedy as the degree of culpability seems to require."[72] Gillem was even more conservative than Ord and apparently had roused up the Radicals by showing too little sympathy for the freedmen and too much for their former Confederate employers.

Ord responded to Grant about two weeks later with a lengthy letter exonerating Gillem of the charge of partiality. As assistant commissioner of the Freedmen's Bureau, Gillem had tried to do justice to the freedmen, Ord wrote, but his force was entirely inadequate. Gillem had reported that he needed twenty additional agents to properly administer the law.[73] Some agents were negligent, as they referred contract-making to civil authorities, did not investigate complaints, and did not arrest offenders as ordered. At Gillem's request, all post commanders had been made agents of the bureau to augment the inadequate staff. Ord pointed out that many arrests had been made and offenders punished for injuring freedmen. He did acknowledge that it was doubtless true that whites abused Negroes on remote plantations beyond the reach of agents without being held accountable for their misdeeds. At the same time, he noted that many frivolous complaints were made by blacks.

The greater part of Ord's letter to Grant was devoted to a thorough discussion of race relations in Mississippi and of some of the complexities of ready adjustment between the blacks and whites. Civil authorities in many parts of the state did ignore the complaints of the Negroes, but, he continued, "it is not easy to eradicate the habits of generations, which has been to allow the master to settle with his servant. . . ."[74] These civil authorities should be removed, but there were counties in the state where there were no intelligent men who could take the required oath of office. If he removed the judges and magistrates who did not do justice to the freedmen, he would have no one to take their places. The nature and magnitude of the problem were eloquently stated by Ord:

> With one Bureau Agent to about every three thousand square miles of forest and swamp, with not loyal northern men enough to fill vacancies occurring in State offices, with scarcely a southern man who can take the oath of office, a portion of the thousand per day of real and imaginary complaints which freedmen in this state may have, must go unheard, and abuses of the simple and ignorant by the powerful and depraved, cannot be prevented.[75]

The general understood the ultimate answer to the problem. Where force could not be maintained to hold the vicious in check, "an enlightened public opinion, the interests of the community, and the selection of good and wise citizens to administer justice," he thought, were the best preventives to the actions of evil men.[76]

In a keen analysis of life as it actually was in Mississippi,

General Ord exposed the fallacy of ultra-Radicalism which would assume a natural enmity between the black man and the white and would take for granted that any gain however small for the black man must be won over the opposition and at the expense of the white. Officers from the North, including agents of the bureau who came into the South, generally associated with the intelligent people of their own color, and they and their associates employed Negroes, as the latter were the only servants in the land. These Northern men did exactly as they would do elsewhere in maintaining proper relations between employer and employee: they encouraged the employee to be industrious. As the freedmen were mostly working for a share of the crop, they were benefitted according to their industry. Thus, did Ord describe the situation as it was. The general brought home to Grant very clearly the absurdity of the extreme Radical position by raising a series of questions. Should the bureau agent not associate with white men, but rather with black? Should he favor the inclination of his black associates rather than their interest, and advise them not to work if they could avoid it? Should he advise them not to keep their contracts, because they thereby added to the white man's wealth? Such advice, if generally followed, said Ord, would result in idleness and poverty for the Negroes and would raise much hostile feeling against them.[77]

In summary view, General Ord had sound advice for the freedmen; he sought to protect them and to give them the full benefits of the laws, state and federal; he encouraged a proper and humane attitude toward Negroes by the white Southerners, but recognized that long-standing habit and prejudice would result in abuse of the blacks. Ord showed remarkable insight and foresight in pointing to the ultimate answer to the problems of race relations: "an enlightened public opinion," and "the selection of good and wise citizens to administer justice."

16

★★★★★

Radicals and Conservatives

GENERAL Edward Ord had in his charge a congressionally mandated political process. Voters were to be registered and elections held as prescribed in the Reconstruction acts. Through it all—or over it all—Ord himself expected to be neutral. Inevitably, political groups formed, and each seemed to expect the general to lend sympathy and render support. As contentiousness increased, Ord was beset from every direction.

Three factions seemed to form naturally under the circumstances. On the one hand, Radical whites—some native, some recent arrivals—undertook to become the political mentors of the Negroes. They would see to it that the freedmen were registered and that they became Republican voters. On the other extreme were the majority of white Southerners, formerly adherents of the Confederate States of America. They were opposed to the congressional plan of Reconstruction and especially to the enfranchisement of the Negroes. Constituting a third element were some moderate Southern whites in between the extremes, who would accept the congressional plan as unavoidable and would vie with the Radicals for control of the Negro electorate.

Ord early stirred the ire of the Radicals when he issued his General Order No. 5 of 15 April advising the Negroes to stay at their work, keep their contracts, and not spend their time in political discussions to the neglect of their business. The Radicals in the district complained to Washington that Ord was trying to prevent the Negroes from forming Republican organizations. Horace Greeley's *New York Tribune* and other radical organs in the North took up the complaint.[1]

On the other side, the conservative *Little Rock Gazette* commented wryly that if Ord did not shape his policies more along Radical lines, "he need not be surprised to be metamorphosed into a 'rebel sympathizer' or a 'disloyal copperhead.'"[2] Other conservative journals came to Ord's defense. James Gordon Bennett's *New York Herald* said that Ord gave more thought to the conscientious discharge of his duties than "to humoring the whims of nigger orators."[3]

Ord's order attracted official notice at a high level. From his eminence at the head of the Freedmen's Bureau in Washington, General Oliver Otis Howard dispatched his chief of staff upon an inspection tour of the Fourth Military District to determine if it were indeed true that the Negroes were being hindered in their political aspirations. The inspector reported that "affairs in General Ord's command are on the whole in very satisfactory condition."[4]

Ord pushed forward with the registration of voters in Mississippi and Arkansas through the months of June, July, and August 1867. Political factions were formed, and conflicts threatened. In June, the general issued an order that when citizens complained to post commanders that they were being persecuted by civil authority for opinion's sake, commanders would investigate, take testimony under oath, and forward a report with affidavits to Ord's headquarters.[5] In September, he prohibited the assembling of any armed organizations or bodies of citizens for any purpose whatever. "The practice of carrying fire arms is prevalent among bullies and cowards—not prevailing in well ordered and civilized communities," Ord instructed all concerned, "and it is the intention of the General Commanding to take all practicable measures to stop it."[6]

In order to gain an understanding of Reconstruction developments, the political factions in Mississippi must be considered. Also, not to be overlooked is the fact that Ord was subjected to their partisan crossfire. A group of moderates, some of them former Whigs, led by William Yerger and Albert Gallatin Brown, accepted the congressional plan and undertook to cooperate with the Negroes politically. Their efforts were doomed from the very outset. The Negroes would not follow whites who so recently had advocated the restrictive Mississippi Black Code, nor would ordinary whites, at least in large numbers, follow aristocratic former Whigs. Vernon L. Wharton, the historian of the Negro in Mississippi, stated that the overwhelming rejection of Negro suffrage by the voters of Ohio in October 1867 convinced Mississippians that the North would go Democratic in 1868 and that patience combined with a "no compromise" position would bring deliverance from the tribulations of Radical Reconstruction. More and more whites, as well as many newspapers previously supporting the moderates, now went over to the ranks of the irreconcilables.[7]

The Republican party in Mississippi was a combination of native and outside elements. Many of the outsiders who rose to positions of leadership in the party were former Union officers who had come South to be planters and merchants. The number of these Carpetbaggers was small. They were generally honest, though there were notable exceptions. They were genuinely bent upon saving the fruits of Northern victory and transforming the South into a progressive section through education and vigorous economic development. Allied with these outsiders was a considerable number of native white Southerners, most of the leaders being former Whigs of wealth and prominence who had generally opposed secession. Historians continue to inquire into the composition of this Scalawag element. Some have found, in addition to the Whig planters, a number of hill country farmers who had also opposed secession and were bitter toward the slavocracy, while others have suggested that the Scalawags represented a cross-section of Mississippi society composed of citizens intent upon reform. These diverse elements found common cause with the conservative business Republicans of the North.[8] Providing the bulk of the voting strength for the party were the thousands of Mississippi Negroes, following their white mentors but developing some leadership of their own.

Ord's lack of sympathy for Radicalism notwithstanding, there were two powerful forces at work in that cause. One of these was the Union League of America, the Radical Republican political machine. The second force was the Freedmen's Bureau.[9] In April 1867, Thomas W. Conway, one-time assistant commissioner of the Freedmen's Bureau in Louisiana, set out on a tour of Southern states at the request of James M. Edmunds, president of the National Council of the Union League of America. In July, Conway made a report of his journey to

Edmunds which was given wide circulation in the *New York Tribune* and other Radical papers of the country. The Republican agent singled out Mississippi as offering a gloomy prospect for the Radicals. The state, he said, was "in a condition of Egyptian darkness." Both Ord and Alvan C. Gillem seemed to have no interest in the Negroes or in the cause of "loyal reconstruction." "The military commanders in the state need reconstructing themselves. . . ," he wrote.[10]

Conservative papers pitched in to defend Ord and to deny the existence of the conditions described by Conway. "We do not believe a word of this," said the *Memphis Appeal* of the Radical report. The Memphis paper went on to say that Ord was "a just, conscientious, honest man, who does not think it becomes him to play the tyrant."[11] Some of the better Carpetbag element in Mississippi came to Ord's defense. General Jonathan Tarbell, a Union officer who had become a planter near Forest, Scott County, promised that a correction would be sent to Horace Greeley's *Tribune*. Tarbell styled himself "a Republican but not a Radical."[12]

In the succeeding weeks prior to the November election, the Republicans perfected their organization, particularly among the freedmen. Efforts of Ord and Alvan C. Gillem to keep the agents of the Freedmen's Bureau neutral were in vain. On 19 October 1867, Gillem issued an order prohibiting all bureau officials and employees in Mississippi from seeking office or taking any active part in politics. To a great extent, the order was ignored.[13]

Conservative white opponents of Radical Reconstruction, calling themselves Constitutional Unionists, were inclined at first to be active. They registered in very substantial numbers. However, many of their leaders were disfranchised, and the group made only feeble efforts to organize. They eventually adopted a policy of boycotting political affairs almost entirely.[14]

★★★★★

The political factions in Arkansas closely paralleled those in Mississippi, and in that state also each group sought to involve Ord in actions to its advantage. Republicans began to organize their forces quite early. In response to a published call, a meeting which styled itself the Union State Convention was held in Little Rock on 2 April 1867. The participation of the

blacks in the deliberations was negligible. The convention advised General Ord to prorogue the legislature, remove the
Supreme Court justices and replace them with loyal men, and
relieve the state treasurer and state auditor of their duties.[15] As
already noted, Ord did only some of these things; most, he did
not do.

In spite of Ord's unwillingness to be their collaborator, the
success of the Radicals in organizing and getting control of the
Negro vote seems to have been complete. The Negroes were
organized and instructed by the Union Leagues or Union Clubs
throughout the state. This work had so far proceeded by the
end of September, according to Staples, "as to place the
freedmen clearly beyond the influence of their Democratic
neighbors."[16]

Most of the white people of Arkansas were opposed to the
congressional Reconstruction and especially to its provision of
Negro suffrage. The Conservative whites, as Staples put it,
were "in confusion." Their natural leaders had been disfranchised, and their organization had been shattered by General
Ord when he dissolved the legislature. They had no platform
and were not unified regarding the course they would follow.[17]

Some prominent Conservatives advocated registering, voting for a convention, and taking the Negroes in hand and
controlling their political power in order to prevent the Radicals
from doing so. A substantial number of Conservatives registered. However, as the November election approached, they
increasingly came to feel that their cause was hopeless. Not
only were the Negroes under Republican control, but also the
registrars were Union men, whose natural affinity would be for
the Radical party. Since the registrars had full power to revise
the voting lists, striking off the names of any persons they
deemed ineligible, it appeared to the Conservatives that the
registrars would control the election itself. Despairing opponents of Reconstruction began to lose interest in political
action.[18]

★★★★★

Ord faced a complex task in the registration of the voters of
Mississippi and Arkansas. He needed three registrars and a
clerk for each of the 116 counties in his district. Every member
of this large and widely scattered staff of 464 men was required

to take the "iron-clad" test oath. In addition to the problem of recruiting registrars, the general had to deal with the great confusion over the eligibility for voting. The Second Reconstruction Act of 23 March 1867 had prescribed an oath to be taken by all registrants. It required that the prospective voter swear that he was at least twenty-one years of age, that he had not been disfranchised for participation in rebellion or for felony, and that he had never held certain state or federal offices and then engaged in rebellion or given aid to the enemies of the United States.[19] A flood of letters poured into Ord's headquarters from people who had served in some minor official capacity before the war asking if they could take the oath.

Henry Stanbery, attorney general of the United States, was called upon to prepare an opinion on voting qualifications, and, although some features of his opinion were public knowledge as early as 29 May,[20] Ord received no official notice of the opinion for weeks. The general could wait no longer. On 10 June he issued his final instructions to boards of registration. Ord directed that each board must register all who took the oath. The opinion of the attorney general finally issued on 20 June affirmed this interpretation of the law. General Grant strongly dissented from the view of Stanbery and Ord, as did Radical Senator Zachariah Chandler of Michigan. Ord defended his order firmly. Few registrants would perjure themselves, Ord said, and these few would have no effect on the outcome of the election.[21]

The Congress, reflecting Radical concern, passed a Third Reconstruction Act on 19 July 1867 providing that registrars might refuse to register a person, or at a specified time prior to the election they might strike from their lists names of persons deemed to be ineligible. Ord ordered registrars to follow the law and revise their work done to date to accord with the new statute.[22]

Ord gave special attention to the registration of Negroes in his district, apparently in response to information that they were being impeded in their efforts to register. In the early part of the registration period, he issued a general order designed to correct mistaken ideas being circulated among the freedmen that the registration was for the purpose of imposing a tax or enrolling them for military service. He directed General Alvan C. Gillem and General C. H. Smith to have their bureau agents visit every important plantation within their reach and, with the registrars, instruct the freedmen correctly on these points.[23]

Ord used the available military force to maintain law and order and to facilitate the process of registration. As registration got under way, additional forces were sent. Altogether, by the close of registration, Ord had approximately 3,500 troops about equally divided between the two states. In Mississippi, the Twenty-fourth Infantry Regiment, headquartered at Vicksburg, had three companies in the garrison, totaling about 270 men. At Jackson, there was one company of that regiment and one company of the Fifth Cavalry, making a garrison of about 160. Single companies, each averaging about 80 men, were posted at Meridian, Winchester, Brookhaven, Natchez and Pass Christian. The Thirty-fourth Infantry Regiment had headquarters at Grenada with a garrison of three companies totaling about 260 men. Columbus, Holly Springs and Corinth each had two companies, making posts of about 160 men at these places. A single company of about 80 was stationed at Greensboro. Yazoo City had a company of the Fifth Cavalry numbering about 80.[24] The garrisons were well distributed on the main roads and rail lines of the state, but it may well be doubted whether they were in sufficient number and strength to police the entire region. Mounted parties could be detached to protect boards of registration or to protect lives and property wherever they might be endangered, but the obstacles in the way of communicating with interior areas made policing difficult.

In Arkansas, one battery of the Fifth Artillery Regiment was stationed in Little Rock. In the capital city were also two companies of the Twenty-eighth Infantry, a garrison of about 250 men. Other companies of this regiment with approximate numbers in garrison were as follows: Princeton, three companies (250); Washington, two companies (160); Batesville, two companies (160); Pine Bluff, one company (80). The Nineteenth Infantry had headquarters and three companies at Fort Smith (250); Dover, two companies (160); Fayetteville, two companies (160); Monticello, one company (80); Madison, one company (80); Burrowsville, one company (80).[25] Again, the garrisons were scattered to utilize available transportation facilities, though remote areas were not within ready reach of the small number of posts.

Special features of the registration peculiar to Mississippi and Arkansas may best be seen by examining each state separately.

The selection of registrars in Mississippi was accomplished in a variety of ways. Gillem's supervisory board sent out a circular to all reliable Union men whose names could be ascertained inviting them to apply for positions as registrars. Judge Robert A. Hill suggested to Ord the registrars to be appointed for his own county, Tishomingo. J. F. H. Claiborne suggested former Union officers, two of whom were appointed for Marion County.[26] In August, the *Jackson Clarion* reported: "It is well known that Gen. Ord was compelled to send Registrars to many of the counties, in consequence of the difficulty which he experienced in finding residents who would take the prescribed oath."[27] The list of registrars shows that there were Southern as well as Northern men on the boards and that only one active army officer was designated as a registrar.

A few complaints were made to Ord's headquarters that Negroes were being deterred from registering. In Newton County, a white man was punished for impeding the registration of Negroes, but this was the only instance of its kind on record in Mississippi. For the accommodation of those Negroes who were hesitant or were being impeded, Judge Hill suggested to Ord that the registrars might give notice and make a second round, and this was done.[28] The results of the registration in Mississippi showed such a preponderance of Negro voters that it must be concluded that the freedmen were not seriously interfered with in their efforts to enroll.

In summary, it appears that a quiet and orderly registration was typical of most of the counties of Mississippi. General Jonathan Tarbell, who was a registrar for Scott County, declared that "it is universally allowed that registration has been conducted with perfect fairness. . . ."[29]

Ord reported Mississippi's preliminary registration figure to Grant in September; by the time of the November election, the number had risen to 139,327. An attempt at analysis of this potential electorate would seem to be called for: Ord estimated that the majority of Negro voters in the state would be about 20,000. This figure may be taken as fairly sound, since Governor Benjamin Grubb Humphreys, quite independently, estimated that there were about 17,000 more blacks than whites registered. The governor further estimated that 4,000 whites voted Republican in the election. This last calculation compares favorably with estimates by modern historians, who have variously fixed the Scalawag numbers of 5,000, 7,000 and 9,000. Since the Carpetbaggers were negligible in number, these Scalawags were a small but important factor in the political picture. As has already been noted, there is still uncertainty about the composition of the Scalawag element.[30]

★★★★★

In selecting registrars in Arkansas, Ord called upon all reliable informants within reach. The general desired that, where possible, two members of each board be former Union officers and the third member a respectable citizen of the county. Governor Murphy was asked to submit names, as were post commanders, and General Powell Clayton, a Carpetbagger, was requested to recommend for his own county, Jefferson. Making further obeisance in the Republican direction, Ord asked Judge J. M. Tibbetts, a prominent member of the Union State Convention, to suggest names. The *Little Rock Gazette* was quick to criticize Ord for thus relying on the Radicals, though it must be noted that there is no evidence to indicate undue influence from this direction. To expedite the selection of registrars, in May, Ord personally made a rapid tour into the southern part of the state to make appointments. To prevent unsatisfactory selections, the general required that Smith and his supervisory board give the antecedents of those whose names were suggested in order that only loyal men would be chosen.[31]

There seemed to be remarkably few complaints from either side about the selection of registrars. The *Gazette* took pains to commend Ord highly for his appointments for Phillips County (Helena). General Smith reported to Ord toward the close of registration that the registrars had been chosen impartially, since, after Ord's stringent orders on the matter of qualification, there were very few unsatisfactory appointments. Apparently, only two active army officers had to be pressed into service as registrars.[32]

Some circumstances and events of the registration in Arkansas are worthy of notice. A military escort consisting of a sergeant and four men was available for any boards requiring it, though how many were called for cannot be said. There were few evidences of attempts to interfere with the registrars. The *Little Rock Gazette* complained that some of the boards had refused to register qualified persons, such as former militia officers, city officials and road overseers. However, only two formal complaints were received by Ord from persons whose names were stricken from the voting lists. The slowness of the freedmen to come forward brought concern to Republican partisans, and they were quick to make protests to Ord. On 9 August, Ord directed General Smith to reregister in all counties where the Arkansas commander thought the freedmen had been seriously impeded. If necessary, Ord said, appoint new boards.[33]

Ord also reported the results of the Arkansas registration to Grant in September. A preliminary tally showed a total of 66,316 enrolled, of whom 43,170 were whites and 23,146 were blacks.[34] There is no way of knowing precisely how many of the whites were Radical partisans. If we assume that all of the Negroes were Republicans and that some eighty-four percent of the Radicals, black and white, voted in the subsequent election (apparently this was the approximate percentage of Radical participation in Mississippi), then about 10,000 white Arkansans might be counted in the Republican ranks. The Conservatives would constitute the remainder of the white registrants, and they would number about 33,000. Thus, if this admittedly crude calculation can be accepted, we can conclude that the two factions had registered about the same number. Some support for these figures may be seen in the fact that in subsequent important elections the two parties polled very close to the same number of votes.[35]

The work of the registrars in Mississippi and Arkansas was controversial because Conservatives, especially in the latter state, charged that they fraudulently carried out their duties in such a way as to insure that the electorate would be safely Republican. However, General Ord apparently did not believe that wholesale fraud had been perpetrated. On the very eve of the election, he issued a general order expressing his sincere thanks to the registrars for the zeal, ability and fidelity shown in performing their "onerous and important" duties. Records in headquarters showed, he said, that the registrars almost without exception had received the esteem and confidence of the most respectable citizens.[36]

Ord issued an order on 26 September 1867, fixing the first Tuesday in November as the date for the elections in Mississippi and Arkansas to determine whether conventions should be held to frame constitutions and establish civil governments and at the same time to elect delegates to be ready to serve, should the convention issue be decided affirmatively.[37]

★★★★★

The election in Mississippi went off smoothly. There were 100 delegates to be elected. Ord sought from C. A. Brougher, secretary of state of Mississippi, information regarding the basis of representation and apportionment of membership in the lower house of the legislature and the number of precincts in each county. Upon this information and upon the registration itself, he apportioned the delegates. The Conservative press made no complaint about his apportionment.[38]

Finding men to serve as judges and clerks of election proved to be as difficult as the previous search for registrars and for the same reason—the "iron-clad" test oath. Ord determined to reduce the difficulty by authorizing the appointment of freedmen, an action which brought down upon him the reproof of the Conservative press. Before the election actually got under way in Mississippi, a few reports reached Ord of interference or threatened interference in the matter of voting. By Ord's order, separate polls for whites and blacks were set up in some places. This, of course, did not forestall a number of efforts to impede Negro voting. The "rebels" were not the only ones offending or threatening to offend. The mayor of Okolona in Chicakasaw County reported the danger of a Negro insurrection on the eve of the election. Ord ordered a detachment of soldiers from Corinth to Okolona to break up armed groups and disarm those threatening the peace.[39]

The results of the election in Mississippi were extraordinary, to say the least. Of the 139,327 registered voters, 76,016 cast votes. Those for a convention numbered 60,739; those against, 6,277. Since a majority of the registered voters voted, and since the majority of votes cast was for a convention, the convention would be held. One hundred delegates were elected. In this number, there were 45 Radicals (including all 17 black delegates), 19 Conservative Radicals, 29 Conservatives, 6 not subject to classification, and 1 convention president who was a Radical.[40] Clearly, the Republicans would have their way.

Any attempt to analyze the election results is hazardous, but a cautious commentary seems warranted. Taking into account Governor Humphreys's statement that there were 17,000 more Negroes than whites registered and that some 4,000 whites voted Republican, the following rough estimates may be made: there were 78,000 black registrants and 61,000 whites; assuming all the blacks were Republicans and adding to their number the 4,000 white Republican voters, we can estimate that party's potential voting strength at about 82,000; the remaining whites, numbering 57,000, would constitute the potential vote of the Conservatives. Accepting these figures provisionally, it is obvious that some 50,000 registered white voters abstained from casting their ballots. The Conservatives had thoroughly boycotted the election.

General Ord ordered the Mississippi convention to meet in the hall of the House of Representatives in Jackson on 7 January 1868.[41]

★★★★★

In preparing for the election in Arkansas, Ord sought information from Secretary of State Robert J. T. White on the number of members in the lower house in 1860 and the number of precincts in each county. According to Staples, Ord based the apportionment as nearly as possible on the registration. There were 75 delegates to be voted on.[42]

The approach of the election caused both Ord and Smith to turn to the matter of security and order. In October, Smith asked Ord if he should issue orders to post commanders to distribute their troops to assist sheriffs and their deputies in keeping order. Ord directed him to issue these orders. When the election got under way, Ord sent to Smith the same order he had sent to Gillem, directing him to report the names of any official or other person who made inflammatory speeches to freedmen or endangered the public peace by inciting one class or race against another.[43]

It was charged at the time of the election that the registrars controlled the outcome of the election in Arkansas by their power to revise the voting lists. Only those not scratched by "their highmightinesses" may vote, said the Little Rock Gazette. Staples found some evidence to indicate that Conservatives were eliminated by erasure of their names,[44] but there is not sufficient data to support the charge that the election was determined by this means.

Conservatives reportedly felt that, since all of the judges and clerks were Radicals, it was useless for them to attempt to vote. Registrars were encouraged to perpetrate fraud, Staples claimed, by the fact that there was no direct civil or military

supervision over them. Conservatives charged that the registrars did not announce the time and place of election, that
Negroes were voted in squads, that repeated voting by Radicals
was encouraged, and that Conservative votes were rejected.
The whites were thoroughly disgusted with the farce of registration and election, said the *Gazette,* and felt that it was useless
to try to vote down the convention. Undoubtedly, there was a
great deal of apathy and abstention from voting on the part of
many Conservatives, as the results of the election showed. It
must be said, however, that general charges of irregularities are
not sufficient to explain the outcome of the election. Fraud
there was, and it was reported to Ord; in every reported instance, he took appropriate action. Perhaps there was much
more of it than that which came to his official notice, but the
evidence is insufficient to conclude that it determined the outcome of the election.[45]

The Arkansas election results proved interesting and at the
same time posed a number of questions. There were 66,805
registered voters on the rolls by election time; and, of this
number, 41,134 cast votes. Votes for the convention numbered
27,576; votes against, 13,555. Since a majority of the registered
voters voted and the majority of votes cast was for a convention, the convention would be held. Seventy-five delegates
were elected, of whom 70 participated. There were 48 Radicals,
17 Conservatives, and 5 nonaligned. The Radical faction was
made up of 23 resident whites (Scalawags), 17 Carpetbaggers
and 8 Negroes. All of the Conservative and nonaligned delegates were Southern whites.[46]

Any commentary on the Arkansas election results must be
based on the uncertain calculations noted above by which the
Republican voting potential was fixed at approximately 33,000
(an estimated 23,000 blacks and 10,000 whites). The Radicals
carried the day by getting out the more than 27,000 votes cast in
favor of a convention. The Conservative whites had a potential
vote roughly equivalent to their opponents, but they polled
only 13,555 votes against the convention. It is obvious that
some 20,000 of the Conservative faction did not vote. As in
Mississippi, abstention was a notable feature of the election.

The Arkansas convention was scheduled by Ord's order to
meet in the hall of the House of Representatives in Little Rock
on 7 January 1868.[47]

17

★★★★★

Ex parte McCardle
and Exit Ord

E VEN as Edward Ord carried through the process of con-gressional Reconstruction, there were judicial challenges to his work. To the Supreme Court of the United States there came, in the spring of 1867, William L. Sharkey and Robert J. Walker, representing the state of Mississippi and seeking leave to file a petition for an injunction to restrain President Andrew Johnson and General Ord from executing the Reconstruction acts of 2 and 23 March on the ground that these laws were unconstitutional. The bill which Sharkey and Walker sought permission to file stated that secession was not legal and that Mississippi was never out of the Union. The Reconstruction acts which President Johnson was about to carry out would annihilate the state and subject it to a military despotism. As Johnson's actions in enforcement of the laws were ministe-rial—that is, duties of administration incumbent upon him by virtue of his position—and as such duties were subject to action of the courts, Mississippi sought an injunction from the Supreme Court to restrain the president from acting. Thus arose the case of *Mississippi* v. *Johnson*. [1] Mississippi presented her best Unionist face before the court. Sharkey, erstwhile provisional governor of the state by Johnson's appointment, and Walker, who had achieved high position in national poli-tics before the Civil War, were distinguished elder statesmen.

The Supreme Court took the Mississippi petition under advisement.

The court did not rule at once on the petition, and, in the latter part of April and early part of May, General Ord committed certain acts in pursuance of his duty which caused the Mississippi attorneys to file a petition to amend their bill. The amendment pointed out to the court that the general had seized the treasury of Arkansas, thus involving the matter of property rights, and that he had dissolved the legislature of the neighboring state. The petition went on to assert that Ord had threatened to depose certain civil officers of Mississippi, to depose or interfere with the legislature, and that he had in mind seizing state property, thereby subjecting it to waste.[2] The *Jackson Daily Clarion,* in printing the text of the amended bill, noted that Ord was "charged with divers and sundry designs upon the treasury, public lands, capitol building and grounds, and other property of the State, no doubt greatly to his astonishment."[3]

It was because of these allegations that Secretary of War Edwin M. Stanton requested Ord to explain his actions in Arkansas and his contemplated actions in Mississippi. The general responded to Stanton on 13 May that he had made no threats to remove any officials in Mississippi except for failure to render impartial justice, and that he had not removed any, unless trials by military commission in effect deposed the civil authorities who otherwise would have tried the cases. He had made no threat to prorogue or interfere with the Mississippi legislature. The general further said that he designed no seizures of state property at present, unless he should find that the laws of Congress could not otherwise be enforced. The motion to amend the Mississippi bill was argued briefly before the Supreme Court on 15 May. Attorney General Henry Stanbery, replying on behalf of the president that the motion to amend should not be received, at the same time officially announced General Ord's denial that he had made the alleged threats against Mississippi.[4]

In its decision on the Mississippi petition, the Supreme Court stated that the duty of the president in this instance was not merely ministerial but executive and political and hence not subject to injunction. The judiciary cannot restrain the executive, but may take cognizance of his acts in appropriate cases. Upon this line of reasoning, the motion by the Mississippi attorneys to file the bill was denied. Justice Robert C. Grier being absent, the motion was rejected by an equally divided court. The implementation of the Reconstruction acts would proceed.[5]

★★★★★

The ready availability to Ord and his subordinates of vast powers under the Reconstruction acts certainly rendered the abuse of those powers a clear possibility. Those in authority had upon them the burden of rational use of powers and the need to exercise great self-control. There were some for whom the responsibility proved too great, as an unfortunate event in Arkansas was to demonstrate all too well.

The town of Camden on the Ouachita River had a newspaper which bore the proud title of *Constitutional Eagle*. To the office of the *Eagle*, on 8 August 1867, came a party of soldiers under the command of Captain George S. Pierce who made a forced entry and carried from the establishment the type and other items which they proceeded to scatter and destroy. This act of vandalism had been done in response to criticism of the soldiers and particularly criticism of the conduct of drunken soldiers on the streets of Camden. Mayor D. Newton of Camden protested this act of barbarity to the post commander, Brevet Colonel C. C. Gilbert, and the colonel passed the mayor's letter on to Ord with a communication of his own. Colonel Gilbert stated that the paper had rendered itself obnoxious to the soldiers by unprovoked attacks and that he considered it well out of the way. The colonel further asserted that the military were the masters and not the servants of the people of Arkansas.[6]

Ord sent Colonel Gilbert a scalding reply: "You will please explain why this act was not prevented by you as post commander. . . ," he began. The general proceeded to lecture the colonel in a classic statement of the place of military power under law.

> Your assertion that the military forces are not the servants of the people of Arkansas, but rather their masters, is unjust to the people and the military and unfounded in fact. The military forces are the servants of the laws, and the laws are for the benefit of the people. . . . The assumption that a party of soldiers can, at their own option, forcibly destroy a citizen's property, and commit a gross violation of the public peace, would not be tolerated under a "Napoleon."[7]

Ord forcefully pointed out that the First Reconstruction Act made it the duty of the district commander to protect citizens in their rights and to preserve the public peace. In an allusion to the military commissions, the general said that, where citizens or soldiers were wronged, there was a mode of redress, and especially was it available to the military. Ord maintained that he had always used the power to the utmost where soldiers had been outraged in line of duty.[8]

A reporter for the *Boston Post* interviewed President Johnson about the incident and quoted the president as saying that Colonel Gilbert's letter was " 'one of the legitimate fruits of the radical teachings of the day. He spoke in flattering terms of General Ord,' the writer continued, 'and heartily approved the noble rebuke which the General administered to Colonel Gilbert.' "[9]

A court-martial ordered by Ord sat at Camden for the trial of Captain Pierce. The captain was found guilty of maliciously causing to be destroyed certain property of the *Constitutional Eagle* and of conduct prejudicial to military discipline. He was sentenced to pay $1,000 damages, forfeit his pay for one year, and was placed in rank below the fifty captains under him in seniority. Ord approved the finding of the court-martial, noting that "Newspaper comments usually are resented only in proportion to their fidelity to the facts."[10]

Ord's actions in this instance had deep significance. In the destruction of the *Eagle*, he was confronted by an act of violence prompted by hatred, one of the rotten fruits of war. Raw military power had carried over into the period of peace and had ridden roughshod over the law and order so essential to a civilized community. To Ord, nothing could be more repugnant. The general, since Appomattox, had risen above pettiness and had evidenced a breadth of spirit from which extended kindness and forgiveness. Ord could see the necessity for law to prevail over the arbitrary violence which is its negative, for only under law can property be secure, expression be free, and other rights be safe. It is under law that military power is restrained and directed. The general expressed these fundamentals in a statement of the first order. His ultimate object was to create good will, to develop the comity of sections, and to make peace and unity real in a nation torn by discord. Blessed are the peacemakers!

The *Eagle* resumed publication after a time. At its masthead was a new motto, Ord's statement to Colonel Gilbert: "the military forces are the servants of the laws, and the laws are for the benefit of the people."[11]

★★★★★

A few weeks after the *Constitutional Eagle* affair, another newspaper editor in Ord's district felt the weight of military force, but in a different way. On 8 November 1867, a lieutenant with a squad of soldiers marched into the office of the *Vicksburg Daily Times*, arrested the editor, Colonel William H. McCardle, and took him to General Alvan C. Gillem's headquarters, where he was confined in the military prison. The arrest was ordered by Ord, who charged the editor with obstructing the execution of the laws of the United States by fomenting disorder and encouraging violence against the agents of the government. The editor was to be held for trial before a military commission. Later, Ord told Gillem that there was no need to keep McCardle in a cell unless there was fear that he might escape.[12]

McCardle had been a colonel in Confederate service and had been on Pemberton's staff at the siege of Vicksburg. A journalist before the war, he had resumed his newspaper career in Vicksburg after the conflict had closed. McCardle had opposed the military Reconstruction at the outset. He had done so forcefully, albeit erratically, and had frequently aroused members of the moderate press to condemn him for his inconsistencies and for his taking extreme stands which, they felt, would merely worsen the plight of the South.

What sort of language had the Vicksburg editor used to bring military arrest upon himself? McCardle referred to the various orders issued by Ord as "the brutal edicts which have fallen from the insolent, vulgar Satrap, who lords it over two States and a million and a half people. . . ." The general's tyranny, he believed, would "attract the attention of the whole civilized world." Of a particular order, the editor taunted: "See, for instance, how his Royal Highness King Otho the 1st, (pray Heaven he may be the last), proclaims *his* law!" The prospective constitutional convention voted into existence about the time of McCardle's arrest the editor described as being "composed, for the most part, of Negroes, foreign adventurers, and domestic renegades. . . ." The constitution expected to emanate from the convention was "born of this bastard concern—born of Radicalism and Ord. . . ."[13]

It was the judgment of J. F. H. Claiborne, native Mississippian, former Democratic congressman, editor and historian, that McCardle had abused the freedom of the press. The epithets which McCardle had applied to General Ord, wrote Claiborne to Federal Judge Robert A. Hill, "were unjust, uncalled for & outrageous, prompted as he was to draw the Genl into a personal rencontre." Claiborne's opinion that McCardle was attempting to provoke Ord to a duel sheds light upon an interesting aspect of the actions of the erratic Vicksburg editor. "Such a purpose is both criminal and absurd," said Claiborne to Judge Hill of McCardle's intention. "Gen. Ord is vested with military and judicial powers, and could no more accept a challenge than your Honor could. . . ."[14]

Counsel for McCardle sent a request to Ord's headquarters that the editor be admitted to bail, offering to give security to any amount. Ord's terse endorsement on the telegram: "Bail refused."[15] To McCardle's attorney, Walker Brooke, the general telegraphed: "I regard McCardle *as an enemy to public peace!* Mainly *responsible* for the feeling which led to the *murder of Duggin.* Having ordered similar proceedings against partizans on the other side who excite discord between races, or sectional hostility, I cannot bail him."[16]

McCardle denied the truth of Ord's statement and vehemently asserted that the general's purpose was to punish him before trial "by thrusting him into a filthy dungeon." Thus, said the editor, Ord would degrade him and have "sweet revenge."[17]

Attorneys for McCardle applied to Federal Judge Robert A. Hill for a writ of habeas corpus. They argued that Ord had created a new offense, that the Reconstruction acts were unconstitutional, and that the general had destroyed the freedom of the press. The judge issued the writ, but explained to Ord that he had made it clear to those applying that its granting was not to be construed as any indication of the court's judgment on the hearing. The writ was served upon General Gillem who had McCardle in custody, and it directed him to produce his prisoner on 21 November and to show cause for his restraint. Gillem asked Ord whether he should obey the writ.[18]

Ord directed Gillem to inform Judge Hill that his writ would be honored and that the prisoner would be sent to

Jackson to appear before his court on 21 November. At the same time, the general wrote the judge that he did not have the law at hand regarding writs for persons arrested under the Reconstruction acts, but it was his personal opinion that United States judges should have the power to issue the writs and that district commanders should obey them in order to curb any feelings of personal hostility which they might have. The general then ordered an existing military commission headed by Colonel Eben Swift to convene on 20 November for McCardle's arraignment.[19] The arrangement of events was such that McCardle would appear before Judge Hill as a prisoner in process of undergoing trial by a military commission already in existence at the time of his arrest.

Federal Judge Robert A. Hill, into whose hands the McCardle matter fell, already noted as an adviser to Ord in Mississippi affairs, was a native of North Carolina, but had been reared in Tennessee, where he was trained to the law and where he had cast his lot with the Whig party. He had moved in 1855 to Jacinto, Tishomingo County, Mississippi. Hill had opposed Mississippi's secession and had taken no part in the war. He had been appointed to his judgeship in 1866.

On the eve of the McCardle hearing, Judge Hill, while noting that, as a matter of course, he could not give any opinion on the case until it was presented, discoursed at considerable length in letters to Ord upon many matters surrounding the legal action. Of Ord's motives in arresting McCardle, the judge said: "No one who knows you supposes that your action is prompted by any personal feeling, however much cause you may have. All admit that you are incapable of such an act." The attacks upon Ord by some of the press Hill described as "wanton and inexcusable" and stated that they were not approved by the "thinking and reflecting."[20] A pertinent question here would be how many Mississippians were in this latter category. The Conservative element was greatly affronted by the arrest of McCardle, and Ord gained the enmity of those not already alienated.[21]

McCardle was charged before Ord's military commission under the authority of the Reconstruction acts with disturbance of the public peace; inciting to insurrection, disorder, and violence; libel; and impeding Reconstruction. Among the more specific charges against McCardle were that he had denounced General Ord as a usurper and despot, that he had defamed the character of a certain agent of the Freedmen's Bureau, and that he had advised voters to remain away from the polls at the time of the election to determine whether or not they desired a convention.[22]

Gillem produced McCardle before Judge Hill in Jackson on 21 November. The judge set the hearing for 25 November. McCardle's counsel were Walker Brooke and Thomas A. Marshall of Vicksburg and the omnipresent William L. Sharkey. These attorneys contended in the hearing that their client had been denied freedom of speech and of the press under the First Amendment. Judge Hill ruled on this point that McCardle had freedom of speech in Mississippi as did citizens in other states, but this did not extend to abuse of public measures or official acts of those entrusted with making or administering the laws.[23]

Judge Hill asserted that it was admitted that McCardle's publications were libelous, and, under the laws of the state, the writer would be subject to punishment. To the contention that no state courts existed, the judge responded that all state courts existed subject to the district commander, and, under the law of Congress, he might choose the tribunal for trial. McCardle denied that his counsel admitted that his publications were libelous. He insisted that what he had printed was true.[24]

Judge Hill's decision in summary was this: the Reconstruction acts were constitutional; General Ord had not exceeded the powers vested in him by law; and McCardle could properly be arrested and tried before a military commission without indictment or jury. McCardle was remanded to Gillem's custody for the continuance of his trial by military commission.

McCardle appealed to the Supreme Court of the United States under a statute of 5 February 1867, which had provided for appeal to the Supreme Court in habeas corpus proceedings whether initiated in state or federal courts. The law seems to have been intended for the protection of former slaves and Southern Unionists but ironically became the resort of a rabid Southern Conservative. Ord would have pressed on with the military trial in spite of the appeal, but, apparently on the advice of the government counsel, the military proceedings were suspended. McCardle was admitted to $1,000 bail.[25]

The "rebel press" of both North and South, said Judge Hill, were firing away at him on account of his decision, but he insisted to the general that the vociferous Vicksburg editor had done Ord more good than harm in Mississippi. He believed that McCardle's course was almost universally condemned.[26] It is difficult at this time to agree with this last-stated belief of the judge. Claiborne congratulated Hill on the decision. A contrary ruling, he thought, would have struck directly at the Congress, would have let loose in Mississippi a "spirit of licentiousness and disorder." Stern military rule was best until the state was restored to its proper place in the Union. At the same time, apparently referring to other aspects of the general's administration, he described Ord's rule as "mild, forbearing & generous." Claiborne continued: "And so far from trampling on the liberty of the press he has done more to protect it than any military man in this nation. I refer particularly to the Arkansas case, for which every editor and every citizen should be grateful to him."[27]

McCardle, in resuming his editorial duties, was naturally harsh. He called Judge Hill's decision a travesty. If the opinion should be upheld, he said, then constitutional government would cease to exist, all liberty would be suppressed, and the military would be all powerful.[28]

The next action in the case of McCardle would be before the Supreme Court of the United States. It was some weeks before the court was ready to hear the case known as *Ex parte McCardle*. One cannot but wonder whether the pending action of the Supreme Court was a result sought by Ord all along. In view of his conservatism, would the general welcome a judicial negative upon the vast powers he wielded in Mississippi and Arkansas?[29]

Radical Senator Lyman Trumbull of Illinois was appointed as one of the government counsel in the McCardle case along with Matthew H. Carpenter, a prominent lawyer of Wisconsin, and James Hughes. Members of McCardle's counsel were the durable Sharkey; Jeremiah S. Black, a former attorney general of the United States; and David Dudley Field, a well-known Northern legal reformer.[30]

Early in the preliminary proceedings Trumbull made a motion to dismiss the case. He argued that there was no precedent for an appeal such as McCardle's and that the editor's offense was a military one over which the court had no jurisdiction. Black and Sharkey countered that the offense was not military and that the court did have jurisdiction. Chief Justice Chase delivered the opinion of the court that McCardle had a right to appeal under the Habeas Corpus Act of 5 February 1867, and the motion to dismiss was denied.[31]

In the course of the preliminary hearing, one of McCardle's incendiary articles was read in which the editor had violently condemned the military authorities and the Reconstruction acts. This brought from McCardle's attorney, Jeremiah S. Black, the admission that the articles would exasperate the friends of General Ord, and it was his private opinion that McCardle's epithets directed at the general were not deserved.[32]

The great concern of the Republicans, meanwhile, was the threat to congressional Reconstruction posed by the McCardle matter. In this legal action lay the possibility that the court would rule military commissions unconstitutional where civil courts were open. A judgment to this effect had already been made by the court in the famous Milligan case.[33] Beyond that limited possibility loomed the larger possibility of a ruling by the court on the constitutionality of the Reconstruction acts.

The court set 3 March 1868 as the date to hear arguments in the case. The *National Intelligencer*, in listing the lineup of contending attorneys, said: "There will be no lack of ability on either side, and the case will be memorable for all time."[34] Indeed, eloquent arguments were made by the lawyers of both sides, and, upon their conclusion, the judges took the case of McCardle under advisement. In the course of this period of deliberation, on 27 March 1868, the Congress did a most remarkable thing by repealing that part of the statute of 5 February 1867 providing for the appeal from lower federal courts to the Supreme Court in habeas corpus proceedings. Clearly, the Republicans felt they could not allow the McCardle case to reach the point of decision by the Supreme Court. The court reconvened and announced a willingness to hear arguments on the effect of the statute of repeal. Sharkey, speaking for McCardle, said that obviously its purpose was to prevent the court from ruling on the matter at hand. To this, Trumbull and Carpenter replied that the statute clearly destroyed the court's jurisdiction over the case and that it was not correct that the act affected only the McCardle matter. It affected all such cases. In the face of the action of the Congress, the judges felt they had no choice. They dismissed McCardle's appeal for want of jurisdiction.[35]

For many years, historians have taken the position that during the Reconstruction period the Supreme Court was intimidated by the Radical Congress, that it failed to assert itself, and that its judicial powers were greatly diminished. Modern scholars have taken issue with this interpretation. Stanley Kutler cites other cases involving habeas corpus in which the court affirmed its power and jurisdiction.[36] William M. Wiecek notes, in a similar vein, that the Congress actually expanded the powers of the court during Reconstruction. He does concede that "the Court . . . emerged from the McCardle affair slightly bloodied but unbowed."[37] Kutler points out further that, with the death of Justice James M. Wayne in July 1867, the eight-member court was evenly divided on the constitutional question of Reconstruction and, for this reason, was unwilling to rule on that overriding issue.[38]

"*Ex parte McCardle*," writes Kutler, "is one of those rare Supreme Court cases, like *Marbury v. Madison* or Dred Scott's, which has had profound political implications in its contemporary setting and persistent relevance to the nature of Judicial power in the American system of government."[39] The initiator of the litigation was General Ord who, in merely doing his duty as he saw it, became a part of a case which promises indeed to be "memorable for all time."

★★★★★

There was much disquiet among the people in Ord's district between the November elections and the beginning of the year 1868. The restlessness seems to have been prompted by economic distress arising from the second successive year of crop failure, complicated by animosity between the races and between the Radical and Conservative political factions.

The situation in Arkansas did not become critical. In that state General Ord extended protection and assistance to the Negroes in various ways, while at the same time ordering them to go to work or be proceeded against as vagrants. These regulations, along with tight military control, sufficed to keep the peace in Arkansas.[40]

Mississippi was another case. In November and December, a steady stream of requests flowed into Ord's headquarters from sheriffs, boards of police and reliable private citizens that troops be sent or retained for the protection of the whites against a threatened Negro revolt.[41]

At Ord's suggestion, Governor Benjamin Grubb Humphreys issued a proclamation dated 9 December admonishing the blacks not to expect to seize land by violence and warning that any attempt to do so could not succeed. Humphreys went on to warn the white race that, as they valued their own constitutional liberties, they must accord to the black race the full measure of their rights under the Constitution and laws of the land.[42]

About the time Humphreys's proclamation was issued, Ord telegraphed to Ulysses S. Grant that large numbers of Negroes in the river counties were armed and plundering for food. Owners were abandoning the country for their safety. "There is reason to fear a war of races," he said, "if the blacks are not fed."[43] The general proposed that Congress appropriate a half million dollars to employ the freedmen in repairing the Mississippi River levees from Tunica to Vicksburg. On 19 December, by a special order, Ord directed Gillem to go to Washington and present to the president and the secretary of war the starving condition of many of the freedmen in Mississippi due to the bankruptcy of the cotton planters. Conditions were decidedly bad, and many men were destitute. Vast acreage was lost by farmers and planters through foreclosure and by sale for taxes. There were predictions of starvation.[44]

President Johnson and his Cabinet, in a meeting on 24 December, discussed the Mississippi question. Grant, sitting in as secretary of war, said he thought the situation was not as bad as it had been represented and that Ord exaggerated. He did not think there was anything to be concerned about.[45]

The violence which seemed to Ord to be so imminent did not materialize. Yet, the possibility of it was there. The general was prone to tackle any problem facing him with all the force at his command. It appears that he simply erred on the side of caution and preparedness in this instance.

★★★★★

General Ord had entered upon his duties as commander of the Fourth Military District with considerable reluctance, and, quite early in his tenure, he began to press the powers in Washington to release him from the distasteful duties of Reconstruction. "I am going to get out of this Dept. now as soon as it can be done with grace—and may *have* to go to the Pacific," he wrote to Placidus in November.[46] In the meeting of 24 December, in which President Johnson and his Cabinet discussed the Mississippi question, Grant reported that Ord wanted to be relieved and indicated his own approval of this wish. "He gave Ord credit of being very honest, but unsteady and fond of change," Gideon Welles recorded.[47] Grant suggested that Ord be sent to the Pacific and Irvin McDowell recalled from there to take his place. Gillem might command in the interim. The matter was raised again in a Cabinet meeting of 27 December with Grant stating that Ord had asked repeatedly to be relieved over the past four or five months. The acting secretary of war urged that Ord be transferred. "The President . . . seemed not anxious to relieve Ord, who appears to be conscientious. . . ," wrote the secretary of the navy.[48] Nevertheless, the president gave his approval. A general order of 28 December 1867 directed Ord to turn over his command to Gillem, which he did on 9 January 1868, and to proceed to San Francisco to take command of the Department of California.[49]

Comments on Ord's removal from command and upon his work of the preceding year began to appear from various quarters. Washington correspondents of the *Baltimore Sun,* the *New Orleans Crescent,* and the *New York Herald* were uncomplimentary, making vague references to "peculiarities and inconsistencies" which suggested "that the scope of the command was rather beyond his calibre."[50] McCardle, in the *Vicksburg Daily Times,* declined to believe the complimentary implication in these dispatches that Ord had been relieved at his own request. "Poor old Ord! The best excuse that can be trumped up for his insolence and tyranny, is his utter want of brains," wrote the Vicksburg firebrand.[51]

To the *Little Rock Gazette,* Ord's transfer came as a surprise. Picking up the tone of the Washington disptaches, the *Gazette* concurred in the view that the general lacked the ability to cope with the problems of the command. Ord's administration had begun very auspiciously, the Arkansas journal said, but he had become a different man when clothed with power. Selfish partisans surrounded him. He rejected them for a while, but they were scheming, and he was weak. They triumphed. Some of Ord's acts were as arbitrary as any committed by Daniel E. Sickles or Philip H. Sheridan. Still, the *Gazette* said with a pensive note, Ord had been so preferable to officers like Sheridan that there could be no rejoicing at his departure. McDowell might be worse. Most Arkansans looked upon Ord with pity rather than enmity, said the Little Rock newspaper. He was "a man of natural good heart" who "allowed himself to become the tool of designing men." Summing up his account with the people of Arkansas: "To much injustice done to free citizens of the United States, a large amount. By credit to greater injuries that he had the power to inflict, but did not, a credit that overbalances the debit side of the account." With wry solicitude, the *Gazette* concluded: "Long live Gen. Ord—in California."[52]

Were these the only voices raised in judgment upon the work of Ord, he might have stood condemned in his own time. There were others, however, close to the scene, men of widely divergent political views, whose testimony must be considered.

Senator Henry Wilson of Massachusetts, a Radical of some moment, and a correspondent of Ord since the days of the Richmond command, witnessed to the general's accomplishments. "It seems to me that you have been wise and true in words and deeds," Wilson wrote to Ord in November 1867.[53] This was in response to a letter from Ord apparently recounting his work of Reconstruction up to the election date, and would be taken as a mark of Radical approval.

From the other extreme of the political spectrum, the words of Governor Humphreys have particular force as they testify to the general's attitude toward those over whom he ruled. The governor was certainly in position to view Ord's work closely. It could hardly be said that he was predisposed to be a friendly witness to the implementation of Radical Reconstruction. Said he of Ord:

> *I am satisfied he entertained the kindest feelings and sentiments toward the people of the South, and though he incurred some odium with some I am also satisfied it was in weakly yielding to pressure from one of our own people. I must say that in all my intercourse with him, I found him invariably guided by a high sense of honor, truth, and gentlemanly bearing, full of gentleness and kindness, and free from all bitterness.*[54]

Ord did indeed arouse the hostility of McCardle and of other bitter Conservatives. Did he provoke them by yielding to the pressure exerted by a Mississippi Radical? The name of Judge Robert A. Hill would come to mind. If the judge determined the general's actions, it does not appear in the evidence. So far as the records show, Ord was his own man.

Further commentaries on General Ord's part in Reconstruction were offered by the two historians who made intensive studies of Reconstruction in the two states in Ord's command. James W. Garner wrote in *Reconstruction in Mississippi* (1901) with reference to the Reconstruction acts that Ord "might have administered them with less rigor and severity."[55] Thomas S. Staples in his *Reconstruction in Arkansas* (1923) said that Ord "faced a problem impossible of solution satisfactory to all concerned." Looking in retrospect upon Ord's work Staples concluded that "he had been too moderate for the Republicans . . . and not moderate enough for the Conservatives."[56]

Ord's own assessment of the work of Radical Reconstruction which he was called upon to direct has more than ordinary significance. In his annual report for 1867 under date of 27 September, the general stated that the extension of suffrage to the freedmen had aroused hostility to them and to Northern men in many places in his district where it had not existed before. This hostility greatly complicated the establishment of governments under the terms set forth by Congress. Of the freedmen's political situation, Ord reported:

> *All their combinations are now conducted by white men, under the protection of the Military; if this protection were withdrawn the white men now contolling would generally withdraw with it, and some of the southern people now exasperated at what they deem the Freedmen's presumption would not be very gentle towards them, so that the presence of a larger military force will be required for some time, to maintain the freedmen in the possession of the right of suffrage.*[57]

A few weeks later, as the election was getting under way in his district, Ord described to Sherman the situation in the South as "the scrape we are in." "I call it a scrape," Ord wrote, "because matters are not improving in the South and the dominancy of freedmen will be a poor attempt to solve the difficulty." Negro suffrage had just about demonstrated its failure already, Ord continued, as the leading Radicals in Mississippi were wondering if they would be able to control the new electorate "after they are turned loose," and if property should be "put entirely under the control of the most ignorant and impulsive labor not very provident or industrious it will simply go to the devil." Ord believed the conditions forebode the same state of affairs he and Sherman had witnessed in Jamaica in 1850, where the emancipation of the very large slave population in 1833 had brought on economic decline. "I don't want to be one of the men who is to be held responsible for bringing such a condition of things upon ten states once so prosperous," he said.[58]

Ord's task of the moment, he told Sherman, was to keep down the "extravagant hopes" of freedmen on the one hand and the "extravagant acts" of those embittered by Negro suffrage on the other. "I am in a breech between two exasperated and hostile elements who are being egged on to pitch in to each other by the knaves and fools of both sides."[59]

The conventions were in the offing, and Ord's commentary on their prospects was revealing: "If these conventions are composed of the ill, bad and extreme as well as knavish demagogues who seem to be taking the lead among the freed population and who ignored the most respectable ex-officers and Union men in the South, they will if not voted down bring on a war of races, and I don't intend to stay here to be the butt of both sides in any such contest."[60]

Ord journeyed to Washington in January shortly after being relieved and there conferred with President Johnson. The *National Intelligencer* reported that Ord told the president that Negro suffrage would meet with little success in the Fourth Military District.[61] This was probably what the conservative president wanted to hear, though it did not mean that Ord saw eye to eye with Johnson. "I have not favored his views lately," the general had written to Placidus Ord in November. "He goes too much for the rebs, who are many of them rebs yet and would shoot you and I through the belly in a minute if they could do so with impunity." The Radicals were not altogether right either, Ord continued. "Both parties are in a passion & both wrong."[62] The general was caught in the middle of a great political struggle, but one commitment was clear: "I do not think any officer of the army who retains his commission has any right to disregard the laws of the present Congress."[63]

The conventions which Ord had helped to bring into being convened in Jackson and Little Rock on 7 January 1868, just about the time he relinquished his command. The general, lingering in Mississippi for personal reasons, was skeptical that any good would emanate from these assemblies and had little confidence in the wisdom or efficacy of what he had wrought in establishing the Radical Reconstruction program.

The Mississippi convention the irrepressible McCardle referred to as "Gen. Ord's fraudulent, bogus Convention," and as "Ord's nigger Convention," while the delegates he styled as "Ord's vagabonds" and "Ord's scavengers."[64] It produced a progressive constitution, but there ensued a period of political turbulence which kept the state unsettled for many months. It was not until 23 February 1870 that Mississippi was readmitted to the Union under Radical Republican rule.

The white Conservatives were determined to oust the Republicans and to eliminate the Negroes from their prominent role in the political life of Mississippi. Through force and economic coercion, the Democrats won a great victory in 1875, and, by the early part of 1876, the "redemption" of Mississippi was virtually completed. In the ensuing years, the mass of Negroes was held in political impotence through fraud and intimidation. By 1890, Mississippi was ready to make white supremacy formal and give it at least a countenance of legality. A constitutional convention assembled in that year and wrote the famous "understanding clause," a literacy test, into the organic law of the state along with other impediments to discourage the registration of Negro electors. Through the 1890's and into the 1900's, the number of Negro voters, soon negligible, steadily dwindled from year to year until it became a mere cipher.[65] Thus did Mississippi become a "white man's state."

★★★★★

By a very narrow margin, the Arkansas constitution was accepted and the Republicans carried the elections. The bill in Congress providing for the readmission of the state became effective on 22 June 1868. Arkansas was the first of the ten former Confederate states included in the military districts to be returned to the Union. Factional quarrels divided the Republicans, and violent confrontations with Democrats made their rule uncertain. The Democrats came into control of both houses of the legislature in 1874 and arranged for the formation of a new constitution. Early in 1875, the Congress and the president let it be known that they would not interfere in Arkansas affairs. Thus was Arkansas "redeemed" from Radical control. In ensuing years, it was said that Negroes in Arkansas were intimidated to prevent their voting. White primaries became the rule. Negroes were not wanted as voters and were not courted by politicians. The result was a low percentage of Negro registrants. Arkansas became a one-party state, and so she remained for many decades.[66]

Ord had prophesied that, upon the withdrawal of the military forces, Negro suffrage would collapse, and so it had. The Negroes were relegated to their "place"—even as Ord in substance had predicted in 1867. There the blacks remained for nearly a century, and a "Second Reconstruction" was required to secure for them the precious rights of citizenship. Ord's keen insight had brought him to the real answer to the problem of civil rights for blacks a century before they were achieved. As he had written to Grant, the maintenance of those rights ultimately would depend upon "an enlightened public opinion, the interests of the community, and the selection of good and wise citizens to administer justice."[67]

18

★★★★★

Pursuit into Mexico

MOLLY Ord and the six children had joined General Edward Ord in Vicksburg after he had taken command of the Fourth Military District, but terribly high rental costs and a none too healthy climate discouraged their continued residence there. During the course of the summer of 1867, Ord had taken his family to Pass Christian for an extended stay on the salubrious Gulf Coast of Mississippi. Then, in October, the general had moved his headquarters to Holly Springs in the hill country in the northern part of the state. Here the family lived for the remainder of Ord's sojourn in Mississippi. The Ords were expecting another child momentarily when the general received his orders of transfer to California. They remained in Holly Springs for Molly's confinement and recovery.[1]

Ord thought of going to California by the plains route, but the odds were against him. He would have to carry a washing machine, milch cows and other necessities to accommodate seven little children under the age of eleven! He gave up the idea of the overland trip and embarked his entourage from New York on 1 April 1868, for a voyage to San Francisco via the Isthmus of Panama.[2] Even that journey must have been a major accomplishment, no doubt expedited by the assistance of servants.

California seemed to draw Ord like a magnet. Since his landing at Monterey in 1847 as a lieutenant, he had "grown up" with the country. He knew it in the Mexican War and the gold rush, in the achievement of statehood and as a developing frontier. He returned as a brigadier general to find that the population had increased from 93,000 in the year of statehood to approximately a half million, less than twenty years later. San Francisco was a brawling, boisterous frontier metropolis growing larger with each passing day. Her population had almost tripled in the decade of the sixties and stood near 150,000. The city was not blessed with all amenities and advantages. "Full of small pox and mud," Ord described it a few weeks after his arrival. All his pay went for board and the hire of servants. Three domestics and a coachman cost thirty dollars each in gold per month, and washing was done out at twenty-five dollars in gold.[3]

Ord's new command, the Department of California with headquarters in San Francisco, was a part of the Military Division of the Pacific commanded by Henry W. Halleck. The department consisted of California, Nevada and Arizona Territory and was manned by six companies of the First Cavalry, eight companies of the Eighth Cavalry, five companies of the Second Artillery, nine companies of the Ninth Infantry, ten companies of the Fourteenth Infantry, and ten companies of the Thirty-second Infantry, a force totaling more than 3,000 men.[4]

Ord was compelled to give most of his attention to Arizona where the Chiricahua Apaches and the capable Chief Cochise, victimized by white treachery, had sworn to fight without ceasing against encroaching settlers. Ord instituted a policy of aggressively pressing the Indians to punish them and keep them on the defensive. Even as he pressed this relentless campaign of extermination, he repeatedly urged upon the secretary of war that steps be taken to protect the rights of the Indians. The reservation system should be tried and whites kept out, the general insisted.[5]

Ord did not agree with Halleck's view that more troops were needed for Arizona. He did not believe the country was worth the million dollars per year required to maintain the additional forces. "Every white man there could be paid and bought out for less money," he said.[6] The inhabitants were mostly "vagabond rebs" who had no respect for the government and fomented Indian wars in order to sell whiskey to the soldiers and to get contracts to supply them.[7]

While the argument went on, the general kept his troops busy rooting out the hostiles. More than 200 were killed between September 1868 and September 1869, mostly by soldiers doggedly pursuing them day and night. Many villages were destroyed, supplies burned and captives taken. Quite a few soldiers were lost, but Ord believed, and correctly, that the Apaches would soon sue for peace. A reservation policy was attempted in the 1870s for these Indians in New Mexico and Arizona, but it required a good many years to tame them and keep them within their assigned limits.[8]

★★★★★

At various times during the course of his long army career, Ord made proposals for the improvement of the military service. He suggested a number of changes in the lot of the enlisted man. As early as 1860, he heartily endorsed a proposed law providing for commissioning from the ranks, an endorsement he was to repeat in the years ahead. Better have fewer graduates from West Point and have some vacancies "as a reward for the distinguished and brave" in the ranks, he said.[9] Ord advocated higher pay, which he believed would secure a better quality soldier and reduce the high rate of desertion. What a relief for the man in the ranks, Ord continued in a recommendation to Edwin M. Stanton in 1866, if he could have a bed rather than an ungainly bunk, a private nook in the quarters, a bathing room, a room with books and newspapers to keep his mind from stagnating and to keep him away from cards and the grog shop, verandas where he might get fresh air in inclement weather, "and above all some chance of rooming with the best or quietest men if he chose to do so, and not forced into the company of the vicious in spite of himself. . . ."[10] Ord thought the private soldier should be able to approach the company commander directly without having to go through the first sergeant. Sergeants of all grades should be better paid, for this would mean noncommissioned officers of better quality.[11]

Medical care of the soldiers absorbed the general's close attention. During the Civil War, a Cincinnati newspaper highly commended him for his careful concern for the welfare of the soldiers in Corinth, Mississippi, and vicinity when he commanded there in the summer of 1862. His regulations for the operation of the hospitals were credited with saving the lives of many soldiers.[12]

The general protested the inequality in justice meted out to officers and enlisted men. Punishment ought to fall on both categories alike. As to the composition of military courts, he thought that enlisted men of the same grade as the accused ought to be detailed on courts-martial, as was the practice in the German army.[13] Having only officers on the courts, he wrote to a House Sub-Committee on Military Affairs, was "a little like the Republicans having the right to select the juries to try the Democrats. . . ."[14]

Ord had constructive suggestions for the improvement of the officer corps. He observed that officers did not ordinarily pursue their professional studies after leaving West Point. He suggested that study could be encouraged by assignment to corps only after service and examination as to fitness before each promotion through the rank of major. Such a system, Ord noted, was working well on the medical staff.[15]

★★★★★

Ord's assignment in San Francisco lasted a little more than three years.[16] There were the usual signs of discontent, and these were not lost on Placidus Ord who predicted that the restless general would seek a new station in the East.[17] A transfer was indeed in the offing, and it was eastward. In the latter part of 1871, Ord was ordered to take command of the Department of the Platte with headquarters in Omaha. Nebraska had achieved statehood only four years before Ord's arrival, and the state was experiencing a rapid growth. From a scant 29,000 in 1860, the population had risen to nearly 123,000 by 1870. Omaha was a bustling commercial center. Her growth had been phenomenal under the impetus of the construction of the Union Pacific Railroad. The linkup of the Union Pacific with the Central Pacific in Utah in 1869 marked the completion of the first transcontinental line. Omaha, with 16,000 people in 1870, was a center for the shipment of cattle and other products of farm and ranch and a busy outlet for Eastern manufacturers.

The Union Pacific Railroad became the attenuated focus of Ord's command. The security of the line and the safety of the people who settled near it were his prime concern. The Department of the Platte extended westward from the peaceful prairies of Iowa to include the young state of Nebraska and the rugged territories of Wyoming and Utah. For more than 1,000 miles, the thin bands of railroad steel stretched through this wilderness, though each year the frontier line of settlement advanced, absorbing country which only recently had been the domain of Indians. Clashes between red and white became more numerous. "Every man plows and mows with his rifle in his hand or at his back," the general wrote in 1872.[18]

Ord had eleven stations from Omaha to the borders of Nevada garrisoned by the Ninth, Thirteenth and Fourteenth Infantry regiments; eight companies of the Second Cavalry and a detachment of the Fifth Cavalry. The Fourth Infantry was added to the command, but the subsequent transfer of the Thirteenth Infantry kept his force the same. For the protection of farms and ranches and of government surveyors, the troops engaged in constant scouting, and there were occasional clashes with marauders.[19] The railroad was an object of continuous concern. "General Ord has maintained admirably the safety of the great Pacific Railway, now one of the grand avenues of travel for the whole world. . . ," General of the Army William T. Sherman reported toward the close of 1874.[20]

★★★★★

Ord became involved with Nebraska citizens in an unexpected and certainly unusual matter. In 1874, the grasshoppers came to Nebraska, millions upon millions of them, stripping the earth of every green thing and leaving in their wake a helpless and starving people. The general was named chairman of the executive committee of the Nebraska State Relief and Aid Society to alleviate the sufferings of the victims of the insect plague. In October 1874, Ord addressed the Chicago Board of Trade on behalf of the relief society. A few days later, he sought and secured authority from the secretary of war to issue rations as well as arms and ammunition to the sufferers. In December, he reported to Secretary of War William W. Belknap that his committee was issuing to about 9,000 people enough food to keep them alive at a cost of $12,000 per month.[21] Ord's "grasshopper work" made him very popular in Nebraska. "I think if you were to run in this state for office," one of his associates in the relief effort wrote, "you could get nine out of every ten votes."[22]

★★★★★

In 1875, Ord began hinting to Sherman that he would be glad to go to California if Schofield wanted to leave there. A few days later, Ord was saying to Sherman that he did not want to change his department, which he thought was an important one, and that he felt he could manage the Sioux. He merely mentioned California, he said, as he hoped it might be his last station before retiring. These stirrings were likely to yield some result, but not necessarily a predictable one. While working on Sherman, Ord was also pressing his friend President Ulysses S. Grant, and it was Grant who determined Ord's next station. Early in 1875, Ord was ordered to take command of the Department of Texas with headquarters in San Antonio.[23]

The general and family were guests at the Vance House in San Antonio for several weeks while they were arranging for a suitable residence. The citizens of the town were cordial, and many offered to assist the Ords in any way possible.[24] Such hospitality was especially gratifying, as Texans had not always had occasion to express kindly feelings toward the federal commanders in their midst. The state had just ousted the Carpetbagger-Scalawag-Negro government in January 1874.

Civil War and Reconstruction had not impeded the phenomenal growth of Texas. San Antonio was a lusty town well beyond the 12,000 population reported in 1870, and each day saw the arrival of more people from areas to the east. The state as a whole, in the census of 1870, reported 564,700 white and 253,475 black inhabitants, an increase of 35 percent since 1860. The state would nearly double in its population in the decade of the seventies. Settlement had reached westward approximately to the 100th meridian. Beyond this line lay the high plains, and, in the extreme western part of the state across the Pecos were towering mountains.[25]

The edge of settlement was marked by a series of military posts lying roughly along the 100th meridian from north to south: Forts Richardson, Belknap, Griffin, Chadbourne, Concho, McKavett and Clark, the latter near Del Rio on the Rio Grande. West of the Pecos were Forts Stockton and Davis. On the lower Rio Grande, below Fort Clark, were Fort Duncan at Eagle Pass, Fort McIntosh at Laredo, Ringgold Barracks near Rio Grande City and Fort Brown at Brownsville near the mouth of the river. This was the vast perimeter of the Department of Texas. To man this line, Ord had about 3,000 soldiers: the Twenty-fourth and Twenty-fifth Infantry regiments and the

Ninth and Tenth Cavalry regiments, all having white officers and Negro soldiers.[26]

The 1870s were turbulent years in Texas. There were stagecoach holdups, Indian attacks and cattle raids. In response, United States soldiers and Texas Rangers would dash in hot pursuit. Ord found the lower Rio Grande to be the most troublesome portion of a troubled frontier. On the Mexican side of the river, armed parties had for years organized to cross over to the stock ranches on the American side to steal cattle. Then a rapid drive back across the Rio Grande would bring them to sanctuary beyond the reach of United States authority. Raiding and murderous assaults had become so common by the time of Ord's arrival that nearly all of the Americans living in the border counties had left their ranches and farms. A further problem affected mainly the Rio Grande frontier above Laredo. Savage Indians from the mountains of Coahuila and Chihuahua crossed the upper river and raided the frontier of west Texas. They murdered settlers and took away livestock and other plunder to their sanctuary in Mexico.[27] Indeed, this promised to be a state of affairs which could absorb even the restless energies of General Ord. From the moment of his arrival, he was in the thick of it.

The general traveled the Rio Grande frontier not long after he assumed the Texas command in order to get acquainted firsthand with the country and the people. The lower 200 miles of the Rio Grande valley he described as a veritable jungle with now and then a small ranch or a hut. The population was Mexican. The soil was rich, and corn, cotton and sugar cane could be grown with little effort. The Mexicans encountered by Ord as he passed along appeared to have no occupation other than keeping in the shade and riding from ranch to ranch. The men were armed, their horses saddled. They "looked sullen at us as we passed," Ord said, "instead of giving the usual 'Buenos dias'. . . ."[28] Americans acquainted with the area told the general that it was impossible to sort out the raiders from the general run of the inhabitants, as the population was changing all the time, and Mexicans claimed residence on either side of the river to suit their convenience.[29]

Texans were not inclined to tolerate the border violations. In the press, the prevailing anarchy along the river was a constant theme, and there were demands that the barbarians responsible for the trouble be punished without mercy. Governor Richard Coke applied to Washington through Ord and directly for adequate United States military force to protect the border. The War Department instructed Ord to aid the state authorities and was inclined to leave the burden of law enforcement upon the local officials.[30]

Ord himself pressed his superiors to take decisive action against the raiders, but nothing was done immediately. This was not Ord's way of handling such matters. He would try a different tack. The general sent a dispatch to Governor Coke on 28 May 1875, marked "confidential," in which he described the Rio Grande situation as critical and affirmed that the state or the United States must act. If the United States didn't, the state might. Ord went on: "If you could authorize me to say at Washington that . . . you would stop the invasion, . . . provided the Government did not—I think I could get the necessary force and authority to use it effectually."[31] On the following day, Coke dispatched to President Grant that, if the United States did not act promptly to defend the border, the state of Texas would do so by raising a thousand men, or more, if necessary.[32] Ord's purpose was clear. He knew that the Washington authorities would not want a large state force operating along an international boundary. Especially would they not want such an army on the Rio Grande, where so much bad blood was known to exist between Mexicans and Texans. Governor Coke's "inspired" message soon had its effect, for, on 7 June, Ord was ordered to report to Washington for a personal conference with the secretary of war. A change of policy was shortly forthcoming when the president ordered the secretary of the navy to have the lower Rio Grande patrolled by steam launches. In addition, the Eighth Cavalry, a white regiment, was ordered to replace the Ninth Cavalry, composed of Negro troopers whom Ord believed to be ineffective.[33]

Crossing the border was the only way to control the raiding. As early as 1 June 1875, Ord had given instructions to his subordinates to cross on a fresh trail. While he thereby assumed a measure of responsibility for the crossings, perhaps he had been given the tacit approval of his superiors. However, Commanding General Sherman apparently was not a party to the matter and did not approve it.[34] Ord was circumspect in using his forces, and his troops were not involved in any border incidents of any consequence during the remainder of 1875.

Ord was in a situation having diplomatic as well as military significance. In the summer of 1875, John Watson Foster, United States minister to Mexico, informed the Mexican minister, José M. Lafragua, that United States land and naval forces were being strengthened in Texas. "I also called his attention to the fact that my Government had assigned the command of the Department of Texas to one of the most prominent and prudent Generals of the army. . . ."[35] Foster warned that continued raiding might well result in crossing of the border by American troops.

★★★★★

At the time of Ord's arrival in Texas there were four Negro regiments in the United States Army, and he had all of them in his command. In Civil War days, he had pretty clearly indicated that he considered black troops to be auxiliary to whites and probably would not have enlisted them at all. He had not changed in the interim. From San Antonio, he pressed his superiors to exchange his black regiments for white, even offering two for one. When, in 1876, a bill was introduced in Congress to scatter black recruits among all regiments, Ord wrote to Lieutenant Colonel William R. Shafter who commanded the Negro Twenty-fourth Infantry: "It gradually makes the Col'd Regts white (I suppose) as was recommended by myself, Genl Sherman & the President."[36] In the latter part of 1877, Senator Ambrose E. Burnside introduced a bill into the Senate to accomplish the same purpose. Ord testified before congressional committees that the difficulty of finding competent noncommissioned officers among the black troops required for black companies double the usual number of commissioned officers. Whether there was a "conspiracy" to eliminate the blacks from the service cannot be said with certainty, but it appears very likely that Ord would have welcomed that eventuality.[37]

★★★★★

From the moment of his arrival in Texas, Ord made repeated requests to Sheridan and Sherman for additional troops. He asked particularly for Ranald S. Mackenzie's Fourth Cavalry. These requests brought no result. The problem was one of numbers. In 1874, the army had been reduced to 25,000 enlisted men. The congressional elections in this same year had resulted in Democratic party control of the House of Representatives. For the military, the future held scant hope of improvement in the strength of the army, for Southern Democrats generally would not vote to augment the Reconstruction occupation force in the Southern states.[38]

Ord was anxious to please Texans and to win their good will, even though most of them had been his "rebel" enemies. At the Travis County Fair in Austin in 1875, Ord joined with two former Confederate generals to judge the military drill of the local militia organizations. Ord presented a sword and a medal to the winning companies in the presence of Governor Coke and other dignitaries. He also attended the ball given in connection with the fair. The following year, he reviewed the Texas militia companies at the state fair in Houston. The general and staff were invited to attend the annual reunion of Hood's Texas Brigade at Palestine in 1879.[39] In 1880, a former Confederate wrote: "The Texas veterans held their annual reunion in San Antonio, 'the Alamo City' on *San Jacinto Day*, 21st of this month. Genl Ord won the hearts of the veterans by his courtesy & kindness to them; such *soldiers* never awake fears in the minds of civilians."[40]

Ord chanced upon Stephen D. Lee, famed as the Confederacy's youngest lieutenant general, and learned that General Braxton Bragg, a Galveston resident, had recently lost his position with a railroad. Lee thought Bragg had no means of supporting his family. Ord told Sherman he would appoint the former full general of the Confederacy as agent to purchase commissary supplies in Galveston at a small annual stipend. Ord asked Sherman to sound out the secretary of war to see if he would force Bragg's discharge on the ground of his "rebel" record. Ord asserted his willingness to assume the responsibility of the appointment, "and let them say Ord did it."[41]

The general's penchant for conciliating ex-Confederates did not always escape critical notice. A member of the Grand Army of the Republic in San Antonio lodged a complaint with the adjutant general in Washington that Ord employed in the civil service at department headquarters a number of "old rebel officers and soldiers."[42] This was not surprising, for Ord had been a consistent conciliator since Appomattox. Said he of the Texans, in his annual report for 1877: "They are reconstructed and about as good American citizens as if they had been born in Maine (some of them were). . . ."[43]

There was more than mere good fellowship in Ord's efforts to gain the favor of Texans. He was quite anxious to gain the cooperation of the Texas delegation in the Congress. He wanted their support for the army. Senator Samuel Bell Maxey and Representatives Gustave Schleicher and John Hancock became his close collaborators. All were Democrats. A further reduction in the size of the nation's military force was being talked of in the early part of 1876, but, by the middle of the year, Ord was able to note that the Texas men had stood by the military. For the moment the army was safe.[44]

The Texas delegation pressed the need for more troops on the border, and a special House committee to look into the matter was established under Schleicher's chairmanship. On 12 February 1876, Ord sat before the Schleicher committee in the Capitol building in Washington to give testimony on the border problems. He faced three former Yankee generals, N. P. Banks and Stephen A. Hurlbut of the Republican side, and Alpheus S. Williams, Democrat; a fourth committee member was Democrat L.Q.C. Lamar, a former Confederate diplomat. Ord told the panel that at least two regiments of the best cavalry should be posted on the lower Rio Grande. The general also affirmed the necessity of their crossing the frontier in large enough force to maintain themselves in the face of any hazards that might be encountered. In pursuance of the committee's report on 29 April 1876, the Congress authorized an increase of troops on the lower river, but omitted the authorization to order crossing of the border. Eventually, Ord's force was augmented by the arrival of the Tenth Infantry (white).[45]

In several instances during 1876, Ord ordered troops to cross into Mexico to protect American citizens there from revolutionist action or from threatened despoilment by bandits. In addition, Ord sent the aggressive lieutenant colonel of the Twenty-fourth Infantry, William R. Shafter, and his able Lieutenant John L. Bullis into Mexico in pursuit of marauding Indians. Bullis commanded a remarkable detachment of Seminole Negro scouts. In their initial foray, they attacked an Indian camp, killed several, captured some and recovered a number of stolen horses. Perhaps Sherman's silence was all the authorization Ord had for ordering Shafter across, though the general did quote Sheridan as saying to him, "Why the devil don't you do it?" at the time the two were in Washington for the House committee hearing. At any rate, Ord considered Shafter's crossing as a sort of icebreaker and meanwhile secured some sort of quiet approval from President Grant.[46]

★★★★★

Porfirio Díaz raised the standard of revolution against President Lerdo de Texada of Mexico early in 1876. There began what Ord called a "cutthroat struggle" which increased the turmoil all along the frontier. Indian raids from Mexico into Texas began to increase considerably in 1876, probably because of the breakdown of authority in Mexico. These raids occasioned the crossings of Shafter and Bullis. On 23 November 1876, Díaz occupied Mexico City and shortly proclaimed himself provisional president. There was a change of administration in the United States in March 1877. Rutherford B. Hayes succeeded Grant as president. The Hayes administration adopted a policy of withholding recognition from the Díaz government until the new Mexican regime should prove its ability to honor all of its obligations to maintain law and order along the Rio Grande frontier. As early as 31 March 1877, the new secretary of state, William M. Evarts, dispatched to Foster in Mexico City that President Hayes might consider ordering pursuit of raiders into Mexico and that he (Foster) should so inform the de facto authorities.[47]

Ord attempted to take advantage of the Mexican situation to influence high state policy to the army's advantage. He believed that if the president would "pacify" the border states of Mexico, as required by the interest of the United States, a majority of the Southern Democrats would vote no reduction in the army. The general told Sherman that he had given up all hope that there were enough sensible men in Mexico to keep the country united and orderly. Ord had written a "plain honest appeal" to the secretary of state, he told Sherman. "Do secure for it serious consideration."[48] In his appeal to Evarts sent through Philip H. Sheridan, Ord asked that serious consideration be given to intervention in Mexico to pacify the border.[49] What Sherman thought of this, or for that matter, what the secretary of state thought of it, does not appear.

There followed more than a month of inaction. Then, on 10 May 1877, Ord insistently requested of Sheridan authority to proceed to Chicago to confer with him. From Chicago, Ord telegraphed to Sherman that he wanted to see him on business, and the commanding general authorized him to come to Washington.[50]

Ord had come to the capital to seek explicit authority of the administration to cross the border in pursuit of marauders. Sheridan had not given formal approval to the object of the journey. Whether or not Ord had to persuade Sherman to his view is not clear, but the commanding general either shared the view or was won over. The two went to Secretary of War George W. McCrary, and then to Secretary of State Evarts. Finally, Sherman introduced Ord to President Hayes himself. Ord earnestly begged for authority to cross the border. Subsequently, the matter was considered by the president and his Cabinet, and the chief executive determined to issue an order of authorization. "It was at my solicitation, I believe, that it was issued," Ord said later.[51] The Hayes administration had for some weeks considered the possibility of such an order, and Ord's zealous petition had brought the matter to a head.

The Ord Order of 1 June 1877, actually contained in a directive from the secretary of war to Sherman, consisted of detailed instructions of President Hayes to General Ord regarding the use of military force to stop the border raids. Ord was directed to invite the cooperation of the local authorities in Mexico and to notify them of the president's desire to join with them to suppress lawlessness. If the Mexican government should continue its failure to prevent the raids, the duty to do so would fall upon the United States government, a duty which "will be performed even if its performance should render necessary the occasional crossing of the border by our troops." Crossings might be made by troops in hot pursuit or upon a fresh trail.[52]

To his colonels on the Rio Grande, Ord issued instructions based upon the 1 June directive. Thomas C. Devin at Fort Brown and Shafter at Fort Clark were to confer with the local Mexican authorities and invite their cooperation. The local officials were to be notified in every instance where possible of the crossing of American troops. "Extend the same cooperation to Mexican troops who may cross into the United States in pursuit of raiders," Ord directed.[53]

On 28 May 1877, Foster in Mexico City had been informed by President Díaz that he would send a prudent general to the frontier with sufficient force to cooperate cordially with General Ord. Of course, news of this decision had arrived too late to affect Hayes's action of 1 June. The secretary of war directed that Ord cooperate with Díaz's officer, meet and correspond with him, and not to be hasty in pursuit across the border except in aggravated cases.[54]

Gerónimo Treviño, general of the military division, line of the north, was the officer selected by Díaz. Treviño was thirty-eight years old, a veteran of revolutionary fighting, and a member of a wealthy and prominent Mexican family. Upon learning of Treviño's arrival in Piedras Negras, Ord telegraphed to him that he would be glad to confer on frontier matters at Piedras Negras or in San Antonio, if Treviño could spare the time to come. Treviño responded that he awaited Ord's orders. Ord went to the border, crossed over to Piedras Negras, and paid a call on Treviño. Ord's fluent Spanish facilitated their communication. The Mexican general and two of his staff were invited over to Fort Clark where Ord had him review the troops. Treviño was impressed by what he saw and by the cordial treatment accorded him.[55]

In their conference, the two generals reached what Ord described as a good understanding on the basis of the instructions of 1 June and agreed that their troops were to cooperate. "He took advantage of our being alone," Ord said of Treviño, "to ask me (as a sort of favor) and privately not to send other than regular troops into Mexico & hoped I would send those under discreet commanders, and this I promised should be done."[56] When newspaper reports of the Ord-Treviño meeting reached Mexico City with Ord's statement that he had a good understanding with Treviño about the border, there was an outcry of protest at what was interpreted as Treviño's humiliating concessions to Ord. The Mexican general's report, however, denied that he had agreed to the Americans' crossing and asserted that he had rejected Ord's proposal for reciprocal crossing.[57]

Foster had an interview with Minister of Foreign Affairs Luis Vallarta on 20 June. Vallarta claimed that he had private information that the American government "had yielded too readily to the representations of General Ord, who was an annexationist and seeking to precipitate a war between the two countries." The Mexican minister went on to speak of the Ord Order of 1 June "with much feeling." He hoped that peace might prevail and said that Treviño was instructed to preserve it, but "if the order to General Ord were carried out and Mexican territory violated, the consequences might be of the gravest character."[58] Foster asked Vallarta how he knew Ord was an annexationist and seeking to precipitate a war. When pressed, the Mexican minister admitted that these were rumors. Foster said they should be discounted: "General Ord, I said, was one of our most distinguished Generals, and had been selected for the important post which he occupied on the frontier on account of his prudence and ability; and that such charges against him were unworthy of consideration in the form in which they came."[59]

It was certainly true that Ord was an occasional advocate of occupation of northern Mexico, and he had given expression to such sentiments in a letter to Sherman a scant three months before. Be it said to his credit: as soon as the Mexican government evinced a genuine willingness to restore order and dispatched Treviño to the Rio Grande, Ord did not at any time thereafter make any statement suggesting that the United States should occupy any part of Mexico. As an earnest of the new Mexican policy, the government to the south began making real efforts to check the cattle raiding on the lower Rio Grande.

In the latter months of 1877, Ord repeatedly sent troops across the border, but it is significant that all of these expeditions were out of Fort Clark, well up the Rio Grande in the vicinity of the mouth of the Pecos. All were in pursuit of marauding Indians and were into the rugged country of Coahuila. The Mexican government bitterly protested these crossings, and there were comments critical of Ord's actions in some American newspapers. In January 1878, a meeting of citizens in Bexar County (San Antonio) passed resolutions deploring such press reports, affirmed the necessity for the crossings, and heartily endorsed the Ord Order and Ord's promptness in carrying out his instructions. The actions of Shafter and Bullis were endorsed and a public subscription was undertaken to purchase swords to be presented to the two officers. The resolutions further supported reciprocal crossing, the maintenance of a large American force on the border, and stability and prosperity in Mexico. Ord may well have inspired the meeting and the resolutions.[60]

★★★★★

Ord had his hands full suppressing marauders and thieves, but there was an additional duty incumbent upon him to enforce the neutrality laws of the United States. The problem, of course, was that the ousted partisans of former President Lerdo were inclined to use Texas soil as a base for their operations or as a refuge when closely pressed by Díaz forces on the Mexican side. Ord was directed from Washington to prevent any armed bodies from invading Mexico. In June 1877, a large Lerdoist party under Colonel Martinez was driven across the border into Texas by Díaz forces and attacked on Texas soil. The Lerdo men took refuge in Fort Brown and after being interned for some days gave their parole not to organize on American soil to disturb the peace of Mexico. An American protest at the crossing of the Díaz troops was well received in Mexico City and an agreeable reply was made. Shortly after this, Ord's troops arrested near Eagle Pass a revolutionary force of forty-six men under Colonel Valdez. The most important action in maintaining neutrality was the arrest in July of General Mariano Escobedo and sixteen officers near Ringgold Barracks. Escobedo was a former war minister in the Lerdo government. Secretary of State Evarts expressed official gratification to the War Department for the manner in which Ord performed his duties in the arrest of Escobedo.[61]

The possible use of Texas volunteer troops along the border was a touchy question for General Ord. Certain Texans, some of them highly placed officially, advocated supplementing the force of regulars with state troops for use as needed. Ord met the question head-on by publicly saying that he did not want Texas volunteers. He cited the well-known animosity on the border between Texans and Mexicans. Old feuds there had been kept going through the years and new ones begun. He thought there would be no surer way to bring on a clash between the nations than to have local troops facing one another and recommended that both governments keep only regulars on the frontier.[62] "Of course, . . . my Texas popularity is over," Ord commented to Sherman with some exaggeration after he had taken his stand on the volunteer question, "except with those who fit in the rebellion, who all say they have had all the war they want."[63]

Consideration of the use of state troops was involved in a larger question. Did Ord have enough troops to properly protect the vast state of Texas and especially to carry out the order of 1 June 1877? He thought not, and he bombarded Sherman in his personal letters with requests for reinforcements. The force in Texas at the time of the issuance of the Ord Order was made up of two regiments of cavalry and three of infantry as follows:

the Eighth Cavalry (white), the Tenth Cavalry (Negro), the Twenty-fourth Infantry (Negro), the Twenty-fifth Infantry (Negro), and the Tenth Infantry (white), the latter being the only reinforcement sent to Ord since he assumed the command in 1875. The total number was about 3,000 men. The army, already reduced to 25,000 men, was still threatened with further reduction at the hands of Congress. The House of Representatives had continued under Democratic control following the campaign of 1876. Former Confederates were strong in the House, and their Northern Democratic brethren were inclined to vote with them against the army. Even the ending of Reconstruction by the withdrawal of the troops from the Southern states by President Hayes in April 1877 did not remove the threat.[64]

Nevertheless, Ord sought more troops and came to the conclusion that Sheridan was the bottleneck.[65] The division commander had problems of his own, for, with a limited force, he had to see after a frontier extending from Canada to the Rio Grande. But it soon developed that the shortage of troops was not the only consideration shaping Sheridan's view of affairs in Texas.

Ord made a formal application to Sheridan on 14 November 1877 for a cavalry regiment, which the division commander passed along to Sherman. At the same time, Sheridan sat down to write the commanding general a personal letter. "There ought to be more troops on the Rio Grande," he said, "but it troubles me greatly where to get a Regiment even." Sheridan went on: "If you will permit me I will say confidentially that it is my belief that we cannot have any quiet or peace on the Rio Grande, as long as Ord is in command of Texas. I have lost confidence in his motives, and his management of his Dept. is a confusion which is demoralizing to his subordinates."[66]

Sherman replied that he had known for some time that Sheridan ascribed much of the clamor about the border to Ord. President Grant had sent Ord to Texas without his assent, Sherman said: "To change Ord *now* under pressure might damage him, but I am more than convinced that a cool and less spasmodic man in Texas, would do more to compose matters on that border than the mere increase of the cavalry, for which now is the cry."[67] Even as Sherman wrote critically of Ord's management of Texas matters, he admitted to Sheridan that the Texas delegation in Congress had saved the army in the special session of Congress then in progress. The Democrats had the power and were resolved to cut the army to 20,000 and to 17,000 in the coming regular session, but the Texans had saved the day. Unless the Texans could be kept pacified, Sherman said, the army would be "slaughtered" in the coming months. Sherman had just testified before the House Military Committee. "I admitted that the Rio Grande border needed 4,000 effective men, half infantry, and half cavalry. . . ," the commanding general told Sheridan.[68] Whatever their other differences, it is clear that Ord, Sherman and Sheridan all agreed that more troops were needed on the Texas border.

On 24 November 1877, the very day Ord explained to Sheridan his need for more cavalry and infantry, he was summoned to Washington. The general conferred with Sherman and Secretary of War George W. McCrary. A few days later, Sheridan directed the Twentieth Infantry, six companies of the Fourth Cavalry (Mackenzie), and four companies of artillery to the Department of Texas, bringing Ord's total to about 5,000.[69] Was the decision to reinforce Ord a reward for the Texas delegation? An earnest of future protection of the border in exchange for future Texas votes in the Congress? Sherman had as much as said so. For all the criticism of Ord by his superiors, perhaps he should be credited with having a part in saving the army. At any rate, Ord came out of the wrangle with about one-fifth of the entire effective force of the United States Army under his command in Texas!

The crux of the difficulty between Ord and Sheridan was that Ord tried to work official matters through personal letters to Sherman. The commanding general bent over backwards not to offend Sheridan and strove mightily to keep Ord working through channels. The very important order of 1 June 1877, was secured by Ord and Sherman. Sheridan had not been consulted, and he had not forgotten it. Ord worked closely with the Texas congressional delegation in army matters, and Sheridan no doubt resented the resulting congressional pressures upon him requiring certain troop dispositions on the Rio Grande. Sheridan's charge of confusion in Ord's management of the Department of Texas is difficult to evaluate. He made the same charge with regard to Ord's handling of the Department of the Platte, but, at the same time, Sherman described Ord's work there of protecting the Union Pacific Railroad as admirable. Ord did not please Sheridan in Chicago with his handling of Texas, but he certainly pleased the Texans.

★★★★★

Hearings began in Congress on border matters, and General Ord testified before the House Committee on Military Affairs on 5 and 6 December and before the House Committee on Foreign Affairs on 7 and 13 December 1877. The reinforcements recently ordered to him would be enough to preserve the peace, he said. In the matter of crossing the border, he pointed out that he had invited Mexican troops to cross to the American side when they were in pursuit and had issued orders that they be treated as our own troops.[70]

Another witness before the Committee on Foreign Affairs was Thomas L. Kane of Pennsylvania, the same who had commanded the "Bucktails" in that long ago action at Dranesville. Kane was interested in railroad promotion in Texas and Mexico and only recently had traveled in that area. Schleicher asked Kane if he thought Ord would be indiscreet in carrying out his orders. Answer: No. Had not Ord been prudent and careful? Answer: Not only had the general been so, but the nation was under great obligation to him for keeping peace on the Texas side of the river as well as Mexican. He had kept down the Texans. "He also has a good manner, which has been useful to us in Texas as well as in Mexico," Kane said. "It is the old Maryland manner. . . ."[71]

President Hayes extended diplomatic recognition to the Díaz government on 9 April 1878. Shortly afterward, on 25 April, the Committee on Foreign Affairs submitted to the House a joint resolution requesting the president to keep 5,000 troops on the border between the mouth of the Rio Grande and El Paso, 3,000 of the number to be cavalry. The Ord Order was justified, the resolution read, to be kept in force until Mexico should agree by treaty to give protection to lives and property. In securing recognition, Díaz had won a partial diplomatic victory. Yet, he had been forced to maintain order on the lower Rio Grande for the past year, and the Ord Order, a thorn in the Mexican flesh, still remained.[72]

True to Sherman's prediction, the army continued to be dependent upon the Texans: "The Texas men and some [other] Democrats saved the 25,000 men, but would go no further," he wrote to Sheridan in May 1878.[73] Perhaps Ord was too useful with the Texans to be relieved from the border command!

CHAPTER

19

★★★★★

A Legacy of Peace

EDWARD Ord had frequently requested that the Fourth Cavalry be sent to Texas. His choice was based chiefly on the character of the regimental commander, Colonel Ranald S. Mackenzie, who had come to be recognized as an Indian fighter without an equal. Ord knew his man, for the colonel had commanded the cavalry of Ord's Army of the James in the Civil War. When Mackenzie's troopers filed into Fort Clark early in 1878 as part of the reinforcements ordered to the Texas border, it was a return for them to a familiar field of action. The regiment had been on the Rio Grande as recently as 1873.[1]

Mackenzie crossed the border in June 1878 in pursuit of cattle thieves, but failed to apprehend the raiders. So disgusted was he with the lawless condition and the lack of cooperation on the part of Mexican authorities that in his report to Ord he bluntly said that war should be declared on Mexico. Higher authority restrained the belligerent colonel. Tense feelings began building up on both sides of the Rio Grande resulting from Mackenzie's crossing and from rumors of aggression by the United States. Mackenzie crossed again in August in pursuit of cattle raiders, but was again unsuccessful. He reiterated his recommendation that war should be declared on Mexico in order to stop the raids. The disgruntled colonel applied for a transfer. Ord placated Mackenzie by saying that it was a bad time to transfer him, as Gerónimo Treviño was enroute to the border with 5,000 troops and the war feeling in Mexico was still strong. In the ensuing weeks, things quieted down generally, and no doubt Mackenzie's presence contributed to this improved state.[2]

Ord continued to conciliate the Mexican military on the frontier on every possible occasion, communicating with Treviño frequently and conferring with him from time to time in person. In the summer of 1878, the Mexican government began a more vigorous effort to control the raiding Indians. Ord notified Colonel B. H. Grierson, Tenth Cavalry, commanding Forts Concho, Davis and Stockton, that Treviño had mounted a campaign and that, if he pushed the Indians hard, they might cross to the American side. He had told Treviño, Ord continued to Grierson, that cooperation would be extended to his troops if they should cross to the United States. This and other efforts on the part of the Mexicans enabled President Rutherford B. Hayes to note in his second annual message that, since the recognition of Porfirio Díaz, much had been done by Mexico to keep down border incursions. He stated his reluctance to have United States forces cross the border and said that he would take the earliest opportunity to recognize Mexico's ability to keep order.[3]

Such a favorable aspect set the stage for social amenities not hitherto possible. On 21 December 1878, William R. Shafter at Fort Clark telegraphed to Ord that Treviño and a staff of thirteen had come over and were en route to San Antonio. The Mexicans were lionized in Ord's headquarters city. Afterward, Treviño and his entourage, as guests of the Galveston, Harrisburg and San Antonio Railroad, along with Ord and some members of his staff, proceeded to Galveston.[4] In that city on the night of 30 December 1878, a great throng gathered at the railroad depot to greet the military dignitaries. The party proceeded to the Tremont Hotel where a grand reception was held. Mayor D. C. Stone gave a speech of welcome to General Treviño, translated by General Ord. The Mexican general delivered a spirited response in Spanish in which he hoped his visit would tend to ease animosities between Mexico and Texas. General Ord was called upon for a speech and expressed the hope that he might remain in Texas for a long time to receive much more of the generous hospitality of its people. Colonel George P. Finlay referred to Treviño as "the favorite of the American people on the Rio Grande" and complimented General Ord for the "masterly fashion in which he has performed the delicate and difficult trust imposed upon him by the United States."[5]

Writing to William T. Sherman a few days later, Ord said that Treviño and staff were very much pleased by their reception. They were feted wherever they went. Commented Ord: "I think they feel very much relieved."[6] Ord went on to detail to Sherman Treviño's successes against the Indians. The Apaches in the San Carlos area had been captured. Some of the Kickapoos were being removed to an interior state, and Treviño intended moving remaining Kickapoos and Lipans to the interior, too far from the frontier to be an annoyance.

"Ive been conciliatory to Genl Treviño as could be, and think he deserves it, as he is earnest and one of the few Mexican Genls that leaves the impression that you can build on him," Ord said to Sherman. "It is to our interest to try and back him with his people and keep him in office."[7] Ord thought it would be a good thing to have the Mexicans, both on the border and in the interior, think that it was through Treviño's efforts that the order of 1 June 1877, had been publicly modified, as Ord believed it was the president's intention to do. He also urged Philip H. Sheridan to endorse this proposal. The general elaborated upon the possibility along this line in his letter to Sherman, suggesting that after the president was assured that the savages had been removed and a sufficient Mexican force stationed on the border to prevent their return, he might declare the Ord Order to be no longer necessary unless the Indians returned. Sherman's laconic endorsement to the secretary of war: should Ord ask officially for modification of the order to cross on a fresh trail?[8] For the time being, this question was held in abeyance.

Sheridan was not slow to respond to Ord's report at the close of 1878 to the effect that the Mexicans seemed to be in earnest about suppressing the Indian raids. In less than a week's time, he was asking Ord if he could spare six companies of Grierson's Tenth Cavalry (Negro) for use in General John Pope's neighboring Department of Missouri. Ord protested, but Sheridan had his way. Three companies of the regiment were eventually sent to Pope.[9]

The Texans in Congress continued to be Ord's mainstay and apparently the key support for the whole army. They insisted that Mackenzie's presence on the Rio Grande was a necessary condition for their voting for the army, so Sherman informed Sheridan in March 1879.[10]

★★★★★

On 1 October 1878, in his annual report, Ord invited attention to the earnest efforts of the Mexican authorities, especially
Generals Treviño and Servando Canales, to prevent raids from
Mexico. "The condition of affairs which rendered necessary the
order of June 1, 1877, to cross the border, in my opinion, no
longer exists. . . ," the general wrote.[11] If the Ord Order
should be withdrawn, he believed the discretionary authority
which he had exercised prior to 1 June 1877, would be adequate, so long as Mexico maintained sufficient force to restrain
the lawless bands. Ord went on to say that a considerable part
of his troops held in reserve to carry out the order of 1 June
had been diverted to exploring wild country and occupying
water holes frequented by raiding Indians from our own reservations.[12]

The ink was scarcely dry on Ord's report before Sheridan
pounced upon this publishable evidence of good order in Texas
to direct Ord to send Mackenzie and the Fourth Cavalry to
Colorado. Ord protested vigorously that the quiet on the border was entirely due to the presence of Mackenzie's column,
and that raiding would be resumed if it were removed. He also
said that the Mexican regiment at Piedras Negras was under
orders to move to the interior which would remove the restrain-
ing force on that side. Hearing nothing from his protest, Ord
telegraphed Sheridan again on 4 October that, if the Fourth
Cavalry were transferred, he would withdraw his recommendation in his annual report for the rescinding of the order
of 1 June 1877.[13]

In Washington, the Texas men went to work, but Sherman
supported Sheridan.[14] To Ord, the commanding general wrote
that he wished the Eighth and Tenth Cavalry to be so used as to
maintain the good order on the Rio Grande which had given so
much satisfaction. The Utes and the Apaches in the Colorado
area were too active to permit Mackenzie's return. "I doubt if
Mackenzie will come back to you this winter, if ever," was
Sherman's cheerless comment.[15]

Ord was not to be pacified so easily. In a private letter to
Sherman on 12 November 1879, he said that a revolution was
brewing in northern Mexico and there was trouble ahead. In
recommending the withdrawal of the order of 1 June 1877, he
presumed that he would continue to have at or near Fort Clark
1,000 men of all arms and discretionary power to cross the

border under authority given by President Ulysses S. Grant. Since the troops had been removed by Sheridan, he now withdrew his recommendation. The general spelled out his views fully in a later dispatch to Sheridan.[16]

President Hayes, upon the recommendation contained in Ord's annual report of 1 October 1879, had decided to withdraw the order of 1 June 1877. As there still remained a little time before the president's message of 1 December was put in final form, the matter was reconsidered by the secretary of war and the president in the light of Ord's letter to Sherman of 12 November. As a result, the secretary's report and the president's message were modified. President Hayes said in this, his third annual message, that he was gratified that "through the judicious and energetic action of the military commanders of the two nations" raids had greatly diminished along the Rio Grande. He expressed confidence that he would soon be able to modify the Ord Order of 1 June 1877.[17]

All of this (and more) brought down upon Ord the censure of both Sherman and Sheridan. The division commander called Ord's attention to his lack of courtesy and violations of army regulations in writing to Sherman personal letters on official matters. Writing to Sherman, Sheridan was critical of Ord for inconsistency in assigning motives for asking for the withdrawal of the order of 1 June 1877. Sheridan went on to express to Sherman rather bitter resentment that the Ord Order had been issued in the first place without any reference to him. Ord's "eccentricity of character" and his "devious methods" had caused Sheridan to question his good intentions.[18]

Sherman came down on Ord for his failure to send officially the information contained in his private letter of 12 November. He, too, questioned the various statements given by Ord of reasons for asking for the withdrawal of the Ord Order and professed to know nothing of the discretionary power to cross the frontier allegedly conveyed to General Ord by President Grant prior to the accession of President Hayes.[19]

Ord defended himself forcefully. His reasons for asking for the withdrawal of the order of 1 June 1877, he said, were not incompatible with one another. He explained that Sheridan knew all about the discretionary power to cross the border which Grant had given Ord and that it had been conveyed at a time when Sherman was absent. Ord further maintained that Sheridan knew of his intention to secure from President Hayes the authority to cross the border, the order of 1 June 1877, and he supposed that the division commander approved it. As for the recommendation for withdrawal of the order, Ord deemed the order unnecessary on 1 October; conditions changed by 12 November, and he so reported. He did so by private letter because the official report he was preparing on the subject would not be ready in time to affect the actions of the secretary of war and the president. Ord went on to say that he had recently conferred in person with Minister John W. Foster, who agreed that this was no time to withdraw the Ord Order and had so dispatched to the secretary of state. Submit this account of the entire matter to the secretary of state, Ord asked Sherman, and see if he does not feel it worthy of commendation rather than censure.[20]

Sherman smoothed things out, saying to Ord that his reply was quite satisfactory, but stressing again that the subject in question was too important to be conveyed only by a private letter. Go through channels, admonished the commanding general.[21]

What now would be done with the Ord Order? It was still officially a part of the Hayes policy toward Mexico, but it remained so only because of Ord's eleventh hour withdrawal of his recommendation to rescind it. In diplomatic channels, there seemed to be corroboration of Ord's position. Minister Foster had come to the Rio Grande frontier in December to see things at firsthand. General Ord, the very personification of evil in the Mexican mind, was invited by the Mexican authorities at Matamoros to attend the festivities held in honor of the minister. Both general and diplomat were warmly welcomed. In reporting his visit officially, Foster noted the improved order on the frontier, but believed the improvement was due to the firmness of American frontier policy rather than to voluntary efforts by Mexico. The Mexicans had been forced to act as a matter of pride, but he thought the prospect for continuance of favorable conditions none too bright. A presidential election which would absorb the government's energies was in prospect in Mexico. More Indian raids were likely. Don't limit the number of troops on the border and don't limit the discretion of the military to cross the border, wrote Foster to William M. Evarts on 27 December 1879.[22]

President Hayes, nevertheless, was intent upon carrying through his determination to withdraw the Ord Order. On 24

February 1880, a letter of the secretary of war informed Sherman that President Hayes desired to recognize the ability of the Mexican government to maintain order on the frontier. The president based his judgment on the recommendation contained in General Ord's annual report of the preceding 1 October and upon other information in the hands of the United States government. The executive directed that the order of 1 June 1877, should no longer be in force; at the same time, General Ord was to be vigilant and cautious. The new order was promulgated by Ord on the border on 8 March 1880.[23]

The Ord Order was famous in its day as a stumbling block in the way of diplomatic intercourse, a cause of ill-feeling between the two republics, even a potential cause of war between them. Yet, as many scholars have recognized, it contributed to peace. It affronted the fierce pride of Mexicans and forced Díaz through Treviño to suppress the raids. Its value may be measured in lives saved and property made secure on the border. Ord and Treviño, those in power closest to the critical border situation, deserve much credit for so skillfully handling their forces as to avoid any incident of conflict that might have triggered a war. The responsibility of choice was upon them. They wisely chose the way of peace.[24]

The friendly cooperation between the two generals continued in the ensuing months. The Apache chief Victorio and his band began to cause trouble west of the Pecos. Driven out of New Mexico into Old Mexico by United States troops, Victorio twice crossed into Texas and on both occasions was intercepted by Colonel Benjamin H. Grierson and his Negro troopers of the Tenth Cavalry and driven back into Mexico. In a final operation, Colonel Joaquin Terrazas, chief of the Mexican forces in Chihuahua, led a force into the Castillo Mountains and attacked Victorio's band on 14 October 1880. Victorio and sixty of his warriors, along with eighteen women and children, were killed, sixty-eight women and children were captured, and two prisoners held by the Indians were recovered. Mexican authorities were indeed pacifying the frontier radically and violently.[25]

★★★★★

There was a happier side of life for the Ords—the life of the family circle where were mingled the warmth of the fireside, the gaiety of young children, and the hopeful aspiration of young adults. In this round of domestic felicity, Bertie Ord was a shining light. Roberta Augusta Ord, eldest daughter of General and Molly Ord, was twenty-three years old, "blonde and dazzlingly beautiful," and "esteemed for her simplicity and goodness of heart." She had attracted the attention of Gerónimo Treviño on those occasions when the Mexican general had visited in San Antonio. Bertie Ord's "many personal charms and high womanly qualities smote the heart of the military chieftain," ran a contemporary account in the style of the time. The two were to be married on 20 July 1880.[26]

"America and Mexico join hearts and hands" and "this is the grand social event of west Texas," began newspaper reports of the "international" nuptials. "There has never before transpired in this State so interesting a wedding event—one which invited more attention at home or excited more general comment abroad."[27] Both Generals Ord and Treviño were determined to make the marriage symbolic of the friendship between the nations.

The wedding was at the Episcopal Cathedral of St. Mark, as Bertie had followed the Protestantism of her mother. The Right Reverend R.W.B. Elliott, bishop of the diocese, and the Reverend Francis R. Starr officiated. Into the great building thronged the elite of San Antonio and many guests from far away. The procession "fairly glittered," as officers of both armies, brilliantly uniformed, escorted the members of the bridal party. Never in west Texas had there been seen such stylish and costly attire for bride and bridesmaids.[28]

Following the ceremony, the party proceeded to the Ord residence on Nacogdoches Street where a reception was given for special friends of the bride and groom. The grounds of the stately residence were illuminated with Chinese lanterns; spanning the walk were evergreen arches festooned with the banners of the United States and Mexico; the home was draped with the colors of both republics, "flags of the countries entwined." The wedding cake was crowned with a parapet, a fortification in miniature. Tiny bronze cannons guarded the ramparts, and the American and Mexican colors floated from each corner.[29]

Treviño was forty-one years of age at the time of his marriage. He was described as a "gentleman of liberal and progressive views," and was given much credit in the Texas newspapers for his important work in pacifying the frontier. The general was a native of Nuevo León, had been educated in

Monterrey, and had had a distinguished career in the Mexican army. His command was the Northern Division embracing the states of Nuevo León, Coahuila, Chihuahua and Durango.[30]

Elaborate preparations were made to accord the couple a grand welcome as they crossed into Mexico and traveled to their future home at San Luis Potosí. The journey was a continuous triumph through the country, as Roberta Augusta Ord de Treviño shared the homage paid to her popular and powerful husband.[31] The personal lives of these two people did indeed symbolize the unity and peace established between Mexico and the United States.

★★★★★

General Ord was intensely interested in railroads and gave assistance to their builders in every way he could. The roads were a great factor in the settlement of the Texas frontier. As Ord put it in one of his annual reports: "Every railroad is not only a rapid civilizer but a sure protector of the frontier penetrated by it. The sight of a locomotive whirling along its train is such *'big medicine'* for the savages that they wilt under its influence. . . ."[32]

Under Ord's direction, a map of west Texas was prepared in 1879 to aid in opening and developing the country. Extensive explorations were made by scouting parties of Grierson's command in the Pecos region, and the information was fed into Ord's headquarters for compilation. In the summer of 1880, Ord arranged for a geologist from the Smithsonian Institution to accompany an expedition into west Texas with the scientist's expenses to be shared equally by three railroad companies. By October 1880, the general noted that some half dozen parties of surveyors were competing to determine which would first chart the best railroad route through the "dangerous district" of the department west of the Pecos.[33]

In time, Ord came to look upon the possible linkup of American and Mexican railroads as not only an important force for economic development, but also a bond making for peace and friendship between the nations. It so happened that one prominent American was in Mexico early in 1880, learning the country anew, cultivating the leading people there, and becoming interested in Mexican railroads. He was former President U. S. Grant. His arrival in Mexico City in February 1880 coincided with the initial announcement that the Hayes administration would withdraw the Ord Order. The Mexicans, elated at this long-awaited event, received Grant with more than ordinary enthusiasm. Matías Romero, former Mexican minister to the United States and long-time advocate of Mexican economic development with United States capital, along with other leaders asked for and received assurance from Grant that he would publicize among American capitalists the opportunities for railroad building in Mexico.[34]

One week after giving this assurance, Grant with his party, which included General Philip Sheridan, reached Galveston, where, at the invitation of the citizens, Ord and staff were invited to participate in a grand welcome for the former president. At a reception in Galveston's Tremont Hotel, Grant received loud and prolonged applause and made a short speech. General Sheridan was introduced and was applauded once during the speech and at the conclusion. General Ord was presented next and "arose, amidst a storm of applause." There was no doubt as to where the affections of Texans lay toward the Yankee triumvirate. A Galveston newspaper correspondent reporting the meeting expressed the hope that Sheridan would continue to "live in Chicago permanently and let Gen. Ord run Texas."[35]

Toward the end of 1880, Ord requested and secured official permission to visit Monterrey, Mexico, ostensibly to interview Generals Canales and Treviño and the governors of Tamaulipas, Nuevo León, and Coahuila to arrange for more effective frontier security. Actually, his proposed tour had another object, as he revealed to Sherman: he had corresponded with Canales and Treviño and thought that he had interested them in railroads.[36] Treviño was soon to take over the portfolio of war in the Mexican cabinet and had gone to Mexico City with his family. This would alter Ord's destination from Monterrey to the capital city. Treviño had offered to send a man-of-war to convey Ord to Mexico in style and to show him a grand time after his arrival, "but I want to avoid all that," Ord wrote to Sherman.[37]

★★★★★

Over the years, Ord had mellowed somewhat in appearance and manner. He was still physically hardy. His iron-gray hair and moustache had changed to white, and he presented a striking outward aspect. He would be outstanding in almost any company. As already noted, he was very popular with Texans and had gone out of his way to cultivate their good feeling toward him. He developed a close friendship with Senator Samuel Bell Maxey and honored the former Confederate with a reception in San Antonio in 1879, inviting army officers and leading citizens. A newspaper reporter interviewed the senator and the general at Ord's headquarters, being quite impressed by the natural and easy manner of both. Neither attempted to put on any style in conversation, the journalist said. A stranger seeing them together might well imagine that they were two well-to-do farmers discussing the crops. The newspaperman drew a contrast with European notables of the same rank who would be quartered in a stately palace, dressed elaborately and attended by numerous flunkies. He was also impressed by Ord's accessiblity. "I would like to see a reporter stroll into the office of a German department commander," he wrote.[38]

Ord had come to Texas in 1875 as a vigorous and active officer at the age of fifty-six. He had a young family. Molly, his wife, was thirteen years his junior. The children had ranged in age from eighteen-year-old Bertie to eight-year-old Ruth. By 1880, the general was still energetic and active, but somehow the calendar had gone awry! On 18 October, he would be sixty-two. This might mean retirement from active military service—though not necessarily so. Section 1244 of the Revised Statutes of the United States provided that the president of the United States at his discretion might retire an officer of the army who had reached the age of sixty-two and had served forty-five or more years. Ord would soon fall in this category. However, Major General Irvin McDowell was older than Ord in years and in point of service. If anyone should be retired, McDowell would seem to be first in line.

Still it might be well if Ord kept his fences mended. Rather early in the year, in April, Guy M. Bryan of Galveston, in a casual postscript in a letter to his friend, President Hayes, hoped that Ord would be kept in Texas, as he was "the right man & in the right place." Texans liked him for his "good sense" and "fitness in every respect."[39]

Perhaps matters would have gone along smoothly but for an event of 24 June 1880 in Cincinnati. On this date, the Democratic party nominated Major General Winfield Scott Hancock to oppose Republican James A. Garfield for the presidency. Previously, Ord had departed from his Democratic allegiance to vote for Grant, but here was an opportunity to return to his accustomed place. The opportunity was more than ordinarily welcome, for not only was Ord very warm and friendly toward Hancock "the Superb," but also he would undoubtedly feel that a Democratic West Pointer in the White House could mean nothing but good for the army! Sherman put the matter of Ord's reaction very well: he "did the impolitic thing of sending Hancock a congratulatory message upon his nomination."[40] While it was clear that Ord hoped for Hancock's election, he did not attempt to influence anyone in a partisan fashion, believing that it was improper for an officer to do so.

Ord had to reckon with another important force in the retirement matter: colonels wanted to be generals, and some of them knew President Hayes quite well. There would be pressure from below from these men and from their friends. Apparently, some of them were not averse to playing upon the political vulnerability of Ord resulting from his telegram to Hancock.

By 1 July 1880, Ord went to work in earnest to stave off the threatened retirement. He appealed naturally to Senator Maxey who thought the shelving of Ord would be an outrageous violation of the spirit of Section 1244. Maxey contacted Texas Senator Richard Coke and Governor Oran M. Roberts and asked them to write the president on Ord's behalf.[41] In a letter to President Hayes, Maxey paid rare tribute to Ord:

> *He is an exceptionally good officer, and can today in my judgment wear out half the young men of the Army, in any work in the Field. He is tough as a pine knot, and his habits being first rate, has at least ten years good work in him.*
>
> *Gen. Ord has the entire confidence of the Texas Delegation in Congress, of the Governor and Civil authorities. My deliberate judgment is that he has no superior in the Army for the position he occupies.*[42]

It was from the railroad executives whom he had befriended that Ord was able to get the bulk of letters to higher authority seeking to stay the president's hand. Collis P. Huntington of the Southern Pacific, R. S. Hayes and H. M. Hoxie of the International and Great Northern, and Thomas A. Scott and John C. Brown of the Texas and Pacific all wrote on Ord's behalf.[43]

The election on 2 November 1880 resulted in victory for Republican nominee James A. Garfield. At this juncture, newspaper reports that Ord would soon be retired were given wide circulation, and Ord was prompted to telegraph an inquiry to Sherman on 11 November. The commanding general replied on this date: "I have never heard a word from President or Secretary of War about your Retirement. Newspapers and aspirants kill us off at will."[44] Ord followed up with a letter in which he acknowledged that there was heavy pressure from below and that the president might feel obliged to accommodate to it. The general felt that he could perform good service for some time to come, and thought the president might so think, but he continued: "I can not count upon the same consideration from a President who does not know me, or my services. For that reason and others that you can guess at I would like to have my retirement during Mr. Hayes administration because I think I can count upon the aid of sundry M C's of present Congress to secure my retirement under law as a Major General."[45]

Ord seemed to be asking for retirement and with good reason. Within four months Hayes would no longer be president and there was that unfortunate congratulatory telegram to Hancock! The victorious Garfield would feel no obligation to retain Ord. Moreover, the composition of the Congress was about to change significantly as a result of the elections of 1880. The new legislative body, instead of being Democratic in both houses and therefore inclined to favor Ord, would be made up of a Republican House and a Senate evenly divided between the parties. "I want to go out with honor, as a Major General," Ord wrote to Sherman.[46] The existing Democratic Congress would be far more likely to accommodate to Ord's wish in this regard than its successor.

Sherman sent Ord's letter to President Hayes with one of his own, saying that to retire Ord and not to retire McDowell would be unjust and unfair. "Of the two Ord has better physical strength, and has always been a more active officer. His record of war service is equal if not better." In addition, Sherman continued, Ord was poor and McDowell rich. "General Ord though not as well known to the President personally has more friends in the army than Genl. McDowell."[47] President Hayes's reply on 18 November 1880 was laconic and noncommittal: "I return the letter of General Ord. It is very manly."[48]

By order of 6 December 1880, President Hayes retired General Ord from active service, effective on that date.[49] However much anticipated the order may have been, the shock felt by the general must have been severe. To put off suddenly the accustomed military associations of a lifetime was, in a way, to die to that existence and to be faced with the necessity of being born anew to another. The pangs of birth and death are unique, as each life is unique. In Ord's retirement was summed up the human predicament: this man—and there was not another like him—had, for forty-five years, given and received orders in the military establishment of the United States; he would never do so again; that life was gone forever.

There did remain one final order, a farewell to the Department of Texas, in itself a sufficient commentary on what he had wrought in that life now coming to a close:

> *In parting with a command he has exercised for almost six years, during a period embracing delicate relations between the United States of America and the United Mexican States,—relations involving the peace and friendship of the two republics,—it is fitting to refer to the zealous and intelligent efficiency of the command, which has passed into history as an example of what tact can do, in preserving the peace and securing the good will of supposed opponents, when on the verge of war. . . .*[50]

From all over Texas came expressions of regret that Ord was being retired, along with remarks highly complimentary of the general personally. "It is with profound sorrow that your correspondent is called upon to chronicle the retirement of Gen. E.O.C. Ord. . . ," so began a San Antonio dispatch to the *Galveston Daily News.*[51] Ord's retirement "meets with unfavorable comment all over the state," said the *Beaumont Enterprise;*[52] Ord had "endeared himself to the people of this state by his uniform courtesy and soldierly bearing, and his retirement is the cause of universal regret," commented the *Luling Signal;*[53] "the people of Texas, regardless of political sentiment, will all unite in the expression of deep regret that President Hayes has removed Gen. E.O.C. Ord. . . ," said the *Meridian Blade.*[54] Complimentary statements were made of Ord's handling of the Texas command, "above all others in the United States requiring the most careful exercise of military judgment, and where his administration has proved eminently satisfactory."[55] The newspapers bore down hard upon President Hayes for what they believed was his partisan political action in retiring Ord because the general had favored Hancock's election.[56] The Galveston paper noted, apropos of McDowell's retention in the service, that he hailed from Ohio, while Ord not only was not from Ohio, he was "from the wrong side of Mason and Dixon's line, being a native of Maryland."[57]

On 16 December 1880, Senator Maxey of Texas introduced a bill authorizing the president to place General Ord on the retired list as a major general, according to his brevet rank, with the pay and emoluments of a major general.[58] This action evoked from Sherman a letter to Senator Maxey: "I noticed that you had introduced a Bill to retire Genl. Ord as a Major General and I thank you for this thoughtful interest in behalf of one of the truest, most unselfish, most meritorious men in the army," wrote the commanding general. Sherman went on to say: "It actually seems 'funny' that I should be forced to appeal to you 'a Rebel' to protect my oldest and best friend against the action of the 'Union President,' but such is the fact. 'Tempora mutantus etc'."[59]

Maxey replied to Sherman the same day: "[I] endorse to the echo everything good you say about Ord." No one, not even Ord, knew of his intention to introduce the bill, he said. When the general took command in Texas, life and property on the frontier were unsafe.

> He has brought order out of chaos, and leaves life and property on the border fairly secure, and the Dept. in splendid condition. . . . It therefore seemed to me not only a graceful thing, but eminently a just thing for a Texan man to present this bill. I have asked Genl Jos. E. Johnston whose opinion of Ord I know, to take charge in the House, and this because it is meet that a Southern man should recognize eminent services, especially since the war to the people of the South.[60]

Thus, did two "rebel" generals undertake to engineer through the Congress a bill to promote the Yankee General Ord. The Congress quickly completed action on Maxey's bill, and, on 28 January 1881, President Hayes signed the measure placing Ord on the retired list as a major general according to his brevet rank effective on that date.[61]

General Ord left behind him a legacy of peace on the Texas-Mexico frontier. Toward the close of 1881, Ord's successor in the Texas command, General Christopher C. Augur, was able to report that the arrangement made by Ord with the Mexican generals along the Rio Grande for friendly cooperation to preserve order had produced desired results. There had been no trouble of any kind along the line.[62]

20

★★★★★

Far from Home and Family

THE Ords had a comfortable domestic establishment in San Antonio, but it was temporary as all their previous arrangements had been. Now the general desired very much to purchase a home for his family and to provide educational and other advantages for his young children. To accomplish these goals he must start anew, for he was without property and without savings. His retirement pay as a major general was $5,625.00 per year, slightly more than his pay as a brigadier.[1] This was a substantial income, but the Ords were accustomed to a comfortable living. The objectives the general had set for himself would require additional money.

Undoubtedly, Ord and his family had lived well over the years. Perhaps in the management of their affairs they had been inclined to extravagance. On the other hand, their resources had been heavily drained by much sickness, the care of aged parents, and the cost of many moves from one command to another.

Ord was faced, at the age of sixty-two, with the necessity of launching into a new career. "He is a pure and thorough officer," William T. Sherman had said to Samuel Bell Maxey, "but singularly unfitted to embark in any civil occupation."[2] Nevertheless, the general was resourceful, and he would try his hand at the unfamiliar ways of the civilian world.

Ord acted promptly and aggressively to find a situation for himself. He went directly from San Antonio to Washington and thence to New York City. In the latter place, he conferred with T. W. Peirce, president of the Galveston, Harrisburg and San Antonio Railway Company, and Collis P. Huntington of the Southern Pacific Railroad. The two were business associates. The general offered to become the agent in Mexico for Huntington's railroad interests. Peirce favored employing Ord in this capacity, but Huntington protested that he was not interested in Mexico and did not care to have a representative there. Disappointed, the general returned to Washington.[3]

A turn of good fortune came to Ord almost immediately, for he received a letter from Peirce saying that he had had several conversations with Huntington on the subject of Mexican railroads and had finally convinced him that he ought to have Ord look into the situation. The proposal was that Ord would probably like to go to Mexico to see his daughter and that Huntington would advance his fare and pay him a stipend of $100 per month. Should Huntington decide to ask for concessions from the Mexican government, Ord's salary would rise to $3,000 per year.[4] Meanwhile, Ord was making an additional business connection. He approached Standard Oil Company officials and was engaged to be the agent of that organization, though in what capacity is not clear. The general returned to Texas to make preparations for his new venture. Leaving Molly and the children in San Antonio, he proceeded to Galveston, from which point he boarded a steamer for Vera Cruz early in March 1881.[5]

★★★★★

Mexico had undergone a political transformation at the close of 1880. Porfirio Díaz, president by revolution, had determined to follow the constitutional form and to allow a presidential election. He was careful to designate his successor, Manuel González, who had been his principal lieutenant in the revolution. González was readily elected and took office in December 1880. Gerónimo Treviño had issued a manifesto in 1879 announcing that he would not be a candidate in the 1880 election. As a González-Díaz partisan, he was rewarded with appointment as minister of war.[6]

In the early part of 1881, General Ord had been invited to be an official guest in Mexico. Thus, he had set out for that country in a dual capacity. He would be guest of the Mexican nation for a time, and then, on a more extended term, agent of the Southern Pacific Railroad and of the Standard Oil Company. His connection with the González administration through Treviño would make him a powerful advocate of the Collis P. Huntington and John D. Rockefeller interests.

★★★★★

Ord's steamer approached Vera Cruz, City of the True Cross, with the massive fortress of San Juan de Úlua in its harbor. The city lay on a sandy plain, hot and humid, with swarms of mosquitoes to plague native and visitor alike. As the general disembarked at the dock, he was immediately caught up in an elaborate official reception. He was met by his daughter, who was, of course, the wife of the minister of war, along with a large party of government officials. As a first hospitality, Ord was lodged in the home of the secretary of the treasury.[7]

The general and his escort boarded a special train for the city of Mexico some 260 miles to the west. En route, the tropical vegetation near the *tierra caliente,* the hot coastal plain, provided grand scenery with orange, lime, citron, banana and pomegranate trees; sugar cane and palms; coffee plants; and a profusion of brilliant flowering trees and shrubs. Ord was keenly interested in the remarkable engineering which enabled the train to ascend from sea level to an altitude of nearly 8,000 feet at Mexico City. At one point, the railroad ran along a mountainside terrace overlooking a valley 3,000 feet below. Several tunnels and a number of bridges were required to overcome the most difficult obstacles. Ord's active imagination was stirred as his train passed within sight of the ancient Pyramids of the Sun and Moon at San Juan Teotihuacán some thirty miles from the heart of Mexico City. In the distance, the towering snow-shrouded peaks of Popocatepetl and Ixtacihuatl added nature's grand monuments to the scene. The general was impressed by the beautiful gardens and plantations as his train neared the capital city.[8]

There was a big reception in Mexico City as Ord's train arrived. There then followed a succession of dinners and what the general described as a "sort of general ovation." Here was Ord, the "blackest nightmare" of Díaz and his government for sending his troops across the border under the instructions of 1 June 1877, now feted as an honored guest and friend! It would

not be seemly for Treviño to lavish the honors upon his own
father-in-law, so President González himself was official host.
The newspapers of Mexico city printed complimentary biographies of Ord and praised him for his moderate and careful
handling of his instructions of 1 June 1877.[9]

On 16 March, a "grand dinner" was given for Ord and was
attended by most of the cabinet members. Toasts and speeches
were made, and the general held his own with his complimentary responses. On the night of 17 March, the main
plaza of Mexico City, the Plaza de la Constitución or Plaza
Mayor, was illuminated, and Ord was honored with a serenade
by three hundred musicians. The scene was one of exceptional
splendor. On the north, dominating the great plaza with lordly
grandeur, was the Cathedral, built on the site of the oldest
Christian church in North America and it, in turn, on the foundation of an Aztec temple. To the east was the massive Palacio
Nacional covering an entire block and fronting 675 feet on the
plaza. The majesty of the occasion and the sense of history
which it evoked were enough to stir the general to the very
center of his being. In subsequent days, an excursion to the
huge caves of Cacahuamilpa was organized for Ord's entertainment by former President Díaz. Over one hundred people
were in the party.[10] "Well I wonder what it is all for, as I only
did my simple duty on the border, and gave these people credit
for having some sense and some honesty," Ord said.[11]

Ord was quite impressed by Mexico City and its prospects
for the future. There, one could get "more and better fruit,
flowers, scenery and society for the money," he wrote, than
could be had anywhere else. He observed plenty of riches and
plenty of poverty. The railroad boom, he thought, would help
to develop the city to huge proportions. The Mexican leaders
were anxious to stand well in the United States, a favorable
omen for American capitalists interested in investing in the
country.[12]

Ord commented at the outset of his stay in Mexico that
General Treviño was one of the ablest members of González's
cabinet, and he believed that his son-in-law was fast assuming
a leading place in the government. The general hoped, in view
of the uncertain tenure of any administration in Mexico, that
Treviño would be a force to hold the government together, at
least for the four-year term to which González had been
elected. Unfortunately, the future was not to develop in the

form the general hoped that it would. Bertie Treviño's health declined, and it was necessary for General Treviño to resign his cabinet post early in 1882 and return to Monterrey, where he resumed his old command of the Northern Division. On 3 September 1882, Bertie gave birth to a son appropriately named Gerónimo Edwardo de Treviño y Ord. General Ord delighted in referring to his grandson as the "international baby." Porfirio Díaz himself was godfather at the baptism of the infant.[13]

About a month after Ord arrived in Mexico, his name appeared on the letterhead of "La Compañia de Petróleo," an oil company headed by Henry Clay Pierce. Ord was listed as vice-president and F. F. Finley as secretary. It is possible that the company was an affiliate of Standard Oil, but Ord's connection with the Rockefeller interests lasted only a year, and nothing more was heard of the Mexican oil company.[14] Ord's tenure in the service of the Huntington railroad interests also was fairly brief. It was with yet another company that the general eventually found a place.

General Ulysses S. Grant had visited Mexico early in 1880 and had become interested in Mexican railroads. He had visited Ord in Galveston and San Antonio shortly afterward, and it is likely that the two generals talked of Mexican railroad prospects. In this same year, Grant's friend Matías Romero had secured a franchise from the governor of the state of Oaxaca to build without subsidy a railroad from Mexico City southward to the city of Oaxaca, with branches to the Gulf and the Pacific, and later extended to other points. The franchise was transferred to Grant, and, on 1 March 1881, the Mexican Southern Railroad was chartered by the legislature of New York. Among the other incorporators were former President Díaz, Russell Sage and Collis P. Huntington. Grant was named president of the road.[15] Subsequently Ord was employed by the Grant road as a civil engineer, probably beginning his duties sometime in 1881.

Ord was engaged in the preliminary survey of the Mexican Southern Railroad route from Mexico City southward toward the city of Oaxaca. Between his trips in the field, he lived quite comfortably in Mexico City, but it was a lonely existence. After a day's work in his office, he would go home in the evenings to a solitary chamber to smoke his pipe and read alone. It was not a "natural" way of life and not what he had promised himself in his old age. He admitted to having a good deal of self-reliance, and had developed a great interest in the reading of history to while away the evening hours. James Anthony Froude's life of Thomas Carlisle, histories of Europe, Mexico, Peru and of America's own War of 1812 kept him awake some nights, he said, until twelve or one o'clock.[16]

His trips in the field were quite another existence. He rode through the jungle on horseback, getting covered with ticks and fleas. On other terrain he was exposed to fierce gales. He slept out in the air, in open boats, or in dirty huts in the midst of "pigs, crying Indian babies and dirt." He ate, as he told one of his sons, "what you never had to."[17] Through it all, he took risks of contracting deadly fevers. He did all of this "to rake together enough to buy Molly and the children a home. Well come to think of it," he wrote, "I believe I *am* happier roughing it and thinking that I am achieving something than I would be settled down in slippers and arm chair with nothing to do but grumble. . . ."[18]

Yet, it was a weary business, and, at other times, he longed for a way out. To Pacificus, he wrote in whimsical vein: "I wish I could put off the harness of this R. Rd. business and had a big ranch to settle on and a big barn to build, and nice fat sheep, & cattle, and blooded horses, and corn bread & hominy and 19 sorts of preserves. Id sit back in my arm chair and smoke the best Vera Cruz Segars, and read all the latest works. . . ."[19]

The general was in the fight for money, as he expressed it, and was able to save about $250 per month of his salary. If Molly Ord in San Antonio would reduce her expenses to $100 per month, he believed he could increase his saving to $400 per month.[20]

Even as he engaged in the fight for money, Ord's mind was crowded with recollections of that other life, that military life of nearly fifty years' duration. Like an old warrior, he chafed at inaction, albeit with waning strength, and longed to be back in that familiar girding for battle. "The French seem bound to get up a row. . . ," he wrote. And again: "The Mexn Govt. may in next 4 or 5 years go back on the R. Rd. people so as to make it necessary for Uncle Sam to show his teeth. . . ."[21] "You see," he told Sherman, "some of these days we old fellows may be needed again."[22]

The general fell into a state of gloom upon receiving news of the death of his brother, William Marcellus Ord, the "Marcy" of Coast Survey days who had assisted him with the

triangulation of the islands off the coast of California. He unburdened himself to Pacificus:

> *Were it not for my anxiety to see my children comfortably settled*
> *in life, Id just as soon quit this sublunary sphere tomorrow*
> *as not. Not that I have not had as good a time as most persons,*
> *and better health, but I am reaching that age now when earths*
> *attractions cease to please. I am getting old enough to begin*
> *to think them like Solomon all vanities, & vexations and I can*
> *understand the feeling of very old men who are full of infirmities*
> *who want to be relieved.* [23]

He was the same restless Ord. Retirement had not
changed him in this respect. His capricious thoughts were
merely typical. It turned out that there was to be no easy chair,
no war, no recall to the colors. As for a man's life, he must live
all of it, and Edward Ord was still very much alive. In the
meantime, there was a railroad to be built.

Ord's company, the Mexican Southern Railroad headed by
Grant, underwent a change in its structure which might have a
significant effect upon Ord's future. On 28 May 1883, the Mexican Southern was consolidated with Jay Gould's Mexican Ori-
ental Railroad under a contract entered into with the Mexican
government. As Gould's line was proposed to extend from
Laredo, Texas, to Mexico City, the consolidated system when
completed would run the full length of Mexico from the American frontier to Guatemala. Ord determined that he would continue with the company only if they would pay him $6,000 per
year. If they would not do so, he would ask for a two months'
leave of absence to return to the States for the purpose of
prospecting for a new position. [24] Apparently, the salary matter
was not settled to the general's satisfaction, for he secured the
leave and left Mexico City bound for Vera Cruz and New York.

On Friday, the thirteenth day of July 1883, at Vera Cruz,
General Ord boarded the steamer *City of Washington*. His
thoughts were of home, and the name of the vessel reminded
him of the city where he spent his boyhood and from which he
departed to enter West Point. The nation's capital was still
home. The general anticipated a pleasant voyage as the steamer
put out from the Mexican coast and pushed steadily northeasterly under a blazing tropical sun. Havana, Cuba, was to be
the first stop. On 14 July, the second day out, several members

of the crew became ill, their ailment diagnosed as the dreaded black vomit—yellow fever! On the sixteenth, General Ord was stricken and on the eighteenth still more members of the crew, including the ship's doctor, as well as another passenger. Ord seemed to recover, apparently entering the second stage of the disease with its deceptive remission from the worst pain of the symptoms. Perhaps he attempted to exert himself, and it would be in character for him to help care for his fellow sufferers. Whatever the circumstances, he suffered a relapse. On the nineteenth, the steamer put into Havana and was quarantined with eighteen crew members and two passengers ill.[25]

The American consul-general in Havana was Adam Badeau, a member of Grant's staff during the Civil War. Badeau took a keen and sympathetic interest in Ord's condition and kept the State Department informed of developments. The consul visited Ord aboard ship, and the desperately ill old warrior, in a brave show of determination, assured Badeau that he would be up and about and would walk down the gangplank to shore as soon as he regained a bit of strength. On the twentieth, the United States medical inspector, Dr. Burgess, who had served under Ord's command in the Civil War, boarded the ship and later consulted with Badeau about bringing Ord ashore. Dr. Burgess indicated that the general's condition would not be worsened by the move, and the two concurred that it should be done. Eleven of the sick, including Ord, were brought to a hospital in Havana called "Casa de Salud Garcini." By the twenty-first, two of these eleven were dead. Meanwhile, three others had died aboard ship, and six slightly ill aboard the vessel were pronounced recovered.[26]

General Ord steadily grew weaker, and Badeau's report of 21 July was not good. Ord's case, he said, was nearly hopeless. The ill were all under the care of Dr. Burgess, and the hospital was among the best in Havana. Nothing would be spared in the way of faithful nursing and medical skill to save the general and his fellow sufferers.[27]

Ord in his sixty-fifth year lay on his death bed in lonely, self-chosen exile, far from home and family. What a pity! And yet, somehow it seemed appropriate that he go down in full stride, fighting as he always had in response to any challenge that might confront him. To be still and await events was not his way. The end came at 7:30 P.M. on Sunday evening, 22 July 1883.[28] The news was conveyed immediately to Molly Ord and the children, to the railroad company and to the War Department.

The response from the company was prompt. A telegram from Grant to Badeau directed him to draw upon the Mexican Southern Railroad Company for all Havana expenses in connection with General Ord's illness and death. A message of condolence to Molly Ord signed by both Grant and Gould informed her of the firm's action and assured her that the company would not forget the general's faithful services.[29]

Far out in the West, at Fort Missoula, Montana Territory, a telegram containing the notice of Ord's death was handed to Sherman. The commanding general sadly set himself to the duty of penning an obituary order: "As his intimate associate since boyhood, the General here bears testimony of him that a more unselfish, manly and patriotic person never lived."[30] He meant it.

General Ord's body was brought to the District of Columbia and interred in Oak Hill Cemetery. There it remained until 1900, when it was removed to the National Cemetery at Arlington, Virginia.[31] It was altogether fitting that General Ord should rest finally on Southern soil just by the Lee mansion. Across the Potomac was Washington, D.C.—home—and dominating the scene was the massive and beautiful dome of the Capitol, symbol of the Union for which E.O.C. Ord had spent his life.

21

★★★★★

In Review

A T the outbreak of the Civil War, Brigadier General E.O.C. Ord was a vigorous and active officer of forty-three years of age. His basic character had been formed upon a solid Catholic foundation and shaped by pride in the heritage of his country and his family. He was honest and upright, devoted to family, and faithful to duty. Essentially, he was a doer rather than a thinker. This is not to say that he was uninformed, for he read considerably. But basically he was a man of action— ambitious, restless; some would say that he was overactive.

Ord had a quick mind, not ordinary in capacity, inventive and resourceful, with an active imagination. He was changeable in some of his views and not always consistent. While holding to a particular opinion, he was strong in asserting it. His individualism was so pronounced as to cause remark, and he was called eccentric. His eccentricity, to be sure, was to be seen in the externals of appearance and dress. He was a nonconformist. But his idiosyncracies were seen in more significant ways in his unusual and sometimes original ideas and actions.

Ord's thinking on military matters, of course, was shaped by his West Point training which was based on French experience. In particular, the writings of Jomini as emphasized at the Military Academy by Dennis Hart Mahan provided the basis of the curriculum. Ord became a thorough professional. He brought to this training his own fine personal qualities and

talents. He was always concerned with the welfare of the men
in the ranks under his command. In general, he had an old-
fashioned, chivalric view of war and eventually superimposed
upon this view a mature recognition that war was an evil to be
moderated or, better still, avoided.

Ord was widely experienced by extensive travel—Brazil,
Chile, Panama, Jamaica, and, in his own country, up and down
both East Coast and West and in much of the hinterland. He
was associated with all sorts of people—the great, the degraded, the unselfish and the depraved. All of this gave him
some breadth of outlook as well as insight into human behavior. More particularly, he had experienced Indian wars,
where he proved himself to be a hard fighter, and yet one who
could treat a defeated enemy humanely. He believed these
wars advanced civilization. With his reputation established as a
soldier, his abilities and accomplishments were recognized in
his appointment as Superintendent of Practical Instruction at
the Artillery School at Fort Monroe.

Born and reared below the Mason-Dixon line, Ord identified himself as a Southerner and a Democrat, confessed to
being at one period a proslavery man, and expressed sympathy
for Southern grievances. But, more important in the long run,
he was a strong Unionist. As the sectional confrontation of
1860–61 developed and centered upon Fort Sumter, Ord asserted his Unionism and called for vigorous Union action to
meet the secession crisis.

General Ord was proud to say in after-years that he commanded in the Civil War at the first Union victory in Virginia at
Dranesville and at the final one at Appomattox. From first to
last, he was a bold, aggressive, self-confident fighter—brave to
the point of foolhardiness. True, in the abortive effort to catch
Stonewall Jackson in the Valley he did not show up well, but
apparently illness hampered his effectiveness then. When he
led troops in battle, he gained their respect and love. Withal, he
showed a becoming modesty.

The general also gained the respect of Ulysses S. Grant,
who very early recognized his competence and dependability.
A "Grant man," Ord rose to high position, as Grant himself
ascended to supreme command. "Brave and prompt," "skillful
in the management of troops," Grant said of him, and, in a war
which witnessed much bravery but little promptness, this was
a fortuitous combination. At Iuka, Ord was prompt and profi-

cient in maneuver; at the Hatchie, aggressive and brave. These battles helped to pave the way for the Federal offensive in the West in 1863. Better than the addition of 10,000 reinforcements, Grant said of Ord's taking command of the Thirteenth Corps at Vicksburg. The experience gained by Ord in handling one of the largest corps in the army at Vicksburg, Jackson, and in the Gulf Department prepared him for larger responsibilities ahead. He balked at taking a small command under Franz Sigel in an expedition he thought ill-advised. Subsequent failure of the operation seemed to bear out his judgment.

Ord was named by Grant to command the Eighteenth Corps shortly after the latter became General-in-Chief. Ord's assault and capture of the great Richmond bastion known as Fort Harrison was an accomplishment of major importance in the military operations before Richmond and Petersburg. The secrecy and speed were important, but, above all, the quality of Ord's leadership in the assault itself evoked high praise from military experts then as well as later. Perhaps he was the best assault leader of the Union army and certainly one of the most proficient in handling troops in a variety of situations.

Ord was elevated by Grant to command the Department of Virginia and the Army of the James, responsibilities encompassing the line before Richmond and the administration of a vital military area. The change placed Ord third in rank in the field in Virginia. In this position, he promoted the restoration of civil government and the return of private property confiscated from Southerners. The General-in-Chief thought of a winter offensive, and, though it never materialized, he had Ord in mind to lead the attack.

General Ord's conservative Democratic background, his racial views, his Virginian wife, and his kinship by marriage with prominent Southerners caused his loyalty to the Union to be questioned. In view of his hard fighting in the cause, this seemed incongruous, but in the strained emotional atmosphere of wartime, zealous partisans nevertheless questioned his devotion to the Union cause. Perhaps the aura of suspicion which surrounded him made it impolitic for Lincoln to appoint him a brigadier general of regulars.

Ord was conservative in his views toward the Negroes. He did not think they were ready for full responsibilities. He believed they would have to be looked after and put to work. As for Negro soldiers, he did not consider them as being on the same footing with the whites. He was accused of discriminating against them, and he apparently would have been pleased to have them eliminated from the army entirely.

At the time Ord undertook his army and departmental command, it became apparent that a large-scale illicit trade through the Union lines and into Confederate territory was supplying many of the needs of Lee's army. At Ord's suggestion, a commission was set up to investigate, and its findings seemed to implicate high Union military authorities. Meanwhile, the general took stringent measures to effectively cut off the traffic.

As the Northern cause became ascendant, General Ord sought for ways to stop the war short of a bloody fight to the finish. At great risk to his considerable position, he initiated negotiations with Longstreet, looking toward an armistice to be made by Grant and Lee, after which political questions, especially the matter of slavery, could be taken up and settled by the civilian leaders. It was a daring scheme, and it almost worked.

When the spring campaign of 1865 got under way, Grant pulled Ord from the Richmond front with a substantial portion of his army and sent him below Petersburg to take part in the operations to force Lee out of that key city. So skillful was Ord in accomplishing this move, that it was five days before Lee reduced his Richmond force and ten days before the Confederate knew positively that Ord was on his flank in the flight to Appomattox. It was Ord's army which occupied Richmond, and Ord's Negro soldiers were the first to enter Petersburg.

At crucial moments, Ord could think and act on his own initiative. After the breakthrough at Petersburg, he sent to Grant for instructions. Receiving none, he directed his own forces and those of the Sixth Corps to close in on the city from the west. Thus he played a major role in causing Lee to evacuate Petersburg. In the pursuit of Lee, a captured dispatch left Ord at Burkeville without orders, but he moved promptly against Lee without orders as soon as he learned the whereabouts of the enemy. These things were no more than a good commander should have done. On the other hand, Ord ordered Theodore Read to disaster at High Bridge. What his responsibility was in this instance cannot be definitely determined. Either Grant was responsible or Ord, or possibly the two jointly.

Grant dispatched Ord from Farmville to get his infantry in front of the Confederates. As the ranking officer of the pursuing column, Ord had command of two corps of infantry and Sheridan's cavalry, about 30,000 men in all. By a forced march of nearly forty miles, which can only be described as a classic in the annals of warfare, Ord planted his two corps of infantry in Lee's path on 9 April. He was just in time to prevent Lee from breaking through Sheridan's cavalry, which could not withstand the Confederate attack.

At Appomattox, Ord could have annihilated Lee's army, but in Grant's absence, he assumed the responsibility of instituting an armistice and humanely stopped the fight until Grant arrived to receive Lee's surrender. With hostilities ended, Ord fostered the "spirit of Appomattox" to reconcile the sections and to unify the nation.

In the occupation of Richmond and of the entire state of Virginia following Lee's surrender, Ord's conservative and conciliatory policies were quite evident. He secured the removal of the Negro Twenty-fifth Corps from the state, no doubt in part to please Virginians. He insisted that the freed people must work as he undertook the staggering task of providing relief and employment to some 100,000 of them throughout the state. He ordered relief to whites, including paroled Confederates, and aided them in a number of ways, even extending personal kindnesses. He encouraged by various means the recovery of business and agriculture. After the assassination of Lincoln, Ord balked at Grant's order to arrest Lee and other paroled Confederates in Richmond. Ord's wishes prevailed, and his efforts to reconcile Northerners and Southerners in Virginia was allowed to continue. It gave him pleasure to expedite General Lee's application for amnesty.

Soon, however, there were grumblings from those of the Radical persuasion who complained of Ord's softness toward ex-Confederates. Some of the general's orders were revoked in Washington, and then, after a tenure of two months in the post-Appomattox Virginia command, he was transferred.

Only for a brief time was Ord away from Southern problems, for in 1866 he was assigned to command in Arkansas. As assistant commissioner of the Freedmen's Bureau, he undertook to protect freedmen from outrage at the hands of whites. He called to the attention of his superiors that the better class of whites treated the Negroes well, but that the poorer ones, who were in the position of competing with the freedmen for a livelihood, were prone to violence toward them. These race relations crossed party lines and did not simply reflect ex-Confederate intransigence. General Ord adopted a middle-of-the-road policy in adjusting relations between planters and Negro tenants with regard to work contracts and between whites and blacks generally where civil rights were concerned. He took his Freedmen's Bureau duties seriously, encouraging efforts toward educating the Negroes and doing what he could to establish them as independent farmers.

Ord's views toward white and black Southerners shaped his attitude toward Reconstruction policies. He was opposed to Negro suffrage in 1866 and to the Radical Republicans who were suggesting it. Black suffrage became a reality in 1867 as a feature of the congressional reconstruction plan, and Ord was appointed to implement that plan in Mississippi and Arkansas. His opposition to the entire scheme was scarcely concealed. He was nevertheless determined to reconstruct these states by the law, and he used the virtually supreme power at his command to execute the Reconstruction acts vigorously. Along with his firmness, he tried to be fair and conciliatory. Though not extreme in his policy, he removed some officials in both states and dissolved the Arkansas legislature; he set aside certain laws deemed incompatible with the statutes he was charged with enforcing; and, on the same basis, he interfered with courts and established military commissions to try certain types of cases. He championed freedom of the press in the *Constitutional Eagle* affair, but he regarded editor McCardle as a dangerous incendiary who incited civil disorder and obstructed Ord's work of executing the Reconstruction acts. He tried to muzzle the Vicksburg firebrand and thereby precipitated the famous case known as *Ex parte McCardle*.

General Ord extended protection to the freed people in various ways. He used military commissions to try those accused of outraging blacks; he protected the freedmen in the division of the crops; he insisted that the poor laws apply to blacks as well as whites, that taxes fall on all alike, and that the bureau agents serving the Negroes be supported and protected. On the other hand, he protected whites against evil agents of the bureau. He opposed the ultra-Radical position which pitted black against white. He believed with real foresight that ultimately an enlightened citizenry rather than federal troops was the surest protection for the Negroes.

In the political contests in Mississippi and Arkansas, he sought to protect all parties. The Radicals complained that he needed to be reconstructed himself, but, on the other hand, Conservatives found little in his work to give them comfort. He tried in vain to keep the bureau agents neutral while giving the Negroes every opportunity to register. He conscientiously saw to the selection of the best registrars available and provided a fair registration and election.

Ord wanted to get out of Mississippi and Arkansas, and, with the elections over and the constitutional conventions set for January 1868, he was relieved. There were mixed opinions about his capabilities and accomplishments in the Fourth Military District, but the judgment that he was too moderate for the Radicals and not moderate enough for the Conservatives seems sound. He felt trapped between two extreme factions, neither of which, he thought, had much virtue. His own tendency was toward conservatism. He was not confident of the Negroes' capacity to govern; he understood very clearly the harsh feelings of Southern whites toward their "presumptuous" former slaves; he did not look for good to come out of the Radical governments; and he believed that, in the final analysis, "enlightened" Southerners must rule themselves.

★★★★★

The improvement of the military service was a matter of concern to General Ord over the forty-five years of his career. He was particularly interested in the rights of enlisted men, their opportunities, their pay, and their living conditions. He believed they should serve on courts-martial. He thought higher pay for sergeants would secure better qualified non-commissioned officers. Commissioned officers, he believed, should be examined to determine their fitness for promotion.

★★★★★

In his frontier service, Ord believed that, in protecting the advancing white settlements and railroads, he was contributing to the spread of civilization. Toward Indians on the warpath, he was ruthless; yet, at the same time, he could recommend a more humane governmental policy for them. Toward marauders, white or red, he was implacable.

Texas in the 1870s provided Ord with a field ready to be pacified and civilized. Raiders from Mexico, white and Indian, had plagued the frontier for years. Ord did not believe the United States government's policy was vigorous enough to cope with the problem. He sought stronger measures, crossed the border informally in pursuit of raiders, and even proposed that the United States occupy and pacify northern Mexico.

All the while, Ord pressed his superiors for more troops and thereby got into difficulties with his immediate commander, Sheridan. Sheridan did not have enough soldiers, and Ord no doubt caused much trouble by his efforts to circumvent the troop dispositions of the division commander. Moreover, Sheridan found Ord's management of his departments confusing and unsatisfactory. In the entire matter of troop disposition, Ord had in mind the welfare of the army as well as that of Texas. The more commotion on the border, the more the Texans in Congress worked to augment Ord's force and to save the army from reduction. They were apparently the key delegation in this endeavor. Ord's work with the Texans was indispensable to the army.

Ord went around Sheridan to his friend Sherman, the commanding general, to have the instructions of 1 June 1877, authorizing the crossing of the border, issued by President Hayes. However, Ord used his authority judiciously in the matter of crossing. He conciliated the Mexican authorities and worked closely with Mexican General Treviño to pacify the Rio Grande. There were no clashes between their forces. With Treviño on the border and the Díaz government making serious efforts to keep order, General Ord did not again suggest American occupation of Mexican territory.

When the Mexican-American frontier was tranquil, Ord sought to have President Hayes withdraw the instructions of 1 June 1877 and give credit to the Mexican generals for the good order prevailing. This was some time before Treviño became his son-in-law, and there is nothing to indicate that this connection figured in his thinking. However, to Sheridan, an orderly frontier meant that he could withdraw troops from Ord to use elsewhere. As Sheridan ordered Mackenzie out of Texas, Ord withdrew his recommendation for the cancellation of the Ord Order, causing a delay in President Hayes's action and, hence, some awkwardness in Sherman's position. Ord defended the withdrawal of his recommendation, but it is possible that he did not handle the matter very well.

The result of Ord's work on the border was peace and security, for which he deserved credit. To further insure the tranquility of Texas, he not only encouraged railroad building, but also encouraged a link-up of Texas and Mexican railroads as a bond of peace and prosperity.

Retirement came unwanted to General Ord in 1880, though he contributed to its coming by his untimely telegram to Winfield Scott Hancock. He seemed to ask retirement from Hayes, and the president accommodated him. From all over Texas came reports of disappointment at Ord's retirement because the "Yankee" general had won the love of Texans by his good will and good services. Senator Maxey paid high tribute to him, and this former Confederate general joined with one of his brother Confederates, Joseph E. Johnston, to have the Congress retire Ord as a major general.

In retirement, Ord went to Mexico as guest of the nation where his son-in-law was minister of war. His grand reception there he believed was due to his friendly and cooperative actions along the border. He remained as a civil engineer in the service of the Grand-Gould railroad interests, a hard life which wearied him at times. When not surveying in the field, he spent his time reading history and biography, which he found absorbing.

General Ord's death came "in service," as it were, for he was stricken with yellow fever while en route home from his duties in Mexico and died in Havana, Cuba, in 1883. A professional soldier to the very core, Ord was an honest man who played an important part in shaping national and even international events in the cause of peace. No man could ask for a nobler epitaph.

Notes

Chapter 1

1 Mary Ord Preston, ed., *Memoranda Concerning James Ord, Who Died at the United States Navy Yard, Washington, D.C., October 12, 1810* (n.p., 1896). The account of James Ord's life is derived principally from this pamphlet, a copy of which may be found in the archives of Georgetown University, Washington, D.C.

2 For treatment of the question of James Ord's parentage by biographers of George IV, *see* Shane Leslie, *George the Fourth* (Boston: Little, Brown and Company, 1926), pp. 109–203; Christopher Hibbert, *George IV, Prince of Wales, 1762–1811* (New York: Harper and Row, 1972), 63n.

3 John Gilmary Shea, *Memorial of the First Centenary of Georgetown College* (Washington: P. F. Collier, 1891), p. 29.

4 In 1833, James Ord the younger read in an account of the marriage of the Prince of Wales to Mrs. Fitzherbert that it was rumored that she had been pregnant. This gave him reason to suppose that he might be the child of this marriage and that he had been sent out of England for political reasons. He consulted with Father William Matthews, rector of St. Patrick's Church, Washington, friend and executor of the elder Ord. Father Matthews advised him to write to Mrs. Fitzherbert, who was still living at the age of seventy-seven. King George IV had died in 1830. The letter addressed to Mrs. Fitzherbert was sent through the State Department under cover to Aaron Vail, United States minister to England, to be given by him to Mrs. Fitzherbert. There was no response to this letter.

5 Details of the life of the younger James Ord are from Mary Ord Preston, ed., *Memoranda Concerning James Ord, Who Died January 25th, 1873* (n.p., 1896), archives of Georgetown University, Washington, D.C.

6 Kenneth P. Bailey, *Thomas Cresap, Maryland Frontiersman* (Boston: Christopher Publishing House, 1944).

7 John J. Jacob, *A Biographical Sketch of the Life of the Late Capt. Michael Cresap* (Cumberland, Maryland: J. J. Miller, 1881); record of the Cresap family in the family Bible of Edward Otho Cresap. (Photostatic copies in possession of the Cresap Society, Port Washington, Ohio.)

8 Record of the Ord family in the family Bible of James Ord. (Copy in possession of Bernarr Cresap.)

9 Sylvanus Thayer to James Hook, 7 March 1835, records of the Adjutant General's Office relating to the United States Military Academy, Record Group 94, National Archives.

10 Richard M. Johnson to Lewis Cass, 2 February 1835, Adjutant General's Office, Record Group 94, National Archives.

11 Ord to Lewis Cass, 18 August 1835, Adjutant General's Office.

Chapter 2

[1] Edward Ord to Placidus Ord, 7 October 1837, Alexander Collection of Ord Papers, in possession of Mrs. Vida Ord Alexander, Washington, D.C.

[2] William A. Gordon, comp., *A Compilation of Registers of the Army of the United States, from 1815 to 1837* (Washington: James C. Dunn, Printer, 1837), pp. 564–65.

[3] Ord to Joseph C. Ives (draft), 17 August 1860, Edward Otho Cresap Ord Correspondence and Papers, 1850–1883, Bancroft Library, Berkeley, California. These papers were given to the Bancroft Library by the late Miss Ellen F. Ord.

[4] Ord to Mrs. Ord, 1 January 1856, Edward Otho Cresap Ord Papers, 1854–1858, Manuscripts Division, Department of Special Collections, C. H. Green Library, Stanford University, Stanford, California.

[5] Information about Ord's class standing and conduct were provided by the librarian of the United States Military Academy from the Academy records.

[6] Returns of the Third Artillery, 1839, Adjutant General's Office, Record Group 94, National Archives.

[7] Ord to Ives (draft), 17 August 1860, Bancroft Library Collection.

[8] *See* John K. Mahon, *History of the Second Seminole War, 1835–1842* (Gainesville: University of Florida Press, 1967).

[9] Annual Report of the Third Artillery, 1840, Adjutant General's Office.

[10] Theophilus F. Rodenbough, comp., *From Everglade to Cañon with the Second Dragoons* (New York: D. Van Nostrand, 1875), pp. 506–507.

[11] Ord to Mrs. Ord, 23 June 1856, Stanford Collection.

[12] Ord to Placidus Ord, 21 December 1841, Alexander Collection.

[13] *House Misc. Docs.*, 45th Cong., 2nd Sess., No. 64 (Serial No. 1820): 26.

[14] Ord to Pacificus Ord, 19 May 1842, Preston Collection of Ord Papers, in possession of Mr. Murray Preston, Chevy Chase, Maryland.

[15] Ord to Pacificus Ord, 19 and 21 July 1842, Preston Collection.

[16] Ord to Pacificus Ord, 27 August and 4 September 1842, Preston Collection.

[17] Ord to Pacificus Ord, 23 and 24 September 1842, Preston Collection.

[18] Ord to Pacificus Ord, 27 December 1843, Preston Collection.

[19] Ord to Pacificus Ord, 5 June 1844, Preston Collection.

[20] Ord to Pacificus Ord, 7 January 1843, Preston Collection.

[21] Ord to Pacificus Ord, 17 May 1843, Preston Collection.

[22] Ord to Pacificus Ord, 5 June 1844, Preston Collection.

[23] Ord to Pacificus Ord, 27 June 1843, Preston Collection.

[24] Ord to Pacificus Ord, 30 December 1844, Preston Collection.

[25] Ord to Pacificus Ord, 6 December 1845, Preston Collection; Ord to Placidus Ord, 27 February and 30 November 1845, Alexander Collection; Returns of the Third Artillery, 1845.

[26] Ord to Placidus Ord, 27 February 1845, Alexander Collection; Ord to Pacificus Ord, 2 March 1846, Preston Collection.

[27] Ord to Placidus Ord, 25 March 1846, Alexander Collection.

[28] Ord to Placidus Ord, 27 February 1845, Alexander Collection.

[29] Ord to Pacificus Ord, 24 January 1846, Preston Collection.

[30] Ord to Placidus Ord, n.d., Alexander Collection.

[31] Ord to Pacificus Ord, 19 May 1846, Preston Collection. Ord misjudged at least the initial warlike response of the people. Polk got more volunteers than he needed. *See* Justin H. Smith, *The War with Mexico*, 2 vols. (New York: Macmillan Company, 1919), 1:192–96. *Also see* the treatment of the Mexican War by various writers including Glenn W. Price, *Origins of the War with Mexico: The Polk-Stockton Intrigue* (Austin: University of Texas Press, 1967).

[32] Ord to Pacificus Ord, 28 May 1846, Preston Collection.

[33] Ibid.

³⁴ Ibid.

³⁵ William T. Sherman, *Personal Memoirs of Gen. W. T. Sherman*, 4th ed. rev. and corr., 2 vols. (New York: Charles L. Webster and Company, 1891), 1:38–39; Returns of the Third Artillery, 1846.

Chapter 3

¹ Edward Ord to Pacificus Ord, 24 September–1 December 1846, Preston Collection of Ord Papers, in possession of Mr. Murray Preston, Chevy Chase, Maryland. Ord's account of the voyage as given in this letter will be followed here except as otherwise noted.

² Returns of the Third Artillery, 1847, Adjutant General's Office, Record Group 94, National Archives.

³ James L. Ord to Pacificus Ord, 16 March 1847, Preston Collection.

⁴ Ord to Pacificus Ord, 28 April 1847, Preston Collection.

⁵ William T. Sherman, *Personal Memoirs of Gen. W. T. Sherman*, 4th ed. rev. and corr., 2 vols. (New York: Charles L. Webster and Company, 1891), 1:48–49.

⁶ Ibid., p. 50; Sherman to Ellen B. Ewing, 1 May 1847, [William T. Sherman], *Home Letters of General Sherman*, ed. M. A. DeWolfe Howe (New York: Charles Scribner's Sons, 1909), pp. 104–105.

⁷ Ord to Pacificus Ord, 16 March and 28 April 1847, Preston Collection.

⁸ James M. Merrill, *William Tecumseh Sherman* (Chicago: Rand McNally and Company, 1971), p. 71.

⁹ Returns of the Third Artillery, 1847, Adjutant General's Office, Record Group 94, National Archives.

¹⁰ *House Executive Documents*, 31st Cong., 1st Sess., No. 17 (Serial No. 573): 603.

¹¹ Ord to James Ord, 2 July 1848, as quoted in James Ord to Placidus Ord, 12 October 1848, Alexander Collection of Ord Papers, in possession of Mrs. Vida Ord Alexander, Washington, D.C.; Ord to Pacificus Ord, 21 October 1848, Preston Collection.

¹² Ord to James Ord, 2 July 1848, as quoted in James Ord to Placidus Ord, 12 October 1848, Alexander Collection.

¹³ Ord to Pacificus Ord, 21 October 1848, Preston Collection. For corroboration of Ord's statement *see* Robert G. Clelland, *From Wilderness to Empire: A History of California*, ed. Glenn S. Dumke (New York: Macmillan Company, 1959), chaps. 11–13.

¹⁴ William T. Sherman, "Old Times in California," *North American Review*, 148 (1889): 271–75; *House Executive Documents*, 31st Cong., 1st Sess., No. 17 (Serial No. 573): 653. For an account of the military government, *see* Theodore Grivas, *Military Governments in California, 1846–1850* (Glendale, California: Arthur H. Clark Company, 1962).

¹⁵ Ord to Pacificus Ord, 21 October 1848, Preston Collection; Ord to Sherman, 27 March 1849, W. T. Sherman Papers, 3, Manuscript Division, Library of Congress.

¹⁶ Ord to Pacificus Ord, 21 October 1848, Preston Collection. Ord prepared a topographical sketch of the gold and quicksilver district of California, dated 25 July 1848, which was lithographed in Washington. It was one of the earliest maps of the gold region.

¹⁷ Ord to Sherman, 27 March 1849, W. T. Sherman Papers, 3.

¹⁸ Ord to Pacificus Ord, 21 October 1848, Preston Collection.

¹⁹ Ibid. A first lieutenant at this time received $30 per month plus $24 for rations and an allowance of $15.50 for a servant.

²⁰ John A. Swan to Sherman, 15 February 1876, W. T. Sherman Papers, 42.

²¹ Merrill, *William Tecumseh Sherman*, p. 76.

²² J. Gregg Layne, "Edward Otho Cresap Ord, Soldier and Surveyor," *Historical Society of Southern California Quarterly*, 17 (1935): 139.

²³ *Senate Executive Documents*, 31st Cong., 1st Sess., No. 47 (Serial No. 558): 126; Minutes of the Ayuntamiento of Los Angeles, as quoted in W. W. Robinson, ed.,

"Story of Ord's Survey as Disclosed by the Los Angeles Archives," *Historical Society of Southern California Quarterly*, 19 (1937): 121–25; William Rich Hutton, *Glances at California, 1847–1853*, ed. Willard O. Waters (San Marino, California: Huntington Library, 1942), pp. 13, 17, 20, 29. The original map of the survey is preserved in the archives of the City of Los Angeles and bears the following inscription: "Plan De la Ciudad de los Angeles, Surveyed and Drawn by E.O.C. Ord, Lt. U.S.A. & Wm. R. Hutton, Asst., August 29, 1849."

24 Edward R. S. Canby to Ord, 1 October 1849, letters of the 10th Military Department, Adjutant General's Office, Record Group 94, National Archives.

25 *Senate Executive Documents*, 31st Cong., 1st Sess., No. 47 (Serial No. 558): 122–25. Except as otherwise noted, Ord's description is from this published report of his reconnaissance. Ord's topographical sketch of the Los Angeles plains and vicinity, August 1849, is printed in this volume.

26 *See* George L. Albright, *Official Explorations for Pacific Railroads, 1853–1855* (Berkeley: University of California Press, 1921), pp. 7–28; Robert R. Russel, *Improvement of Communication with the Pacific Coast as an Issue in American Politics, 1783–1864* (Cedar Rapids, Iowa: Torch Press, 1948), chap. 11.

27 Sherman, *Memoirs*, 1:109–10.

28 Ord to Sherman, 14 August 1863, W. T. Sherman Papers, 12.

29 Jefferson Davis's resolution, 3 July 1850, as quoted in Dunbar Rowland, ed., *Jefferson Davis, Constitutionalist*, 10 vols. (Jackson, Mississippi: Printed for the Mississippi Department of Archives and History, 1923), 1:403.

30 *Congressional Globe*, 32nd Cong., 2nd Sess. (27 January 1853), pp. 422–23.

31 Albright, *Official Explorations for Pacific Railroads, 1853–1855*, pp. 102–18. The present route of the Atchison, Topeka, and Santa Fe Railroad from the Rio Grande through Cajon Pass along the thirty-fifth parallel follows Whipple's survey very closely. *See* Grant Foreman, ed., *A Pathfinder in the Southwest: The Itinerary of Lieutenant A. W. Whipple* (Norman, Oklahoma: University of Oklahoma Press, 1941).

32 Ord's Diary (1850–1853), 16 July 1850, Edward Otho Cresap Ord Correspondence and Papers, 1850–1883, Bancroft Library, Berkeley, California.

33 Ibid., 19 and 21 July 1850.

34 Ibid., 26–29 July 1850.

35 Ord to Placidus Ord, 14 October 1851, Alexander Collection; Ord to Pacificus Ord, 7 April 1851, Preston Collection.

36 Oscar F. Winship to Francis O. Wyse (copy), 10 February 1852, with Ord's endorsement of 25 June 1852, Bancroft Library Collection.

37 *Senate Executive Documents*, 33rd Cong., 1st Sess., No. 14 (Serial No. 704): 58.

38 *Senate Executive Documents*, 33rd Cong., 2nd Sess., No. 10 (Serial No. 757): 81.

39 William H. T. Huie, comp., "The Family," a typewritten manuscript of the genealogy of the Thompson and allied families, Library of the Sons of the American Revolution, San Francisco, California.

40 James Ord to Placidus Ord, 2 October 1855, Alexander Collection.

41 Erasmus D. Keyes, *Fifty Years' Observation of Men and Events, Civil and Military* (New York: Charles Scribner's Sons, 1884), p. 263.

42 Mary Ord Preston, ed., *Memoranda Concerning James Ord, Who Died January 25th, 1873* (n.p., 1896), p. 6. In 1857, James and Rebecca Ord were presented by their sons with a beautiful rancho located about six miles south of Santa Cruz.

43 Ord to James Ord, 18 December 1853, Alexander Collection.

Chapter 4

1 *See* Oscar O. Winther, *The Great Northwest, A History* (New York: Alfred A. Knopf, 1948), pp. 171–78; John W. Caughey, *History of the Pacific Coast* (Los Angeles: Privately printed by the author, 1933), pp. 347–51; Robert M. Utley, *Frontiersmen in Blue: The United States Army and the Indian, 1848–1865* (New York: Macmillan Company, 1967), chap. 9.

2 Major Gabriel J. Rains's report, 1 December 1855, Letters Received, Adjutant General's Office, Record Group 94, National Archives.

3 Ibid.; Returns of the Third Artillery, 1855, Adjutant General's Office, Record Group 94, National Archives; Philip H. Sheridan, *Personal Memoirs of P. H. Sheridan,* 2 vols. (New York: C. L. Webster and Company, 1888), 1:63–64, 68.

4 Edward Ord to Mrs. Ord, 21 November 1855, Edward Otho Cresap Ord Papers, 1854–1858, Manuscripts Division, Department of Special Collections, C. H. Green Library, Stanford University, Stanford, California.

5 Sheridan, *Personal Memoirs,* 1:68–69.

6 Ibid.

7 *Olympia Pioneer and Democrat,* 26 October 1855, 15 February and 11 April 1856; *San Francisco Daily Herald,* 7 November 1855, 22 February 1856; *New York Herald,* 17 February 1856; *Harper's New Monthly Magazine,* 13 (1856): 522–26. Utley says in *Frontiersmen in Blue* (p. 101) that "the origins of nearly every Indian disturbance could be traced clearly to undisguised white aggression."

8 Ord to James Ord (copy), 23 March 1856, Alexander Collection of Ord Papers, in possession of Mrs. Vida Ord Alexander, Washington, D.C.

9 *Harper's New Monthly Magazine,* 13:523.

10 Edward Ord's Diary (1856), 20–21 March 1856, Edward Otho Cresap Ord Correspondence and Papers, 1850–1883, Bancroft Library, Berkeley, California.

11 Ord's report, 27 March 1856, Letters Received, Adjutant General's Office. This account of the expedition is from Ord's report except where otherwise noted.

12 Ord to James Ord (copy), 28 March 1856, Alexander Collection.

13 Ord's Diary (1856), 26 March 1856, Bancroft Library Collection.

14 Ibid., 27 March 1856.

15 *San Francisco Daily Herald,* 18 April 1856.

16 Ord to Mrs. Ord, 7 May 1856, Stanford Collection; Returns of the Third Artillery, 1856.

17 Ord to James Ord, 23 May 1856, Alexander Collection; Ord to Mrs. Ord, 23 May 1856, Stanford Collection.

18 Ord's Diary (1856), 30 May and 8 June 1856, Bancroft Library Collection.

19 Ord to one of his brothers, 7 July 1858, Stanford Collection.

20 Ord's Diary (1856), 10 June 1856, Bancroft Library Collection.

21 Ibid., 6 June 1856.

22 Robert C. Buchanan to David R. Jones, 24 June 1856, Letters Received, Adjutant General's Office.

23 Ord's Diary (1856), 23 June–6 July 1856, Bancroft Library Collection.

24 Stanton A. Coblentz, *Villians and Vigilantes* (New York: Thomas Yoseloff, 1957); Special Orders, No. 84, Department of the Pacific (copy), 13 August 1856, Bancroft Library Collection. In the latter part of July 1856, Ord was ordered to Southern California, as he had been in 1849, to determine the need for an army post to restrain marauding Indians in the vicinity of San Bernardino. For Ord's account of this journey, *see The City of the Angels and the City of the Saints,* ed. Neal Harlow (San Marino, California: Huntington Library, 1978).

25 Returns of the Third Artillery, 1858; Colonel George Wright's reports, 19 and 31 August 1858, Letters Received, Adjutant General's Office.

26 Ord to Mrs. Ord, 1 September 1858, Stanford Collection.

27 Wright's report, 2 September 1858, Letters Received, Adjutant General's Office. The account of the battle is from Wright's report except as otherwise noted.

28 Ord to Mrs. Ord, 15 September 1858, Stanford Collection.

29 Wright's report, 6 September 1858, Letters Received, Adjutant General's Office. The account of the battle is from Wright's report except as otherwise noted.

30 Ord to Mrs. Ord, 15 September 1858, Stanford Collection.

31 Ibid.

[32] Wright's reports, 9, 10, 15, 21, and 30 September 1858, Letters Received, Adjutant General's Office.

[33] Returns of the Third Artillery, 1858, 1859.

Chapter 5

[1] Edward Ord to W. T. Sherman, 18 April 1882, W. T. Sherman Papers, 57, Manuscript Division, Library of Congress.

[2] In getting at the views and characteristics of Ord as an officer, the studies of Russell Weigley have been closely followed, as they set forth the French influence and, particularly, the Jomini influence in the teaching and writing of Sylvanus Thayer, Dennis Hart Mahan and Henry W. Halleck. *See* Weigley's *Towards an American Army: Military Thought from Washington to Marshall* (New York: Columbia University Press, 1962), pp. 45–67; *History of the United States Army* (New York: Macmillan Company, 1967), pp. 147–52.

[3] Robert M. Utley, *Frontiersmen in Blue: The United States Army and the Indian, 1848– 1865* (New York: Macmillan Company, 1967), p. 29.

[4] Ibid., p. 23.

[5] Ord to Mrs. Ord, 11 July 1858, Edward Otho Cresap Ord Papers, 1854–1858, Manuscripts Division, Department of Special Collections, C. H. Green Library, Stanford University, Stanford, California.

[6] Ibid., 7 May 1856.

[7] Ord's Diary, 12 August 1850, Edward Otho Cresap Ord Correspondence and Papers, 1850–1883, Bancroft Library, Berkeley, California.

[8] Ord's essay on annexation (draft), April 1859, Bancroft Library Collection.

[9] Ord's Diary, 18 August 1850, Bancroft Library Collection.

[10] Ord's essay on annexation (draft), April 1859, Bancroft Library Collection.

[11] Ibid.

[12] E. D. Townsend to Ord, 17 October 1859, Bancroft Library Collection.

[13] Joseph Roberts to Samuel Cooper, 18 October 1859, Letters Received, Adjutant General's Office, Record Group 94, National Archives.

[14] Oswald Garrison Villard, *John Brown, 1800–1859: A Biography Fifty Years After* (Boston: Houghton Mifflin Company, 1910), chaps. 11–15; Hill Peebles Wilson, *John Brown, Soldier of Fortune: A Critique* (Lawrence, Kansas: Hill P. Wilson, 1913), chaps. 12–17; C. Vann Woodward, *The Burden of Southern History* (New York: Random House, 1961), chap. 3; Allan Keller, *Thunder at Harper's Ferry* (Englewood Cliffs, New Jersey: Prentice-Hall, 1958); Stephen B. Oates, *To Purge This Land with Blood: A Biography of John Brown* (New York: Harper and Row, 1970), chaps. 14–22.

[15] Robert E. Lee to Samuel Cooper, 18 October 1859, Letters Received, Adjutant General's Office.

[16] *Washington Daily National Intelligencer*, 23 and 30 November, 1 December 1859.

[17] Villard, *John Brown*, pp. 511–28; Wilson, *John Brown, Soldier of Fortune*, pp. 383–94; Keller, *Thunder at Harper's Ferry*, pp. 238–44.

[18] Samuel Cooper to Justin Dimick (copy), 28 November 1859, Bancroft Library Collection; Keller, *Thunder at Harper's Ferry*, pp. 249–53.

[19] Ord to Placidus Ord, 11 December 1859, Alexander Collection.

[20] Ibid.

[21] Ibid. For further explanation of the need for a large security force at Harpers Ferry from the time of the raid to the execution of the raiders, *see* Barton H. Wise, *The Life of Henry A. Wise of Virginia, 1806–1876* (New York: Macmillan Company, 1899), pp. 255–61. *See also* Allan Nevins, *The Emergence of Lincoln*, 2 vols. (New York: Scribner, 1950), 2:91–97; Boyd B. Stutler, "The Hanging of John Brown," *American Heritage*, 6 (1955): 4–9.

[22] Ord to Sherman, 14 August 1863, W. T. Sherman Papers, 12.

[23] Ord's Diary, 31 July, 1–3 August 1850, Bancroft Library Collection.

[24] Ibid., 16 August 1850.

[25] Ibid., 29 November 1850.

[26] Ord to Pacificus Ord, 7 April 1851, Preston Collection.

[27] Ord to one of his brothers, 7 July 1858, Stanford Collection.

[28] Ord to Placidus Ord, 11 December 1859, Alexander Collection.

[29] James G. Randall and David Donald, *The Civil War and Reconstruction*, 2nd ed. (Boston: D. C. Heath and Company, 1961), chap. 7. *See also* Frank Wysor Klingberg, "James Buchanan and the Crisis of the Union," *Journal of Southern History*, 9 (1943): 455–74; Philip S. Klein, *President James Buchanan: A Biography* (University Park, Penn.: Pennsylvania State University Press, 1962), chaps. 27–29.

[30] *See* Philip G. Auchampaugh, *James Buchanan and His Cabinet on the Eve of Secession* (Lancaster, Penn.: Privately printed, 1926), pp. 155–56; Roy Meredith, *Storm over Sumter, the Opening Engagement of the Civil War* (New York: Simon and Schuster, 1957); Kenneth M. Stampp, *And the War Came: The North and the Secession Crisis, 1860–1861* (Baton Rouge: Louisiana State University Press, 1950); W. A. Swanberg, *First Blood: The Story of Fort Sumter* (New York: Scribner, 1957).

[31] Ord to Robert Anderson, 26 November 1860, Robert Anderson Papers, Manuscript Division, Library of Congress. Anderson took note of Ord's warning, but stated that he knew of no attempts to tamper with his men. See *The War of the Rebellion: A Compilation of the Official Records of the Union and Confederate Armies*, 129 vols. and index (Washington: Government Printing Office, 1880–1901), Ser. 1, 1:82.

[32] Ord to Anderson, 26 November 1860, Robert Anderson Papers.

[33] Ord to John Sherman, 28 January 1861, John Sherman Papers, Manuscript Division, Library of Congress.

[34] James Buchanan, *Mr. Buchanan's Administration on the Eve of the Rebellion* (New York: D. Appleton and Company, 1866), pp. 165–66.

[35] Ord to John Sherman, 28 January 1861, John Sherman Papers.

[36] Ibid.

[37] Ord to John Sherman, 29 January 1861, John Sherman Papers.

[38] John Sherman to Winfield Scott, 3 February 1861, John Sherman Papers; General Winfield Scott's "Views," 29, 30 October 1860, Appendix to Buchanan, *Mr. Buchanan's Administration*, pp. 287–90. Secretary of the Navy Gideon Welles wanted to hold the Norfolk Navy Yard, but Lincoln hesitated to make any move which might excite fear in the South. The ships were scuttled and the yard abandoned by the United States after Virginia left the Union. *See* Gideon Welles, *The Diary of Gideon Welles, Secretary of the Navy under Lincoln and Johnson*, ed. John T. Morse, 3 vols. (Boston: Houghton Mifflin Company, 1911), 1:41–54.

[39] Returns of the Third Artillery, 1860, Adjutant General's Office Record Group 94, National Archives; Samuel Cooper to Winfield Scott, 30 October 1860, Letters Sent, Adjutant General's Office, Record Group 94, National Archives.

[40] Louis Garesché, *Biography of Lieut. Col. Julius P. Garesché, Assistant Adjutant-General, U.S. Army* (Philadelphia: J. B. Lippincott Company, 1887), pp. 357–58. Only about one-fourth of the West Point graduates in service at the outbreak of the Civil War became general officers.

[41] Ibid., p. 358. Ord felt under great obligation to Garesché and named one of his sons for him. The Garesché name was ill-starred, for Ord's friend took the field as assistant adjutant general to Major General William S. Rosecrans and was killed at the battle of Murfreesboro in 1862. His namesake, Julius Garesché Ord, fell in action at San Juan Hill in 1898.

Chapter 6

[1] Edward Ord's Diary (1861–64), 6–11 November 1861, Radford Collection of Ord Papers, in possession of Mrs. Rebecca Ord Radford, La Jolla, California.

[2] J. H. Stine, *History of the Army of the Potomac*, 2nd ed. (Washington: Gibson Bros., Printers and Bookbinders, 1893), p. 37.

³ Placidus Ord to James and James L. Ord, 30 December 1861, Alexander Collection of Ord Papers, in possession of Mrs. Vida Ord Alexander, Washington, D.C.

⁴ Carl Russell Fish, *The American Civil War, An Interpretation*, ed. William E. Smith (New York: Longmans, Green and Company, 1937), pp. 277-78. *See* Bruce Catton, *Mr. Lincoln's Army* (Garden City, New York: Doubleday and Company, 1951) for the story of the Army of the Potomac under McClellan.

⁵ William S. Hammond, "The Battle of Dranesville, Va.," *Southern Historical Society Papers*, 52 vols. (Richmond: The Southern Historical Society, 1876–1959), Old Series, 35 (1907): 72. *See also* Osmund R. H. Thomson and William H. Ranch, *History of the "Bucktails"* (Philadelphia: Electric Printing Company, 1906), pp. 72–81.

⁶ *The War of the Rebellion: A Compilation of the Official Records of the Union and Confederate Armies*, 129 vols. and index (Washington: Government Printing Office, 1880–1901), Ser. 1, 5:480–81. For a full account of the Civil War, *see* Bruce Catton's *Centennial History of the Civil War*, 3 vols. (New York: Doubleday and Company, 1961–65). Other useful accounts are Richard E. DuPuy and Trevor N. DuPuy, *The Compact History of the Civil War* (New York: Collier Books, 1960); W. Birkbeck Wood and J. E. Edmunds, *A History of the Civil War in the United States, 1861–5* (London: Methuen and Company, 1905); James Ford Rhodes, *History of the Civil War, 1861–1865*, ed. E. B. Long (New York: Frederick Ungar Publishing Company, 1961); and Shelby Foote, *The Civil War: A Narrative*, 3 vols. (New York: Random House, 1958–74).

⁷ *Official Records*, 5:715.

⁸ Ibid., pp. 477–78.

⁹ Ibid., pp. 490–91. For the battle of Dranesville as recounted by Stuart's biographers, *see* John W. Thomason, Jr., *Jeb Stuart* (New York: Charles Scribner's Sons, 1934), pp. 124–28; Burke Davis, *Jeb Stuart, the Last Cavalier* (New York: Rinehart and Company, 1957), pp. 82–83; Henry B. McClellan, *I Rode with Jeb Stuart: The Life and Campaigns of Major General J.E.B. Stuart*, ed. Burke Davis (Bloomington, Indiana: Indiana University Press, 1958).

¹⁰ *Official Records*, 5:478.

¹¹ Ibid., pp. 490–91; Hammond, "The Battle of Dranesville, Va.," *Southern Historical Society Papers*, o.s. 35:74–75.

¹² *Official Records*, 5:478–79.

¹³ Ibid., p. 479.

¹⁴ Ord to Sherman, 18 April 1882, W. T. Sherman Papers, 57, Manuscript Division, Library of Congress.

¹⁵ *Official Records*, 5:491–92.

¹⁶ Ibid., pp. 479, 481; George G. Meade to Mrs. George G. Meade, 21 December 1861, George Meade, comp., *The Life and Letters of George Gordon Meade*, ed. George Gordon Meade, 2 vols. (New York: Charles Scribner's Sons, 1913), 1:237–38. *See* Freeman Cleaves, *Meade of Gettysburg* (Norman: University of Oklahoma Press, 1960), pp. 59–60; Edwin A. Glover, *Bucktailed Wildcats: A Regiment of Civil War Volunteers* (New York: Thomas Yoseloff, 1960).

¹⁷ *Official Records*, 5:492.

¹⁸ Ibid., p. 479.

¹⁹ Ibid., pp. 475, 479.

²⁰ Ibid., pp. 479–80, 494.

²¹Ibid., pp. 66, 476–77. The *New York Herald*, 21 December 1861, termed the battle "a splendid little affair." The *New York Times*, 21 December 1861, reported that it gave "great elation to all classes here." *See also* James Longstreet, *From Manassas to Appomattox* (Philadelphia: J. B. Lippincott Company, 1896), p. 63; Horace Greeley, *The American Conflict*, 2 vols. (Hartford: O. D. Case and Company, 1864–67), 1:626; Alexander Kelly McClure, *Abraham Lincoln and Men of War Times* (Philadelphia: Times Publishing Company, 1892), pp. 394–95; Hammond, "The Battle of Dranesville, Va.," *Southern Historical Society Papers*, o.s. 35:72; Warren W. Hassler, Jr., *General George B. McClellan, Shield of the Union* (Baton Rouge: Louisiana State University Press, 1957), pp. 45–46; Stine, *History of the Army of the Potomac*, pp. 40–41; Josiah R. Sypher,

History of the Pennsylvania Reserve Corps (Lancaster, Pennsylvania: Elias Barr and Company, 1865), pp. 142–43.

22 Meade, comp., *Life and Letters of George Gordon Meade*, 1:240.

23 As quoted in Henry Coppée, *Grant and His Campaigns: A Military Biography* (New York: Charles B. Richardson, 1866), p. 132.

24 Placidus Ord to Julianne Ord, 25 April and 25 June 1862, Alexander Collection. Placidus was a faithful informant, not neglecting to mention minute details to his wife: "Even the General (Ord) wears the *medal* of the Virgin Mary ever around his neck, still believing that relying on her, he feels safe from the balls of the enemy." (5 March 1862, Alexander Collection.)

25 *Official Army Register for August, 1862* (Washington: Government Printing Office, 1862), p. 27.

26 Meade to Mrs. George G. Meade, 10 May 1862, Meade, comp., *Life and Letters of George Gordon Meade*, 1:265.

27 As quoted in Edward J. Nichols, *Toward Gettysburg: A Biography of General John F. Reynolds* (University Park, Pennsylvania: Pennsylvania State University Press, 1958), p. 93.

28 Placidus Ord to Julianne Ord, 18 May 1862, Alexander Collection.

29 *Official Records*, 12, pt. 3:196; Ord to Samuel W. Holladay (copy), 9 September 1862, Edward Otho Cresap Ord Correspondence and Papers, 1850–1883, Bancroft Library, Berkeley, California; Ord to Stanton (copy), 3 June 1862, Bancroft Library Collection. For McDowell's lack of courtesy, *see* George F. Noyes, *The Bivouac and the Battlefield: Or, Campaign Sketches in Virginia and Maryland* (London: Sampson Low, Son, and Marston, 1863), p. 24.

30 Comte de Paris, *History of the Civil War in America*, ed. Henry Coppée, 4 vols. (Philadelphia: Porter and Coates, 1875–88), 1:629; Jefferson Davis, *The Rise and Fall of the Confederate Government*, 2 vols. (New York: D. Appleton and Company, 1881), 2:105.

31 James G. Randall and David Donald, *The Civil War and Reconstruction*, 2nd ed. (Boston: D. C. Heath and Company, 1961), p. 212. Great excitement was created in New York state by the call for militia to defend the capital. *New York Herald*, 28 May 1862.

32 *Official Records*, 12, pt. 3:219, 235, 244–45, 252. Opinions vary as to the wisdom of Lincoln's and Stanton's direction of operations at this time. *See* Kenneth P. Williams, *Lincoln Finds a General: A Military Study of the Civil War*, 5 vols. (New York: Macmillan Company, 1949–59), 1:171–213; Allan Nevins, *The War for the Union*, 4 vols. (New York: Scribner, 1959–71), 2:123–28; T. Harry Williams, *Lincoln and His Generals* (New York: Alfred A. Knopf, 1952), pp. 87–110.

33 *Official Records*, 12, pt. 3:245; Ed.Schriver to Ord, 28 May 1862, Bancroft Library Collection.

34 *Official Records*, 12, pt. 3:294; George F. R. Henderson, *Stonewall Jackson and the American Civil War*, authorized American ed. (New York: Longmans, Green and Company, 1943), p. 271; Frank E. Vandiver, *Mighty Stonewall* (New York: McGraw-Hill Book Company, 1957), chap. 12.

35 *Official Records*, 12, pt. 3:291.

36 *Report of the Joint Committee on the Conduct of the War*, 3 parts (Washington: Government Printing Office, 1863), pt. 1, p. 265.

37 Comte de Paris, *History of the Civil War in America*, 2:47. Major General William B. Franklin called the detention of McDowell "The First Great Crime of the War," his article in *Annals of the War* (Philadelphia: Times Publishing Company, 1879), p. 81.

38 Ord to Stanton (copy), 3 June 1862, Bancroft Library Collection.

39 *Official Records*, 12, pt. 3:349.

40 Ibid.

41 Ibid., p. 352. Ord's contention in this case was that, should he fail to take command, he would be guilty of neglect and of tolerating disorder and would render himself liable to court-martial under the 62nd article of war. *See* George B. Davis, *A Treatise*

on the Military Law of the United States, 2nd ed. rev. (New York: John Wiley and Sons, 1906), pp. 472–78.

[42] Ord to Samuel W. Holladay (copy), 9 September 1862, Bancroft Library Collection.

[43] Ibid. See T. Harry Williams, Lincoln and the Radicals (Madison, Wisconsin: University of Wisconsin Press, 1944), pp. 28–34, 56, 85–86, 131–33; George B. McClellan, McClellan's Own Story (New York: C. L. Webster and Company, 1887), pp. 155–59.

[44] General Edward O. C. Ord's report, 1 February 1864, Generals' Reports, p. 695, Adjutant General's Office, Record Group 94, National Archives.

Chapter 7

[1] The War of the Rebellion: A Compilation of the Official Records of the Union and Confederate Armies, 129 vols. and index (Washington: Government Printing Office, 1880–1901), Ser. 1, 52, pt. 1:259; Placidus Ord to Julianne Ord, 25 June 1862, Alexander Collection of Ord Papers, in possession of Mrs. Vida Ord Alexander, Washington, D.C.

[2] Edward Ord to Alexander D. Bache (draft), 8 July 1862, Edward Otho Cresap Ord Correspondence and Papers, 1850–1883, Bancroft Library, Berkeley, California.

[3] Ulysses S. Grant, Personal Memoirs of U. S. Grant, 2 vols. (New York: C. L. Webster and Company, 1885–86), 1:405; John F. C. Fuller, The Generalship of Ulysses S. Grant (New York: Dodd, Mead, and Company, 1929), p. 116. For an account of Major General Henry W. Halleck's work in the West see Stephen E. Ambrose, Halleck, Lincoln's Chief of Staff (Baton Rouge: Louisiana State University Press, 1962), chaps. 2–5.

[4] Official Records, 17, pt. 2:206.

[5] Ibid., pt. 1:120–21. See William T. Sherman, Personal Memoirs of Gen. W. T. Sherman, 4th ed. rev. and corr., 2 vols. (New York: Charles L. Webster and Company, 1891), 1:288; Archer Jones, Confederate Strategy from Shiloh to Vicksburg (Baton Rouge: Louisiana State University Press, 1961).

[6] Official Records, 17, pt. 1:65; Comte de Paris, History of the Civil War in America, ed. Henry Coppée, 4 vols. (Philadelphia: Porter and Coates, 1875–88), 2:401.

[7] Official Records, 17, pt. 1:65; see Bruce Catton, Grant Moves South (Boston: Little, Brown and Company, 1960), chap. 15; Francis Vinton Greene, The Mississippi, Campaigns of the Civil War, vol. 8 (New York: Charles Scribner's Sons, 1882), chap. 2.

[8] Official Records, 17, pt. 1:66, 117–18; Grant, Memoirs, 1:407–11.

[9] Ibid.

[10] Official Records, 17, pt. 1:118; Dabney H. Maury, "Recollections of Campaign against Grant in North Mississippi in 1862–63," Southern Historical Society Papers, 52 vols. (Richmond: The Southern Historical Society, 1876–1959), o.s. 13 (1885): 287.

[11] Official Records, 17, pt. 1:67, 118–19.

[12] Ibid., p. 119.

[13] Ibid.

[14] Ibid., pp. 67–68.

[15] Ibid., p. 122. Badeau recounts the story that Price had been informed by a spy of Rosecrans's failure to block the Fulton Road. The Confederate then withdrew the bulk of his forces from Ord's front to oppose Rosecrans. Adam Badeau, Military History of Ulysses S. Grant, 3 vols. (New York: D. Appleton and Company, 1885) 1:114n.

[16] Grant, Memoirs, 1:412.

[17] Official Records, 17, pt. 1:68.

[18] Ibid., p. 64.

[19] Ibid., p. 119.

[20] See Robert G. Hartje, Van Dorn: The Life and Times of a Confederate General (Nashville:

Vanderbilt University Press, 1967), chap. 10; Comte de Paris, *History of the Civil War in America*, 2:404; Sherman, *Memoirs*, 1:290.

21 *Official Records*, 17, pt. 1:378.

22 Ibid., p. 158.

23 Hartje, *Van Dorn*, chaps. 9 and 10; Thomas L. Livermore, *Numbers and Losses in the Civil War in America, 1861–1865* (Boston: Houghton Mifflin and Company, 1900), p. 94.

24 *Official Records*, 17, pt. 1:305.

25 Ibid.

26 Ibid., p. 158; Badeau, *Military History of Ulysses S. Grant*, 1:119.

27 Grant, *Memoirs*, 1:417–18; Comte de Paris, *History of the Civil War in America*, 2:397.

28 *Official Records*, 17, pt. 1:380.

29 Ord's Diary (1861–1864), 4 and 5 October 1862, Radford Collection of Ord Papers, in possession of Mrs. Rebecca Ord Radford, La Jolla, California.

30 *Official Records*, 17, pt. 1:302.

31 Ibid., pp. 302, 380; Livermore, *Numbers and Losses*, pp. 94n, 95n.

32 W. B. Cummins to Alexander B. Sharpe, 30 October 1862, Bancroft Library Collection.

33 *Official Records*, 17, pt. 1:302, 306, 312, 322–23.

34 Ord's strength at Davis Bridge has been variously estimated, but the general himself gave the figure as "5,000 all told." Ord to Samuel W. Holladay (copy), —— October 1862, Bancroft Library Collection.

35 *Official Records*, 17, pt. 1:303.

36 Ord's Diary (1861–1864), 5 October 1862, Radford Collection.

37 Ibid., 6 October 1862; Ord to Samuel W. Holladay (copy), —— October 1862, Bancroft Library Collection.

38 *Official Records*, 17, pt. 1:301–302, 306, 380.

39 Ibid., p. 302.

40 Ibid., pp. 303–304; Livermore, *Numbers and Losses*, pp. 94n, 95n. For a detailed account of the battles of Iuka and Corinth *see* Kenneth P. Williams, *Lincoln Finds a General: A Military Study of the Civil War*, 5 vols. (New York: Macmillan Company, 1949–59, 4: chap. 4.

41 *Official Records*, 17, pt. 1:155, 158, 306. The portion of Rosecrans's pursuing force under McPherson hit the rear of Van Dorn's column at Young's Bridge over the Tuscumbia River late on 5 October. *See* Hartje, *Van Dorn*, p. 238. For a careful defense of Rosecrans's part in the battles at Iuka and Corinth *see* William M. Lamers, *The Edge of Glory: A Biography of General William S. Rosecrans* (New York: Harcourt, Brace and World, 1961), pp. 103–180.

42 *Official Records*, 17, pt. 2:268. "The complimentary part [of the order] was entirely unexpected," Ord wrote. (Ord to Samual W. Holladay (copy), —— October 1862, Bancroft Library Collection.)

43 The phrase "Grant men" was used by Robert R. McCormick in *Ulysses S. Grant; The Great Soldier of America* (New York: D. Appleton-Century Company, 1934), pp. 70–72. Grant seemed to have lacked the ability to choose able subordinates in civilian life.

44 Ord to Samuel W. Holladay (copy), —— October 1862, Bancroft Library Collection. Ord's antipathy toward newspaper reporters is quite evident here. Rosecrans was profusely cordial to reporters and kept a "publicity agent." *See* James G. Randall, "The Newspaper Problem in Its Bearing upon Military Secrecy during the Civil War," *American Historical Review*, 23 (1917–18): 308n.

45 Ord to Holladay (copy), —— October 1862; Garesché to Ord, 13 October 1862, Bancroft Library Collection.

46 Ord's Diary (1861–1864), 6 October 1862, Radford Collection.

47 Placidus Ord to Julianne Ord, 10 October 1862, Alexander Collection.

48 Ord to Holladay (copy), —— October 1862, Bancroft Library Collection.

Chapter 8

[1] Edward Ord's Diary (1861–1864), 10 and 17 November 1862, Radford Collection of Ord Papers, in possession of Mrs. Rebecca Ord Radford, La Jolla, California.

[2] *War of the Rebellion: A Compilation of the Official Records of the Union and Confederate Armies*, 129 vols. and index (Washington: Government Printing Office, 1880–1901), Ser. 1, 16, pt. 1:7.

[3] Lew Wallace, *Lew Wallace, An Autobiography*, 2 vols. (New York: Harper and Brothers, 1906), 2:643. *See* Don Carlos Buell, *Statement of Major General Buell* (n.p., 1863); James B. Fry, *Operations of the Army under Buell from June 10th to October 30, 1862, and the "Buell Commission"* (New York: D. Van Nostrand, 1884); Irving McKee, *"Ben Hur" Wallace: The Life of General Lew Wallace* (Berkeley: University of California Press, 1947), pp. 63–64.

[4] Ord to W. T. Sherman, 14 January 1875, W. T. Sherman Papers, 38, Manuscript Division, Library of Congress.

[5] Ord to Sherman, 8 February 1863, W. T. Sherman Papers, 12; Ord to Henry W. Halleck (draft), 22 May 1863, Edward Otho Cresap Ord Correspondence and Papers, 1850–1883, Bancroft Library, Berkeley, California; *Official Records*, 24, pt. 3:351.

[6] Placidus Ord to Julianne Ord, 11 June 1863, Alexander Collection of Ord Papers, in possession of Mrs. Vida Ord Alexander, Washington, D.C.

[7] For detailed accounts of Grant's Vicksburg campaign, *see* Kenneth P. Williams, *Lincoln Finds a General: A Military Study of the Civil War*, 5 vols. (New York: Macmillan Company, 1949–59), 4: chaps. 12–13; Frances Vinton Greene, *The Mississippi*, Campaigns of the Civil War, vol. 8 (New York: Charles Scribner's Sons, 1882), chap. 6; Earl S. Miers, *The Web of Victory: Grant at Vicksburg* (New York: Alfred A. Knopf, 1955).

[8] John F. C. Fuller, *The Generalship of Ulysses S. Grant* (New York: Dodd, Mead and Company, 1929), pp. 152–55; Joseph E. Johnston, *Narrative of Military Operations* (New York: D. Appleton and Company, 1874); Comte de Paris, *History of the Civil War in America*, ed. Henry Coppée, 4 vols. (Philadelphia: Porter and Coates, 1875–88), 2:369.

[9] *Official Records*, 24, pt. 1:103.

[10] Ibid., pp. 102–103.

[11] Quoted in Adam Badeau, *Military History of Ulysses S. Grant*, 3 vols. (New York: D. Appleton and Company, 1885), 1:364n.

[12] Grant to Charles A. Dana, 5 August 1863, Charles A. Dana Papers, Manuscript Division, Library of Congress. For an account of the Vicksburg campaign which is more friendly to Major General John A. McClernand *see* Allan Nevins, *The War for the Union*, 4 vols. (New York: Scribner, 1959–71), 2:376–428.

[13] *Official Records*, 24, pt. 2:149–51; Badeau, *Military History of Ulysses S. Grant*, 1:351–52.

[14] *Official Records*, 24, pt. 1:106–107.

[15] Ibid., pp. 107–108.

[16] Ibid., pp. 108–109, 111; pt. 2:175. On 1 July Ord reported to Grant that "one of the rebels who gave himself up" was confined at his headquarters. The soldier lived about three miles away, was poor and "without servants," and had a sick wife who he expected would die soon. The man had behaved well and was anxious to be paroled to be with his wife. "Can I parole him, as I should do if it were left to me?" asked Ord. "Exercise your own judgment," was Grant's reply. (Ord to Grant and Grant to Ord, 1 July 1863, Bancroft Library Collection.)

[17] Charles A. Dana, *Recollections of the Civil War* (New York: D. Appleton and Company, 1898), p. 93.

[18] *Official Records*, 24, pt. 3:457.

[19] Horace Greeley, *The American Conflict*, 2 vols. (Hartford, Conn.: O.D. Case and Company, 1864–67), 2:314n; Comte de Paris, *History of the Civil War in America*, 3:370–72; Edward S. Gregory, "Vicksburg during the Siege," *The Annals of the War*

(Philadelphia: Times Publishing Company, 1879), 111ff; Badeau, *Military History of Ulysses S. Grant*, 1:366. *See* Peter F. Walker, *Vicksburg: A People at War, 1860–65* (Chapel Hill: University of North Carolina Press, 1960).

[20] John C. Pemberton, "The Terms of Surrender," *Battles and Leaders of the Civil War*, 4 vols. (New York: Century Company, 1884–1888), 3:543; *Official Records*, 24, pt. 1:114–15. On 3 July Ord telegraphed to Grant: "Shall I notify my men of the enemy's offer? It will renew their energy after the momentary relaxation by indicating the hold we have on the enemy." "Certainly, let them know it," answered Grant. (Ord to Grant and Grant to Ord, 3 July 1863, Bancroft Library Collection.)

[21] Ord to Badeau (draft), 21 July 1867, Bancroft Library Collection. It will be noted that Ord's account was written to Badeau four years after the surrender of Vicksburg and might have suffered somewhat from the general's imagination in the interim.

[22] Ibid.

[23] Ibid. Ord stated that the reduction of the efficiency of Grant's troops and the weakness of the Federal line on the extreme left made a Confederate breakthrough a real possibility. On the matter of the withdrawal of troops from Grant, the latter was ordered to send the Ninth Corps to Kentucky. *See* Ulysses S. Grant, *Personal Memoirs of U. S. Grant*, 2 vols. (New York: C. L. Webster and Company, 1885–86), 1:567, 579–80.

[24] *Official Records*, 24, pt. 3:460. In his *Memoirs*, 1:560–62, Grant claimed authorship of the terms, but this claim hardly accords with his dispatch to David D. Porter. Dana in his *Recollections* (p. 97) wrote that all of Grant's generals except Steele favored the plan of parole.

[25] Circular Thirteenth Army Corps, 4 July 1863; Ord to Grant, 4 July 1863, Bancroft Library Collection.

[26] Grant, *Memoirs*, 1:567, 572.

[27] *Official Records*, 24, pt. 3:461–62. For a detailed account of Sherman's Jackson campaign *see* Kenneth P. Williams, *Lincoln Finds a General*, 5:54–78.

[28] *Official Records*, 24, pt. 2:574, 587–88; pt. 3:470, 481.

[29] Ibid., 24, pt. 2:521, 574; pt. 3:482; Johnston, *Narrative of Military Operations*, p. 202.

[30] Leander Stillwell, *The Story of a Common Soldier of Army Life in the Civil War, 1861–1865*, 2nd ed. (n.p.: Franklin Hudson Publishing Company, 1920), pp. 144–46.

[31] *Official Records*, 24, pt. 1:200; pt. 2:521; Comte de Paris, *History of the Civil War in America*, 3:374–75; Johnston, *Narrative of Military Operations*, pp. 197–200, 205.

[32] *Official Records*, 24, pt. 2:574; pt. 3:496, 503–504; Comte de Paris, *History of the Civil War in America*, 3:394.

[33] Comte de Paris, *History of the Civil War in America*, 3:394–95.

[34] *Official Records*, 24, pt. 2:525, 575; Jefferson Davis, *The Rise and Fall of the Confederate Government*, 2 vols. (New York: D. Appleton and Company, 1881), 2:425.

[35] *Official Records*, 24, pt. 2:575.

[36] Ibid., pp. 523, 525–26, 575. Ord's action in relieving Lauman was approved by Sherman.

[37] Ibid., pt. 1:108.

[38] Ibid., pt. 3:515.

[39] Ibid., pt. 2:526, 534, 576; pt. 3:460, 496.

[40] Ibid., pt. 2:575–76, 598; pt. 3:510.

[41] Ibid., pt. 2:528; pt. 3:522.

[42] Ibid., pt. 2:529, 576.

[43] Placidus Ord to Julianne Ord, 19 July 1863, Alexander Collection.

[44] *Official Records*, 24, pt. 2:576.

[45] Ibid., p. 550.

[46] Ibid., pt. 3:544, 560, 580.

[47] Ord to Sherman, 14 August 1863, W. T. Sherman Papers, 12.

[48] Placidus Ord to Julianne Ord, 5 September 1863, Alexander Collection.

49 Ord to Sherman, 14 August 1863, W. T. Sherman Papers, 12.

50 Placidus Ord to Julianne Ord, 5 September 1863, Alexander Collection.

51 *Official Records,* 26, pt. 1:381, 760; Comte de Paris, *History of the Civil War in America,* 4:396–97. For discussion of the decision to invade Texas, *see* Kenneth P. Williams, *Lincoln Finds a General,* 5: chap. 4. *See also* Fred H. Harrington, *Fighting Politician: Major General N. P. Banks* (Philadelphia: University of Pennsylvania Press, 1948), chap. 11.

52 *Official Records,* 26, pt. 1:762.

53 Ibid., pp. 334n, 339, 771.

54 Richard B. Irwin, "The Red River Campaign," *Battles and Leaders of the Civil War,* 4:346.

55 James Russell Soley, "Gulf Operations in 1862 and 1863," *Battles and Leaders of the Civil War,* 3:571.

56 Ord to Halleck, 30 November 1863, Letters Received, Headquarters of the Army, Record Group 108, National Archives.

57 *Official Records,* 34, pt. 2:103–104, 114–15, 287–88, 310, 343.

58 Ibid., pp. 102, 119, 156, 353–54.

59 Napoleon J. T. Dana to Ord, 10 February 1864, Bancroft Library Collection.

60 Ord to President Abraham Lincoln, 19 February 1864, Letters Received, Headquarters of the Army.

61 *Official Records,* 34, pt. 2:378, 400–401.

Chapter 9

1 Edward Ord to Adjutant General Lorenzo Thomas, 10 March 1864, Edward O. C. Ord's Personal File, Adjutant General's Office, Record Group 94, National Archives.

2 Henry W. Halleck stepped down to the position of chief of staff.

3 *The War of the Rebellion: A Compilation of the Official Records of the Union and Confederate Armies,* 129 vols. and index (Washington: Government Printing Office, 1880–1901), Ser. 1, 32, pt. 3:246. General Ulysses S. Grant's military operations of 1864–65 are told in Bruce Catton, *A Stillness at Appomattox* (New York: Pocket Books, 1958).

4 Ord to Grant, 9 April 1864, Letters Received, Headquarters of the Army, Record Group 108, National Archives; Ord to Grant (draft), 17 April 1864, Edward Otho Cresap Ord Correspondence and Papers, 1850–1883, Bancroft Library, Berkeley, California; Franz Sigel, "Sigel in the Shenandoah Valley in 1864," *Battles and Leaders of the Civil War,* 4 vols. (New York: Century Company, 1884–88), 4:487.

5 T. Harry Williams, *Lincoln and the Radicals* (Madison, Wisconsin: University of Wisconsin Press, 1941), pp. 3–18, 223.

6 Ord was not sympathetic toward newspaper reporters, and it may be that these attacks were from newspapers whose reporters had been severely dealt with by him. Randall and Donald say: "The papers hurt the cause [of the North] by undermining confidence in some of the best generals, who were wary of reporters, puffing the reputations of others less worthy who courted the press. . . ." (James G. Randall and David Donald, *The Civil War and Reconstruction,* 2nd ed. (Boston: D. C. Heath and Company, 1961), p. 496.

7 Ord to Samuel W. Holladay (copy), 9 September 1862, Bancroft Library Collection.

8 Ibid.

9 Ord to Halleck, 17 April 1863, Letters Received, Headquarters of the Army.

10 *New York Times,* 2 and 9 August 1863. *See* Hudson Strode, *Jefferson Davis, Confederate President* (New York: Harcourt, Brace and Company, 1959), pp. 351, 419, 486.

11 *New York Times,* 16 August 1863.

12 Ord to Sherman, 14 August 1863, W. T. Sherman Papers, 12, Manuscript Division, Library of Congress.

13 Ord to Placidus Ord, 23 May 1864, Alexander Collection of Ord Papers, in possession of Mrs. Vida Ord Alexander, Washington, D.C.

14 Ibid., Ord to Edwin M. Stanton, 23 May 1864, Edwin M. Stanton Papers, Manuscript Division, Library of Congress.

15 Official Records, 37, pt. 1:526–27; Ord to Stanton, 23 May 1864, Stanton Papers.

16 Ord to Placidus Ord, 23 May 1864, Alexander Collection.

17 Ord to Placidus Ord, 27 and 30 June 1864, Alexander Collection.

18 Official Records, 37, pt. 2:98.

19 Ibid., p. 119.

20 Ibid., p. 156.

21 See Frank E. Vandiver, Jubal's Raid: General Early's Famous Attack on Washington in 1864 (New York: McGraw-Hill Book Company, 1960); George E. Pond, The Shenandoah Valley in 1864 (New York: Charles Scribner's Sons, 1883), chaps. 4–5; Jubal Anderson Early, War Memoirs: Autobiographical Sketch and Narrative of the War between the States, ed. Frank E. Vandiver (Bloomington, Indiana: Indiana University Press, 1960), chap. 39; Irving McKee, "Ben Hur" Wallace: The Life of General Lew Wallace (Berkeley: University of California Press, 1947), pp. 71–74.

22 Official Records, 37, pt. 2:214.

23 Ord to Mayor J. Lee Chapman (draft), 11 July 1864, Bancroft Library Collection; Baltimore Sun, 12 July 1864; New York Herald, 14 July 1864.

24 New York Times, 13 July 1864; Official Records, 37, pt. 2:247–48.

25 New York Herald, 14 July 1864.

26 Official Records, 37, pt. 1:349; pt. 2:247, 249. See Bradley T. Johnson, "My Ride around Baltimore in Eighteen Hundred and Sixty-Four," Southern Historical Society Papers, 52 vols. (Richmond: The Southern Historical Society, 1876–1959), o.s. 30 (1902): 215–25.

27 Official Records, 37, pt. 2:345; 40, pt. 3:361, 577.

28 See Hans L. Trefousse, Ben Butler, the South Called Him Beast (New York: Twayne Publishers, 1957); Robert S. Holzman, Stormy Ben Butler (New York: Macmillan Company, 1954). For a defense of Butler, see Richard S. West, Jr., Lincoln's Scapegoat General: A Life of B. F. Butler, 1818–1883 (Boston: Houghton Mifflin Company, 1965).

29 Official Records, 40, pt. 1:83, 86, 134, 140, 147, 178, 707; pt. 3:407–408, 549.

30 Thomas L. Livermore, Days and Events, 1860–1866 (Boston: Houghton Mifflin Company, 1920), pp. 384–85.

31 Adelbert Ames to Ord, 30 July 1864, Bancroft Library Collection.

32 Official Records, 40, pt. 1:167; Douglas Southall Freeman, Lee's Lieutenants: A Study in Command, 3 vols. (New York: Charles Scribner's Sons, 1942–44), 3:543.

33 Official Records, 40, pt. 1:172; New York Times, 3 and 4 August 1864.

34 Official Records, 40, pt. 1:42–129, 84. See Henry Pleasants and George H. Straley, Inferno at Petersburg (Philadelphia: Chilton Company, Book Division, 1961).

35 Official Records, 42, pt. 2:136.

36 Official Records, 40, pt. 1:457.

37 New York Times, 1 October 1864.

38 August V. Kautz, "Reminiscences of the Civil War," pp. 88–89, typescript, Manuscript Division, Library of Congress; Official Records, 42, pt. 1:793; pt. 2:1082–1088.

39 Official Records, 42, pt. 1:793–95. Except as otherwise noted, the account of the attack upon Fort Harrison is from Ord's report.

40 See Edward H. Ripley, Vermont General: The Unusual War Experiences of Edward Hastings Ripley, 1862–1865, ed. Otto Eisenschiml (New York: Devin-Adair Company, Publishers, 1960), pp. 241–55.

41 See S. Millett Thompson, Thirteenth Regiment of New Hampshire Volunteer Infantry (Boston: Houghton Mifflin Company, 1888), pp. 458–507.

42 New York Herald, 2 October 1864.

43 Horace Porter, Campaigning with Grant (New York: Century Company, 1897), p. 301.

44 Ibid.

45 *See* John F. C. Fuller, *The Generalship of Ulysses S. Grant* (New York: Dodd, Mead and Company, 1929), p. 57. Andrew A. Humphreys gives the losses in Stannard's division as 594 in *The Virginia Campaign of '64 and '65; the Army of the Potomac and the Army of the James*, Campaigns of the Civil War, vol. 12 (New York: Charles Scribner's Sons, 1883), p. 286.

46 Fuller, *The Generalship of Ulysses S. Grant*, p. 305. Robert R. McCormick noted the suggestion of "some writers" that, if Ord had not been wounded at Fort Harrison, he would have captured Fort Gilmer, "the key to Richmond." Robert R. McCormick, *Ulysses S. Grant, the Great Soldier of America* (New York: D. Appleton-Century Company, 1934), p. 257.

47 *Official Records*, 42, pt. 3:162; 46, pt. 1:30.

48 John B. Jones, *A Rebel War Clerk's Diary*, ed. Earl Schenck Miers (New York: Sagamore Press, 1958), pp. 427–28.

49 *Official Records*, 42, pt. 3:162–63; Freeman, *Lee's Lieutenants*, 3:590–91. Clifford Dowdey wrote that Lee's failure to recapture Fort Harrison may have been the moment when he realized the Confederacy was doomed. See *Lee's Last Campaign: The Story of Lee and His Men against Grant—1864* (Boston: Little, Brown and Company, 1960), p. 370.

50 *New York Times*, 2 October 1864.

51 Placidus Ord to Julianne Ord, 2 October 1864, Alexander Collection.

52 *New York Herald*, 3 December 1864.

53 *Official Records*, 42, pt. 1:111n, 113n. "The XXV Corps . . . remains the largest Negro unit ever activated by the American Army," noted L. D. Reddick, in "The Negro Policy of the United States Army, 1775–1945," *Journal of Negro History*, 34 (1949): 17. *See* Fred A. Shannon, "The Federal Government and the Negro Soldier, 1861–1865," *Journal of Negro History*, 11 (1926): 563–83; Bell I. Wiley, *Southern Negroes, 1861–1865* (New York: Rinehart and Company, 1938), chap. 15.

54 *Official Records*, 42, pt. 3:802.

Chapter 10

1 Edward Ord to William T. Sherman, 14 August 1863, W. T. Sherman Papers, 12, Manuscript Division, Library of Congress. Radicals in Congress blocked the promotion of Democratic or conservative officers whose political expressions, particularly on emancipation, did not agree with theirs. *See* T. Harry Williams, *Lincoln and the Radicals* (Madison: University of Wisconsin Press, 1941), pp. 74, 223.

2 Placidus Ord to Julianne Ord, 28 March 1865, Alexander Collection of Ord Papers, in possession of Mrs. Vida Ord Alexander, Washington, D.C.

3 Senators and representatives from the states of the Pacific slope to Edwin M. Stanton, 8 January 1865, Ord's Personal File, Adjutant General's Office, Record Group 94, National Archives.

4 Ulysses S. Grant to Stanton, 4 January 1865, Benjamin F. Butler Papers, Manuscript Division, Library of Congress. *See* William D. Mallam, "The Grant-Butler Relationship," *Mississippi Valley Historical Review*, 41 (1954–55): 259–76.

5 Grant to President Lincoln, 6 January 1865, Butler Papers; *The War of the Rebellion: A Compilation of the Official Records of the Union and Confederate Armies*, 129 vols. and index (Washington: Government Printing Office, 1880–1901), Ser. 1, 46, pt. 2:61.

6 August V. Kautz, "Reminiscences of the Civil War," p. 97, typescript, Manuscript Division, Library of Congress; *New York Herald*, 11 January 1865.

7 *New York Herald*, 10 January 1865.

8 Ibid., 17 January 1865; *New York Times*, 16 January 1865; *Alexandria* (Va.) *Gazette*, 17 and 28 January 1865; *Official Records*, 46, pt. 2:366, 421.

9 Leander Stillwell, *The Story of a Common Soldier of Army Life in the Civil War, 1861–1865*, 2nd ed. (n.p.: Franklin Hudson Publishing Company, 1920), pp. 102–103.

[10] Morris Schaff, *The Sunset of the Confederacy* (Boston: John W. Luce and Company, 1912), pp. 186–87.

[11] William E. Rachal, ed., "The Occupation of Richmond, April 1865: The Memorandum of Events of Colonel Christopher Q. Tompkins," *Virginia Magazine of History and Biography*, 73 (1965): 196.

[12] Erasmus D. Keyes, *Fifty Years' Observation of Men and Events, Civil and Military* (New York: Charles Scribner's Sons, 1884), p. 263.

[13] Ord to Samuel W. Holladay (copy), 9 September 1862, Edward Otho Cresap Ord Correspondence and Papers, 1850–1883, Bancroft Library, Berkeley, California.

[14] Ord to Stanton, 14 December 1864, Simon Gratz Collection, Historical Society of Pennsylvania, Philadelphia, Pennsylvania.

[15] Ibid.

[16] Placidus Ord to Julianne Ord, 10 January 1865, Alexander Collection.

[17] John Gibbon, *Personal Recollections of the Civil War* (New York: G. P. Putnam's Sons, 1928), pp. 277–78.

[18] Godfrey Weitzel to Butler, 25 January 1865, Butler Papers.

[19] Kautz, "Reminiscences," pp. 100–101. After the Civil War, Kautz was again under Ord's command. He was insubordinate, and Ord preferred charges against him. Kautz was court-martialed, found guilty, and sentenced to be reprimanded. The sentence was remitted, apparently in view of the general's service during the war. Some time after 1883, Kautz wrote his "Reminiscences," but, as they contain a good many errors and in view of his hostility to Ord, they have been used with caution.

[20] John W. Turner to Butler, 30 January 1865 and 23 March 1865, Butler Papers.

[21] Charles K. Graham to Butler, 22 January 1865, Butler Papers.

[22] Fred Martin to Butler, 26 January 1865, Butler Papers.

[23] William P. Webster to Butler, 1 February 1865, Butler Papers.

[24] Francis H. Pierpont, *Letter of Governor Pierpoint to His Excellency the President and the Honorable Congress of the United States on the Subject of the Abuse of Military Power in the Command of General Butler in Virginia and North Carolina* (Washington: McGill and Witherow, 1864), pp. 10–12, 39–41, 43–46; Charles H. Ambler, *Francis H. Pierpont, Union War Governor of Virginia and Father of West Virginia* (Chapel Hill: University of North Carolina Press, 1937), pp. 231–47.

[25] Petition of citizens of Norfolk, with Lincoln's endorsement of 28 January 1865, Bancroft Library Collection. For the Butler-Pierpont controversy as seen by President Lincoln, *see* James G. Randall and Richard N. Current, *Lincoln the President*, 4 vols. (New York: Dodd, Mead and Company, 1945–55), 4:286–93.

[26] Pierpont's speech, 16 February 1865, was printed in pamphlet form, a copy of which may be found in the Butler Papers. It is used here as the source of the account of the Mechanics Hall meeting.

[27] Ord to Lincoln (draft), n.d., Bancroft Library Collection.

[28] Benjamin F. Butler, *Butler's Book* (Boston: A. M. Thayer and Company, 1892), pp. 828–29.

[29] Ord to John A. Rawlins (draft), —— July 1865, Bancroft Library Collection. Butler's military savings bank was absorbed by the Freedmen's Savings Bank. *See* Walter L. Fleming, *The Freedmen's Savings Bank: A Chapter in the Economic History of the Negro Race* (Chapel Hill: University of North Carolina Press, 1927), p. 33.

[30] Ord to John Coughlin, 2 February 1865, Letters sent, Department of Virginia, Record Group 98, National Archives.

[31] Ord to Rawlins (draft), —— July 1865, Bancroft Library Collection. Butler's anti-Semitism and harsh treatment of Jews are set forth in Bertram W. Korn, *American Jewry and the Civil War* (Philadelphia: Jewish Publication Society of America, 1951), pp. 164–66.

[32] *Official Records*, 46, pt. 2:94; Ord to George H. Gordon, 19 February 1865; Ord to Coughlin, 15 March 1865, Letters Sent, Department of Virginia.

[33] Butler, *Butler's Book*, pp. 838–39.

34 George R. Bentley, *A History of the Freedmen's Bureau* (Philadelphia: University of Pennsylvania Press, 1955), p. 25; Louis S. Gerteis, *From Contraband to Freedman: Federal Policy toward Southern Blacks, 1861–1865* (Westport, Conn.: Greenwood Press, 1973), pp. 11–44. See Tinsley L. Spraggins, "Mobilization of Negro Labor for the Department of Virginia and North Carolina, 1861–1865," *North Carolina Historical Review*, 24 (1947): 160–97; Benjamin Quarles, *The Negro in the Civil War* (Boston: Little, Brown and Company, 1953).

35 Ord to Horace Porter (draft), 5 February 1865, Bancroft Library Collection; Gerteis, *From Contraband to Freedman*, pp. 44–45.

36 Porter to Ord, 13 February 1865, Bancroft Library Collection. See William T. Alderson, Jr., "The Freedmen's Bureau and Negro Education in Virginia," *North Carolina Historical Review*, 29 (1952): 64–90.

37 Ord to Henry Wilson (draft), 20 February 1865, Bancroft Library Collection.

38 Ord to Coughlin, 20 March 1865, Letters Sent, Department of Virginia.

39 Ord to Captain Coffin, 21 February 1865; Ord to Thomas Mulcahy, 21 February 1865, Letters Sent, Department of Virginia; General Orders, No. 26, 22 February 1865, Department of Virginia, Record Group 98, National Archives.

40 Ord to Gordon, 7 March 1865; Ord to Coffin, 10 March 1865, Letters Sent, Department of Virginia; *Official Records*, 46, pt. 2:975–76.

41 Porter to Ord, 13 February 1865, Bancroft Library Collection.

42 Charles A. Dana to Grant, 16 January 1865, Letters Received, Headquarters of the Army, Record Group 108, National Archives. Various investigations by historians have revealed widespread speculation and profiteering, some of it involving men high in the counsels of the nation. See E. Merton Coulter, "Commercial Intercourse with the Confederacy in the Mississippi Valley, 1861–1865," *Mississippi Valley Historical Review*, 5 (1918–19): 377–95; A. Sellew Roberts, "The Federal Government and Confederate Cotton," *American Historical Review*, 32 (1926–27): 262–75; Thomas H. O'Connor, "Lincoln and the Cotton Trade," *Civil War History*, 7 (1961): 20–35; Ludwell H. Johnson, "Northern Profit and Profiteers: The Cotton Rings of 1864–1865," *Civil War History*, 12 (1966): 101–115.

43 *Official Records*, 46, pt. 2:181; Special Orders, No. 19, 19 January 1865, Department of Virginia, Record Group 98, National Archives.

44 *Official Records*, 46, pt. 2:181.

45 For information bearing directly on the Virginia trade, see Ludwell H. Johnson, "Contraband Trade during the Last Year of the Civil War," *Mississippi Valley Historical Review*, 49 (1962–63): 635–52. See also Hans L. Trefousse, *Ben Butler, the South Called Him Beast* (New York: Twayne Publishers, 1957), pp. 122–24, 166.

46 Special Orders, No. 15, 15 January 1865; No. 16, 16 January 1865, Department of Virginia; General Orders, No. 7, 15 January 1865, Department of Virginia; Special Orders, No. 43, 10 March 1865, Headquarters of the Army; *New York Herald*, 22 January 1865.

47 William P. Webster to Butler, 26 February 1865, Butler Papers.

48 See Johnson, "Contraband Trade during the Last Year of the Civil War," *Mississippi Valley Historical Review*, 49:643.

49 Webster to Butler, 1 February 1865, Butler Papers.

50 Webster to Butler, 1 and 8 February 1865, Butler Papers; Gordon to Ord, 8 February 1865, Bancroft Library Collection; General Orders, No. 21, 9 February 1865; Special Orders, No. 44, 13 February 1865, Department of Virginia.

51 Brief of the report of the Gordon commission, 20 March 1865, Letters Received, Headquarters of the Army, Document File 1865, Box No. 81, Record Group 108, National Archives. The account given here except as otherwise noted is from this brief. See also George H. Gordon, *A War Diary of Events in the War of the Great Rebellion, 1863–1865* (Boston: J. R. Osgood and Company, 1882), pp. 377–80.

52 Stanton to Ord, 5 May 1865; Stanton to Ord, 9 May 1865; Ord to Gordon, 8 June 1865, Bancroft Library Collection.

53 Webster to Butler, 22 June 1865, Butler Papers.

Chapter 11

1 Edward Ord to William Henry Seward, 16 December 1864, William Henry Seward Collection, University of Rochester Library, Rochester, New York.

2 Ord to Seward, 17 December 1864, Seward Collection. That Ord was a correspondent of Seward at this time is significant in view of Seward's moderation on the questions of slavery and reunion. *See* Glyndon G. Van Deusen, *William Henry Seward* (New York: Oxford University Press, 1967), chap. 26.

3 *The War of the Rebellion: A Compilation of the Official Records of the Union and Confederate Armies*, 129 vols. and index (Washington: Government Printing Office, 1880–1901), Ser. 1, 46, pt. 2:259, 267.

4 Ibid., p. 290.

5 Ibid., pp. 292, 297.

6 Ibid., pp. 302, 507–508.

7 *New York Times*, 3 February 1865. *See* Carl Sandburg, *Abraham Lincoln, The War Years*, Sangamon ed., 4 vols. (New York: Charles Scribner's Sons, 1947), 4:37.

8 George Gordon Meade to Mrs. Meade, 1 February 1865, George Meade, comp., *The Life and Letters of George Gordon Meade*, 2 vols. (New York: Charles Scribner's Sons, 1913), 2:259–60.

9 Ibid.

10 Alexander H. Stephens, *A Constitutional View of the Late War between the States*, 2 vols. (Philadelphia: National Publishing Company, 1868–1870), 2:607–608; message of President Jefferson Davis to the Confederate Congress, 13 March 1865, as quoted in John A. Campbell, *Reminiscences and Documents Relating to the Civil War during the Year 1865* (Baltimore: J. Murphy and Company, 1887), pp. 51–53.

11 Stephens, *Constitutional View of the Late War*, 2:607–608. *See* Henry G. Connor, *John Archibald Campbell, Associate Justice of the United States Supreme Court, 1853–1861* (Boston: Houghton Mifflin Company, 1920), chap. 6; Edward C. Kirkland, *The Peacemakers of 1864* (New York: Macmillan Company, 1927), chap. 5; Henry H. Simms, *Life of Robert M. T. Hunter: A Study in Sectionalism and Secession* (Richmond: William Byrd Press, 1935), pp. 197–99; Rudolph R. Von Abele, *Alexander H. Stephens, A Biography* (New York: Alfred A. Knopf, 1946), chap. 4.

12 *Official Records*, 41, pt. 2:363; *New York Herald*, 8 February 1865.

13 Gideon Welles, *Diary of Gideon Welles, Secretary of the Navy under Lincoln and Johnson*, ed. John T. Morse, 3 vols. (Boston: Houghton Mifflin Company, 1911), 2:237.

14 Julia Dent Grant, *The Personal Memoirs of Julia Dent Grant*, ed. John Y. Simon (New York: G. P. Putnam's Sons, 1975), p. 141.

15 *Official Records*, 41, pt. 2:1259; James Longstreet, *From Manassas to Appomattox* (Philadelphia: J. B. Lippincott Company, 1896), pp. 583–84. *See* Donald B. Sanger and Thomas R. Hay, *James Longstreet* (Baton Rouge: Louisiana State University Press, 1952), p. 288.

16 Longstreet, *From Manassas to Appomattox*, p. 584.

17 Ibid., pp. 584–85; Davis's message to the Confederate Congress, 13 March 1865, as quoted in Campbell, *Reminiscences and Documents Relating to the Civil War*, pp. 51–53.

18 *Official Records*, Ser. 2, 8:315.

19 *Official Records*, Ser. 1, 46, pt. 2:1275–76.

20 Ibid., p. 1276.

21 Longstreet, *From Manassas to Appomattox*, p. 585.

22 *Official Records*, 46, pt. 2:1264.

23 Ibid., pp. 824–25.

24 Ibid., pp. 801–802.

25 Ward H. Lamon, *Recollections of Abraham Lincoln, 1847–1865*, ed. Dorothy Lamon Teillard (Washington: Published by the editor, 1911), pp. 249–50.

26 Ibid., pp. 250–51.

27 Ibid., p. 251.

28 Ibid.

29 *Official Records*, 46, pt. 2:802.

30 Ibid. For a slightly different account of Lincoln's reaction to Grant's telegram, *see* Benjamin P. Thomas and Harold M. Hyman, *Stanton: The Life and Times of Lincoln's Secretary of War* (New York: Alfred A. Knopf, 1962), p. 348. *See also* James G. Randall and Richard N. Current, *Lincoln the President*, 4 vols. (New York: Dodd, Mead and Company, 1945–55), 4:349–50.

31 *Official Records*, 46, pt. 2:823–25.

32 Clarence E. McCartney stressed Grant's responsibility, affirming that Grant did lead Ord to believe that a military convention might succeed where the politicians had not. See *Grant and His Generals* (New York: McBride Company, 1953), p. 333.

33 Sylvanus Cadwallader, *Three Years with Grant as Recalled by War Correspondent Sylvanus Cadwallader*, ed. Benjamin P. Thomas (New York: Alfred A. Knopf, 1956), p. 334.

34 *Official Records*, 46, pt. 3:716.

35 Julia Dent Grant, *Personal Memoirs*, p. 141. Mrs. Grant very positively stated that that part of Ord's proposal regarding the participation of the ladies did not emanate from General Grant.

36 Placidus Ord to Julianne Ord, 10 March 1865, Alexander Collection of Ord Papers, in possession of Mrs. Vida Ord Alexander, Washington, D.C.

37 *New York Herald*, 24 and 29 March 1865.

38 John S. Barnes, "With Lincoln from Washington to Richmond in 1865," *Appleton's Magazine*, 13 vols. (New York and Philadelphia, 1903–1909), 9 (1907): 523.

39 Ibid.

40 Philip Van Doren Stern, *An End to Valor: The Last Days of the Civil War* (Boston: Houghton Mifflin Company, 1958), pp. 92–93.

41 John S. Barnes's account as cited in Stern, *An End to Valor*, p. 93.

42 Adam Badeau's account as cited in Stern, *An End to Valor*, p.94.

43 Barnes's account as cited in Stern, *An End to Valor*, p. 93.

44 Badeau's account as cited in Stern, *An End to Valor*, p. 95.

45 Ibid. Captain Barnes gave an account of the incident involving Mrs. Lincoln to Sherman shortly after it happened. *See* William T. Sherman, *Personal Memoirs of Gen. W. T. Sherman*, 4th ed. rev. and corr., 2 vols. (New York: Charles L. Webster and Company, 1891), 2:332. Mrs. Grant's story of the affair in her *Personal Memoirs* (p. 146) is not very convincing in some details.

46 *Official Records*, 46, pt. 2:79.

47 Ibid., pp. 318–19.

48 Ibid., pp. 356, 679.

49 Ibid., p. 552.

50 Ibid., pp. 588, 597, 605; pt. 3:43.

51 *New York Herald*, 18 February 1865.

52 Ibid., 20 February 1865.

53 *Official Records*, 46, pt. 3:65–66.

54 General Orders, No. 28, 6 March 1865; Special Orders, No. 79, 20 March 1865, Department of Virginia, Record Group 98, National Archives.

55 John W. Turner to Benjamin F. Butler, 23 March 1865, B. F. Butler Papers, Manuscript Division, Library of Congress.

56 *Official Records*, 46, pt. 2:663–64; Special Orders, No. 77, 18 March 1865; No. 79, 20 March 1865; No. 82, 23 March 1865, Department of Virginia; August V. Kautz, "Reminiscences of the Civil War," pp. 102, 104, typescript, Manuscript Division, Library of Congress.

Chapter 12

[1] *The War of the Rebellion: A Compilation of the Official Records of the Union and Confederate Armies*, 129 vols. and index (Washington: Government Printing Office, 1880–1901), Ser. 1, 36, pt. 1:52.

[2] Ibid., p. 53. For accounts of the final campaign in Virginia, *see* Bruce Catton, *A Stillness at Appomattox* (New York: Pocket Books, 1958), chap. 6; Burke Davis, *To Appomattox: Nine April Days, 1865* (New York: Rinehart and Company, 1959).

[3] *Official Records*, 36, pt. 1:52.

[4] *Official Records*, 46, pt. 1:1160.

[5] Ibid., pt. 3:210–11; *New York Herald*, 3 April 1865.

[6] Placidus Ord to Julianne Ord, 28 March 1865, Alexander Collection of Ord Papers, in possession of Mrs. Vida Ord Alexander, Washington, D.C.; *Official Records*, 46, pt. 3:236.

[7] William T. Sherman, *Personal Memoirs of Gen. W. T. Sherman*, 4th ed. rev. and corr., 2 vols. (New York: Charles L. Webster and Company, 1891), 2:325.

[8] *Official Records*, 46, pt. 1:1160–61, 1173.

[9] Ibid., pp. 52–53; pt. 3:268.

[10] Ibid., pt. 1:53, 1160, 1173; pt. 3:243–44; Ulysses S. Grant to Edward Ord, 30 March 1865, Edward Otho Cresap Ord Correspondence and Papers, 1850–1883, Bancroft Library, Berkeley, California; *New York Herald*, 3 April 1865. *See* Freeman Cleaves, *Meade of Gettysburg* (Norman: University of Oklahoma Press, 1960), chap. 24.

[11] Douglas Southall Freeman, *Lee's Lieutenants: A Study in Command*, 3 vols. (New York: Charles Scribner's Sons, 1942–44), 3:657–71. Freeman estimated Philip Sheridan's total force at 30,000 and Pickett's at 10,000. *See* A. A. Humphreys, *The Virginia Campaign of '64 and '65: The Army of the Potomac and the Army of the James*, Campaigns of the Civil War, vol. 12 (New York: Charles Scribner's Sons, 1883), pp. 324–62.

[12] Freeman, *Lee's Lieutenants*, 3:675.

[13] Grant to Ord, 1 April 1865, Bancroft Library Collection.

[14] Grant to Ord (2 dispatches), 1 April 1865, Bancroft Library Collection; *Official Records*, 46, pt. 3:430.

[15] Ord to John Gibbon, 1 April 1865, Bancroft Library Collection.

[16] Wright to Ord, 2 April 1865, Bancroft Library Collection; *Official Records*, 46, pt. 1:54, 1161, 1174; pt. 3:446, 492–93, 495.

[17] *Official Records*, 46, pt. 3:450, 494.

[18] Humphreys, *The Virginia Campaign of '64 and '65*, pp. 367–69.

[19] Wright to Ord, Ord to Grant, 2 April 1865, Bancroft Library Collection; *Official Records*, 46, pt. 3:494.

[20] *Official Records*, 46, pt. 1:1161, 1174, 1179; John Gibbon, *Personal Recollections of the Civil War* (New York: G. P. Putnam's Sons, 1928), pp. 300–301; Freeman, *Lee's Lieutenants*, 3:682.

[21] Freeman, *Lee's Lieutenants*, 3:680–83.

[22] *Official Records*, 46, pt. 3:511, 532; Grant to Ord, Ord to Grant, 3 April 1865, Bancroft Library Collection.

[23] *Official Records*, 46, pt. 3:532; Freeman, *Lee's Lieutenants*, 3:683–87.

[24] *Official Records*, 46, pt. 3:534; Gibbon, *Personal Recollections*, p. 302; Ulysses S. Grant, *Personal Memoirs of U. S. Grant*, 2 vols. (New York: C. L. Webster and Company, 1885–1886), 2:318–20.

[25] *Official Records*, 46, pt. 1:1227; pt. 3:212, 439. Ord's associate of the Indian fighting of the 1850s, Gabriel J. Rains, had become a Confederate brigadier general and superintendent of the torpedo bureau and did much to develop land mines.

[26] Ibid., pt. 1:1227–28; Rembert W. Patrick, *The Fall of Richmond* (Baton Rouge:

Louisiana State University Press, 1960), pp. 41–68; John B. Jones, *A Rebel War Clerk's Diary*, ed. Earl Schenck Miers (New York: Sagamore Press, 1958), pp. 528–32. *See also* Edward Hastings Ripley, *Vermont General: The Unusual War Experiences of Edward Hastings Ripley, 1862–1865*, ed. Otto Eisenschiml (New York: The Devin-Adair Company, Publishers, 1960), pp. 296–309.

27 *Official Records*, 46, pt. 1:1227.

28 Ibid.; Patrick, *Fall of Richmond*, pp. 70–73, 101–102.

29 Patrick, *Fall of Richmond*, pp. 70–73, 101–102.

30 William P. Webster to Benjamin F. Butler, 8 April 1865, B. F. Butler Papers, Manuscript Division, Library of Congress.

31 *Official Records*, 46, pt. 3:573.

32 Ibid., p. 535.

33 Ord to Godfrey Weitzel, 4 April 1865, Bancroft Library Collection.

34 *Official Records*, 46, pt. 1:55, 1245; pt. 3:545; Freeman, *Lee's Lieutenants*, 3:689–90.

35 Humphreys, *The Virginia Campaign of '64 and '65*, p. 374.

36 *Official Records*, 46, pt. 1:1180; pt. 3:557, 573.

37 *New York Herald*, 10 April 1865.

38 *Official Records*, 46, pt. 3:573.

39 Ibid., p. 582.

40 *New York Herald*, 10 April 1865.

41 Freeman, *Lee's Lieutenants*, 3:691–97.

42 *Official Records*, 46, pt. 1:1174; *New York Herald*, 10 April 1865.

43 *Official Records*, 46, pt. 3:577, 583; *New York Herald*, 10 April 1865; Humphreys, *The Virginia Campaign of '64 and '65*, p. 375; Freeman, *Lee's Lieutenants*, 3:698; Allen P. Tankersley, *John B. Gordon: A Study in Gallantry* (Atlanta: Whitehall Press, 1955), pp. 194–95; Douglas S. Freeman, *R. E. Lee: A Biography*, 4 vols. (New York: Charles Scribner's Sons, 1934), 4:78.

44 *Official Records*, 46, pt. 1:1161.

45 Ibid.

46 Ibid., pt. 3:611.

47 Ibid., pt. 1:1161–62.

48 Ibid., p. 1162; Freeman, *Lee's Lieutenants*, 3:707–708.

49 Freeman, *Lee's Lieutenants*, 3:708–709. For comment on Theodore Read's death by a survivor of the fight, *see* S. Millett Thompson, *Thirteenth Regiment of New Hampshire Volunteer Infantry* (Boston: Houghton Mifflin and Company, 1888), p. 586.

50 *Official Records*, 46, pt. 3:609, 611.

51 Grant, *Memoirs*, 2:331.

52 *Official Records*, 46, pt. 1:1162.

53 Ibid., pp. 55, 1180.

54 Freeman, *Lee's Lieutenants*, 3:698–711.

55 *Official Records*, 46, pt. 3:611.

56 Freeman, *Lee's Lieutenants*, 3:612–16; Freeman, *R. E. Lee*, 4:93–99.

57 Freeman, *Lee's Lieutenants*, 3:712; Humphreys, *The Virginia Campaign of '64 and '65*, pp. 387–88.

58 *Official Records*, 46, pt. 1:56, 1162.

59 Freeman, *Lee's Lieutenants*, 3:715–16.

60 Horace Porter, "The Surrender at Appomattox Court House," *Battles and Leaders of the Civil War*, 4 vols. (New York: Century Company, 1884–88), 4:729–30; Gibbon, *Personal Recollections*, pp. 305–307; *New York Herald*, 14 April 1865.

61 *Official Records*, 46, pt. 3:619.

62 Ibid.

63 Ibid., p. 641.

⁶⁴ Ibid., pt. 1:56.

⁶⁵ Ibid., pt. 3:640; Porter, "The Surrender at Appomattox Court House," *Battles and Leaders*, 4:731.

⁶⁶ *New York Herald*, 14 April 1865; Gibbon, *Personal Recollections*, p. 308.

⁶⁷ *Official Records*, 46, pt. 1:1162; pt. 3:621.

Chapter 13

¹ *New York Herald*, 10 April 1865.

² Joshua L. Chamberlain, *The Passing of the Armies: An Account of the Final Campaign of the Army of the Potomac* (New York: G. P. Putnam's Sons, 1915), pp. 226, 378. See William H. Powell, *The Fifth Army Corps* (New York: G. P. Putnam's Sons, 1896); Willard M. Wallace, *Soul of the Lion: A Biography of General Joshua L. Chamberlain* (New York: Thomas Nelson and Sons, 1960).

³ Maine Infantry, 11th Regiment, 1861–1866, *The Story of One Regiment, the Eleventh Maine Infantry Volunteers in the War of the Rebellion* (New York: J. J. Little and Company, 1896), p. 326.

⁴ *New York Herald*, 14 April 1865; John Gibbon, *Personal Recollections of the Civil War* (New York: G. P. Putnam's Sons, 1928), pp. 309–310; *The War of the Rebellion: A Compilation of the Official Records of the Union and Confederate Armies*, 129 vols. and index (Washington: Government Printing Office, 1880–1901), Ser. 1, 46, pt. 3:653.

⁵ *Official Records*, 46, pt. 1:56; Douglas Southall Freeman, *Lee's Lieutenants: A Study in Command*, 3 vols. (New York: Charles Scribner's Sons, 1942–44), 3:722–25.

⁶ *Official Records*, 46, pt. 3:641.

⁷ Ibid., p. 664.

⁸ Horace Porter, *Campaigning with Grant* (New York: Century Company, 1897), p. 466.

⁹ *New York Herald*, 14 April 1865.

¹⁰ Philip H. Sheridan, *Personal Memoirs of P. H. Sheridan*, 2 vols. (New York: C. L. Webster and Company, 1888), 2:191.

¹¹ *New York Herald*, 14 April 1865; *Official Records*, 46, pt. 1:841.

¹² Freeman, *Lee's Lieutenants*, 3:726–28; *New York Herald*, 14 April 1865; *Official Records*, 46, pt. 1:841, 1162, 1175, 1181.

¹³ *New York Herald*, 14 April 1865; *Official Records*, 46, pt. 1:1175, 1181, 1246.

¹⁴ *Official Records*, 46, pt. 1:1181, 1243.

¹⁵ Ibid., p. 1236.

¹⁶ Ibid., pp. 1215, 1236.

¹⁷ Ibid., pp. 841, 1109; *New York Herald*, 14 April 1865.

¹⁸ Freeman, *Lee's Lieutenants*, 3:729–30; Douglas Southall Freeman, *R. E. Lee: A Biography*, 4 vols. (New York: Charles Scribner's Sons, 1934), 4:120–28; *Official Records*, 46, pt. 3:664.

¹⁹ *New York Herald*, 14 April 1865.

²⁰ *Official Records*, 46, pt. 3:1181, 1215.

²¹ *New York Herald*, 14 April 1865.

²² Chamberlain, *Passing of the Armies*, pp. 236–38.

²³ *New York Herald*, 14 April 1865.

²⁴ *Official Records*, 46, pt. 1:1163.

²⁵ Freeman, *Lee's Lieutenants*, 3:733–36; Morris Schaff, *The Sunset of the Confederacy* (Boston: John W. Luce and Company, 1912), pp. 239–46; John Brown Gordon, *Reminiscences of the Civil War* (New York: Charles Scribner's Sons, 1903), chap. 29.

²⁶ Charles S. Wainwright, *A Diary of Battle: The Personal Journals of Colonel Charles S. Wainwright, 1861–1865*, ed. Allan Nevins (New York: Harcourt, Brace and World, 1962), p. 521.

[27] *Official Records,* 46, pt. 1:1163.

[28] Chamberlain, *Passing of the Armies,* p. 243.

[29] *Official Records,* 46, pt. 1:1110.

[30] *New York Herald,* 14 April 1865.

[31] Ibid.; Henry Edwin Tremain, *The Last Hours of Sheridan's Cavalry* (New York: Bonnell, Silver and Bowers, 1904), pp. 258–60.

[32] Chamberlain, *Passing of the Armies,* pp. 244–45.

[33] Porter, *Campaigning with Grant,* p. 467; Sheridan, *Memoirs,* 2:198–99.

[34] *New York Herald,* 14 April 1865; Edward Ord to George G. Meade (draft), 9 April 1865, Edward Otho Cresap Ord Correspondence and Papers, 1850–1883, Bancroft Library, Berkeley, California; Tremain, *The Last Hours of Sheridan's Cavalry,* pp. 371–75.

[35] *New York Times,* 14 April 1865. For comment on Ord's humane conduct in suspending hostilities, *see* Clifford Dowdey, *Lee* (Boston: Little, Brown and Company, 1965), pp. 575–76.

[36] Andrew A. Humphreys, *The Virginia Campaign of '64 and '65: The Army of the Potomac and the Army of the James,* Campaigns of the Civil War, vol. 12 (New York: Charles Scribner's Sons, 1883), pp. 392–95.

[37] Ibid.

[38] Porter, *Campaigning with Grant,* pp. 466–67; *Official Records,* 46, pt. 3:665.

[39] Walter H. Taylor, *Four Years with General Lee* (Bloomington: Indiana University Press, 1962), p. 152.

[40] *Official Records,* 46, pt. 3:666.

[41] Ibid.

[42] Ord to Robert E. Lee (photocopy), 9 April 1865, Radford Collection of Ord Papers, in possession of Mrs. Rebecca Ord Radford, La Jolla, California. This dispatch apparently has been unknown to writers who have previously described the events of 9 April at Appomattox.

[43] *Official Records,* 46, pt. 3:665.

[44] Ord to Meade (draft), 9 April 1865, Bancroft Library Collection. This dispatch has not hitherto figured in accounts of events at Appomattox. Even if it were not sent, its contents would still cast important light on the happenings of 9 April.

[45] Ord to Ulysses S. Grant, 9 April 1865, Edwin M. Stanton Papers, Manuscript Division, Library of Congress. This dispatch also brings new information to bear upon the events leading up to the surrender of Lee's army. It is not known how this document became part of the personal papers of the secretary of war. General Joshua L. Chamberlain recalled that he received orders at this time to prepare for action. (*Passing of the Armies,* p. 245.)

[46] Freeman, *R. E. Lee,* 4:131–33; *Official Records,* 46, pt. 3:605.

[47] Freeman, *R. E. Lee,* 4:133–34. *See* Charles Marshall, *An Aide-de-Camp of Lee, Being the Papers of Colonel Charles Marshall,* ed. Major General Sir Frederick Maurice (Boston: Little, Brown and Company, 1927).

[48] The timing of events of 9 April is confusing. The chronology as set forth here seems reasonable in the light of available evidence. *See* Philip Van Doren Stern, *An End to Valor: The Last Days of the Civil War* (Boston: Houghton Mifflin Company, 1958), p. 394n.

[49] Porter, *Campaigning with Grant,* pp. 468–73; Ulysses S. Grant, *Personal Memoirs of U. S. Grant,* 2 vols. (New York: C. L. Webster and Company, 1885–1886), 2:340. Grant recalled that, upon his arrival, Sheridan wanted to attack the Confederates, but that he (Grant) "had no doubt about the good faith of Lee." If Grant's memory served him correctly, it would have to be concluded that Ord would not let Sheridan "go in." (Grant, *Memoirs,* 2:340.)

[50] Porter, *Campaigning with Grant,* pp. 475–83; Grant, *Memoirs,* 2:342–46; *Official Records,* 46, pt. 3:665–66.

[51] Porter, *Campaigning with Grant,* p. 481.

52 Ibid., p. 486.

53 Ibid., pp. 486–87. General Ord later presented the table to Mrs. Grant, who modestly refused it, insisting that Mrs. Ord should have it. The table remained the property of the Ords until after General Ord's death. Mrs. Ord sold the table to Charles F. Gunther, a Chicago manufacturer and collector, in 1887 for $1,000. In 1920, the Chicago Historical Society came into possession of the table when it purchased Gunther's entire collection. The foregoing information was provided by Paul M. Angle, secretary and director of the Chicago Historical Society, in a letter to the author, 21 October 1960. See Mary A. Benjamin, "Tale of a Table," *American Heritage*, 16 (1965): 100–101; 17 (1966): 100.

54 *Official Records*, 46, pt. 3:677.

55 Ibid., pt. 1:1162.

56 William T. Sherman to Samuel B. Maxey, 21 December 1880, Bancroft Library Collection. James Longstreet's biographers say flatly: "It was Ord who trapped Lee." Donald B. Sanger and Thomas R. Hay, *James Longstreet* (Baton Rouge: Louisiana State University Press, 1952), p. 306.

57 *New York Herald*, 14 April 1865; *Official Records*, 46, pt. 1:1279; pt. 3:666–68, 685, 687, 696, 706, 734, 796.

58 *Official Records*, 46, pt. 1:581–99.

59 Grant, *Memoirs*, 2:348; Porter, *Campaigning with Grant*, pp. 489–92.

60 *Official Records*, 46, pt. 3:1163. See Ulysses S. Grant III, "Appomattox, Where Grant and Lee Made Peace with Honor a Century Ago," *National Geographic Magazine*, 127 (1965): 435–69.

Chapter 14

1 Edward Ord to Mrs. Ord (draft), 12 April 1865, Edward Otho Cresap Ord Correspondence and Papers, 1850–1883, Bancroft Library, Berkeley, California.

2 *Danville Register*, 5 April 1865, as quoted in *New York Herald*, 15 April 1865.

3 See U. S. Signal Corps photographs, Brady Collection, National Archives; James D. Horan, *Mathew Brady: Historian with a Camera* (New York: Crown Publishers, 1955), p. 59.

4 Placidus Ord to James Cresap Ord, 11 April 1865, Alexander Collection of Ord Papers, in possession of Mrs. Vida Ord Alexander, Washington, D.C.

5 *The War of the Rebellion: A Compilation of the Official Records of the Union and Confederate Armies*, 129 vols. and index (Washington: Government Printing Office, 1880–1901), Ser. 1, 46, pt. 3:835.

6 Ibid., pp. 718, 724; Diary of Marsena R. Patrick, 13 April 1865, Manuscript Division, Library of Congress.

7 *Official Records*, 46, pt. 1:1236; pt. 3:545.

8 William Birney to Benjamin F. Butler, 23 April 1865, B. F. Butler Papers, Manuscript Division, Library of Congress.

9 Godfrey Weitzel to Butler, 26 April 1865, Butler Papers.

10 Ibid.

11 *Official Records*, 46, pt. 3:1062. See James E. Sefton, *The United States Army and Reconstruction, 1865–1877* (Baton Rouge: Louisiana State University Press, 1967), pp. 51–52.

12 *Official Records*, 46, pt. 3:748.

13 James A. Bishop, *The Day Lincoln Was Shot* (New York: Harper and Brothers, 1955), pp. 200–201. See Theodore Roscoe, *The Web of Conspiracy: The Complete Story of the Men Who Murdered Abraham Lincoln* (Englewood Cliffs, N.J.: Prentice-Hall, 1959).

14 *Official Records*, 46, pt. 3:745.

15 Ibid., p. 762.

16 Ibid.

17 Ibid. By a proclamation of 2 May 1865, President Andrew Johnson charged that a conspiracy of Confederate leaders had been behind the assassination of Lincoln. He offered a reward for the arrest of the ringleaders See James D. Richardson, comp., A Compilation of the Messages and Papers of the Presidents, 20 vols. (New York: Bureau of National Literature, c. 1897–1927), 8:3505–3506.

18 Official Records, 46, pt. 3:763.

19 Ibid. Elihu B. Washburne was eventually numbered among the Radical partisans.

20 Ibid., pp. 796–97.

21 Ibid., p. 749.

22 Ibid., p. 835. For post-war conditions in Virginia and for treatment of the entire Reconstruction period, see the volumes of Ellis P. Oberholtzer, A History of the United States since the Civil War, 5 vols. (New York: Macmillan Company, 1926–31).

23 Edwin M. Stanton to Ord (copy), 19 April 1865, Bancroft Library Collection.

24 Official Records, 46, pt. 3:882–84.

25 Ibid., p. 826.

26 Ibid., p. 836.

27 Ibid.

28 Ibid., p. 833.

29 Ibid., p. 941.

30 Ibid., pp. 1063, 1076–1077.

31 Ibid., pp. 1077, 1133.

32 Henry W. Halleck to Ord, 2, 8, 22, 30 May and 3 June 1865; Stanton to Ord, 22 May 1865, Bancroft Library Collection.

33 Richardson, comp., Messages and Papers of the Presidents, 8:3508–3510.

34 Douglas Southall Freeman, R. E. Lee: A Biography, 4 vols. (New York: Charles Scribner's Sons, 1934), 4:200–207.

35 Rufus Ingalls to Ord, 10 June 1865, Bancroft Library Collection.

36 Official Records, 46, pt. 3:1275–76, 1286–87.

37 Congressional Record, 93 Cong., 2 Sess., vol. 120, pt. 3:3831–3834. In 1970, a century after Robert E. Lee's death, the missing oath was found among records in the National Archives. Senator Harry F. Byrd, Jr., of Virginia introduced into the Congress a resolution providing for the restoration of citizenship rights to General Lee. A joint resolution of the 94th Congress, 1st Session, restored Lee's citizenship effective 13 June 1865. President Gerald R. Ford signed the resolution on 5 August 1975.

38 Official Records, 46, pt. 3:1213, 1215.

39 Ibid., pp. 797, 881–82; Hartsuff to Ord, 16 April 1865, Bancroft Library Collection.

40 Official Records, 46, pt. 3:1205; Special Orders, No. 111, 24 April 1865, Department of Virginia, 22:243, Record Group 98, National Archives; E. V. Sumner, Jr., to E. W. Smith, 15 May 1865; Alvin C. Voris to N. M. Curtis, 29 May 1865, Bancroft Library Collection.

41 Official Records, 46, pt. 3:888, 956–57, 1131.

42 Ibid., pp. 1143, 1147–48, 1162–63, 1249.

43 Ibid., pp. 1062, 1180, 1219, 1225; Ord to Halleck, 14 May 1865, Letters Sent, Department of Virginia, 13:263, Record Group 98, National Archives.

44 Official Records, 46, pt. 3:961; Ord to John B. Howard, 1 May 1865, Letters Sent, Department of Virginia, 13:230.

45 Louis S. Gerteis, From Contraband to Freedman: Federal Policy Toward Southern Blacks, 1861–1865 (Westport, Conn.: Greenwood Press, 1973), pp. 11–44.

46 Sumner to E. W. Smith, 15 May 1865, Bancroft Library Collection.

47 Official Records, 46, pt. 3:932.

48 Ibid., p. 1205.

⁴⁹ Ibid., pp. 1156–58; Alvin C. Voris to N. M. Curtis, 29 May 1865, Bancroft Library Collection. *See* Henderson H. Donald, *The Negro Freedman: Life Conditions of the American Negro in the Early Years after Emancipation* (New York: Henry Schuman, 1952); Robert G. H. Kean, *Inside the Confederate Government: The Diary of Robert Garlick Hill Kean,* ed. Edward Younger (New York: Oxford University Press, 1957), pp. 207–43; Alrutheus Ambush Taylor, *The Negro in the Reconstruction of Virginia* (Washington: Association for the Study of Negro Life and History, 1926); John P. McConnell, *Negroes and Their Treatment in Virginia from 1865 to 1867* (Pulaski, Va.: B. D. Smith and Brothers, 1910).

⁵⁰ *Official Records,* 46, pt. 3:932–33, 1235–36; Ord to Hartsuff, 28 April 1865; Ord to Voris, 4 May 1865, Letters Sent, Department of Virginia, 13:235, 239–40.

⁵¹ *Official Records,* 46, pt. 3:961, 1116.

⁵² G. W. Davis to Curtis, 20 May 1865; Ord to John A. Rawlins (draft), —— July 1865, Bancroft Library Collection.

⁵³ Ord to Gordon, 12 May 1865, Letters Sent, Department of Virginia, 13:255–56.

⁵⁴ *Official Records,* 46, pt. 3:1116.

⁵⁵ Ibid., p. 1215.

⁵⁶ Ibid., pp. 1224–25.

⁵⁷ Ibid., p. 1133.

⁵⁸ Burnham Wardwell to Butler, 19 April 1865, Benjamin F. Butler, *Private and Official Correspondence of General Benjamin F. Butler,* 5 vols. (Norwood, Mass.: Plimpton Press, 1917), 5:598.

⁵⁹ Wardwell to Butler, 26 July 1865, Butler Papers. *See* J. T. Trowbridge, *A Picture of the Desolated States and the Work of Restoration, 1865–1868* (Hartford: L. Stebbins, 1868), pp. 176–77.

⁶⁰ Birney to Butler, 19 April 1865, Butler Papers.

⁶¹ *Official Records,* 46, pt. 3:896.

⁶² Patrick's Diary, 7 June 1865.

⁶³ Sallie A. Putnam, *In Richmond during the Confederacy* (New York: Robert M. McBride Company, 1961), p. 386. Myrta L. Avery recounts a number of instances in which the kindness of General and Mrs. Ord was expressed toward Richmond citizens. *See* Myrta Lockett Avery, *Dixie after the War* (Boston: Houghton Mifflin Company, 1937), pp. 69, 112.

⁶⁴ *Official Records,* 46, pt. 3:1269, 1277, 1279. For the reconstruction of Virginia, *see* Hamilton J. Eckenrode, *The Political History of Virginia during the Reconstruction* (Baltimore: The Johns Hopkins Press, 1904).

Chapter 15

¹ *The War of the Rebellion: A Compilation of the Official Records of the Union and Confederate Armies,* 129 vols. and index (Washington: Government Printing Office, 1880–1901), Ser. 1, 46, pt. 3:1298–99; 49, pt. 2:1074.

² Petition of senators to President Andrew Johnson, —— April 1866; Edward Ord to E. D. Townsend, 15 August 1866, Edward O. C. Ord's Personal File, Adjutant General's Office, Record Group 94, National Archives; *Official Army Register for 1866* (Washington: Adjutant General's Office, 1866), p. 3.

³ Ord to William T. Sherman, 19 September 1866, Letters and Telegrams Sent, Department of the Arkansas, 3:139, Record Group 98, National Archives; Ord to Placidus Ord, 22 September 1866, Alexander Collection of Ord Papers, in possession of Mrs. Vida Ord Alexander, Washington, D.C.; Orville W. Taylor, *Negro Slavery in Arkansas* (Durham: Duke University Press, 1958), p. 53.

⁴ David Y. Thomas advanced this suggestion of possible competition between white and black labor. It seems significant in view of the racial competition present during Reconstruction. *See* David Y. Thomas, *Arkansas in War and Reconstruction, 1861–1874*

(Little Rock: Arkansas Division, United Daughters of the Confederacy, 1926), p. 19.

5 Ibid., pp. 12–27.

6 Ord's report to Oliver Otis Howard, 21 December 1866, Bureau Records for Arkansas, Reports of Operations, 1866–67, Records of the Bureau of Refugees, Freedmen, and Abandoned Lands, Record Group 105, National Archives.

7 Ord to Sherman, 31 December 1866, Letters and Telegrams Sent, Department of the Arkansas, 3:268.

8 Thomas S. Staples, Reconstruction in Arkansas, 1862–1874, Columbia University Studies in History, Economics and Public Law, vol. 109, whole no. 245 (New York: Columbia University, 1923), p. 109; General Orders, No. 8, 14 September 1866, Department of the Arkansas, 20:264, Record Group 98, National Archives.

9 See Walter L. Fleming, ed., Documentary History of Reconstruction, 2 vols. in one (Gloucester, Mass.: P. Smith, 1960), 1:319–26.

10 Staples, Reconstruction in Arkansas, p. 202.

11 The Arkansas civil rights act provided only limited rights to blacks. Negroes had all of the rights of whites except to intermarry with whites, serve on juries, vote, and attend schools with whites. For the full text of the law, see Fleming, ed., Documentary History of Reconstruction, 1:274–75.

12 Ord to Howard (draft), 27 October 1866, Edward Otho Cresap Ord Correspondence and Papers, 1850–1883, Bancroft Library, Berkeley, California. For a statement of General Howard on outrages on freedmen throughout the South, see John A. Carpenter, Sword and Olive Branch: Oliver Otis Howard (Pittsburgh: University of Pittsburgh Press, 1964), pp. 131–32. See also Oliver O. Howard, Autobiography of Oliver Otis Howard, Major General, United States Army, 2 vols. (New York: Baker and Taylor Company, 1907).

13 Ord to post commanders, 16 December 1866; Ord to Sherman, 31 December 1866, Letters and Telegrams Sent, Department of the Arkansas, 3:254, 268; Circular No. 30, 14 December 1866, Bureau Records for Arkansas, Circular Orders, Assistant Commissioners, 22:35–37; J. S. Taylor's report, 2 March 1867, Bureau Records for Arkansas, Reports of Operations, 1866–67.

14 Ord to Howard (copy), 22 February 1867, Bancroft Library Collection.

15 Ibid.

16 Circular No. 7, 6 March 1867, Bureau Records for Arkansas, Circular Orders, Assistant Commissioners, 2:45–46.

17 Nathan Cole to Ord, 26 October 1866, Letters Received, Department of the Arkansas, 8, Record Group 98, National Archives; E. G. Barker's report, 30 November 1866, Bureau Records for Arkansas, Reports of Operations, 1866–67; Ord to Howard (draft), 27 January 1867, Bancroft Library Collection.

18 Circular No. 7, 6 March 1867, Bureau Records for Arkansas, Circular Orders, Assistant Commissioners, 2:45–46; H. Sweeney's report, 30 November 1866; J. T. Watson's report, 31 December 1866; C. H. Smith's report, 24 April 1867, Bureau Records for Arkansas, Reports of Operations, 1866–67; George W. Mallett to Ord, Bureau Records for Arkansas, Letters Received, 1866 (General).

19 George R. Bentley, A History of the Freedmen's Bureau (Philadelphia: University of Pennsylvania Press, 1955), chap. 11; Barker's report, 30 November 1866, Bureau Records for Arkansas, Reports of Operations, 1866–67. For further information on work contracts, see Martin Abbott, "Free Land, Free Labor, and the Freedmen's Bureau," Agricultural History, 30 (1956): 150–56.

20 See Ira V. Brown, "Lyman Abbott and Freedmen's Aid, 1865–1869," Journal of Southern History, 15 (1949): 22–38; Carpenter, Oliver Otis Howard, pp. 157–68; Larry W. Pearce, "The American Missionary Association and the Freedmen's Bureau in Arkansas, 1866–68," Arkansas Historical Quarterly, 30 (1971): 242–59.

21 Staples, Reconstruction in Arkansas, pp. 208–209; William Preston Vaughn, Schools for All: The Blacks and Public Education in the South, 1865–1877 (Lexington: University Press of Kentucky, 1974), pp. 34–46.

22 William M. Colby's report for March 1867, Bureau Records for Arkansas, Reports of Operations, 1866–67.

23 Colby's report, 21 December 1866; William Brian to Ord, 4 January 1867; H. E. Habicht's report, 31 March 1867; Smith's report, 24 April 1867, Bureau Records for Arkansas, Reports of Operations, 1866–67; Circular No. 28, 6 December 1866, Bureau Records for Arkansas, Circular Orders, Assistant Commissioners, 22:33–34; Ord's report of 22 February 1867, Bureau Records, Commissioner Howard's Office, Letters Received, 9 (A–F), Records of the Bureau of Refugees, Freedmen, and Abandoned Lands, Record Group 105, National Archives.

24 Staples, *Reconstruction in Arkansas*, pp. 315, 323.

25 *United States Statutes at Large*, 14:66–67; Carpenter, *Oliver Otis Howard*, pp. 106–121; Paul W. Gates, "Federal Land Policy in the South, 1866–1888," *Journal of Southern History*, 6 (1940): 303–310; Bentley, *Freedmen's Bureau*, p. 145; W. W. Granger's report, 30 November 1866, Bureau Records for Arkansas, Reports of Operations, 1866–67; Howard to Ord, 6 March 1867, Bureau Records for Arkansas, Letters Received, 1866 (General); Ord's report, 22 February 1867, Bureau Records, Commissioner Howard's Office, Letters Received, 9 (A–F).

26 In the considerable literature on Reconstruction, *see* James Ford Rhodes, *History of the United States from the Compromise of 1850*, 9 vols. (New York: Macmillan Company, 1909–1922), 5, 6, 7; William A. Dunning, *Reconstruction, Political and Economic, 1865–1877* (New York: Harper and Brothers, 1907); James G. Randall and David Donald, *The Civil War and Reconstruction*, 2nd ed. (Boston: D. C. Heath and Company, 1961); E. Merton Coulter, *The South during Reconstruction, 1865–1877* (Baton Rouge: Louisiana State University Press, 1947); LaWanda Cox and John H. Cox, *Politics, Principle, and Prejudice, 1865–1866* (New York: Free Press of Glencoe, 1963); Kenneth M. Stampp, *The Era of Reconstruction, 1865–1877* (New York: Alfred A. Knopf, 1965); Rembert W. Patrick, *The Reconstruction of the Nation* (New York: Oxford University Press, 1967); Avery Craven, *Reconstruction: The Ending of the Civil War* (New York: Holt, Rinehart and Winston, 1969).

27 Ord to Sherman, 27 January 1866, W. T. Sherman Papers, 18, Manuscript Division, Library of Congress.

28 Ord to William H. Seward, 22 June 1866, William H. Seward Collection, University of Rochester Library, Rochester, New York.

29 Ord to Seward, 17 July 1866, William H. Seward Collection.

30 General Orders, No. 10, 11 March 1867, Adjutant General's Office, Record Group 94, National Archives. George F. Milton indicated that Andrew Johnson relied on Edwin M. Stanton and Ulysses S. Grant in choosing the five commanders for the military districts. See *The Age of Hate: Andrew Johnson and the Radicals* (New York: Coward-McCann, 1930), p. 433; Benjamin P. Thomas and Harold M. Hyman, *Stanton: The Life and Times of Lincoln's Secretary of War* (New York: Alfred A. Knopf, 1962), p. 531. Sefton takes Gideon Welles to task for assuming that Ord was a Stanton partisan at the time of his appointment. *See* James E. Sefton, *The United States Army and Reconstruction, 1865–1877* (Baton Rouge: Louisiana State University Press, 1967), p. 115.

31 First Reconstruction Act of 2 March 1867, as quoted in Fleming, ed., *Documentary History of Reconstruction*, 1:401–403.

32 James D. Richardson, comp., *A Compilation of the Messages and Papers of the Presidents*, 20 vols. (New York: Bureau of National Literature, c. 1897–1927), 8:3696–3709.

33 Ord referred to his letter to Henry Wilson and to Grant's report in a letter to Sherman of 14 January 1875, W. T. Sherman Papers, 38.

34 Ord to Sherman, 8 March 1867, W. T. Sherman Papers, 20.

35 Ord to Sherman, 2 April 1867, W. T. Sherman Papers, 21.

36 *Little Rock Daily Arkansas Gazette*, 9 April 1867.

37 James Wilford Garner, *Reconstruction in Mississippi* (New York: Macmillan Company, 1901), pp. 12, 13, 15n.

38 Ibid., pp. 75–95.

39 Percy L. Rainwater, ed., "The Autobiography of Benjamin Grubb Humphreys, August 26, 1808–December 20, 1882," *Mississippi Valley Historical Review*, 21 (1934): 249.

40 *Jackson Daily Clarion*, 27 April 1867.

41 William K. Scarborough, "Heartland of the Cotton Kingdom," *A History of Mississippi*, ed. Richard Aubrey McLemore, 2 vols. (Hattiesburg: University and College Press of Mississippi, 1973), 1:310–351.

42 General Orders, No. 1, 26 March 1867, Fourth Military District, 16:53, Record Group 98, National Archives; *Little Rock Gazette*, 3 April 1867.

43 *Jackson Daily Clarion*, 6 April 1867.

44 Third Reconstruction Act of 19 July 1867, as quoted in Fleming, ed., *Documentary History of Reconstruction*, 1:415–18; Garner, *Reconstruction in Mississippi*, p. 163.

45 Special Orders, Nos. 112–216, 27 August–31 December 1867, Fourth Military District, 13:172–287, Record Group 98, National Archives. As records are confusing, precise figures for removals and appointments are difficult to determine. The figures given were arrived at after careful examination of the records, and they are substantially correct. *See* Garner, *Reconstruction in Mississippi*, pp. 163–64; Staples, *Reconstruction in Arkansas*, pp. 133–34.

46 Special Orders, No. 135, 18 September 1867, Fourth Military District, 13:196; Vernon L. Wharton, *The Negro in Mississippi, 1865–1890*, The James Sprunt Studies in History and Political Science, vol. 28 (Chapel Hill: University of North Carolina Press, 1947), pp. 38–42, 145. There is some question as to whether Ord appointed Benjamin T. Montgomery or his son, Isaiah T. Montgomery, to be justice of the peace. Special Orders show that Benjamin T. Montgomery was the appointee.

47 Ord to L. B. Cunningham, 4 April 1867; Ord to Stanton, 13 May 1867, Letters Sent, Fourth Military District, 1:77, 101, Record Group 98, National Archives; Cunningham to Ord, 11 April 1867; Stanton to Ord, 10 May 1867, Letters Received, Fourth Military District, 3:88, 605, Record Group 98, National Archives; Ord to Isaac Murphy, 21 August 1867, Letters Sent, Civil Affairs, Fourth Military District, 25:177, Record Group 98, National Archives; Ord to Cunningham (copy), 23 May 1867, Andrew Johnson Papers, vol. 113 (1867), Manuscript Division, Library of Congress; Ord to Sherman, 21 May 1867, W. T. Sherman Papers, 21. *See* Staples, *Reconstruction in Arkansas*, pp. 81, 135, 150.

48 Staples, *Reconstruction in Arkansas*, pp. 149–52. The expenses of the constitutional convention of 1868 were eventually paid by order of Ord's successor through sale of $50,000 of the United States bonds.

49 A. W. Bishop and others to Ord, 13 August 1867, Letters Received, Civil Affairs, Fourth Military District, 29:57, Record Group 98, National Archives; *Fort Smith New Era*, 31 July 1867, as quoted in Staples, *Reconstruction in Arkansas*, p. 136.

50 *Van Buren Press*, 5 July and 9 August 1867, as quoted in Staples, *Reconstruction in Arkansas*, p. 136.

51 Garner, *Reconstruction in Mississippi*, pp. 164–67.

52 Ord to Isaac Murphy, 15 April 1867, as quoted in *Little Rock Gazette*, 27 April 1867; Ord to Stanton, 13 May 1867, Letters Sent, Fourth Military District, 1:101.

53 Ord to Sherman, 21 May 1867, W. T. Sherman Papers, 21.

54 Staples, *Reconstruction in Arkansas*, pp. 92, 113–14; *Little Rock Gazette*, 26 July 1867.

55 Staples, *Reconstruction in Arkansas*, pp. 110–11, 132; R. C. Brinkley to Ord, 6 August 1867, Letters Received, Civil Affairs, Fourth Military District, 29:55; Ord to Brinkley, 17 August 1867, Letters Sent, Civil Affairs, Fourth Military District, 25:170.

56 General Orders, Nos. 12 and 15, 12 and 27 June 1867, Fourth Military District, 16:65–69; Staples, *Reconstruction in Arkansas*, p. 139. Ord's interference with the judiciary caused the three judges of the High Court of Errors and Appeals in Mississippi to resign.

57 Ord to Charles H. Smith, 29 October 1867, Letters Sent, Civil Affairs, Fourth Military District, 25:318; Staples, *Reconstruction in Arkansas*, pp. 81, 132–33.

⁵⁸ General Orders, No. 19, 13 August 1867, Fourth Military District, as quoted in Bureau Records for Arkansas, Circular Orders, Assistant Commissioners, 2:65–66; Ord to Grant, 24 December 1867, Letters Sent, Civil Affairs, Fourth Military District, 25:443.

⁵⁹ General Orders, No. 9, 16 May 1867; No. 25, 6 September 1867; Nos. 38 and 39, 5 December 1867, Fourth Military District, 16:59–60, 79, 94–96; General Orders, No. 19, as quoted in Bureau Records for Arkansas, Circular Orders, Assistant Commissioners, 2:65–66; Ord to Stanton, 7 June 1867, Letters Sent, Fourth Military District, 1:125; W. E. Satterfield and others to Ord, 28 March 1867, Letters Received, Fourth Military District, 3:495; Daniel Williamson to Ord, 20 June 1867, Letters Received, Civil Affairs, Fourth Military District, 28:661; Smith to Ord, 27 September 1867, Letters Received, Civil Affairs, Fourth Military District, 29:592.

⁶⁰ General Court-Martial Orders, Nos. 4–32, 10 June–1 December 1867, General Orders, Fourth Military District, 16:287–461.

⁶¹ General Orders, No. 5, 15 April 1867, Fourth Military District, 16:55.

⁶² *Little Rock Gazette,* 20 April 1867; *Jackson Daily Clarion,* 20 April 1867.

⁶³ Ord to Ulysses S. Grant (draft), 8 December 1867, Bancroft Library Collection.

⁶⁴ General Orders, No. 19, 13 August 1867, Fourth Military District, as quoted in Bureau Records for Arkansas, Circular Orders, Assistant Commissioners, 2:65–66.

⁶⁵ General Orders, No. 25, 6 September 1867, Fourth Military District, 16:79.

⁶⁶ General Orders, No. 15, 27 June 1867, Fourth Military District, 16:68–69; Stephen Eggleston to Ord, 21 April 1867; James M. Ellis to Ord, 6 May 1867, Letters Received, Fourth Military District, 3:153; Ord to James R. Kidd, 6 September 1867, Letters Sent, Civil Affairs, Fourth Military District, 25:212. For analysis of the Mississippi Black Code *see* Wharton, *The Negro in Mississippi, 1865–1890,* pp. 84–89.

⁶⁷ G. W. Benson to Ord, 19 August 1867; Robert E. Craig to Ord, 11 September 1867; F. P. Walker to Ord, 25 September 1867, Letters Received, Civil Affairs, Fourth Military District, 29:56, 117, 121; Ord to Alvan C. Gillem, 19 August 1867, Letters Sent, Fourth Military District, 1:169; *Little Rock Gazette,* 18 December 1867.

⁶⁸ —— to Ord, 5 August 1867; L. L. Casey to Ord, 5 August 1867; K. H. Clease to Ord, 13 August 1867, Letters Received, Civil Affairs, Fourth Military District, 29:52, 92, 96; Ord to ——, 22 August 1867, Letters Sent, Civil Affairs, Fourth Military District, 25:180. *See* Wharton, *The Negro in Mississippi, 1865–1890,* pp. 227–29.

⁶⁹ Ord to Mrs. John B. Coleman, 18 April 1867; Ord to Gillem, 2 May 1867, Letters Sent, Fourth Military District, 1:71, 85.

⁷⁰ Wharton, *The Negro in Mississippi, 1865–1890,* p. 244.

⁷¹ Ord to Gillem, 29 October 1867; 13 December 1867, Letters Sent, Civil Affairs, Fourth Military District, 25:319, 416; Ord to Arthur Allyn, 25 November 1867, Letters Sent, Fourth Military District, 1:285.

⁷² Grant to Ord, 30 July 1867, Bancroft Library Collection.

⁷³ Gillem to Ord, 8 August 1867, Letters Received, Fourth Military District, 3:203.

⁷⁴ Ord to Grant (copy), 12 August 1867, Bancroft Library Collection.

⁷⁵ Ibid.

⁷⁶ Ibid.

⁷⁷ Ibid.

Chapter 16

¹ *Chicago Tribune* as quoted in *Little Rock Gazette,* 7 May 1867; *New York Tribune* as quoted in *Gazette,* 14 June 1867; *Little Rock Gazette,* 12 June 1867.

² *Little Rock Gazette,* 12 June 1867.

³ *New York Herald* as quoted in *Jackson Weekly Clarion,* 13 June 1867.

⁴ *Jackson Weekly Clarion,* 13 June 1867. For discussion of conflicting views as to Edward Ord's Radicalism or Conservatism, *see* James E. Sefton, *The United States Army and*

Reconstruction, 1865–1877 (Baton Rouge: Louisiana State University Press, 1967), p. 174.

5 General Orders, No. 12, 12 June 1867, Fourth Military District, 16:66, Record Group 98, National Archives.

6 General Orders, No. 28, 9 Spetember 1867, Fourth Military District, 16:81.

7 Vernon L. Wharton, *The Negro in Mississippi, 1865–1890,* The James Sprunt Studies in History and Political Science, vol. 28 (Chapel Hill: University of North Carolina Press, 1947), pp. 143–44.

8 William C. Harris, "The Creed of the Carpetbaggers: The Case of Mississippi," *Journal of Southern History,* 40 (1974): 199–203, 209–24; David Donald, "The Scalawag in Mississippi Reconstruction," *Journal of Southern History,* 10 (1944): 447–60; Allen W. Trelease, "Who Were the Scalawags?" *Journal of Southern History,* 29 (1963): 458n; "Historical News and Notices," *Journal of Southern History,* 30 (1964): 253–57; Otto H. Olsen, "Reconsidering the Scalawags," *Civil War History,* 12 (1966): 304–20; William C. Harris, "A Reconsideration of the Mississippi Scalawag," *Journal of Mississippi History,* 32 (1970): 38–41; Warren A. Ellem, "Who Were the Mississippi Scalawags?" *Journal of Southern History,* 38 (1972): 240.

9 George R. Bentley, *A History of the Freedmen's Bureau* (Philadelphia: University of Pennsylvania Press, 1955), pp. 186–87; John A. Carpenter, *Sword and Olive Branch: Oliver Otis Howard* (Pittsburgh: University of Pittsburgh Press, 1964), pp. 135–56.

10 Thomas W. Conway's report as quoted in *Little Rock Gazette,* 10 August 1867.

11 *Memphis Appeal* as quoted in *Little Rock Gazette,* 14 July 1867.

12 Jonathan Tarbell to O. D. Greene, 20 July 1867, Edward Otho Cresap Ord Correspondence and Papers, 1850–1883, Bancroft Library, Berkeley, California.

13 Bentley, *A History of the Freedmen's Bureau,* pp. 198–99.

14 Wharton, *The Negro in Mississippi, 1865–1890,* pp. 144–46; James Wilford Garner, *Reconstruction in Mississippi* (New York: Macmillan Company, 1901), p. 178.

15 Thomas S. Staples, *Reconstruction in Arkansas, 1862–1874,* Columbia University Studies in History, Economics, and Public Law, vol. 109, whole no. 245 (New York: Columbia University, 1923), pp. 162–66; *Little Rock Gazette,* 5 April 1867. See Powell Clayton, *The Aftermath of the Civil War in Arkansas* (New York: Neale Publishing Company, 1915).

16 Staples, *Reconstruction in Arkansas,* pp. 168–69.

17 Ibid., pp. 127, 129, 169–71.

18 Ibid., pp. 169–70, 174.

19 Walter L. Fleming, ed., *Documentary History of Reconstruction,* 2 vols. in one (Gloucester, Mass.: P. Smith, 1960), 1:408.

20 *Jackson Daily Clarion,* 29 May 1867. Edwin M. Stanton's biographers, Thomas and Hyman, stated that Ord's threat to disperse the Andrew Johnson legislatures of Mississippi and Arkansas prompted Henry Stanbery to disclose to the Cabinet his preliminary opinion in May as to voting qualifications. See Benjamin P. Thomas and Harold M. Hyman, *Stanton: The Life and Times of Lincoln's Secretary of War* (New York: Alfred A. Knopf, 1962), pp. 539–40.

21 Ord's circular to boards of registration, 10 June 1867, as printed in *Little Rock Gazette,* 28 June 1867; opinion of the attorney-general, 20 June 1867, James D. Richardson, comp., *A Compilation of the Messages and Papers of the Presidents,* 20 vols. (New York: Bureau of National Literature, c. 1897–1927), 8:3726–3729; Ulysses S. Grant to Ord, 23 June 1867, Letters Sent (1867), Headquarters of the Army, 286, Record Group 108, National Archives; Ord to Grant (rough draft), c. 30 June 1867, Bancroft Library Collection; Ord to Zachariah Chandler, 16 September 1867, Zachariah Chandler Papers, Manuscript Division, Library of Congress. Sefton believes that Grant was in error in assuming that Ord could interpret the law in the matter of registration qualifications instead of relying on Stanbery. See Sefton, *The United States Army and Reconstruction, 1865–1877,* p. 133.

22 Fleming, ed., *Documentary History of Reconstruction,* 1:415–18; Ord's circular to boards of registration, 6 August 1867, as printed in *Jackson Daily Clarion,* 8 August 1867.

23 General Orders, No. 16, 29 June 1867, Fourth Military District, as quoted in Bureau Records for Arkansas, Circular Orders, Assistant Commissioners, 2:60–61, Records of the Bureau of Refugees, Freedmen, and Abandoned Lands, Record Group 105, National Archives.

24 Ord's annual report, 27 September 1867, Letters Sent, Fourth Military District, 1:215–19, Record Group 98, National Archives; Garner, *Reconstruction in Mississippi*, pp. 171, 171n.

25 Ord's annual report, 27 September 1867, Letters Sent, Fourth Military District, 1:219–20; Staples, *Reconstruction in Arkansas*, pp. 159n. 160n.

26 Ord to C. H. Smith, 27 May 1867, Letters Sent, Civil Affairs, Fourth Military District, 25:35, Record Group 98, National Archives; Robert A. Hill to Ord, 2 May 1867; J.F.H. Claiborne to Ord, 11 May 1867, Letters Received, Fourth Military District, 3:1, 89, Record Group 98, National Archives; *Natchez Courier* and *Holly Springs Reporter*, quoted in *Jackson Daily Clarion*, 10 and 11 May 1867; *Jackson Weekly Clarion*, 13 June 1867.

27 *Jackson Weekly Clarion*, 29 August 1867.

28 August V. Kautz to Ord, 26 June 1867; Arthur W. Allyn to Ord, 8 July 1867, Letters Received, Civil Affairs, Fourth Military District, 28:22, 294, Record Group 98, National Archives; General Court-Martial Orders, Nos. 4–32, 10 June–1 December 1867, General Orders, Fourth Military District, 16:365; *Jackson Weekly Clarion*, 4 July 1867; Hill to Ord, 4 July 1867, Bancroft Library Collection.

29 Jonathan Tarbell to O. D. Greene, 20 July 1867, Bancroft Library Collection.

30 Ord to Grant, 24 September 1867, Letters Sent, Civil Affairs, Fourth Military District, 25:262; Percy L. Rainwater, ed., "The Autobiography of Benjamin Grubb Humphreys, August 26, 1808–December 20, 1882," *Mississippi Valley Historical Review*, 21:249. *See* the articles by Donald, Trelease, Olsen, Harris, and Ellem cited in note 8 above.

31 Ord to Smith, 15 April 1867; Ord to Isaac Murphy, 15 April 1867; Ord to J. M. Tibbetts, 15 April 1867; Ord to Clayton, 27 April 1867, Letters Sent, Fourth Military District, 1:67, 69, 78; Ord to Smith, 27 May 1867, Letters Sent, Civil Affairs, Fourth Military District, 25:35; *Little Rock Gazette*, 17 April 1867; Staples, *Reconstruction in Arkansas*, pp. 154–55.

32 *Little Rock Gazette*, 25 May 1867; Smith to Ord, 20 August 1867, Bancroft Library Collection.

33 Albert W. Bishop to Ord, 6 August 1867; Henry St. John to Ord, 6 August 1867; Ernest Wiedman to Ord, 7 August 1867; L. W. Hopkins to Ord, 19 November 1867; Murphy to Ord, 29 November 1867, Letters Received, Civil Affairs, Fourth Military District, 29:3, 47, 53, 236, 279; Ord to Smith, 9 August 1867; Ord to Murphy, 9 December 1867, Letters Sent, Civil Affairs, Fourth Military District, 25:159, 402; Staples, *Reconstruction in Arkansas*, pp. 159–60; *Little Rock Gazette*, 1 October 1867.

34 Ord to Grant, 24 September 1867, Letters Sent, Civil Affairs, Fourth Military District, 25:262; Eugene B. Feistman, "Radical Disfranchisement in Arkansas, 1867–1868," *Arkansas Historical Quarterly*, 12 (1953): 158–59.

35 The risky analogy between the Arkansas and Mississippi elections seems to be the only way to get even a rough approximation of the numbers in the two Arkansas factions. Other election statistics are of little help in verifying the analysis of the Arkansas electorate as it stood in 1867. Of possible significance is the fact that, in the presidential contests of 1868 and 1872, there was only a difference of about 3,000 votes between the polls of the two parties. *See* W. Dean Burnham, *Presidential Ballots, 1836–1892* (Baltimore: The Johns Hopkins University Press, 1955), pp. 254–55.

36 General Orders, No. 35, 4 November 1867, Fourth Military District, 26:91.

37 General Orders, No. 31, 26 September 1867, Fourth Military District, 26:83–86.

38 Ord to C. A. Brougher, 25 April 1867 and 6 May 1867, Letters Sent, Fourth Military District, 1:74, 90; Ord to editor of *Vicksburg Republican*, 26 September 1867, Letters Sent, Civil Affairs, Fourth Military District, 25:270; James T. Currie, "The Beginnings of Congressional Reconstruction in Mississippi," *Journal of Mississippi History*, 35 (1973): 274–78. Garner, in his *Reconstruction in Mississippi* (p. 187), charged Ord with

pro-Radical favoritism in the apportionment of delegates. Currie takes issue with Garner, saying that the figures he used to arrive at this conclusion were "both irrelevant and erroneous" (pp. 275–76). Continued Currie (p. 278): "Indeed, the apportionment within the 1868 Constitutional Convention was probably fairer and more equitable than that of any legislature that met in Mississippi until 1966."

[39] *Vicksburg Herald* as quoted in Garner, *Reconstruction in Mississippi*, p. 177n; Tarbell to Ord, 25 September 1867; Walton C. Brewer to Ord, 25 September 1867; E. T. Hulaniski to Ord, 2 October 1867; W. Ben Cunningham to Ord, 10 October 1867; Jerre Hansen to Ord, 28 October 1867; T. W. Hammond to Ord, 9 November 1867; Abel Alderson to Ord, 11 November 1867; A. A. McArthur to Ord, 13 November 1867; John E. McKee to Ord, 28 November 1867; Andrew Thomas to Ord, 18 December 1867, Letters Received, Civil Affairs, Fourth Military District, 29:130, 172, 175, 189, 263, 353, 435, 506, 588, 667B; Ord to Lloyd Wheaton, 6 November 1867; Ord to Alvan C. Gillem, 8 November 1867, Letters Sent, Civil Affairs, Fourth Military District, 25:337, 342.

[40] General Orders, No. 42, 16 December 1867, Fourth Military District, 16:98–102; Currie, "The Beginnings of Congressional Reconstruction in Mississippi," *Journal of Mississippi History*, 35:281–82. Currie's figures are used here as representing the latest close scrutiny of the pertinent documents. For somewhat different figures, *see* Wharton, *The Negro in Mississippi, 1865–1890*, pp. 146–47; and Garner, *Reconstruction in Mississippi*, p. 187.

[41] General Orders, No. 37, 5 December 1867, Fourth Military District, 16:93.

[42] Ord to Robert J. T. White, 6 May 1867, Letters Sent, Fourth Military District, 1:89, 90; Ord to Smith, 26 September 1867, Letters Sent, Civil Affairs, Fourth Military District, 25:268; Staples, *Reconstruction in Arkansas*, p. 175.

[43] Smith to Ord, 20 August and 12 November 1867, Bancroft Library Collection; Ord to Smith, 8 November 1867, as quoted in *Little Rock Gazette*, 10 November 1867; Smith to Ord, 19 October 1867, Letters Received, Fourth Military District, 3:410; Ord to Smith, 21 October 1867, Letters Sent, Fourth Military District, 1:248.

[44] *Little Rock Gazette*, 17 November 1867; Staples, *Reconstruction in Arkansas*, pp. 162, 177.

[45] *Little Rock Gazette*, 8 and 12 November 1867; Staples, *Reconstruction in Arkansas*, pp. 174, 177–78; William F. Grove to Ord, 13 November 1867, Letters Received, Civil Affairs, Fourth Military District, 29:43.

[46] General Orders, No. 43, 21 December 1867, Fourth Military District, 16:102–104; Richard L. Hume, "The Arkansas Constitutional Convention of 1868: A Case Study in the Politics of Reconstruction," *Journal of Southern History*, 39 (1973): 192. Hume's figures on the composition of the Arkansas convention are relied upon here because they derive from the latest examination of the relevant documents, but *see* Staples's figures in *Reconstruction in Arkansas*, pp. 219–21. *See also* Joseph M. St. Hilaire, "The Negro Delegates in the Arkansas Constitutional Convention of 1868: A Group Profile," *Arkansas Historical Quarterly*, 33 (1974): 38–69.

[47] General Orders, No. 37, 5 December 1867, Fourth Military District, 16:93.

Chapter 17

[1] *United States Supreme Court Reports* (1867), *Mississippi v. Johnson*, 4 Wall. 475.

[2] *Jackson Daily Clarion*, 16, 17, and 22 May 1867.

[3] Ibid., 22 May 1867.

[4] Edward Ord to Edwin M. Stanton, 13 May 1867, Letters Sent, Fourth Military District, 1:101–102, Record Group 98, National Archives; *Jackson Daily Clarion*, 17 May 1867.

[5] *Mississippi v. Johnson*, 4 Wall. 481–97; Stanley I. Kutler, *Judicial Power and Reconstruction Politics* (Chicago: University of Chicago Press, 1968), pp. 96–100. Kutler believes that the Mississippi case was weak in that it sought to attack the president and set him against the Congress, thus producing an impossible situation. He further notes that had Justice Robert C. Grier been present, he would have sided with the

plaintiffs, and a case would have developed. As the case did not develop, the question of the constitutionality of the Reconstruction acts did not arise.

6 C. C. Gilbert to Ord, 15 August 1867, Letters Received, Fourth Military District, 3:105, Record Group 98, National Archives; Thomas S. Staples, *Reconstruction in Arkansas, 1862–1874*, Columbia University Studies in History, Economics, and Public Law, vol. 109, whole no. 245 (New York: Columbia University, 1923), pp. 148–49; James E. Sefton, *The United States Army and Reconstruction, 1865–1877* (Baton Rouge: Louisiana State University Press, 1967), pp. 151-52.

7 Ord to Gilbert, 4 September 1867, Letters Sent, Fourth Military District, 1:187.

8 Ibid., pp. 187–88.

9 *Boston Post* as quoted in *Little Rock Gazette*, 8 October 1867.

10 As quoted in Staples, *Reconstruction in Arkansas*, p. 149.

11 Margaret Ross, "Retaliation against Arkansas Newspaper Editors during Reconstruction," *Arkansas Historical Quarterly*, 21 (1972): 153–54.

12 Ord to Alvan C. Gillem, 8 November 1867, Letters Sent, Civil Affairs, Fourth Military District, 25:341, Record Group 98, National Archives; James Wilford Garner, *Reconstruction in Mississippi* (New York: Macmillan Company, 1901), p. 168.

13 *Vicksburg Weekly Times*, 11 December 1867.

14 J.F.H. Claiborne to Robert A. Hill, 4 December 1867, Edward Otho Cresap Ord Correspondence and Papers, 1850–1883, Bancroft Library, Berkeley, California.

15 William H. McCardle's counsel to Ord, 12 November 1867, Bancroft Library Collection.

16 Ord to Walker Brooke, 12 November 1867, as quoted in *Vicksburg Weekly Times*, 11 December 1867. A man named Duggin, a Radical partisan, was killed by Charles W. Vick, who shared McCardle's extreme views. Vick was convicted and sentenced to five years in prison.

17 *Vicksburg Weekly Times*, 11 December 1867.

18 Hill to Ord, 12 November 1867; Gillem to Ord, 13 November 1867, Letters Received, Civil Affairs, Fourth Military District, 29:269, 430, Record Group 98, National Archives; George C. McKee to Ord, 18 November 1867, Bancroft Library Collection, Many writers have erroneously stated that McCardle was denied the writ and that he thereupon appealed to the Supreme Court.

19 Ord to Gillem, 16 November 1867; Ord to Hill, 16 November 1867, Letters Sent, Civil Affairs, Fourth Military District, 25:358, 362–63; Special Orders, No. 184, 16 November 1867, Fourth Military District, 13:250, Record Group 98, National Archives.

20 Hill to Ord, 20 November 1867, Bancroft Library Collection.

21 James T. Currie, "The Beginnings of Congressional Reconstruction in Mississippi," *Journal of Mississippi History*, 35 (1973): 269.

22 *United States Supreme Court Reports* (1868), *Ex parte McCardle*, 6 Wall. 320; Garner, *Reconstruction in Mississippi*, p. 168.

23 *Ex parte McCardle*, 6 Wall. 320; *Jackson Daily Clarion*, 29 November 1867.

24 *Jackson Daily Clarion*, 29 November 1867.

25 *Ex parte McCardle*, 6 Wall. 320; Ord to Major D. G. Swain, 26 November 1867, Letters Sent, Civil Affairs, Fourth Military District, 25:380; Garner, *Reconstruction in Mississippi*, p. 168; William M. Wiecek, "The Great Writ and Reconstruction: The Habeas Corpus Act of 1867," *Journal of Southern History*, 36 (1970): 540–41.

26 Hill to Ord, 11 December 1867, Bancroft Library Collection.

27 Claiborne to Hill, 4 December 1867, Bancroft Library Collection.

28 *Vicksburg Weekly Times*, 11 December 1867.

29 When Ord was assistant commissioner of the Freedmen's Bureau in Arkansas, General Oliver O. Howard asked Ord and other assistant commissioners in a "strictly confidential" letter if they could have a federal judge take a case by writ of habeas corpus from a military commission and have it appealed to the Supreme Court in order to test the judicial powers of the bureau. There is evidence that Ord sought to develop such a case, but all efforts were interrupted shortly by passage of

the Reconstruction acts. The parallel possibilities in the McCardle matter would not be lost upon Ord. *See* Howard to Ord, 30 January 1867, Bancroft Library Collection; Ord to William D. Hale, 13 February 1867, Bureau Records for Arkansas, Letters Sent, Assistant Commissioners, 11:104, Records of the Bureau of Refugees, Freedmen, and Abandoned Lands, Record Group 105, National Archives; George R. Bentley, *A History of the Freedmen's Bureau* (Philadelphia: University of Pennsylvania Press, 1955), pp. 164–65.

[30] *See* Sever L. Eubank, "The McCardle Case: A Challenge to Radical Reconstruction," *Journal of Mississippi History,* 18 (1956): 111–27. For details of the effect of the McCardle case on the struggle between President Johnson on the one hand and Stanton and Ulysses S. Grant on the other, *see* Benjamin P. Thomas and Harold M. Hyman, *Stanton: The Life and Times of Lincoln's Secretary of War* (New York: Alfred A. Knopf, 1962), pp. 566–67.

[31] *Ex parte McCardle,* 6 Wall. 321–24.

[32] *Vicksburg Daily Times,* 4 February 1868.

[33] *United States Supreme Court Reports* (1866), *Ex parte Milligan,* 4 Wall. 2.

[34] *National Intelligencer,* 20 February 1868, as quoted in *Vicksburg Daily Times,* 26 February 1868.

[35] *Ex parte McCardle,* 7 Wall. 506–15; William Norwood Brigance, *Jeremiah Sullivan Black, A Defender of the Constitution and the Ten Commandments* (Philadelphia: University of Pennsylvania Press, 1934), pp. 171–79; Stanley I. Kutler, *"Ex parte McCardle: Judicial* Impotency? The Supreme Court and Reconstruction Reconsidered," *American Historical Review,* 72 (1966–67): 835–51; Charles Warren, *The Supreme Court in United States History,* rev. ed., 2 vols. (Boston: Little, Brown and Company, 1935), 2: chap. 30.

[36] Kutler, *Judicial Power and Reconstruction Politics,* pp. 104–108.

[37] William M. Wiecek, "The Great Writ and Reconstruction: The Habeas Corpus Act of 1867," *Journal of Southern History,* 36:531, 543.

[38] Kutler, *Judicial Power and Reconstruction Politics,* p. 100.

[39] Ibid.

[40] Staples, *Reconstruction in Arkansas,* p. 181; *Little Rock Gazette,* 22 December 1867.

[41] Ord to Gillem, 8 August 1867; Ord to George Haller, 9 August 1867, Letters Sent, Fourth Military District, 1:161, 164; Ord to Gillem, 14 November 1867, Letters Sent, Civil Affairs, Fourth Military District, 25:353; W. Epperson to Ord, 5 October 1867, Letters Received, Fourth Military District, 3:155; A. L. Dabney to Ord, 13 November 1867, Letters Received, Civil Affairs, Fourth Military District, 29:143–44.

[42] Benjamin Grubb Humphreys's proclamation, 9 December 1867, as quoted in *Jackson Daily Clarion,* 19 December 1867. When the Radical-dominated Mississippi convention met in January, it undertook to investigate the truth of the reports on which the governor's proclamation was based.

[43] Ord to Grant, 7 December 1867, Letters Sent, Civil Affairs, Fourth Military District, 25:400–401. Stanley Horn noted that it was out of fear of Negro insurrection at the time of Humphreys's proclamation that the whites turned to the Ku Klux Klan. See *Invisible Empire: The Story of the Ku Klux Klan, 1866–1871* (Boston: Houghton Mifflin Company, 1939), pp. 148–49.

[44] Gillem to Ord, 10 December 1867, as quoted in *Jackson Daily Clarion,* 29 December 1867; Special Orders, No. 208, 19 December 1867, Fourth Military District, 13:280; Ord to Humphreys, 27 December 1867, Governor's Archives, Series E, Numbers 80–82, Mississippi Department of Archives and History, Jackson; William C. Harris, "The Reconstruction of the Commonwealth, 1865–1870," *A History of Mississippi,* ed. Richard Aubrey McLemore, 2 vols. (Hattiesburg: University and College Press of Mississippi, 1973), 1:552.

[45] Orville H. Browning, *The Diary of Orville Hickman Browning,* eds. Theodore C. Pease and James G. Randall, Collections of the Illinois State Historical Library, vols. 20 and 22 (Springfield: Trustees of the Illinois State Historical Library, 1927–33), 22:170.

[46] Ord to Placidus Ord, 26 November 1867, Alexander Collection of Ord Papers, in possession of Mrs. Vida Ord Alexander, Washington, D.C.

⁴⁷ Gideon Welles, *Diary of Gideon Welles, Secretary of the Navy under Lincoln and Johnson*, ed. John T. Morse, 3 vols. (Boston: Houghton Mifflin Company, 1911), 3:245.

⁴⁸ Ibid., pp. 245, 249.

⁴⁹ Memorandum of claim to pay in Ord's Personal File, Adjutant General's Office, Record Group 94, National Archives. Hans L. Trefousse indicates that President Johnson's transfer of Ord, John Pope and Wager Swayne from Southern commands on 28 December 1867, along with his quarrel with Grant, stiffened the disposition of Congress to be hostile toward the president. Trefousse says a majority of the Republican Party believed Johnson must be deposed if Reconstruction was to succeed. See Hans L. Trefousse, *Impeachment of a President: Andrew Johnson, the Blacks and Reconstruction* (Knoxville: University of Tennessee Press, 1975), p. 140.

⁵⁰ *Baltimore Sun* as quoted in *Jackson Daily Clarion*, 7 January 1868; *New Orleans Crescent* and *New York Herald* as quoted in *Vicksburg Daily Times*, 1 and 5 January 1868.

⁵¹ *Vicksburg Daily Times*, 5 January 1868.

⁵² *Little Rock Gazette*, 4 and 5 January 1868.

⁵³ Henry Wilson to Ord, 8 November 1867, Bancroft Library Collection.

⁵⁴ Percy L. Rainwater, ed., "The Autobiography of Benjamin Grubb Humphreys, August 26, 1808–December 20, 1882," *Mississippi Valley Historical Review*, 21 (1934–35): 249.

⁵⁵ Garner, *Reconstruction in Mississippi*, pp. 171, 181–82.

⁵⁶ Staples, *Reconstruction in Arkansas*, pp. 127–28, 180.

⁵⁷ Ord's annual report, 27 September 1867, Letters Sent, Fourth Military District, 1:220–21.

⁵⁸ Ord to William T. Sherman, 6 November 1867, W. T. Sherman Papers, 21, Manuscript Division, Library of Congress.

⁵⁹ Ibid.

⁶⁰ Ibid.

⁶¹ *National Intelligencer*, 18 January 1868, as quoted in *Vicksburg Daily Times*, 25 January 1868.

⁶² Ord to Placidus Ord, 26 November 1867, Alexander Collection.

⁶³ Ord to Placidus Ord, 29 March 1868, Alexander Collection.

⁶⁴ *Vicksburg Daily Times*, 9 January 1868.

⁶⁵ Garner, *Reconstruction in Mississippi*, pp. 372–413; Vernon L. Wharton, *The Negro in Mississippi, 1865–1890*, The James Sprunt Studies in History, Economics, and Public Law, vol. 28 (Chapel Hill: University of North Carolina Press, 1947), pp. 181–215. See John R. Lynch, *The Facts of Reconstruction* (New York: Neale Publishing Company, 1913).

⁶⁶ Staples, *Reconstruction in Arkansas*, pp. 424–40; Paul Lewinson, *Race, Class, and Party: A History of Negro Suffrage and White Politics in the South* (New York: Russell and Russell, 1963), pp 120–21, 203–213; V. O. Key, Jr., *Southern Politics in State and Nation* (New York: Random House, 1949), p. 183. See John M. Harrell, *The Brooks and Baxter War: A History of the Reconstruction Period in Arkansas* (St. Louis: Slawson Printing Company, 1893); C. Vann Woodward, *Origins of the New South, 1877–1913* (Baton Rouge: Louisiana State University Press, 1966).

⁶⁷ Ord to Grant (copy), 12 August 1867, Bancroft Library Collection.

Chapter 18

¹ Edward Ord to Placidus Ord, 16 March 1867 and 17 January 1868, Alexander Collection of Ord Papers, in possession of Mrs. Vida Ord Alexander, Washington, D.C.; O. D. Greene to Ord, 17 July 1867; Ord to Ulysses S. Grant, 8 October 1867, Letters Sent, Fourth Military District, 1:143, 235, Record Group 98, National Archives.

² Ord to William T. Sherman, 27 February 1868, W. T. Sherman Papers, 22, Manu-

script Division, Library of Congress; Ord to Placidus Ord, 29 March 1868, Alexander Collection.

3 Ord to Placidus Ord, 31 December 1868, Alexander Collection.

4 Ord's annual report, 27 September 1868, Letters Received, Adjutant General's Office (1868), Record Group 94, National Archives.

5 Ibid.; Ord's annual report, 10 October 1870, Letters Received, Adjutant General's Office.

6 Ord to John A. Rawlins (draft), 17 February 1868, Edward Otho Cresap Ord Correspondence and Papers, 1850–1883, Bancroft Library, Berkeley, California.

7 Ord to Sherman, 12 May 1870, Miscellaneous Manuscripts. New York Historical Society, New York, New York; Henry W. Halleck to the Adjutant General, 5 April and 14 May 1869, Letters Received, Adjutant General's Office (1869).

8 Ord's annual report, 27 September 1869, Letters Received, Adjutant General's Office (1869); Ralph H. Ogle, Federal Control of the Western Apaches, 1848–1886 (Albuquerque: University of New Mexico Press, 1970), pp. 72–79; Morris Edward Opler, An Apache Life-Way: The Economic, Social, and Religious Institutions of the Chiricahua Indians (Chicago: University of Chicago Press, 1941), pp. 1–4.

9 Ord to Joseph Ives (draft), 17 August 1860, Bancroft Library Collection.

10 Ord to Edwin M. Stanton (copy), —— March 1866, Bancroft Library Collection.

11 Most of Ord's suggestions were made in his annual reports during the 1870s. See Jack D. Foner, The United States Soldier between Two Wars: Army Life and Reforms, 1865–1898 (New York: Humanities Press, 1970), pp. 15–68.

12 Cincinnati Catholic Telegraph, 16 March 1864.

13 Ord's annual report, 13 October 1873, Letters Sent, Department of the Platte, 3:470, Record Group 98, National Archives. The Articles of War, effective 1 February 1949 provided for enlisted men to serve on courts-martial. This provision was included in the Uniform Code of Military Justice (Article 25) enacted by the Congress and made effective on 31 May 1951. See William B. Aycock and Seymour W. Wurfel, Military Law under the Uniform Code of Military Justice (Chapel Hill: University of North Carolina Press, 1955), pp. 24, 373, 375; William T. Generous, Jr., Swords and Scales: The Development of the Uniform Code of Military Justice (Port Washington, N.Y.: Kennikat Press, 1973).

14 Ord to Levi Maish, Edward S. Bragg and Harry White (draft), 14 February 1878, Bancroft Library Collection.

15 Ord to Ives (draft), 17 August 1860, Bancroft Library Collection. Statutes requiring such examinations were passed by Congress in 1890 and 1892. See George B. Davis, A Treatise on the Military Law of the United States, 2nd ed. rev. (New York: John Wiley and Sons, 1906), p. 230.

16 General Ord was identified with the history of California over a period of some twenty-five years. Fort Ord, the large army reservation near Monterey, commemorates this long connection as well as the general's services to the United States. A government reserve since 1917, the post was named Camp Ord in 1933 and Fort Ord in 1940. It consists of 28,600 acres.

17 Placidus Ord to Julianne Ord, 16 August 1869, Alexander Collection.

18 House Executive Documents, 42nd Cong., 3rd Sess., No. 1 (Serial No. 1558): 51–52. For a general account of the part played by the army in the settlement of the trans-Mississippi West following the Civil War, see Robert G. Athearn, William Tecumseh Sherman and the Settlement of the West (Norman: University of Oklahoma Press, 1956). See also Allan Nevins, The Emergence of Modern America, 1865–1878 (New York: Macmillan Company, 1927).

19 House Executive Documents, 42nd Cong., 3rd Sess., No. 1 (Serial No. 1558): 51; Ord's annual report, 13 October 1873, Letters Sent, Department of the Platte, 3:468, 470–71. See Loring B. Priest, Uncle Sam's Stepchildren: The Reformation of the United States Indian Policy, 1865–1887 (New York: Octagon Books, 1969); James C. Olson, Red Cloud and the Sioux Problem (Lincoln, Neb.: University of Nebraska Press, 1965).

20 House Executive Documents, 43rd Cong., 2nd Sess., No. 1 (Serial No. 1635): 3–4. Ord established Fort Hartsuff on the North Loup in 1874. The county seat of Valley

County, Nebraska, near the fort was surveyed in the same year and named Ord in honor of the general.

21 Gary D. Olsen, ed., "Relief for Nebraska Grasshopper Victims: The Official Journal of Lieutenant Theodore E. True," *Nebraska History*, 48 (1967): 119–40; Everett Dick, *The Sod-House Frontier, 1854–1890* (New York: D. Appleton-Century Company, 1937), pp. 202–212; Fred A. Shannon, *The Farmer's Last Frontier: Agriculture, 1860–1897* (New York: Farrar and Rinehart, 1945), pp. 152–53; *Chicago Tribune*, 23 October 1874; Ord to post commanders and Ord to the adjutant general, 27 October 1874; Ord to Secretary of War William W. Belknap, 19 December 1874, Letters Sent, Department of the Platte, 26:3, 4, 27.

22 James S. Brisbin to Ord, 27 July 1875, Bancroft Library Collection.

23 Ord to Sherman, 4 and 7 May 1875, W. T. Sherman Papers, 36. General Ord's domestic establishment in Omaha included his aged father, a widower since 1860. Here in 1873, the elder Ord died at about the age of eighty-six. In a world of anomalies, his career still excites remark. In this picturesque Western frontier town, there passed from the scene James Ord, native of England, sometime Jesuit, veteran of both the naval and military service of the United States.

24 Placidus Ord to James C. Ord, 17 April and 17 May 1875, Alexander Collection.

25 For an account of the development of the area, *see* Carl Coke Rister, *The Southwestern Frontier, 1865–1881* (Cleveland: Arthur H. Clark Company, 1928).

26 Francis P. Prucha, *A Guide to the Military Posts of the United States, 1789–1895* (Madison: State Historical Society of Wisconsin, 1965). For the activities of the Negro cavalry regiments, *see* William H. Leckie, *The Buffalo Soldiers: A Narrative of the Negro Cavalry in the West* (Norman: University of Oklahoma Press, 1967); for the infantry regiments, *see* Arlen L. Fowler, *The Black Infantry in the West, 1869–1891* (Westport, Conn.: Greenwood Publishing Corporation, 1971).

27 James M. Callahan, *American Foreign Policy in Mexican Relations* (New York: Macmillan Company, 1932), pp. 341–49, 357–61; J. Fred Rippy, *The United States and Mexico*, rev. ed. (New York: F. S. Crofts and Company, 1931), pp. 282–90; Carl Coke Rister, *Robert E. Lee in Texas* (Norman: University of Oklahoma Press, 1946), pp. 106–128; *House Executive Documents*, 44th Cong., 2nd Sess., No. 1 (Serial No. 1674): 95. For other general accounts, *see* William H. Leckie, *The Military Conquest of the Southern Plains* (Norman: University of Oklahoma Press, 1963); Karl M. Schmitt, *Mexico and the United States, 1821–1973: Conflict and Coexistence* (New York: John Wiley and Sons, 1974).

28 Ord to Sherman, 25 August 1875, W. T. Sherman Papers, 40.

29 *House Executive Documents*, 44th Cong., 2nd Sess., No. 1 (Serial No. 1674): 95.

30 Ibid.; *Galveston Daily News*, 25 March and 13 April 1875.

31 Ord to Richard Coke, 28 May 1875, Letters Sent (1875), Department of Texas, p. 903, Record Group 98, National Archives.

32 Coke to Ord, 29 May 1875, Letters Received (1875), Department of Texas, p. 481, Record Group 98, National Archives.

33 E. D. Townsend to Ord, 7 June 1875, Ord's Personal File, Adjutant General's Office, Record Group 94, National Archives; Ord to Coke (draft), 16 June 1875, Bancroft Library Collection; *Galveston Daily News*, 12 and 22 June 1875. *See* Michael G. Webster, "Intrigue on the Rio Grande: The *Rio Bravo* Affair, 1875." *Southwestern Historical Quarterly*, 74 (1970): 149–64.

34 Ord to his headquarters, 1 June 1875, Letters Received (1875), Department of Texas; *House Misc. Documents*, 45th Cong., 2nd Sess., No. 64 (Serial No. 1820): 103; Sherman to Ord, 14 July 1875, Sherman-Ord Correspondence, Missouri Historical Society, St. Louis, Missouri (used by permission).

35 John W. Foster to Hamilton Fish, 7 July 1875, no. 317, Mexican Dispatches, vol. 54, Department of State, Record Group 59, National Archives. For Secretary of State Fish's views on the Mexican problem *see* Allan Nevins, *Hamilton Fish: The Inner History of the Grant Administration*, rev. ed., 2 vols. (New York: Frederick Ungar Publishing Company, 1957), 2: appendix 1, 912–13.

36 Ord to William R. Shafter, 1 April 1876, William R. Shafter Papers, Manuscripts

Division, Department of Special Collections, C. H. Green Library, Stanford University, Stanford, California.

[37] Ord to Shafter, 3 January 1877 [1878?], Shafter Papers; Fowler, *The Black Infantry in the West*, pp. 116–39; Jack D. Foner, *Blacks and the Military in American History: A New Perspective* (New York: Praeger Publishers, 1974), pp. 53–62; John M. Carroll, ed., *The Black Military Experience in the American West* (New York: Liveright, 1971), pp. 261–63.

[38] *House Executive Documents*, 43rd Cong., 2nd Sess., No. 1 (Serial No. 1635): 3.

[39] *Galveston Daily News*, 13 November 1875 and 14 April 1876; Robert Burns to Ord, 30 May 1879, Letters Received (1879), Department of Texas, p. 520.

[40] Guy M. Bryan to Rutherford B. Hayes, 27 April 1880, Rutherford B. Hayes Papers, Rutherford B. Hayes Library, Fremont, Ohio.

[41] Ord to Sherman, 2 June 1876, W. T. Sherman Papers, 43.

[42] Adjutant General to Ord, 17 September 1875, Letters Received (1875), Department of Texas, p. 251.

[43] *House Executive Documents*, 45th Cong., 2nd Sess., No. 1 (Serial No. 1794): 80.

[44] *Galveston Daily News*, 18 January 1876; Ord to Sherman, 15 January and 2 June 1876, W. T. Sherman Papers, 42, 43; Louise Horton, *Samuel Bell Maxey: A Biography* (Austin: University of Texas Press, 1974), pp. 78, 99, 100.

[45] *House Reports*, 45th Cong., 2nd Sess., No. 701 (Serial No. 1824): 161, 173–79; Foster to Fish, 25 and 29 April 1876, nos. 404 and 405, Mexican Dispatches, vol. 56; *Galveston Daily News*, 11 January and 9 April 1876.

[46] Shafter to Ord, 31 July 1876, Letters Received (1876), Department of Texas, p. 296; Ord to Shafter, 14 August 1876, Letters Sent (1876), Department of Texas, p. 465; Ord to Sherman, 27 June 1876, W. T. Sherman Papers, 44. For further accounts of John L. Bullis's scouts, *see* Clarence C. Clendenen, *Blood on the Border: The United States Army and the Mexican Irregulars* (London: Collier-Macmillan, 1969), p. 76; Edward S. Wallace, "General John Lapham Bullis, the Thunderbolt of the Texas Frontier," *Southwestern Historical Quarterly*, 54 (1951): 452–61 and 55 (1952): 77–85; Kenneth W. Porter, "The Seminole Negro-Indian Scouts, 1870–1881," *Southwestern Historical Quarterly*, 55 (1952): 358–77.

[47] Callahan, *American Foreign Policy in Mexican Relations*, pp. 371–74. For brief accounts of Hayes's Mexican policy *see* Harry Barnard, *Rutherford B. Hayes and His America* (Indianapolis: Bobbs-Merrill, 1954), pp. 443–44; Hamilton J. Eckenrode, *Rutherford B. Hayes, Statesman of Reunion* (New York: Dodd, Mead and Company, 1930), pp. 282–83.

[48] Ord to Sherman, 2 April 1877, W. T. Sherman Papers, 46.

[49] Ord to Philip H. Sheridan, 3 April 1877, Letters Sent (1877), Department of Texas, p. 180.

[50] Ord to Sheridan, 10 and 11 May 1877, Letters Sent (1877), Department of Texas, pp. 253–57; Ord to Sherman, 22 May 1877; Sherman to Ord, 23 May 1877, Ord's Personal File, Adjutant General's Office.

[51] *House Reports*, 45th Cong., 2nd Sess., No. 701 (Serial No. 1824): 15. *See* Ord to Sherman, 27 December 1879, Alexander Collection. The Hayes administration was apparently sensitive to the congressional pressures which constituted a censure of the weak Mexican policy of Grant.

[52] Ord to Shafter, 8 June 1877, Letters Sent (1877), Department of Texas, p. 315.

[53] Ord to Thomas C. Devin and Shafter, 9 June 1877, Letters Sent (1877), Department of Texas, pp. 318–19.

[54] Sherman to Ord, 10 June 1877, Letters Received (1877), Department of Texas, p. 166. *See* Robert M. Utley, *Frontier Regulars: The United States Army and the Indians, 1866–1891* (New York: Macmillan Company, 1974), p. 352.

[55] Gerónimo Treviño to Ord, 11 June 1877, Letters Received (1877), Department of Texas, p. 171; Ord to Treviño, 11 June 1877; Ord to Sheridan, 19 June 1877, Letters Sent (1877), Department of Texas, pp. 331, 354.

[56] Ord to Sherman, 25 October 1877, W. T. Sherman Papers, 46.

⁵⁷ Callahan, *American Foreign Policy in Mexican Relations*, p. 382; Foster to William M. Evarts, 13 July 1877, no. 573, Mexican Dispatches, vol. 59.

⁵⁸ Foster to Evarts, 20 June 1877, no. 550, Mexican Dispatches, vol. 59.

⁵⁹ Ibid.

⁶⁰ Ord to Shafter, 6 July and 6 August 1877; Ord to the Adjutant General, 7 July 1877; Shafter to Ord, 27 September 1877; Ord to Sheridan, 2 October 1877, Letters Sent (1877), Department of Texas, pp. 54–55, 70, 393, 395, 502; copy of resolutions adopted at the meeting of citizens of Bexar County, 5 January 1878, Shafter Papers.

⁶¹ *House Executive Documents*, 45th Cong., 2nd Sess., No. 1 (Serial No. 1794): 81; Callahan, *American Foreign Policy in Mexican Relations*, p. 385; Ord to Shafter, 4 August 1877; Ord to Sheridan, 25 July 1877; Ord to Benavides, 14 August 1877, Letters Sent (1877), Department of Texas, pp. 466, 499–500, 533; W. R. Price to Ord, 21 July 1877; Sheridan to Ord, 24 August 1877, Letters Received (1877), Department of Texas, pp. 380, 591.

⁶² Gustave Schleicher to Ord, 16 September 1877, Bancroft Library Collection; *House Executive Documents*, 45th Cong., 2nd Sess., No. 1 (Serial No. 1794): 80–81.

⁶³ Ord to Sherman, 25 October 1877, W. T. Sherman Papers, 46.

⁶⁴ William A. Ganoe, historian of the army, described the period between 1865 and 1880 as "The Army's Dark Ages." *See* his *The History of the United States Army*, rev. ed. (Ashton, Md.: Eric Lundberg, 1964), chap. 9; and Russell F. Weigley, *History of the United States Army* (New York: Macmillan Company, 1967), chap. 12.

⁶⁵ Ord to Sherman (draft), 13 November 1876, Bancroft Library Collection.

⁶⁶ Sheridan to Sherman, 24 November 1877, W. T. Sherman Papers, 47.

⁶⁷ Sherman to Sheridan, 29 November 1877, W. T. Sherman Papers, Letterbook, 1872–78.

⁶⁸ Ibid.

⁶⁹ *Galveston Daily News*, 5 December 1877; Sheridan to Ord, 8 December 1877, Letters Received (1877), Department of Texas, p. 367.

⁷⁰ *House Reports*, 45th Cong., 2nd Sess., No. 701 (Serial No. 1824): 3–15.

⁷¹ Ibid., p. 19.

⁷² Ibid., xlii; Rippy, *The United States and Mexico*, pp. 307–308; Carlton Beals, *Porfirio Díaz, Dictator of Mexico* (Philadelphia: J. B. Lippincott Company, 1932), pp. 236–37; Callahan, *American Foreign Policy in Mexican Relations*, p. 392; Foster to Evarts, 2 May 1878, no. 699, Mexican Dispatches, vol. 62.

⁷³ Sherman to Sheridan, 26 May 1878, Philip H. Sheridan Papers, Manuscript Division, Library of Congress.

Chapter 19

¹ Edward S. Wallace, "General Ranald Slidell Mackenzie, Indian Fighting cavalryman," *Southwestern Historical Quarterly*, 56 (1953): 378–96; Edward S. Wallace, "Border Warrior," *American Heritage*, 9 (1958): 22–25, 101–105; Ernest Wallace, *Ranald S. Mackenzie on the Texas Frontier* (Lubbock, Tex.: West Texas Museum Association, 1964), pp. 175–81; Robert G. Carter, *On the Border with Mackenzie: Or Winning West Texas from the Comanches* (New York: Antiquarian Press, 1961).

² Ranald S. Mackenzie to Edward Ord, 25 June, 5 July, 19 August, and 9 September 1878, Letters Received (1878), Department of Texas, pp. 44, 417, 490, 537; Mackenzie to Ord, 1, 2, 8, 9 July 1878, Letters Received (1878), Department of Texas, Doc. Box No. 36, 8075–8078 DT 78 filed with 4155 DT 78, Record Group 98, National Archives; Ord to Mackenzie, 24 August and 4 October 1878, Letters Sent (1878), Department of Texas, pp. 200, 300–314, Record Group 98, National Archives; Edward S. Wallace, "Border Warrior," *American Heritage*, 9:104.

³ Ord to B. H. Grierson, 6 November 1878; Ord to Lewis C. Hunt, 20 November 1878, Letters Sent (1878), Department of Texas, pp. 396, 423–24; James D. Richardson, comp., *A Compilation of the Messages and Papers of the Presidents*, 20 vols. (New York: Bureau of National Literature, c. 1897–1927), 9:4449.

4 William R. Shafter to Ord, 21 December 1878, Letters Received (1878), Department of Texas, p. 528; Ord to D. C. Stone, 27 December 1878, Letters Sent (1878), Department of Texas, p. 498.

5 *Galveston Daily News,* 31 December 1878.

6 Ord to William T. Sherman, 3 January 1879, W. T. Sherman Papers, 49, Manuscript Division, Library of Congress.

7 Ibid.

8 Ibid.; Philip H. Sheridan to Sherman, 12 December 1879, W. T. Sherman Papers, 51.

9 Sheridan to Ord, 30 December 1878, Letters Received (1878), Department of Texas, p. 533; Ord to Sheridan, 30 December 1878, Letters Sent (1878), Department of Texas, p. 511.

10 Sherman to Sheridan, 9 March 1879, Philip H. Sheridan Papers, Manuscript Division, Library of Congress; Sherman to Samuel Bell Maxey, 31 March 1879, W. T. Sherman Papers, Letterbook, 1878–79.

11 *House Executive Documents,* 46th Cong., 2nd Sess., No. 1 (Serial No. 1903): 93.

12 Ibid., pp. 90,93.

13 Ord to Sheridan, 3 and 4 October 1879, Letters Sent (1879), Department of Texas, pp. 44, 46.

14 Sherman to Maxey, 17 October 1879; Maxey to Sherman, 30 October 1879, W. T. Sherman Papers, 50, and Letterbook, 1878–79.

15 Sherman to Ord, 25 October 1879, W. T. Sherman Papers, Letterbook, 1878–79.

16 Ord to Sheridan, 28 November 1879, Letters Sent (1879), Department of Texas, p. 169. The substance of Ord's letter to Sherman of 12 November 1879 was referred to in other communications, but the letter itself has not been found.

17 Sherman to Ord, 5 January 1880, Alexander Collection of Ord Papers, in possession of Mrs. Vida Ord Alexander, Washington, D.C.; Richardson, comp., *Messages and Papers of the Presidents,* 10:4521.

18 Sheridan to Sherman, 12 December 1879, W. T. Sherman Papers, 51.

19 Ord to Sherman (draft), 27 December 1879, Alexander Collection.

20 Ibid.

21 Sherman to Ord, 5 January 1880, Alexander Collection.

22 John W. Foster, *Diplomatic Memoirs,* 2 vols. (Boston: Houghton Mifflin Company, 1909), 1:135; Foster to Ord, 8 January 1880, Edward Otho Cresap Ord Correspondence and Papers, 1850–1883, Bancroft Library, Berkeley, California; Foster to William M. Evarts, 27 December 1879, no. 1078, Mexican Dispatches, vol. 69, Records of the State Department, Record Group 59, National Archives.

23 Secretary of War Alexander Ramsey to Sherman, 24 February 1880, General Orders, No. 4, 8 March 1880, Department of Texas, Record Group 98, National Archives; Herbert I. Priestley, *The Mexican Nation, A History* (New York: Macmillan Company, 1924), p. 377.

24 Robert D. Gregg, *The Influence of Border Troubles on Relations between the United States and Mexico, 1876–1910,* Johns Hopkins University Studies in Historical and Political Science, Series 45, no. 3 (Baltimore: Johns Hopkins University Press, 1937), pp. 64–65; Chester L. Barrows, *William M. Evarts, Lawyer, Diplomat, Statesman* (Chapel Hill: University of North Carolina Press, 1941), p. 362; J. Fred Rippy, *The United States and Mexico,* rev. ed. (New York: F. S. Crofts and Company, 1931), p. 310; James M. Callahan, *American Foreign Policy in Mexican Relations* (New York: Macmillan Company, 1932), pp. 403–404, 418, 420; J. Fred Rippy, "Some Precedents of the Pershing Expedition into Mexico," *Southwestern Historical Quarterly,* 24 (1921): 313.

25 Ord to Sheridan, 11 August and 26 October 1880; Ord to C. O., District of Nueces, 2 August 1880, Letters Sent (1880), Department of Texas, pp. 26, 63–65, 315–16; *see* William H. Leckie, *The Buffalo Soldiers: A Narrative of the Negro Cavalry in the West* (Norman: University of Oklahoma Press, 1967), chaps. 6–8; Dan L. Thrapp, *The Conquest of Apacheria* (Norman: University of Oklahoma Press, 1967), pp. 182–210.

26 *San Antonio Daily Express*, 21 July 1880; *Galveston Daily News*, 24 July 1880; Daniel Cosío Villegas, *The United States versus Porfirio Díaz* (Lincoln: University of Nebraska Press, 1963), p. 209.

27 *San Antonio Daily Express*, 21 July 1880; *Galveston Daily News*, 21 July 1880.

28 Ibid.; *Galveston Daily News*, 24 July 1880.

29 *San Antonio Daily Express*, 21 July 1880.

30 Ibid.; *Galveston Daily News*, 21 July 1880.

31 *San Antonio Daily Express*, 21 July 1880; Cosío Villegas, *The United States versus Porfirio Díaz*, p. 210.

32 *House Executive Documents*, 46th Cong., 3rd Sess., No. 1 (Serial No. 1952): 112. *See* James P. Baughman, "The Evolution of Rail-Water Systems of Transportation in the Gulf Southwest, 1836–1890," *Journal of Southern History*, 34 (1968): 357–81.

33 Ord to Collis P. Huntington, 12 January 1880; Ord to Horatio G. Wright, 21 May 1880; Ord to John C. Brown, 11 June 1880, Letters Sent (1880), Department of Texas, pp. 32, 369–70, 450–51; Brown to Ord, 15 March 1880, Letters Received (1880), Department of Texas, p. 225; Ord to Brown (draft), 14 October 1880, Bancroft Library Collection; Ord to Adjutant General of the Army (copy), 16 April 1879, Benjamin H. Grierson Papers, Newberry Library, Chicago, Illinois; Ord to Wright (copy), 31 May 1880; Wright to Spencer F. Baird, 1 June 1880, Secretarial Records, 1863–1907, R. U. 28, Box 21, Smithsonian Institution Archives, Washington, D.C.

34 David M. Pletcher, *Rails, Mines, and Progress: Seven American Promoters in Mexico, 1867–1911* (Ithaca, N.Y.: Cornell University Press, 1958), pp. 155–59.

35 *Galveston Daily News*, 25 and 28 March 1880.

36 Ord to W. D. Whipple, 5 November 1880, Ord's Personal File, Adjutant General's Office, Record Group 94, National Archives; Ord to Sherman, 28 November 1880, W. T. Sherman Papers, 53.

37 Ord to Sherman, 28 November 1880, W. T. Sherman Papers, 53.

38 *Galveston Daily News*, 21 and 23 September 1879.

39 Guy M. Bryan to Rutherford B. Hayes, 27 April 1880, Rutherford B. Hayes Papers, Rutherford B. Hayes Library, Fremont, Ohio.

40 As quoted in *Galveston Daily News*, 9 December 1880. *See* Glen Tucker, *Hancock the Superb* (Indianapolis: Bobbs-Merrill, 1960), pp. 301–304.

41 Maxey to Ord, 4 July 1880, Bancroft Library Collection.

42 Maxey to Hayes, 5 July 1880, Hayes Papers.

43 Huntington to John Sherman, 6 July 1880; R. S. Hayes and H. M. Hoxie to Rutherford B. Hayes, 8 July 1880, Ord's Personal File, Adjutant General's Office; Alexander Ramsey to J. J. Dull, 16 July 1880; George McCrary to Dull, 18 July 1880; Dull to Ord, 17 and 21 July 1880, Bancroft Library Collection; Thomas A. Scott to James A. Garfield (copy), 29 November 1880; Scott to Rutherford B. Hayes, 2 December 1880, Hayes Papers.

44 Sherman to Ord, 11 November 1880, Ord's Personal File, Adjutant General's Office.

45 Ord to Sherman, 11 November 1880, W. T. Sherman Papers, 53.

46 Ibid.

47 Sherman to Rutherford B. Hayes, 18 November 1880, W. T. Sherman Papers, Letterbook, 1880–81.

48 Hayes to Sherman, 18 November 1880, W. T. Sherman Papers, Letterbook, 1880–81.

49 Hayes's order, 6 December 1880, Ord's Personal File, Adjutant General's Office.

50 General Orders, No. 19, 6 December 1880, Department of Texas.

51 *Galveston Daily News*, 8 December 1880.

52 *Beaumont Enterprise* as quoted in *Galveston Daily News*, 16 December 1880.

53 *Luling Signal* as quoted in *Galveston Daily News*, 19 December 1880.

54 *Meridian Blade* as quoted in *Galveston Daily News*, 22 December 1880.

55 *Galveston Daily News*, 9 December 1880.

56 *See* reports quoted in *Galveston Daily News*, 16, 19, and 22 December 1880. Hayes noted in his diary on 23 January 1881 that he had temporarily lost the friendship of General Sherman, attributing this to several matters including the retirement of Ord. The president wrote that he had no intention of slighting General Sherman. *See* Charles Richard Williams, ed., *Diary and Letters of Rutherford Birchard Hayes, Nineteenth President of the United States*, 5 vols. (Columbus: Ohio State Archeological and Historical Society, 1922–26), 5:640.

57 *Galveston Daily News*, 9 December 1880.

58 Maxey's bill, 16 December 1880, Ord's Personal File, Adjutant General's Office.

59 Sherman to Maxey, 17 December 1880, W. T. Sherman Papers, Letterbook, 1880–81.

60 Maxey to Sherman, 17 December 1880, W. T. Sherman Papers, 54. There is one impressive monument in Texas to mark Ord's services there. In 1876, Lieutenant George Wheeler of the Engineers, exploring west of the Pecos, named "Ord Peak" or Mt. Ord for the general. *See* Wheeler to Ord, 24 February 1876, Bancroft Library Collection.

61 *Congressional Record*, 46th Cong., 3rd Sess., 11, pt. 2:1056; Hayes's order, 5 February 1881, Ord's Personal File, Adjutant General's Office. Ord understood that his commission dated from 13 March 1865, the date of his brevet as major general. This would make him senior to Irvin McDowell when the latter retired. *See* Ord to Sherman, 8 May 1882, Ord's Personal File, Adjutant General's Office.

62 *House Executive Documents*, 47th Cong., 1st Sess., No. 1 (Serial No. 2010): 128.

Chapter 20

1 *Official Army Register for January, 1880* (Washington: Adjutant General's Office, 1880).

2 William T. Sherman to Samuel Bell Maxey, 21 December 1880, Edward Otho Cresap Ord Correspondence and Papers, 1850–1883, Bancroft Library, Berkeley, California.

3 T. W. Peirce to Edward Ord, 14 January 1881, Bancroft Library Collection.

4 Ibid.

5 Edward Ord to Sherman, 3 March 1881, W. T. Sherman Papers, 44, Manuscript Division, Library of Congress.

6 Gerónimo Treviño's manifesto, 11 May 1879, Letters Received (1879), Department of Texas, p. 474, Record Group 98, National Archives; James M. Callahan, *American Foreign Policy in Mexican Relations* (New York: Macmillan Company, 1932), p. 405.

7 Ord to Pacificus Ord, 17 March 1881, Preston Collection of Ord Papers, in possession of Mr. Murray Preston, Chevy Chase, Maryland; Daniel Cosío Villegas, *The United States versus Porfirio Díaz* (Lincoln: University of Nebraska Press, 1963), pp. 211–12.

8 Ibid.

9 Ibid.

10 Cosío Villegas, *The United States versus Porfirio Díaz*, p. 211.

11 Ord to Pacificus Ord, 17 March 1881, Preston Collection.

12 Ibid.

13 Ord to Pacificus Ord, 22 April 1881 and 14 June 1883, Preston Collection; Placidus Peter Ord to _____, 26 February 1882, Alexander Collection of Ord Papers, in possession of Mrs. Vida Ord Alexander, Washington, D.C.; Cosío Villegas, *The United States versus Porfirio Díaz*, p. 215. Bertie Treviño died in 1883.

14 Ord to Pacificus Ord, 22 April 1881, Preston Collection; W. P. Thompson to Ord, 29 May 1882, Bancroft Library Collection.

15 Osgood Hardy, "Ulysses S. Grant, President of the Mexican Southern Railroad," *Pacific Historical Review*, 24 (1955): 114–17; David M. Pletcher, *Rails, Mines, and Progress: Seven American Promoters in Mexico, 1867–1911* (Ithaca, N.Y.: Cornell University Press, 1958), pp. 152–69; Fred Wilbur Powell, *The Railroads of Mexico* (Boston:

Stratford Company, Publishers, 1921), pp. 145–47; William B. Hesseltine, *Ulysses S. Grant, Politician* (New York: Frederick Ungar Publishing Company, 1957), pp. 444–45.

[16] Ord to James T. Ord, 17 June 1883, Radford Collection of Ord Papers, in possession of Mrs. Rebecca Ord Radford, La Jolla, California.

[17] Ord to one of his sons, n.d., Bancroft Library Collection.

[18] Ord to Pacificus Ord, 5 March 1883, Preston Collection.

[19] Ibid.

[20] Ord to James T. Ord, 17 June 1883, Radford Collection.

[21] Ord to _____, n.d., Ord's Personal File, Adjutant General's Office, Record Group 94, National Archives.

[22] Ord to Sherman, 18 April 1882, W. T. Sherman Papers, 57.

[23] Ord to Pacificus Ord, 28 May 1882, Preston Collection.

[24] Hardy, "Ulysses S. Grant, President of the Mexican Southern Railroad," *Pacific Historical Review*, 24:118; Ord to James T. Ord, 17 June 1883, Radford Collection; Ord to Pacificus Ord, 4 July 1883, Preston Collection. *See* Julius Grodinsky, *Jay Gould: His Business Career, 1867–1892* (Philadelphia: University of Pennsylvania Press, 1957).

[25] Adam Badeau to John Davis (copy), 21 July 1883, Ord's Personal File, Adjutant General's Office.

[26] Ibid.

[27] Ibid.

[28] Badeau to Davis, 26 July 1883, Ord's Personal File, Adjutant General's Office.

[29] Ulysses S. Grant to Badeau (copy), 25 July 1883; Grant and Jay Gould to Mrs. Ord (copy), 25 July 1883, Bancroft Library Collection.

[30] General Orders, No. 54, 24 July 1883, Headquarters of the Army, Adjutant General's Office (extract in Ord's Personal File).

[31] Public Law No. 34, 8 March 1900. See *Congressional Record*, 56th Cong., 1st Sess., index to 33:99. Joseph Pacificus Ord, son of Judge Pacificus Ord, was instrumental in having General Ord's remains moved to Arlington National Cemetery and also had the remains of the following members of the Ord family interred in the same place: James Ord, the general's father; the following children of the general: Captain James Thompson Ord, Lieutenant Julius Garesché Ord (killed at San Juan Hill in 1898), and Roberta Augusta Ord de Treviño. The remains of Rebecca Cresap Ord, the general's mother, were removed from the Mission Santa Cruz, California, and buried at Arlington through the agency of her grandson, Edmund Burke Holladay. Mary Mercer Thompson Ord, wife of the general, died in San Antonio in 1894 and is buried in the National Cemetery in that city.

Bibliography: Critical Essay on Authorities

In his long and active life, most of it in military service, E.O.C. Ord went many places and left many records both public and private. His biographer has had no problem with paucity of sources, rather a task of getting at these Ord materials in depositories scattered from coast to coast. This bibliographical essay does not attempt to list all of the works cited in footnotes, but rather those manuscripts and printed sources which were significant in revealing Ord's career. Books and articles containing only bits of useful information are not listed here.

Manuscript Collections

Members of the Ord family have collected papers indispensable to the writing of the present volume. The late Miss Ellen F. Ord, granddaughter of the general, gathered an extensive collection of drafts of Ord's letters, letters to Ord, his diaries and various other documents. This collection was presented by Miss Ord to the Bancroft Library, Berkeley, California, and is designated as follows: Edward Otho Cresap Ord Correspondence and Papers, 1850–1883. Mrs. Vida Ord Alexander of Washington, D.C., granddaughter of Placidus Ord, has letters especially valuable for the Civil War period. Placidus served on the general's staff during the war and, from this point of vantage, dispatched letters to his wife about his brother's activities. Mr. A. Murray Preston of Washington, D.C., great-grandson of Judge Pacificus Ord, the general's brother, has a collection containing the letters of the general to the judge extending over forty years. Mrs. Rebecca Ord Radford of La Jolla, California, granddaughter of the general, has a diary, important letters of Ord relating to the Appomattox surrender, and other items.

Important are letters of Ord to his wife in the Edward Otho Cresap Ord Papers, 1854–1858, in the Manuscripts Division, Department of Special Collections, C. H. Green Library, Stanford University, Stanford, California. The letters are especially useful for the

Indian wars on the Pacific Coast. The William R. Shafter Papers in the same depository include letters of Ord.

Other papers of General Ord and papers relating to him are located in the Manuscript Division of the Library of Congress. Especially valuable are Ord's letters in the W. T. Sherman Papers. The close friendship of Ord and Sherman lasted from their meeting at West Point to Ord's death and, over this forty-seven-year period, produced a voluminous correspondence. Particularly useful also are the Benjamin F. Butler Papers, the typescript copy of August V. Kautz's "Reminiscences of the Civil War," and the Marsena R. Patrick Diary. Important collections containing a few Ord items are: Robert Anderson Papers, Zachariah Chandler Papers, Charles A. Dana Papers, Andrew Johnson Papers, Philip H. Sheridan Papers, John Sherman Papers and Edwin M. Stanton Papers.

The Rutherford B. Hayes Papers in the Rutherford B. Hayes Library, Fremont, Ohio, include a few letters relating to Ord's retirement. The Sherman-Ord Correspondence, 1865–82, in the Missouri Historical Society, St. Louis, consists of a number of Sherman's letters to Ord. The William Henry Seward Collection in the University of Rochester Library, Rochester, New York, contains letters of Ord to Seward.

Records of General Ord's military career spanning forty-five years are found in abundance in the National Archives. The Records of the Adjutant General's Office, Record Group 94, include those relating to Ord's entry into West Point; Regimental Returns of the Third Artillery account for his early military activities. Other records include his Personal File, Letters Sent, Letters Received, and General Orders. Records of the Headquarters of the Army, Record Group 108, embrace Letters Sent and Letters Received. Records of the Army Commands, Record Group 98, provide Letters Sent, Letters Received, and General and Special Orders of the following commands held by Ord: Military Departments of Virginia, the Arkansas, the Platte, and Texas, and the Fourth Military District. The Records of the Bureau of Refugees, Freedmen, and Abandoned Lands, Record Group 105, were used in two categories. First, for Arkansas, were Reports of Operations; Circular Orders, Assistant Commissioners; and Letters Received (General). Second, were those for Commissioner Howard's Office, Letters Received. The Mexican Dispatches of the Department of State, Record Group 59, comprise in part the diplomatic exchanges between Mexico City and Washington during the border troubles of the 1870s.

Two miscellaneous manuscript records were helpful. Ord's record as a West Point cadet was provided from the records of the United States Military Academy, West Point, New York. A single item of some consequence, a letter from General Ord to Governor Benjamin Grubb Humphreys, was gleaned from the Governor's Archives, Series E, No. 80–82, Mississippi Department of Archives and History, Jackson.

Printed Government Documents

Indispensable for its reports and dispatches of Civil War operations is the *War of the Rebellion: A Compilation of the Official Records of the Union and Confederate Armies,* 129 vols. and index (Washington: Government Printing Office, 1880–1901). Various aspects of Ord's early career are included in the following *Senate Executive Documents:* 31st Cong., 1st Sess., No. 47 (Serial No. 558); 33rd Cong., 1st Sess., No. 14 (Serial No. 704); 33rd Cong., 2nd Sess., No. 10 (Serial No. 757); and *House Executive Documents,* 31st Cong., 1st Sess., No. 17 (Serial No. 573). Annual Reports of Ord and others of operations in the Department of the Platte and Texas are in *House Executive Documents,* 42nd Cong., 3rd Sess., No. 1 (Serial No. 1558); 43rd Cong., 2nd Sess., No. 1 (Serial No. 1635); 44th Cong., 1st Sess., No. 1 (Serial No. 1674); 45th Cong., 2nd Sess., No. 1 (Serial No. 1903); 46th Cong., 3rd Sess., No. 1 (Serial No. 1952); 47th Cong., 2nd Sess., No. 1 (Serial No. 2010). Texas border problems are dealt with in *House Reports,* 45th Cong., 2nd Sess., No. 701 (Serial No. 1824) and *House Miscellaneous Documents,* 45th Cong., 2nd Sess., No. 64 (Serial No. 1820).

Important Supreme Court cases of the Reconstruction period in which Ord was involved are found in the *United States Supreme Court Reports* for 1867 and 1868 as follows: *Mississippi* v. *Johnson,* 4 Wall. 475–501; *Ex parte McCardle,* 6 Wall. 318–27, 7 Wall. 506–515.

A number of pertinent items relating to Ord's career are in James D. Richardson, comp., *A Compilation of the Messages and Papers of the Presidents,* 20 vols. (New York: Bureau of National Literature, Inc., c. 1897–1927). The *Congressional Record,* 46th Cong., 3rd Sess. (1880–1881), contains the action of Congress in the retirement of General Ord.

Memoirs, Letters, Diaries and Other Printed Sources

For various phases of Ord's early life, several works are particularly helpful. Two pamphlets concerned with the parentage of James Ord, father of the general, may be found in the archives of Georgetown University. Twenty-five copies of each were privately printed. These are: Mary Ord Preston, ed., *Memoranda Concerning James Ord, Who Died at the United States Navy Yard, Washington, D.C., October 12, 1810* (n.p., 1896); and *Memoranda Concerning James Ord, Who Died January 25th, 1873* (n.p., 1896). Quite important for early and also later aspects of Ord's life are William T. Sherman, *Personal Memoirs of Gen. W. T. Sherman,* 4th ed. rev. and corr., 2 vols. (New York: Charles L. Webster and Company, 1891); William T. Sherman, "Old Times in California," *North American Review,* 148 (1889): 269–79; and Philip H. Sheridan, *Personal Memoirs of P. H. Sheridan,* 2 vols. (New York: C L. Webster & Company, 1888). Ord's survey of Los Angeles is covered in W. W. Robinson, ed., "Story of Ord's Survey

As Disclosed by the Los Angeles Archives," Historical Society of Southern California *Quarterly*, 19 (1937): 121–31.

Memoirs, letters and other printed items of special significance of Ord's associates of the Civil War period are: Benjamin F. Butler, *Butler's Book* (Boston: A. M. Thayer and Company, 1892); Benjamin F. Butler, *Private and Official Correspondence of General Benjamin F. Butler*, 5 vols. (Norwood, Mass.: Plimpton Press, 1917); Joshua L. Chamberlain, *The Passing of the Armies: An Account of the Final Campaign of the Army of the Potomac* (New York: G. P. Putnam's Sons, 1915); John Gibbon, *Personal Recollections of the Civil War* (New York: G. P. Putnam's Sons, 1928); Ulysses S. Grant, *Personal Memoirs of U. S. Grant*, 2 vols. (New York: C. L. Webster and Company, 1885–86); James Longstreet, *From Manassas to Appomattox* (Philadelphia: J. B. Lippincott Company, 1896); George Meade, comp., *The Life and Letters of George Gordon Meade*, ed. George Gordon Meade, 2 vols. (New York: C. Scribner's Sons, 1913); Francis H. Pierpoint (sometimes Pierpont), *Letter of Governor Pierpoint to His Excellency the President and the Honorable Congress on the Subject of the Abuse of Military Power in the Command of General Butler in Virginia and North Carolina* (Washington: McGill and Witherow, 1864); Horace Porter, *Campaigning with Grant*, (New York: The Century Company, 1897); Gideon Welles, *Diary of Gideon Welles, Secretary of the Navy under Lincoln and Johnson*, ed. John T. Morse, 3 vols. (Boston: Houghton Mifflin Company, 1911); Julia Dent Grant, *The Personal Memoirs of Julia Dent Grant*, ed. John Y. Simon (New York: G. P. Putnam's Sons, 1975).

Also of some importance are the following which provided limited but useful information: John S. Barnes, "With Lincoln from Washington to Richmond in 1865," *Appleton's Magazine*, 9 (Jan.–June, 1907): 515–24; Joseph E. Johnston, *Narrative of Military Operations* (New York: D. Appleton and Company, 1874); John B. Jones, *A Rebel War Clerk's Diary*, ed. Earl Schenck Miers (New York: Sagamore Press, 1958); Ward H. Lamon, *Recollections of Abraham Lincoln, 1847–1865*, ed. Dorothy Lamon Teillard (Washington: Pub. by the editor, 1911); Edward Hastings Ripley, *Vermont General: The Unusual War Experiences of Edward Hastings Ripley, 1862–1865*, ed. Otto Eisenschiml (New York: The Devin-Adair Company, Publishers, 1960); Morris Schaff, *The Sunset of the Confederacy* (Boston: John W. Luce and Company, 1912); Leander Stillwell, *The Story of a Common Soldier of Army Life in the Civil War, 1861–1865*, 2nd ed. (n.p.: Franklin Hudson Publishing Company, 1920); Charles S. Wainwright, *A Diary of Battle: The Personal Journals of Colonel Charles S. Wainwright, 1861–1865*, ed. Allan Nevins (New York: Harcourt, Brace and World, Inc., 1962). Articles by some of Ord's Civil War contemporaries in the following compilations are of some value: *The Annals of the War* (Philadelphia: Times Publishing Company, 1879); Robert Underwood Johnson and Clarence Clough Buel, eds., *Battles and Leaders of the Civil War*, 4 vols. (New York: Century Company, 1884–88).

The following listed recollection is useful for the period of the Richmond occupation immediately following Lee's surrender: Sallie

A. Putnam, *In Richmond during the Confederacy* (New York: Robert M. McBride Company, 1961).

Of great assistance in dealing with the Reconstruction period is Walter L. Fleming, ed., *Documentary History of Reconstruction*, 2 vols. in one (Gloucester, Mass.: P. Smith, 1960). For its direct commentary on Ord's part in Mississippi's Reconstruction, of special value is Percy L. Rainwater, ed., "The Autobiography of Benjamin Grubb Humphreys, August 26, 1808–December 20, 1882," *Mississippi Valley Historical Review*, 21 (1934–35): 231–55.

Newspapers

The *San Francisco Daily Herald* has a few items relating to Ord's part in the Indian wars of the 1850s along the Pacific Coast. For the Civil War years, the *New York Herald* and the *New York Times* are particularly helpful. Correspondents of these papers accompanied Ord's army in the Appomattox campaign and wrote firsthand accounts of the operations. The principal newspapers of Mississippi and Arkansas are valuable for Ord's part in the Reconstruction of these states. These are the *Jackson Daily Clarion* and *Weekly Clarion* and the *Little Rock Daily Arkansas Gazette*. Also useful are the *Vicksburg Daily Times* and *Weekly Times*. For Ord's Texas years (1875–1880), the *Galveston Daily News* is indispensable and the *San Antonio Daily Express* helpful.

Secondary Works

Ord's ancestry is set forth in John J. Jacob, *A Biographical Sketch of the Life of the Late Capt. Michael Cresap* (Cumberland, Md.: J. J. Miller, 1881); and John Gilmary Shea, *Memorial of the First Centenary of Georgetown College* (Washington and New York: P. F. Collier, 1891).

The French influence and particularly the Jomini influence which were powerful in the West Point curriculum when Ord was there are seen in two works of Russell Weigley: *Towards an American Army: Military Thought from Washington to Marshall* (New York: Columbia University Press, 1962) and *History of the United States Army* (New York: Macmillan Company, 1967).

Useful information on various aspects of Ord's early career was secured from the following: Theophilus F. Rodenbough, comp., *From Everglade to Cañon with the Second Dragoons* (New York: D. Van Nostrand, 1875) for the Seminole Indian war; Robert M. Utley, *Frontiersmen in Blue: The United States Army and the Indian, 1848–1865* (New York: Macmillan Company, 1967) for Ord in the Indian wars of the Pacific Coast; George L. Albright, *Official Explorations for Pacific Railroads, 1853–1855* (Berkeley: University of California Press, 1921); and J. Gregg Layne, "Edward Otho Cresap Ord, Soldier and Surveyor," Historical Society of Southern California *Quarterly*, 17 (1935):

139–42, on Ord as explorer and surveyor; Oswald Garrison Villard, *John Brown, 1800–1859, A Biography Fifty Years After* (Boston: Houghton Mifflin Company, 1910); and Hill Peebles Wilson, *John Brown, Soldier of Fortune: A Critique* (Lawrence, Kansas: Hill P. Wilson, 1913), for John Brown's raid.

A number of military studies of the Civil War are especially valuable for delineating Ord's part in the great sectional struggle: Adam Badeau, *Military History of Ulysses S. Grant,* 3 vols. (New York: D. Appleton and Company, 1885); Comte de Paris, *History of the Civil War in America*, ed. Henry Coppée, 4 vols. (Philadelphia: Porter and Coates, 1875–88); Douglas Southall Freeman, *Lee's Lieutenants: A Study in Command,* 3 vols. (New York: Charles Scribner's Sons, 1942–44); John F. C. Fuller, *The Generalship of Ulysses S. Grant* (New York: Dodd, Mead, and Company, 1929); Francis Vinton Greene, *The Mississippi*, Campaigns of the Civil War, vol. 8 (New York: Charles Scribner's Sons, 1882); William S. Hammond, "The Battle of Dranesville, Va.," *Southern Historical Society Papers*, 52 vols. (Richmond: The Southern Historical Society, 1876–1959), Old Series, 35 (1907): 69–78; Andrew A. Humphreys, *The Virginia Campaign of '64 and '65: The Army of the Potomac and the Army of the James*, Campaigns of the Civil War, vol. 12 (New York: Charles Scribner's Sons, 1883); Rembert W. Patrick, *The Fall of Richmond* (Baton Rouge: Louisiana State University Press, 1960); Philip Van Doren Stern, *An End to Valor: The Last Days of the Civil War* (Boston: Houghton Mifflin Company, 1958); Kenneth P. Williams, *Lincoln Finds a General: A Military Study of the Civil War,* 5 vols. (New York: The Macmillan Company, 1949–59); T. Harry Williams, *Lincoln and His Generals* (New York: Alfred A. Knopf, 1952); Bruce Catton, *A Stillness at Appomattox* (New York: Pocket Books, Inc., 1958).

Special aspects of the Civil War are covered in James A. Bishop, *The Day Lincoln Was Shot* (New York: Harper and Brothers, 1955); Ludwell H. Johnson, "Contraband Trade during the Last Year of the Civil War," *Mississippi Valley Historical Review,* 49 (1962–63): 635–52; Thomas L. Livermore, *Numbers and Losses in the Civil War in America, 1861–1865* (Boston: Houghton Mifflin and Company, 1900); James G. Randall and David Donald, *The Civil War and Reconstruction,* 2nd ed. (Boston: D. C. Heath and Company, 1961); T. Harry Williams, *Lincoln and the Radicals* (Madison: University of Wisconsin Press, 1941); and, for the Richmond occupation in 1865, Myrta Lockett Avery, *Dixie after the War* (Boston: Houghton Mifflin Company, 1937).

The following biographies were especially helpful because of Ord's close association with the subjects: Louis Garesché, *Biography of Lieut. Col. Julius P. Garesché, Assistant Adjutant-General, U.S. Army* (Philadelphia: J. B. Lippincott Company, 1887); Charles H. Ambler, *Francis H. Pierpont, Union War Governor of Virginia and Father of West Virginia* (Chapel Hill: University of North Carolina Press, 1937); Freeman Cleaves, *Meade of Gettysburg* (Norman: University of Oklahoma Press, 1960); Douglas Southall Freeman, *R. E. Lee, A Biography,* 4 vols. (New York: Charles Scribner's Sons, 1934); Robert R. McCormick, *Ulysses S. Grant, The Great Soldier of America* (New York:

D. Appleton-Century Company, 1934); Donald B. Sanger and Thomas R. Hay, *James Longstreet* (Baton Rouge: Louisiana State University Press, 1952); and Benjamn P. Thomas and Harold M. Hyman, *Stanton: The Life and Times of Lincoln's Secretary of War* (New York: Alfred A. Knopf, 1962).

Three works highly essential to the story of Reconstruction as Ord was involved in it are James Wilford Garner, *Reconstruction in Mississippi* (New York: Macmillan Company, 1901); Thomas S. Staples, *Reconstruction in Arkansas, 1862–1874*, Columbia University Studies in History, Economics, and Public Law, vol. 109, whole no. 245 (New York: Columbia University, 1923); and Vernon L. Wharton, *The Negro in Mississippi, 1865–1890*, The James Sprunt Studies in History and Political Science, vol. 28 (Chapel Hill: University of North Carolina Press, 1947). In addition, these are quite useful for important aspects of Reconstruction: George R. Bentley, *A History of the Freedmen's Bureau* (Philadelphia: University of Pennsylvania Press, 1955); John A. Carpenter, *Sword and Olive Branch: Oliver Otis Howard* (Pittsburgh: University of Pittsburgh Press, 1964); James E. Sefton, *The United States Army and Reconstruction, 1865–1877* (Baton Rouge: Louisiana State University Press, 1967); James T. Currie, "The Beginnings of Congressional Reconstruction in Mississippi," *Journal of Mississippi History*, 35 (1973): 267–86.

For an understanding of the case *Ex parte McCardle*, two works by Stanley I. Kutler are essential: *Judicial Power and Reconstruction Politics* (Chicago: University of Chicago Press, 1968); "*Ex parte McCardle*: Judicial Impotency? The Supreme Court and Reconstruction Reconsidered," *American Historical Review*, 72 (1966–67): 835–51. *See also* William M. Wiecek, "The Great Writ and Reconstruction: The Habeas Corpus Act of 1867," *Journal of Southern History*, 36 (1970): 530–48; Sever Eubank, "The McCardle Case: A Challenge to Radical Reconstruction," *Journal of Mississippi History*, 18 (1956): 111–27.

Texas border troubles in which Ord figured prominently are treated in James M. Callahan, *American Foreign Policy in Mexican Relations* (New York: Macmillan Company, 1932); Daniel Cosío Villegas, *The United States versus Porfirio Díaz* (Lincoln: University of Nebraska Press, 1963); Robert D. Gregg, *The Influence of Border Troubles on Relations between the United States and Mexico: 1876–1910*, The Johns Hopkins University Studies in Historical and Political Science, Series 55, no. 3 (Baltimore: The Johns Hopkins University Press, 1937); J. Fred Rippy, *The United States and Mexico*, rev. ed. (New York: F. S. Crofts & Co., 1931); Robert M. Utley, *Frontier Regulars: The United States Army and the Indians, 1866–1891* (New York: Macmillan Company, 1974).

The Mexican business ventures with which Ord was connected in retirement are described in Osgood Hardy, "Ulysses S. Grant, President of the Mexican Southern Railroad," *Pacific Historical Review*, 24 (1955); 111–120; and David M. Pletcher, *Rails, Mines, and Progress: Seven American Promoters in Mexico, 1867–1911* (Ithaca: Cornell University Press, 1958).

Index